Lecture Notes in Computer Science 13642

More information about this series at https://link.springer.com/bookseries/558

Martin Schulz · Carsten Trinitis ·
Nikela Papadopoulou · Thilo Pionteck (Eds.)

Architecture of Computing Systems

35th International Conference, ARCS 2022
Heilbronn, Germany, September 13–15, 2022
Proceedings

Springer

Editors
Martin Schulz
Technical University of Munich
Garching, Germany

Nikela Papadopoulou
Chalmers University of Technology
Gothenburg, Sweden

Carsten Trinitis ⓘ
Technical University of Munich
Heilbronn, Germany

Thilo Pionteck ⓘ
Otto-von-Guericke-Universität Magdeburg
Magdeburg, Germany

ISSN 0302-9743   ISSN 1611-3349 (electronic)
Lecture Notes in Computer Science
ISBN 978-3-031-21866-8   ISBN 978-3-031-21867-5 (eBook)
https://doi.org/10.1007/978-3-031-21867-5

This Springer imprint is published by the registered company Springer Nature Switzerland AG
The registered company address is: Gewerbestrasse 11, 6330 Cham, Switzerland

Preface

The 35th International Conference on Computer Architecture (ARCS 2022) was hosted at the Technical University of Munich in Heilbronn, Germany, during September 13–15 2022. It was organized by the special interest group on "Architecture of Computing Systems" of the GI (Gesellschaft für Informatik e. V.) and ITG (Informationstechnische Gesellschaft im VDE).

After the 2020 conference unfortunately had to be canceled due to COVID-19 and could only take place virtually in 2021, we were very pleased to be able to hold a physical meeting again this year. Despite all the manifold options of virtual conferences, we believe that nothing beats face-to-face meetings and exchanges of ideas. Besides the discussion in the sessions, we see the personal exchange during the social events as elementary for the scientific discourse.

The ARCS conference series has 35 years of tradition reporting leading edge research in computer architecture, operating systems, and other related low-level system software, as well as a wide range of software techniques and tools required to exploit and build new hardware systems efficiently. ARCS addresses the complete spectrum from fully integrated, self-powered embedded systems up to plant-powered high-performance systems and provides a platform covering new emerging and cross-cutting topics, such as autonomous and ubiquitous systems, reconfigurable computing and acceleration, neural networks, and artificial intelligence, as well as outlooks on future topics like quantum computing and organic computing.

ARCS 2022 attracted 35 submissions from authors in eight countries, including Finland, India, and the USA. Each submission was reviewed by a diverse and dedicated Program Committee in a double-blind process. Almost all papers received four qualified reviews. A total of 135 reviews were completed, of which 112 were provided by the members of the Program Committee while 23 originated from external reviewers. The Program Committee selected 18 submissions to be presented at ARCS and published in the proceedings, which correspond to a 51% paper acceptance rate.

The accepted papers formed five entertaining sessions with 30-minute slots per presentation: Energy Efficiency (three papers), Advanced Computing Techniques (two papers), Applied Machine Learning (two papers), Hardware and Software System Security (three papers), and Reliable and Fault-tolerant Systems (2 papers). In addition to the papers from the main conference, this year we were lucky to organize a Special Track on "Organic Computing" with two additional sessions, one on Learning Capabilities (three papers) and one on Systems and Applications (three papers).

There is no successful conference without keynote talks. In ARCS 2022, we were delighted to host two very interesting keynotes, one on "SpMV: An embarrassing kernel for modern compute devices" by Georgios Goumas, Associate Professor at the National Technical University of Athens, and the other on "Low-level fun with parallel runtime systems" by Michael Klemm, CEO of the OpenMP Architecture Review Board and Principal Member of Technical Staff in the HPC Center of Excellence at AMD.

We further thank all authors for submitting their work to ARCS and presenting accepted papers. The special track on Organic Computing was organized and coordinated by Sven Tomforde and Anthony Stein. Thanks to all these individuals and all the many other people who helped in the organization of ARCS 2022. Finally, we thank MEGWARE and Springer for sponsoring this year's conference.

September 2022

Martin Schulz
Carsten Trinitis
Nikela Papadopoulou
Thilo Pionteck

Organization

General Chairs

Carsten Trinitis — Technical University of Munich, Heilbronn, Germany
Martin Schulz — Technical University of Munich, Germany

Program Chairs

Nikela Papadopoulou — Chalmers University of Technology, Sweden
Thilo Pionteck — Otto-von-Guericke University Magdeburg, Germany

Workshop and Special Session Co-chairs

Stefan Lankes — RWTH Aachen, Germany
Jens Breitbart — Bosch Driver Assistance, Germany

Web and Publicity Chair

Lars Bauer — Karlsruhe Institute of Technology, Germany

Publication Chair

Thilo Pionteck — Otto-von-Guericke University Magdeburg, Germany

Program Committee

Lars Bauer — Karlsruhe Institute of Technology, Germany
Mladen Berekovic — Universität zu Lübeck, Germany
Jürgen Brehm — Leibniz University Hannover, Germany
Andre Brinkmann — Johannes Gutenberg University Mainz, Germany
Uwe Brinkschulte — Goethe-Universität Frankfurt am Main, Germany
Joao Cardoso — Universidade do Porto, Portugal
Thomas Carle — Institute de Recherche en Informatique de Toulouse, France
Ahmed El-Mahdy — Egypt-Japan University of Science and Technology, Egypt

Pierfrancesco Foglia	Universitá di Pisa, Italy
Roberto Giorgi	University of Siena, Italy
Christian Gruhl	University of Kassel, Germany
Jan Haase	Universität Lübeck, Germany
Joerg Haehner	University of Augsburg, Germany
Heiko Hamann	Universität Lübeck, Germany
Andreas Herkersdorf	Technical University of Munich, Germany
Christian Hochberger	Technische Universität Darmstadt, Germany
Gert Jervan	Tallinn University of Technology, Estonia
Wolfgang Karl	Karlsruhe Institute of Technology, Germany
Jörg Keller	FernUniversität in Hagen, Germany
Peter Kogge	University of Notre Dame, USA
Erik Maehle	Universität zu Lübeck, Germany
Lena Oden	FernUniversität in Hagen, Germany
Alex Orailoglu	University of California, San Diego, USA
Mario Porrmann	Osnabrück University, Germany
Reza Salkhordeh	Johannes Gutenberg University Mainz, Germany
Toshinori Sato	Fukuoka University, Japan
Wolfgang Schröder Preikschat	Friedrich-Alexander-Universität Erlangen-Nürnberg, Germany
Martin Schulz	Technical University of Munich, Germany
Leonel Sousa	Universidade de Lisboa, Portugal
Benno Stabernack	Fraunhofer Institute for Telecommunications, Germany
Walter Stechele	Technical University of Munich, Germany
Jürgen Teich	Friedrich-Alexander-Universität Erlangen-Nürnberg, Germany
Theo Ungerer	University of Augsburg, Germany
Daniel Versick	NORDAKADEMIE Hochschule der Wirtschaft, Germany
Klaus Waldschmidt	Goethe-Universität Frankfurt am Main, Germany
Stephan Wong	Delft University of Technology, The Netherlands

Special Track on Organic Computing

Program Chairs

Anthony Stein	University of Hohenheim, Germany
Sven Tomforde	Kiel University, Germany
Stefan Wildermann	Friedrich-Alexander-Universität Erlangen-Nürnberg, Germany

Program Committee

Thomas Becker	Karlsruhe Institute of Technology, Germany
Kirstie Bellman	Topcy House Consulting, USA
Uwe Brinkschulte	Goethe-Universität Frankfurt am Main, Germany
Frank Dürr	University of Stuttgart, Germany
Christian Gruhl	University of Kassel, Germany
Heiko Hamann	Universität zu Lübeck, Germany
Martin Hoffmann	Bielefeld University of Applied Sciences, Germany
Christian Krupitzer	University of Hohenheim, Germany
Chris Landauer	Topcy House Consulting, USA
Erik Maehle	Universität zu Lübeck, Germany
Gero Mühl	University of Rostock, Germany
Mathias Pacher	University of Frankfurt, Germany
Hella Ponsar	University of Augsburg, Germany
Marc Reichenbach	Friedrich-Alexander-Universität Erlangen-Nürnberg, Germany
Wolfgang Reif	University of Augsburg, Germany
Hartmut Schmeck	Karlsruhe Institute of Technology, Germany
Gregor Schiele	University of Duisburg-Essen, Germany
Anthony Stein	University of Hohenheim, Germany
Jürgen Teich	Friedrich-Alexander-Universität Erlangen-Nürnberg, Germany
Sven Tomforde	Kiel University, Germany
Sebastian von Mammen	University of Würzburg, Germany
Torben Weis	University of Duisburg-Essen, Germany
Stefan Wildermann	Friedrich-Alexander-Universität Erlangen-Nürnberg, Germany

Keynote Talks

SpMV: An Embarrassing Kernel for Modern Compute Devices

Georgios Goumas

National Technical University of Athens, Greece

Abstract: Sparse Matrix-Vector Multiplication (SpMV) is a ubiquitous and critical kernel for a large variety of applications. Despite the mass of technical and research work that it has attracted over the last decades, the kernel's performance remains embarrassingly low across all modern compute devices. In this talk we will shed light into the reasons why the performance of SpMV is so low, present a few concepts and approaches towards optimizing it using algorithmic engineering, and conclude by discussing current state and future perspectives towards a co-designed,truly optimized execution environment for SpMV.

Georgios Goumas is an Associate Professor at the School of ECE of the National Technical University of Athens. He graduated from the Dept. of Electrical and Computer Engineering of the National Technical University of Athens (NTUA) (1999). He received a PhD Degree from the School of Electrical and Computer Engineering of NTUA in January 2004. He is currently a senior researcher at the Computing Systems Laboratory (CSLab) in the School of Electrical and Computer Engineering of NTUA. His research interests include high-performance computing and architectures, cloud computing, resource allocation policies, resource-demanding applications, sparse algebra, automatic parallelizing compilers, parallel programming models, etc. He has published more than 80 research papers in journals, international conferences and peer-reviewed workshops. He has worked in several European and National R&D programs in the field of High Performance Computing, Cloud Computing, Networking and Storage for IT systems.

Low-level Fun with Parallel Runtime Systems

Michael Klemm

OpenMP ARB, Germany

Abstract: In this talk, we will have a look at how a parallel programming model interacts with contemporary multi-core and many-core processors. When thinking about low-level runtime implementations, you will see that the traditional assumptions of parallel programming may not hold and why a slightly different perspective on topic and how to obtain performance is required. After a quick recap of some OpenMP API features and how a compiler implements this programming model. Then, we will turn towards interesting runtime questions. We will show what problem waiting threads impose on waking them up again. We also will exemplify several algorithms (for, e.g., locks and barriers) and show how the processor design influences these algorithms. We will discuss some interesting effects of the modern cache hierarchy on the performance on such algorithms.

Michael Klemm is the Chief Executive Officer of the OpenMP Architecture Review Board as well as a long-time technical contributor and sub-committee chair in the OpenMP Language Committee. Michael is also a Principal Member of Technical Staff in the HPC Center of Excellence at AMD, where he is working on High Performance and Throughput Computing on AMD EPYC Processors and AMD Instinct Accelerators. Michael holds a Doctor of Engineering degree in Computer Science from the Friedrich-Alexander-University Erlangen-Nuremberg, Germany. His research focus is on compilers and runtime optimizations for distributed and heterogeneous systems. Michael is author and co-author of more than 50 scientific publications. He is co-author of the book "High Performance Parallel Runtimes" and holds a teaching position at Technical University of Munich, Germany.

Contents

Energy Efficiency

Energy Efficient Frequency Scaling on GPUs in Heterogeneous HPC Systems

Karlo Kraljic[1,2]([⊠]) [iD], Daniel Kerger[1] [iD], and Martin Schulz[2] [iD]

[1] Hewlett Packard Enterprise, Herrenberger Straße 140, 71034 Böblingen, Germany
{karlo.kraljic,daniel.kerger}@hpe.com
[2] Technical University of Munich, Chair of Computer Architecture and Parallel Systems, Boltzmannstraße 3, 85748 Garching, Germany
karlo.kraljic@tum.de, schulzm@in.tum.de

Abstract. With most major corporations and research institutions having pledged to support sustainability goals for High Performance Computing (HPC), energy efficiency is a critical factor when evaluating heterogeneous HPC systems. However, many popular hardware performance & energy measurement frameworks, such as LIKWID, and benchmarks, such as the STREAM or the hipBone benchmark, do not or not fully support execution on heterogeneous systems containing AMD or NVIDIA Graphical Processing Units (GPUs), leading to a gap with regards to the understanding the relationship between frequency, performance and energy. We aim at closing this gap by extending the performance measurement framework LIKWID to support both AMD and NVIDIA GPUs. We run the STREAM and hipBone benchmark on AMD and NVIDIA GPUs at different GPU core frequencies. We show that the minimum period between two measurements for our GPU is at least 100ms and that GPUs have a sweet spot with regards to energy consumption at approximately 75% of their maximum frequency with energy savings up to 30% at a performance overhead between 0.72% and 3.12%.

Keywords: Energy awareness · Heterogeneous computing · High Performance Computing

1 Motivation, Problem Statement and Key Contributions

1.1 Motivation

The computational power of Graphics Processing Units (GPUs) in High Performance Computing (HPC) systems has become a crucial factor with regards to performance gains. GPUs have a significantly higher computation rate for certain workloads at the cost of a typically significantly higher Thermal Design Power (TDP) compared to many Central Processing Units (CPUs). The GPUs that are currently built into systems in the TOP500 and the respective TDPs are: NVIDIA A100 with a TDP of 300/400 W (PCIe/ SXM), NVIDIA V100 with 250/300 W (PCIe/ SXM), NVIDIA GV100 with 250 W (PCIe), and AMD

MI250X with 500 W (OAM). In contrast, the CPUs built into the systems of the TOP500 list and their respective TDPs are: IBM POWER9 with 190 W, AMD EPYC 7763 with 280 W, and Intel XEON E5-2692v2 with 130 W.

These numbers show the increasing importance of GPUs with regards to energy efficiency in HPC systems.

1.2 Problem Statement and Key Contributions

Even though work has been performed to analyze NVIDIA GPUs with regards to energy efficiency, as shown in Sect. 2.3, there still is a lack in both, performance & energy measurement frameworks and benchmarks to perform research on AMD GPUs. Comparing performance and energy results among GPU vendors and architectures is difficult as performance and energy events may be vendor specific or vary among architectures.

This work addresses these issues with the following key contributions:

1. Introducing a methodology to get comparable results among different vendors, architectures, and programming models
2. Extending the Like I Knew What IWas Doing (LIKWID) [26] performance & energy efficiency measurement framework to support energy measurements on NVIDIA GPUs and performance & energy measurements on AMD GPUs
3. Discussing insights with regards to dynamic frequency scaling and its impact on energy efficiency for the STREAM and hipBone (GPU port of Nekbone) benchmark running on both, AMD and NVIDIA GPUs

2   Related Work and Background

2.1 Performance and Energy Measurement Tools

Several tools, e.g., Performance Application Programming Interface (PAPI) [15], LIKWID [26], rocm-smi [3], rocprof [4], NVIDIA Management Library (NVML) [1], or nvidia-smi [17] expose low-level hardware performance counters to the user.

PAPI is an interface for performance and energy counters of a system [25]. It consists of a high-level and a low-level interface. The high-level interface exposes events via event sets to the user. The low-level interface needs programming to access the performance counters, but has more features to operate more precisely with them [21]. PAPI supports all common architectures, like AMD, ARM and Intel. Furthermore, GPUs of AMD and NVIDIA are supported [14].

LIKWID is a collection of command-line tools that is able to perform performance & energy efficiency measurements by accessing lower level hardware counters and system libraries, as described in Sect. 3 [26]. In contrast to PAPI, it provides a timeline mode which is able to read performance and energy counters of a system without having to modify the source code of an application.

rocprof and rocm-smi are command line utilities that access lower level AMD libraries to get the values of lower level performance & energy counters [3,4].

rocprof is responsible for data that varies during run time of an application such as instruction counts or current power draw, while rocm-smi is responsible for managing static information such as the GPU frequency or voltage.

Similarly, NVIDIA exposes run time information using NVML [1], while static information is presented via nvidia-smi [17].

2.2   Benchmarks

Table 1. Comparison of benchmarking applications

Name	Type	GPU support	Focus
STREAM	Microbenchmark [12]	HIP [12]	Memory (MB/s) [12]
BabelSTREAM	Microbenchmark [22]	CUDA, OpenCL [22]	Memory (MB/s) [22]
HPCG	Microbenchmark [8]	CUDA, HIP, OpenCL [8,18]	Memory (MB/s) [8]
HPL	Kernel benchmark [20]	CUDA, HIP, OpenCL [18,20]	Compute, Memory (PFLOPS/s, MB/s) [20]
SPEC (Accel/CPU)	Benchmark suite (real applications) [24]	CUDA, OpenCL [24]	Memory, Compute (SPEC scores) [24]
Coral-2	Proxy application suite [2]	CUDA, HIP [2]	Memory, Compute, Network (PFLOPS/s, MB/s) [2]
FIRESTARTER	Kernel benchmark [10]	CUDA, HIP [10]	Power (watts) [10]
MVAPICH (OSU Micro-Benchmarks)	Benchmark suite [16]	CUDA, HIP [16]	Network, Latency (μs) [16]
NAS Parallel Benchmarks	Benchmark suite (real applications) [5]	N/A [5]	Memory, Compute (PFLOPS/s, mwords) [5]
Exascale Proxy Apps	Proxy application suite [9]	Some MPI, HIP, OpenCL [9]	Memory, Compute, (PFLOP/s, MB/s) [9]

Table 1 provides an overview of commonly used benchmarks and their current GPU support. Only a fraction of the benchmarks fully support heterogeneous systems equipped with GPUs.

2.3   Energy Efficiency on Graphics Processing Units

Several research works have been on energy efficiency on GPUs. Most of the works are developed/performed on NVIDIA GPUs, resulting in nearly no results for AMD GPUs. Kasichayanula et al. [13] developed a measurement approach for NVIDIA GPUs with NVML. The resulting power model predicts the power consumption of the GPU within execution time with an error of 10%. Similar models predicting the energy were conducted by [11,19,27]. Further work investigates the power draw and energy consumption within different memory and core frequency on NVIDIA GPUs. Coplin [7] found that changing a program's frequency alters the energy, power, and performance by a factor of two or higher. On the other hand, Suda [23] investigated the impact on the non-working and working threads on NVIDIA GPUs, resulting in a 71% power consumption of

non-working threads concerning working threads. Further work inspected the
energy efficiency on a heterogeneous system but dealt with drawbacks, like the
impact of cooling effects on the measured energy data [6].

3   Methodology

The target of this work is to analyze the impact of frequency scaling on different workloads and compare the results among architectures. To achieve this
goal, we are taking the following three steps: preparation, execution, evaluation.
Within the preparation, the measurement framework LIKWID is extended with
GPU support. LIKWID consists of two layers, as shown in Fig. 1. The first layer
are applications written in Lua exposing the functionality of LIKWID to the
user. likwid-topology shows topology information, i.e., information about the
architecture and the components of the underlying system. likwid-perfctr provides the interface to either measure the performance and energy efficiency of the
underlying system by making use of the timeline mode or the marker Application
Programming Interface (API). likwid-bench is a set of micro benchmarks for
testing and verifying the installation of LIKWID, and performing minor benchmarking on a system. The second layer is the core of LIKWID: it contains the
source code for accepting calls from the **Command Line Interface (CLI)
commands/ Tools** layer, reading the system topology, managing the performance & energy backends, and communicating with underlying layers such as
vendors specific drivers, referred to as **3rd Party Libraries**.

To measure energy related hardware events on NVIDIA GPUs, we extended
the second layer of LIKWID to support calls to the **nvml! (nvml!)** [1]. This
required changes in the Marker API, Lua interface, and the counter backend.
The likwid-perfctr CLI was extended to support energy related information.

To support performance and energy related hardware events on AMD GPUs,
we implemented new libraries for LIKWID to perform calls to the AMD backend. The AMD backend consists of the HIP, Rocprofiler, and ROCm SMI system
libraries. Besides making calls to the backend, these libraries expose the entry
points for the first layer and manage all data structures to define, get, and print
the desired performance & energy counters to the user. We implemented other
supportive functionality, i.e., integration tests, to verify the functional correctness of LIKWID. In the first layer, we have extended all necessary CLI tools
accordingly. Figure 1 provides an overview of LIKWID. All changes of LIKWID
to fully support GPUs are put in orange boxes. All changes were open sourced.

The execution and evaluation steps consist of performing benchmarks and
analysing the energy consumption on the systems under analysis, listed in
Table 2. The benchmarks STREAM and hipBone are executed on the three
nodes in Table 2. The STREAM benchmarks stresses the memory bandwidth,
while the hipBone benchmark stresses the compute units of the GPU. Since
these two benchmarks cover the two main components of a GPU, we expect to
see different results with regards energy efficiency while changing the frequencies on the GPU. The monitoring occurs with the LIKWID CLI for the CPU

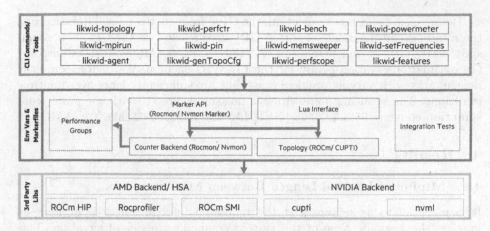

Fig. 1. Overview of LIKWID. Changes for extending LIKWID to support the NVIDIA energy counters and AMD performance & energy counters are put in orange boxes. (Color figure online)

Table 2. Overview of systems under analysis

	NVIDIA Node 1	AMD Node	NVIDIA Node 3
CPU	AMD EPYC Rome 7402	Intel Xeon CPU E5-2660 v4	AMD EPYC Milan 7413
GPU	NVIDIA A100	AMD MI100	NVIDIA A100
GPU Software Stack	CUDA 11.1.TC455_06.29190527_0	ROCm 5.1.2.50102-55	CUDA 11.1.TC455_06.29190527_0
Memory	515G	128G	515G
Operating System	RHEL-8.5	Ubuntu 20.04.2	RHEL-8.5
Kernel	4.18.0-348.23.1.el8_5.x86_64	5.4.0-99-generic	4.18.0-372.9.1.el8.x86_64

or with a daemon for the GPU. The CPU CLI-command includes the iteration length in ms, monitored performance counters, the output file, and the targeted benchmark. The iteration length defines the time in ms, after which LIKWID persists the performance counters values. A reset of the counters follows with the start of the next period. Instead of the CLI, the LIKWID daemon conducts the GPU measurements. Therefore, the requirements are the GPU id of the targeted GPU, the frequency, the monitored performance counters of rocm-smi and rocprof, and the output file. After fulfilling these prerequisites, the benchmark execution is monitored by the LIKWID daemon.

For the period analysis, the iteration length of LIKWID varies from 10 ms up to 250 ms. The targeted LIKWID hardware performance counters are defined for CPU and GPUs. The benchmark execution and monitoring start for each iteration length, generating the needed period timestamps. With these timestamps, the percentage difference to the mathematically calculated timestamp is calculated with the following formula:

$$deviation = (\frac{measured\_timestamp}{i * period} - 1) * 100, i \in [1, n\_periods]$$

This value is our definition of the term deviation.

Before each benchmark execution, the GPU frequency is pinned iteratively to the minimal and maximal supported GPU frequencies via the CLI-tools rocm-smi (AMD GPUs) and nvidia-smi (NVIDIA GPUs). Afterwards, we discover the optimal observation period for the LIKWID daemon. We then execure the benchmarks with varying problem sizes that are sufficiently large over multiple iterations. The resulting power draw is measured directly with the power consumption counters POWER_USAGE (NVIDIA) and RSMI_POWER_AVE[0] (AMD).

4 Results

4.1 Minimum Interval Length Between Measurements

It is essential to make sure that the minimum interval length is at least as long as the response time of the system component under observation. This section discusses the measurement results for defining the minimum interval length between measurements on the targeted systems.

Figure 2 shows the results for the minimum interval length analysis for NVIDIA Node 1. All frequencies show a similar behaviour: the deviation peaks for small amounts of iterations and small frequencies and converges to a specific deviation. It is in the nature of software-based measurement tools to expose an overhead to the system under observation. At the start of an application, software-based measurement tools have to load dynamically linked libraries or create internally required data structures, which creates a constant overhead. The same holds true for driver and firmware components, hence there is a high probability of getting false measurement results at low iteration counts. Higher frequencies do not show an initial peak as initial overheads are already compensated at the point of measurement: loading required libraries and creating data structures takes a smaller fraction of the initial observation period and is hence not blocking LIKWID to read the performance counters of the corresponding system component.

However, there is a difference in the value of the deviation: smaller frequencies have a significantly higher deviation compared to large frequencies, i.e., the deviation of a frequency of 10 ms converges to approximately 75%, while the deviation of a frequency of 250 ms converges to approximately 2%. At run time, measurement tools collect system information, i.e., performance or energy related counters, and thus have to either perform firmware or driver calls. These calls lead to false or timely decoupled results if the response time of the driver, firmware, or hardware of the targeted device is slower than the observation period of the application under analysis (Fig. 2).

The results of NVIDIA Node 2 are similar to the results of NVIDIA Node 1. This behaviour holds true for varying benchmarks executed on the GPU, which are omitted due to space reasons. LIKWID is running on the CPU, storing its data structures in the Random Access Memory (RAM) of the system, and only performing calls to the AMD resp. NVIDIA drivers. The minimum observation period of a software measurement tool, i.e., LIKWID, thus depends on the characteristics of the CPU, RAM, Peripheral Component Interconnect express

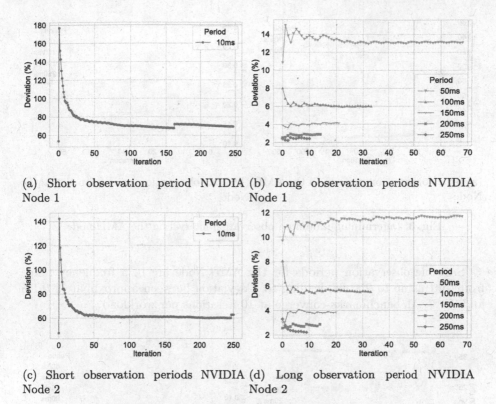

(a) Short observation period NVIDIA Node 1

(b) Long observation periods NVIDIA Node 1

(c) Short observation periods NVIDIA Node 2

(d) Long observation period NVIDIA Node 2

Fig. 2. Determining minimum observation interval on the NVIDIA nodes

(PCIe) bus, and the response time of the GPU. As performance & energy counters are typically independent from the compute units, the response time is not affected by the workload being executed on the GPU. Hence, evaluating the minimum interval length between measurements is a one-time effort for a specific system and may be reused in similar nodes. If one wants to perform multi-node measurements, the latency of the network becomes an additional factor that is affecting the minimal observation period.

Suitable observation periods for NVIDIA Node 1 and NVIDIA Node 2 are in a frequency range from 100 ms up to 250 ms, leading to a deviation between approximately 2% and 6%. All benchmarks converge at 10 iterations per workload.

Similar conclusions can be made on systems consisting of AMD GPUs. Small frequencies have a fairly high peak for small iterations and converge at approximately 10 iterations towards their final deviation. Small frequencies have a higher deviation that larger frequencies. However, AMD GPUs have smaller deviations compared to NVIDIA GPUs: for larger frequencies, there is a deviation of under 1% on AMD based systems, while NVIDIA based systems are never under 2%.

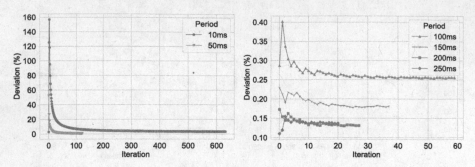

(a) Short observation periods on the AMD (b) Long observation periods on the AMD
Node   Node

Fig. 3. Determining minimum observation interval on the AMD node

Suitable observation periods for the AMD Node are in a frequency range
from 100 ms up to 250 ms, leading to a deviation between approximately 0.1%
and 0.4%. All benchmarks converge at 10 iterations per workload.

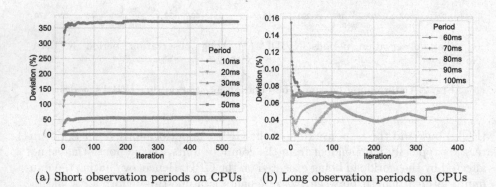

(a) Short observation periods on CPUs   (b) Long observation periods on CPUs

Fig. 4. On Central Processing Units

Regarding the CPU deviations in Fig. 4a and 4b, the overall deviation is
much lower than the GPU. Measurement frequencies lower than 60ms have a
deviation from 20% up to 350%. Higher frequencies, such as 60ms and above,
are steady with their deviations between 0.02% and 0.10%. This shows that the
optimal frequency for CPUs is at 60 ms up to 100 ms with a converging deviation
rate at 20 iterations.

The minimum interval length between measurements of a heterogeneous system is defined as the highest lower bound of an observation interval of all system components under observation. In this specific case, the lowest upper bound
with an acceptable deviation is provided by the NVIDIA based systems with an

observation period of 100 ms. All following benchmarks are executed with an observation period of 100 ms.

4.2 Frequency Scaling

The following section compares the effect of frequency scaling on the power draw and the execution time on the STREAM and hipBone benchmark running on different GPU architectures.

STREAM. Figure 5 provides an overview of the results gathered for STREAM. All lines depicted in these figures show a similar pattern: all lines raise immediately to their maximum followed by a fall to a lower power draw level. Both NVIDIA GPUs show a similar behaviour, as these are identical GPUs: their idle power draw is at 40 W. The maximum power draw is at 180 W for both nodes. The execution script only tunes the core clock speed and not the memory clock speed. The maximum power draw at 180 W and the tuning of the core clock speed show the memory boundness of the STREAM benchmark: At a certain point in time, compute units are waiting for their input from the memory leading to a plateau with regards to power consumption. The maximum power draw is reached at maximum frequency, while the smallest frequency has a power draw of 85 W. Increasing the frequency from 210 Mhz to 330 Mhz decreases the execution from approximately 6.5 s (NVIDIA Node 1) resp. 6.1 s (NVIDIA Node 2) to 4.8 s (NVIDIA Node 1) resp. 4.5 s (NVIDIA Node 2). Additional increasements of the frequency only provide minor improvements of the overall execution, i.e., changing the frequence from 330 MHz to 1410 MHz MHz decreases the execution from 4.8 s to 4.2 s (NVIDIA Node 1) resp. 4.5 s to 4.1 s (NVIDIA Node 2).

The AMD GPU reaches its maximum power draw at 250 W at a frequency of 1502 MHz MHz, also not reaching its TDP. The execution time is 7.3 s at this frequency level. The run time for the STREAM benchmark running on a frequency of 300 MHz is approximately 28 s reaching a maximum power draw of 95 W. In contrast to the NVIDIA GPU, the AMD GPU has four frequency levels leading to significant changes with regards to execution time and power draw: at 300 MHz (power draw: 95 W) with an execution time of 28 s, at 495 MHz (power draw: 105 W) with an execution time of 14.5 s, at 731 MHz (power draw: 120 W) with an execution time of 10 s, and at 1500 MHz (power draw: 245 W) with an execution time of 8 s.

The best execution on the NVIDIA GPU took 4.2 s, while the best execution on the AMD GPU took 8 s. The NVIDIA GPU outperforms the AMD GPU with regards to execution time. Since the STREAM benchmark is specifically designed to test the memory bandwidth of a specific architecture, differences with regards to the execution time point into a better memory bandwidth within NVIDIA GPUs.

HipBone. The hipBone benchmark has not been executed on NVIDIA Node 2 due to library incompatibilities.

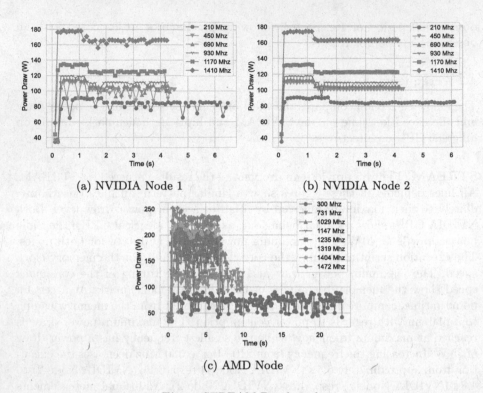

(a) NVIDIA Node 1   (b) NVIDIA Node 2

(c) AMD Node

Fig. 5. STREAM Benchmark

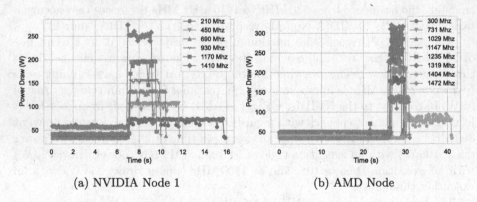

(a) NVIDIA Node 1   (b) AMD Node

Fig. 6. hipBone Benchmark

The execution time of hipBone consists of two phases: a setup phase and an execution phase, as shown in Fig. 6. On both nodes, the power draw steadies at 50 W within the first execution half. On NVIDIA Node 1, the power draw reaches its maximum after 7 s and plateaus for several seconds, depending on the frequency set. The longest plateau time is approximately 9 s at the lowest frequency, i.e., 210 MHz. The smallest plateau time is approximately 2.5 s at the maximum frequency, i.e., 1410 MHz. On the AMD Node, the setup phased is finished after 27 s and reaching its maximum power draw. Please note that at a certain point in time, the power draw is suddenly dropping, even though there are currently high frequencies set on the GPU. At this point in time, the GPU is being throttled.

In both cases, the GPUs are coming closer to their respective TDP, while the NVIDIA GPU still outperforms the AMD GPU.

Summary. All of these figures, benchmarks, and architectures show that there is a relationship between execution time and frequency: the higher the frequency, the faster the execution. However, it also shows the relationship between frequency and power draw: the higher the frequency, the higher the power draw. Increasing a low frequency to a mid frequency has a potentially greater impact than increasing a mid-ranged frequency to a high frequency.

4.3   Frequency vs. Total Energy Consumption

Figure 7 shows the total energy consumption of all benchmarks executed on the various platforms. Again, both NVIDIA based GPUs show a similar behaviour for the STREAM benchmark: for very low frequencies, the total energy consumption is at approximately 5 J. For mid ranged frequencies, the total energy consumption shrinks to approximately 4.1 J up to a frequency of 1050 MHz. Starting at a frequency of 1050 MHz, the total energy consumption raises up to 6.2 J. A similar pattern holds true for the hipbone benchmark executed on NVIDIA Node 1: It start at 8.05 J, decreases to 6.2 J, and starting at a frequency of 1050 MHz the total power consumption starts to rise while reaching its maximum of 8.4 J at a frequency of 1410 MHz.

The AMD Node shows a similar behaviour with regards to the STREAM benchmark as both NVIDIA nodes. The overall energy consumption is higher, and the maximum frequency of the low-energy plateau is at 1283 MHz. Its energy consumption is not at the maximum frequency of 1502 MHz (total energy consumption: 15.1 J), but at the lowest frequency of 300 MHz (total energy consumption: 16.5 J). The hipBone benchmark total energy consumption reaches at 962 MHz with a total energy consumption of 16.5 J without having an initial drop in total energy consumption. It reaches its maximum total energy consumption of 23 J at a frequency of 1363 MHz. After this point, the system throttles the GPU leading to a significant drop with regards total energy consumption.

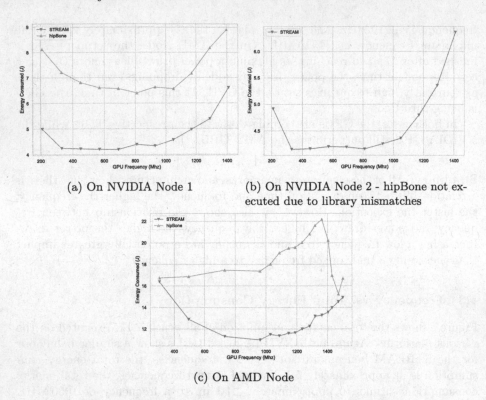

(a) On NVIDIA Node 1

(b) On NVIDIA Node 2 - hipBone not executed due to library mismatches

(c) On AMD Node

Fig. 7. Total Energy Consumption of different benchmarks on different GPUs

5   Summary, Future Research and Conclusion

We modified LIKWID in heterogeneous system to measure both, performance and energy efficiency: extend the nvmon with the necessary energy backend and implement both, a performance and a energy efficiency backend for the ROCm software stack. We discussed the reasons for selecting the STREAM benchmark, i.e., being memory focused and the hipBone benchmark, i.e., being compute focused and ported both benchmarks to support both programming models, HIP and CUDA. By utilizing LIKWID, we determine a minimum observation period on heterogeneous systems with AMDs MI100 and NVIDIA A100 of 100ms. There is a relationship between execution time, frequency, and power draw: the higher the frequency, the faster the execution time and the higher the frequency, the higher the power draw. The relationship between these dimensions is non-trivial. The sweet spot with regards to total energy consumption is, regardless of the underlying architecture and running workload, at approximately 75% of the maximum frequency of a GPU. The performance impacts are acceptable when running at 75% of the maximum frequency, i.e., at 1050 MHz, are in a range from 0.72% (STREAM) to 3.12% (hipBone) on systems with NVIDIA GPUs. On systems with AMD GPUs, the overhead is 2.6% (STREAM). Due to throttling effects on the AMD GPU, the overhead could not be calculated with respect to the maximum frequency. Future work consists of understanding and overcoming the throttling effect on the AMD GPUs. This work observes the impact of tuning the core frequency of GPUs. We show that there are much more degrees of freedom requiring a more sophisticated analysis regarding their impact on energy efficiency, such as the GPU memory frequency. Future work will on the one hand identify all variables and on the other hand quantify their impact on the total energy consumption. Besides the inherent characteristics of a GPU, the inherent characteristics of a specific benchmark and its executed instructions are additional parameters that define the power consumption of the system. It is necessary to understand what are the most important contributors with regards to energy consumption in order to identify a new way of optimizing with regards to energy efficiency.

References

1. NVML API Reference Guide: GPU Deployment and Management Documentation. http://docs.nvidia.com/deploy/nvml-api/index.html
2. Advanced Simulation and Computing: Coral-2 benchmarks (15062022). https://asc.llnl.gov/coral-2-benchmarks
3. AMD: Radeonopencompute/rocm_smi_lib: Rocm smi lib (27062022). https://github.com/RadeonOpenCompute/rocm_smi_lib
4. AMD: Rocm-developer-tools/rocprofiler: Roc profiler library. profiling with perf-counters and derived metrics (27062022). https://github.com/ROCm-Developer-Tools/rocprofiler
5. Bailey, D., Harris, T., Saphir, W.: The NAS parallel benchmarks 2.0 (1995)
6. Collange, C., Defour, D., Tisserand, A.: Power consumption of GPUs from a software perspective. In: Allen, G., Nabrzyski, J., Seidel, E., van Albada, G.D., Dongarra, J., Sloot, P.M.A. (eds.) ICCS 2009. LNCS, vol. 5544, pp. 914–923. Springer, Heidelberg (2009). https://doi.org/10.1007/978-3-642-01970-8_92
7. Coplin, J., Burtscher, M.: Energy, power, and performance characterization of GPGPU benchmark programs. In: 2016 IEEE International Parallel and Distributed Processing Symposium Workshops (IPDPSW), pp. 1190–1199 (2016). https://doi.org/10.1109/IPDPSW.2016.164
8. Dongarra, J., Heroux, M.A., Luszczek, P.: High-performance conjugate-gradient benchmark: a new metric for ranking high-performance computing systems. Int. J. High Perform. Comput. Appl. **30**(1), 3–10 (2016). https://doi.org/10.1177/1094342015593158
9. ECP Proxy Applications: Ecp proxy applications (16062022). https://proxyapps.exascaleproject.org/
10. Hackenberg, D., Oldenburg, R., Molka, D., Schone, R.: Introducing firestarter: a processor stress test utility. In: 2013 International Green Computing Conference Proceedings. IEEE (2013). https://doi.org/10.1109/igcc.2013.6604507
11. Hong, S., Kim, H.: An integrated GPU power and performance model. In: Proceedings of the 37th Annual International Symposium on Computer Architecture, pp. 280–289. ISCA 2010, Association for Computing Machinery, New York (2010). https://doi.org/10.1145/1815961.1815998

12. McCalpin, J.D.: Memory bandwidth and machine balance in high performance computers (1995)
13. Kasichayanula, K., Terpstra, D., Luszczek, P., Tomov, S., Moore, S., Peterson, G.D.: Power aware computing on GPUs. In: 2012 Symposium on Application Accelerators in High Performance Computing, pp. 64–73 (2012). https://doi.org/10.1109/SAAHPC.2012.26, iSSN: 2166-515X
14. Kozhokanova, A.: Papi: Performance API introduction & overview (17062022). https://www.vi-hps.org/cms/upload/material/tw39/PAPI.pdf
15. Mucci, P.J., Browne, S., Deane, C., Ho, G.: PAPI: a portable interface to hardware performance counters. In: In Proceedings of the Department of Defense HPCMP Users Group Conference, pp. 7–10 (1999)
16. MVAPICH: Mvapich 2-2.3.6-userguide (15062022). http://mvapich.cse.ohio-state.edu/static/media/mvapich/mvapich2-2.3.6-userguide.pdf
17. NVIDIA: nvidia-smi documentation. https://developer.download.nvidia.com/com-pute/DCGM/docs/nvidia-smi-367.38.pdf
18. NVIDIA: Nvidia hpc-benchmarks — nvidia ngc (15062022). https://catalog.ngc.nvidia.com/orgs/nvidia/containers/hpc-benchmarks
19. Payvar, S., Pelcat, M., Hämäläinen, T.D.: A model of architecture for estimating GPU processing performance and power. Des. Autom. Embedded Syst. 25(1), 43–63 (2021). https://doi.org/10.1007/s10617-020-09244-4
20. Petitet, A., Whaley R. C., Dongarra, J., Cleary A.: Hpl - a portable implementation of the high-performance linpack benchmark for distributed-memory computers (862019). https://www.netlib.org/benchmark/hpl/
21. Mucci, P. J., Browne, S., Deane, C., Ho, G.: PAPI: A Portable Interface to Hardware Performance Counters (1999)
22. Reddy Kuncham, G.K., Vaidya, R., Barve, M.: Performance study of GPU applications using SYCL and CUDA on tesla V100 GPU. In: 2021 IEEE High Performance Extreme Computing Conference (HPEC). IEEE (2021). https://doi.org/10.1109/hpec49654.2021.9622813
23. Ren, D.Q., Suda, R.: Modeling and estimation for the power consumption of matrix computation on multi-core platform. In: 2009 International Joint Conference on Computational Sciences and Optimization. vol. 1, pp. 42–46 (2009). https://doi.org/10.1109/CSO.2009.451
24. SPEC: Spec benchmarks (14062022). https://www.spec.org/benchmarks.html
25. Terpstra, D., Jagode, H., You, H., Dongarra, J.: Collecting performance data with PAPI-C. In: Müller, M.S., Schulz, A., Nagel, W.E., Resch, M. (eds.) Tools for high performance computing 2009, vol. 14, pp. 157–173. Springer, Cham (2010). https://doi.org/10.1007/978-3-642-11261-4_11
26. Treibig, J., Hager, G., Wellein, G.: LIKWID: lightweight performance tools. In: 2010 39th International Conference on Parallel Processing Workshops, pp. 207–216 (2010). https://doi.org/10.1109/ICPPW.2010.38, http://arxiv.org/abs/1104.4874, arXiv: 1104.4874
27. Wang, Q., Li, N., Shen, L., Wang, Z.: A statistic approach for power analysis of integrated GPU. Soft. Comput. 23(3), 827–836 (2019). https://doi.org/10.1007/s00500-017-2786-1

Dual-IS: Instruction Set Modality for Efficient Instruction Level Parallelism

Kari Hepola[✉], Joonas Multanen, and Pekka Jääskeläinen

Tampere University, Tampere, Finland
{kari.hepola,joonas.multanen,pekka.jaaskelainen}@tuni.fi

Abstract. Exploiting *instruction level parallelism* (ILP) is a widely used method for increasing performance of processors. While traditional *very long instruction word* (VLIW) processors can exploit ILP energy-efficiently thanks to static instruction scheduling, they suffer from bad code density with serial parts that cannot utilize the multi-issue capabilities. *Transport triggered architecture* (TTA) is a variation of the VLIW paradigm with an *exposed datapath* that improves scaling of VLIW processors with the cost of even wider instructions by exposing the datapath interconnection network to the programmer.

To this end, we propose Dual-IS, an architecture that implements a TTA multi-issue and RISC-V compatible single-issue instruction-set modes by means of a microcoded control path. By utilizing the instruction set modality, the TTA mode can be used in codes that benefit from ILP, while a single-issue RISC-V ISA mode reduces instruction stream energy and code size for sequential programs. Thanks to the TTA programming model, the static multi-issue mode can be implemented without additional register file ports.

The processor was synthesized on a 28 nm ASIC technology. For this design point, when instruction-set mode was selected based on energy-delay product at the program granularity, with CHStone benchmarks, Dual-IS had on average 14% lower energy-delay product compared to a single-mode TTA processor with a similar datapath, while only adding a 3% overhead in the core area. Dual-IS achieved on average 15% and in the best case 33% smaller run times than a single-issue RISC-V implementation by running programs in the TTA mode only when it was beneficial in terms of performance.

Keywords: Instruction level parallelism · Microcode · Multiple instruction set architecture · Transport triggered architecture

1 Introduction

In order to achieve higher performance, processors exploit *instruction level parallelism* (ILP) either statically in *very long instruction word* (VLIW) style or dynamically in *superscalar* processors. The benefit of the VLIW style is simplified hardware implementation acquired by static scheduling which yields better results in terms of energy efficiency and area in digital signal processing applications compared to dynamically scheduled processors. However, VLIWs suffer

© The Author(s), under exclusive license to Springer Nature Switzerland AG 2022
M. Schulz et al. (Eds.): ARCS 2022, LNCS 13642, pp. 17–32, 2022.
https://doi.org/10.1007/978-3-031-21867-5_2

from high instruction stream energy and code size in programs that cannot utilize ILP. This is caused by the use of *no-operation* instructions (NOPs) when the VLIW instruction packet cannot be completely filled with useful operations.

To make designs more flexible, designers have incorporated multiple heterogeneous cores that can be used depending on the desired use case into their *system-on-chips* (SoCs). While this results in increased flexibility, it is not an optimal solution from an area utilization point of view as it effectively adds "dark silicon" [18] to the design.

Exposed datapath processors [12] provide an instruction-set that exposes low-level aspects of the datapath to the programmer. *Transport triggered architectures* (TTAs) are highly modular architectures that follow the exposed datapath paradigm, which makes them an interesting base for VLIW processor designs. In TTAs, the programming interface is based on *moves* that transport operands and execute operations as a side-effect. Their key drawback is that like traditional VLIW processors, TTAs suffer from high code size and instruction stream energy in sequential programs. In addition, the low-level programming interface exposes more information in the instruction format which correspondingly requires more bits in the instruction word. However, the programming interface of TTAs allows efficient exploitation of ILP thanks to optimizations enabled by exposing the interconnection network to the programmer.

With the aim to provide the best of two worlds, we introduce Dual-IS, a processor that implements both a RISC-V single-issue and an exposed datapath VLIW instruction set. Dual-IS enables optimizing execution of programs in terms of performance, code size and energy efficiency by supporting two different instruction sets. We maximize the reuse of the core's datapath resources by implementing the RISC-V mode with the use of microcode that maps and sequences transport triggered move instructions for the exposed datapath. Thanks to the exposed datapath architecture, we can support a multi-issue instruction set with a *register file* (RF) complexity of a single-issue implementation.

This paper makes the following contributions:

- A novel dual-mode (RISC-V single-issue and an exposed datapath VLIW) instruction set for exploiting instruction level parallelism statically when available in the program, but not suffering from the VLIW's poor code density when there's a lack of it.
- Datapath resource sharing between the RISC-V and exposed datapath ISAs via a low-level microcode-based control implementation.
- A proof-of-concept implementation and ASIC synthesis of the dual-mode instruction set architecture as well as its performance and energy efficiency evaluation.

2   Related Work

There have been various instruction set processor approaches in the past. Lin et al. [17] proposed a unified processor architecture that had both a scalar MIPS-like *reduced instruction set computer* (RISC) instruction set and a 4-way VLIW mode. The mode was set by a dedicated mode encoding that was specified for each instruction. To minimize code size, the architecture formed 512-bit bundles that could contain both VLIW and RISC instructions. In their approach, the VLIW mode did not implement control instructions and therefore control instructions were always executed in RISC mode.

Hou et al. [11] built on this concept with their FuMicro processor. In their approach, the processor had a superscalar and VLIW ARM mode. The two modes had a different issue width: The superscalar mode had an issue width of two to minimize dependency checking while the VLIW mode was a 7-issue architecture. The instructions were fetched in 256-bit packets that could contain 16- or 32-bit instructions.

Contrary to the previous two processors, Karaki et al. [13] proposed a processor that could run both ARM and x86 instructions on shared hardware. The processor utilized a hardware interpreter that translated and sequenced ARM micro-operations from x86 instructions which enabled sharing the processor datapath between instruction-set modes. This concept is quite interesting as it combines two completely different ISA design philosophies: reduced and *complex instruction set computer* (CISC).

Crepaldi et al. [4] presented a multi-one instruction set computer that followed the *one instruction set computer* (OISC) principle. The processor had two modes that could be selected during startup. The first mode was a standard OISC mode that was based around the *subleq* instruction. The second mode was called CISC mode and it could change between 14 different run modes depending on a control register value that was explicitly stated in each instruction. In their work, however, the different modes were not used to exploit ILP.

Another interesting architecture utilizing multiple modes is Nvidia's Denver project [2]. Denver implemented a traditional hardware-decoder mode that decoded two ARM instructions per cycle and executed them in parallel if possible. The second mode, microcode mode, was used together with dynamic code optimization that formed optimized packets of micro-operations in software. In this mode, hardware-decoder was bypassed and the optimized micro-operation packets were passed directly to the in-order hardware scheduler to execute up to 7 instructions per cycle. This architectural concept is quite close to the one introduced in this paper. However, we use a an exposed datapath as the statically scheduled multi-issue instruction set together with a microcode unit that implements the RISC-V frontend for the processor core.

VLIWs have also been used in commercial designs together with code translation. For example, the Crusoe processor [14] that implemented x86 compatibility with the use of software translation to run native VLIW code. The concept is quite different from our work, as we add hardware decoding support for both instruction sets instead of using software to translate code during runtime.

Some previous work regarding microcoded control design with the RISC-V ISA has been done. Albartus et al. [1] introduced a RISC-V implementation using microcoded control logic. In their work, the datapath of the processor only allowed one transaction per cycle to occur which meant that execution of RISC-V instructions required multiple cycles due to operand transportations. Klemmer and Große [15] used an OISC microarchitecture to implement the RISC-V ISA through microcoded control logic. In their work, they implemented the RISC-V instructions as a chain of subleq micro-operations with the use of microcode. Because of this microarchitecture, multiple cycles were needed to implement single RISC-V instructions.

Previous work on microcoded RISC-V design is close to the concept of control logic design used in this work except that the internal microarchitecture is a transport triggered architecture. In our microarchitecture, we directly map the RISC-V instructions to equivalent operations in the function units without implementing them as a chain of operations and use the microcoded control logic for operand transportations on the exposed datapath. In addition, the operand transports are sequenced in parallel to minimize cycle counts when executing instructions. Contrary to previous work, we also make use of the microcoded control logic design by using it to support multiple instruction set modes.

3   Transport Triggered Architectures

Transport triggered architectures are highly modular exposed datapath processors. Like traditional VLIW processors, TTAs are statically scheduled and allow programmers to directly exploit ILP. However, programming TTAs differs vastly from the traditional "operation triggered" architectures [9]. The TTA programming model is based on data moves on the datapath *interconnection* (IC) network which executes operations as a side-effect as demonstrated in Fig. 1. That is, the programmer is exposed to the datapath connections of the processor. The additional degrees of freedom in the programming model, however, leads to wider instruction words [12].

Compared to traditional operation triggered multi-issue machines that require a notorious amount of register file IO to support concurrent operations, transport triggered architectures can exploit ILP with reduced register file connectivity and port amount. This is thanks to the *function unit* (FU) ports being registered, and can therefore be used to store values between clock cycles. Hoogerbrugge and Corporaal [8] showed that transport triggered architecture required an average amount of 0.5 read and 0.35 write ports per operation, compared to two read and one write ports of traditional operation triggered architectures. This difference becomes quite substantial when designing VLIW architectures as increased register file complexity affects the area, timing and energy efficiency of the processor core. Multiple TTA-specific optimizations contribute to the reduced register file traffic:

- **Operand sharing** is used when two sequential operations share the same operand. This potentially saves one register file read as the input operand has already been transported to the function unit input register.
- **Software bypassing** [5] allows programmer to directly move data from function unit output port to function unit input port without routing the data through the register file.

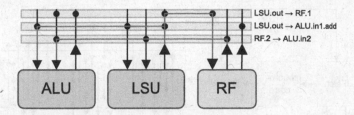

Fig. 1. Example of TTA programming model. Colored lines describe moves on the exposed datapath between function units and a register file which triggers an add operation as a side-effect. (Color figure online)

- **Dead result elimination** reduces redundant register writes when an output operand is not needed to be written to the register file. This happens when a software bypass is used to transport the output operand to a function unit and the value is no longer needed.

In addition to reduced register file IO requirements, TTAs can be implemented with a reduced datapath connectivity when compared to operation triggered VLIWs [3]. Contrary to dynamic data hazard detection implemented in operation triggered architectures, TTAs solve data hazards in compile time which reduces hardware complexity together with static software bypasses. In addition, software bypassing eases customization of the interconnect network as the programmer is aware of the connections of the processor datapath.

The low-level programming interface of TTAs allows efficient use of latency hiding with delay slot filling where delay slots of pipelined operations can be used statically by the programmer to execute other operations.

Due to additional state data in function unit ports, external interrupts and exceptions are expensive to implement in TTA processors. However, this is not an issue when a TTA is used as a programmable accelerator as interrupts are rarely justified in this type of use case. The problem of context saving during interrupts can be solved with the concepts introduced in this work where the RISC-V mode can be used for traditional register file base context saving.

4   Dual-IS Processor

Dual-IS processor combines both a RISC-V single-issue mode for sequential code and a TTA-based VLIW mode for exploitation of ILP. An overview of the processor structure is presented in Fig. 2. From the instruction set modality point of view, the most important component is the microcode unit that translates and sequences RISC-V instructions to TTA instructions during run time. In our approach, using microcoded control logic for a RISC architecture enables the processor to share resources with the TTA mode due to the exposed datapath programming model.

The microcode unit is a crucial component that connects the two instruction set interfaces of Dual-IS processor. In addition to instruction translation and

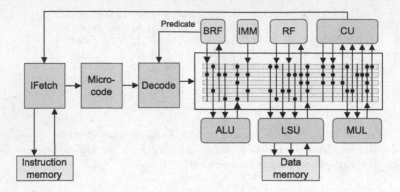

Fig. 2. Overview of the Dual-IS structure with a microcode unit between the instruction fetch and decode components.

micro-operation sequencing, the microcode unit implements all the operation triggered features that are not found in transport triggered architectures, for example, dynamic data hazard detection. In our work, we automatically generate the microcode RTL based on a high-level architecture definition which enables to heavily customize the instruction set of the TTA mode.

The internal structure of the microcode unit is presented in Fig. 3. As seen in the figure, the microcode unit is split into multiple subcomponents that implement parts of the decoding and control logic of the processor. The internal structure of the microcode unit is explored in greater detail in later sections.

By using TTA for the VLIW mode, we could expand the processor datapath without adding register file IO due to the decreased register file usage as discussed in Sect. 3. This enables to extend a traditional single-issue processor with a VLIW mode with relatively inexpensive hardware changes. A traditional operation triggered VLIW would need the minimum of 2 write and 4 read ports to support the same amount of peak issue width as Dual-IS.

4.1 Instruction Translation

Inside the microcode unit is a translation table that translates RISC-V instructions to TTA instructions. The translation table holds entries for each RISC-V operation and format combination that correspond to parallel moves on the exposed datapath. As the translation table does not need to be reprogrammed, it is constructed purely of combinatorial logic to minimize the hardware overhead.

To reduce the amount of entries, register file indexes and immediate values are not stored in the translation table. Instead, when a RISC-V instruction arrives to the microcode unit, bits representing register file indexes and immediate values are sliced from the instruction which leaves only the function unit and operation codes. This information is sufficient for the translation table to translate the correct function unit and socket encodings that control function unit port multiplexers. After the instruction is read from the translation table, register file indexes are inserted to the translated instruction.

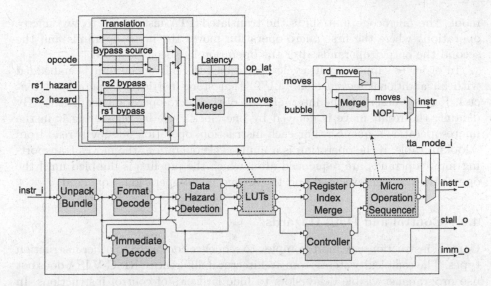

Fig. 3. Dual-IS microcode unit combines instruction translation and dynamic micro-operation sequencing. Data hazards are solved during run time with bypass lookup tables and dynamic data hazard detection. The microcode unit supports instruction set modality with the use of a control signal that is used to bypass the microcode.

Immediate values require more attention, as supporting the full immediate ranges of RISC-V instruction formats takes a considerable amount of encoding space from TTA instructions. To optimize this, the immediate values are sliced from RISC-V instructions and assigned directly to the interconnect immediate signals by bypassing the decoder. This allows having different immediate ranges between different instruction-set modes to preserve encoding space on TTA instruction formats.

4.2 Micro-operation Sequencing

Vast differences between the programming interfaces of operation and transport triggered architectures, as mentioned in Sect. 3, require the translated instruction to be split into multiple micro-operations. The reason behind this are the explicit moves that transport result operands on the exposed datapath after the operation has been executed. An example of such a phenomenon is a simple RISC register *add* instruction that requires a minimum of two separate instructions on a TTA:

```
Cycle 0: RF.1 → ALU.in2, RF.2 → ALU.in1.add.
Cycle 1: ALU.out → RF.3
```

On the first cycle, the input operands are transported to the ALU and the add operation is triggered. On the next cycle, the result operand is transported to the register file. To implement this feature dynamically on the Dual-IS RISC-V mode, the microcode unit splits the translated TTA instruction to two micro-operations where the first micro-operation moves the input operands and the second the output operands after the operation has been executed.

In order to support multi-cycle operations, the microcode unit is embedded with an additional *lookup table* (LUT) that stores entries for operation latencies. Figure 3 describes the internal logic of the micro-operation sequencing. By default, the result move is delayed by one clock cycle by registering it in the micro-operation sequencer. For each instruction, operation latency is read from a lookup table. If the operation is a multi-cycle operation, the moves transporting input operands are sequenced after which the pipeline is bubbled until the operation has been executed and the second micro-operation sequenced.

4.3   Control and Data Hazards

Control instructions are more complex to sequence compared to other instruction types. The complexity stems from architectural differences: RISC-V ISA does not use programmer visible delay slots to hide latencies of control instructions. In order to preserve delay slots, and to follow the TTA programming model for the TTA mode, the microcode unit is embedded with a controller that solves control hazards during the execution of control instructions by stalling the processor pipeline. The execution of control instructions could be improved with the use of a branch predictor but we chose not to include one to minimize the amount of RISC-V specific hardware.

The programming interface of RISC-V enables manipulation of the program counter register directly without routing the data through the later stages of the processor pipeline. This is especially beneficial when the control instruction does not have a dependency on the register file. In Dual-IS, direct RISC-V jump instructions are implemented by bypassing the interconnect which reduces operation latency by one clock cycle when executing them in RISC-V mode.

In addition to control hazards, solving data hazards requires additional hardware in the microcode unit due to the static software bypasses used in TTAs. To implement dynamic bypasses in the Dual-IS processor, the microcode unit is embedded with additional lookup tables. A LUT is required for each of the register operands. These LUTs contain the bypass move from the source function unit output port to the target function unit input port for the hazard operand.

As there can be multiple function units, a third LUT that maps operations to function units is required. To support bypass moves between multiple different function units, the two LUTs containing bypass moves must be two-dimensional where the operation encoding and the source function unit form a set of keys.

Figure 3 presents the dynamic bypass feature in more detail. The LUT component contains the translation, bypass source and operand bypass LUTs that are constructed of purely combinatorial logic. When a data hazard is detected, the register file move on the data hazard bus is discarded by multiplexing it with the move read from the bypass lookup table. This way, the correct operand value is moved directly to the function unit input port by bypassing the register file.

4.4 Mode Switching

Supporting multiple instruction sets induces problems for the *instruction fetch* (IF) design. The main challenge is how to support the different instruction word sizes of different instruction-set with minimal complexity. In our approach, we chose to bundle the RISC-V instructions to a wider instruction packet that is fetched at a time. The width of the packet corresponds to one TTA instruction width which allows simple instruction fetch design. Effectively this restricts the TTA instruction word to be a multiple of the single-issue instruction word size while minimizing the hardware overhead.

This design choice, however, does not come without issues because branches between non-bundle-aligned addresses must be supported. This also has an overhead in terms of fetched instruction bits because when jumping between non-bundle-aligned addresses, redundant instructions are fetched. This problem could be minimized by aligning all jump targets with the cost of larger code size.

In Dual-IS, the instruction-set mode is controlled by a signal that is visible in the hardware interface of the processor. The mode switching itself requires very little additional logic because the RISC-V mode shares the same decoder with the TTA mode. In the microcode unit, the translated and sequenced micro-operations are multiplexed with the fetched instruction which enables to bypass the microcoding and execute TTA instructions as demonstrated in Fig. 3. Because we chose to decode RISC-V immediate values directly in the microcode unit to save encoding space in TTA instruction formats, the decoder requires an additional multiplexer that discards the immediate value output by the microcode unit and assigns the one produced by the decoder instead. Overall, the additional hardware changes required by mode switching are relatively small.

5   Evaluation

For evaluation, we generated multiple designs that are discussed in more depth in Sect. 5.1. The generated designs were synthesized with Synopsys Design Compiler and a 28 nm ASIC technology to acquire post-synthesis properties of the cores. In addition, the cores were benchmarked with the widely used CHStone benchmark suite [6] in ModelSim RTL simulation to acquire cycle counts and switching activity information for power estimation.

5.1   Evaluated Designs

We used the open-source OpenASIP toolset [7] to generate and design our evaluated cores. OpenASIP supports customization, generation, simulation and programming of TTA-based *application-specific instruction-set processors* (ASIPs). It ships with an automatically retargeting LLVM-based compiler that supports heavy customization of the processor architecture.

To evaluate the overhead of multiple instruction-set modes, an in-order 4-stage single-issue RISC-V core with hardware multiplier support was designed with the toolset by using a TTA with a reduced interconnect network connectivity and hardware resources as the internal microarchitecture together with a generated microcode unit. Similarly, a TTA core was generated without the RISC-V mode and the RISC-V specific branch, call and auipc instructions that cannot be utilized by the OpenASIP's compiler. The architectures were targeted for small embedded applications without floating point computation.

Both Dual-IS and single-mode TTA processors have five interconnect buses and concurrently accessible function units which enables the execution of a memory, an arithmetic and a control flow operation in parallel. The TTA instruction set has an instruction width of 64 bits that is double the width of RISC-V instruction word which enables to bundle instructions without using padding bits. For the single-mode TTA and Dual-IS, instruction memories consisted of 64-bit banks to match the instruction fetch width. The instruction memory of the single-issue processor consisted of 32-bit elements.

To optimize the critical path, load and multiply operations were implemented as 2-cycle operations. For the single-issue instruction sets, execution of these operations caused one stall cycle. The TTA instruction sets, thanks to their low-level programming model, were able to utilize static latency hiding to minimize the overhead of multi-cycle operations. In addition to multi-cycle load and multiply operations, control operations had programmer-visible delay slots that could be exploited by the TTA instruction set.

5.2   Synthesis Results

Out of the three designs, the single-issue core achieved the highest clock frequency of 2.08 GHz. The maximum clock frequency for the single-mode TTA design was 2.04 GHz and for Dual-IS 2.00 GHz. The negligible overhead of Dual-IS comes from the more complex control unit that adds additional multiplexers to the interconnect which has a small effect on timing. The additional hardware of Dual-IS, however, was not directly on the critical path of the design.

Table 1 lists the area utilization and breakdown of the designs. Dual-IS utilized 3% more area than the single-mode TTA core and compared to the RISC-V core, the area overhead was 17%. In Dual-IS, the microcode unit itself utilized 3% of the area and in the single-mode RISC-V design only 2%. The larger area overhead of the microcode unit in Dual-IS was due to the additional multiplexers that are required to switch instruction-set modes. Overall, the area overhead of the microcode unit was negligible.

5.3   Performance

In this work, we utilized instruction set modality only at program scope which allowed to use the same program binaries for Dual-IS and single-mode architectures. While in-program mode switching would offer more flexibility and gain from the Dual-IS architecture, choosing the instruction set mode at program scope works well for applications that are clearly either control oriented or parallel. Thereby, Dual-IS instruction set runs have the same clock cycle counts as

Table 1. Area breakdown of the cores.

	Dual-IS	TTA	RISC-V
Area (μm^2)	12900	12500	11000
RFs	37%	40%	42%
FUs	35%	40%	38%
IF	8%	3%	8%
Decoder	5%	5%	3%
IC	10%	12%	8%
Microcode	3%	–	2%

the matching single-mode processors as the instruction set modality does not have an overhead in terms of cycle counts. The clock cycles of TTA and RISC-V instruction sets are presented in Table 2.

Running programs with the TTA instruction set reduced clock cycle counts by 17% on average and 21% if mips was excluded. The most notable improvement was seen in the blowfish benchmark which had a 35% reduction in clock cycles when run with the TTA instruction set. The control-oriented mips benchmark did not benefit from ILP, which is why cycle counts were 15% higher than in RISC-V mode. The use of branches and lower jump latency contributed to the lower clock cycle count as the TTA instruction set used a slower predicate + direct jump to implement branches. Run times followed the same trend as the clock cycles. However, as the single-mode RISC-V and TTA implementations are able to achieve higher clock frequencies, Dual-IS runs suffer a run time overhead of 4 and 2% when compared to their matching single-mode TTA and RISC-V implementations. With Dual-IS, when running mips in RISC-V mode and other benchmarks in TTA mode, the run time was only 0.4% higher on average

Table 2. Cycle counts and instruction code sizes.

Benchmark	TTA cycles	RISC-V cycles	TTA code size	RISC-V code size
adpcm	138480	168448	13 kB	8 kB
aes	23753	25894	12 kB	5 kB
blowfish	542882	837995	7 kB	6 kB
gsm	13058	17518	11 kB	6 kB
mips	37670	32839	5 kB	2 kB
motion	2140	2641	6 kB	3 kB
sha	428790	602243	12 kB	7 kB
jpeg	2262176	2617326	85 kB	44 kB

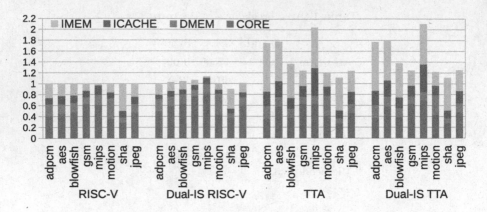

Fig. 4. Energy consumption relative to single-mode RISC-V baseline.

compared to the single-mode TTA architecture. Compared to the single-mode RISC-V architecture, the run time was on average 15% lower.

5.4 Energy Efficiency

Energy consumption of the processors was evaluated by generating *switching activity information files* (SAIFs) in RTL simulation and using them to generate power reports for the synthesized designs. As a 128 kB instruction memory was required to successfully compile all the benchmarks, we evaluated the system with that instruction memory size. For the instruction cache, we chose a direct-mapped 2 kB cache with a line size of 16 bytes. The data memory size was 64 kB because that was sufficient for compiling all the benchmarks.

We evaluated the instruction and data stream energy by generating memory access traces in RTL simulation and used Cacti [16] for generating estimates of the access energies. The memory access traces generated in RTL simulation were processed with a cache simulator to find the amount of accesses to the instruction cache and memory. The evaluated energies at maximum clock frequencies are described in Fig. 4 where energy foot print of the core, data memory, instruction cache and instruction memory are separated.

From the instruction stream energy point of view, bundling the RISC-V instructions to packets of two was beneficial as wider banks have lower access energy per bit which lowered the instruction stream energy of the Dual-IS RISC-V runs by 29% on average. Dual-IS had the same amount of cache misses as the single-mode RISC-V processor because the bundles never exceed cache lines. Furthermore, even though Dual-IS fetched more bytes from the cache due to excess instructions that are fetched in the bundle during jumps, it had the same amount of fetched bytes from the instruction memory because during a cache miss the whole line is replaced in the cache.

The reduced energy achieved by bundling instructions compensates for the energy overhead of the more complex datapath and control logic of Dual-IS. In

Dual-IS RISC-V runs, the core itself, however, consumed 27% more energy on average compared to the single-mode RISC-V core. The energy overhead of the core is expected due to the underlying multi-issue microarchitecture that executes the single-issue RISC-V instructions. In addition, Dual-IS function units are more complex compared to the single-mode RISC-V implementation because extra registers are required to store values in the function unit input ports between cycles to implement the transport triggering behaviour for the TTA mode.

The TTA instruction set suffered a significant overhead in terms of energy consumption in benchmark applications that expose little ILP. This is expected due to the wider instruction word that contained NOPs when move slots could not be utilized for operand transports. Furthermore, the programmer-visible delay slots increased the number of redundant instructions when they could not be utilized for operations in sequential code. On average, compared to the single-mode RISC-V processor, the single-mode TTA processor consumed 48% more energy in total. Dual-IS TTA mode consumed 1% more energy in total compared to the single-mode TTA processor due to the extra hardware that is required for the RISC-V instruction set and switching of instruction sets but the overhead was also compensated by the slightly lower clock frequency of Dual-IS.

With Dual-IS, it is beneficial to run benchmarks in RISC-V mode when frequent instruction cache misses and lack of ILP cause the instruction stream energy to be significant. *Energy-delay product* (EDP) [10] is a widely used metric that combines energy efficiency and execution speed of circuits. When instruction set was chosen based on the lowest EDP value, Dual-IS had 14% lower EDP compared to the single-mode TTA design. This way, the run time was 6% higher than with the TTA processor but energy consumption was lowered by 18%.

Power breakdown of different components is listed in Table 3. In the single-mode RISC-V core, the microcode unit consumed on average 6% power. In Dual-IS, the equivalent power consumption was 9%. The difference is due to the additional multiplexers that are needed to switch between RISC-V and TTA modes. When running Dual-IS on TTA mode, the microcode unit consumed 4% of the total power due to multiplexers responsible for mode switching.

Table 3. Power breakdown of the designs.

Component	RISC-V	Dual-IS RISC-V	TTA	Dual-IS TTA
Register Files	15%	16%	13%	13%
Function Units	31%	34%	47%	42%
Instruction Fetch	7%	7%	5%	7%
Decoder	11%	14%	14%	15%
Interconnect	16%	15%	18%	16%
Microcode	6%	9%	–	4%

5.5 Discussion

With the evaluated benchmark set we were able to reduce cycle counts on average by 17% with the TTA instruction set. Higher average performance improvement could be acquired by concentrating on benchmarks with more exploitable ILP. However, it should be noted that this benchmark set was chosen to evaluate the benefit of flexible architectures and their efficient use in the minimization of the instruction stream energy in statically scheduled multi-issue machines when ILP is scarce. Additional improvements to minimize the TTA instruction stream energy could be done by using a loop oriented L0 cache such as a loop buffer that would fit the program hot spots. That would steer the design towards using the TTA mode mostly for loop kernels and the RISC-V mode for control oriented parts and to retain binary compatibility with unmodified RISC-V binaries.

6 Conclusions

In this paper, we introduced Dual-IS, a processor that provides both a single-issue RISC-V and exposed datapath VLIW instruction-set modes with shared resources. To support the two instruction sets in the same microarchitecture, we implemented the RISC-V mode with the use of microcode-based control that extends the exposed datapath core with decoding and control logic. By using an exposed datapath instruction set for the TTA mode, we could implement the core with the same level of register file complexity as a single-issue implementation. Instruction set modality of Dual-IS enables to select instruction-set modes to optimize performance, energy efficiency or code size which adds flexibility.

Dual-IS achieved on average 15% and in the best case 33% smaller run times than a single-issue RISC-V processor when instruction-set modes were selected at the program scope to optimize performance. Compared to a single-mode TTA processor, when selecting the instruction set modes of Dual-IS based on energy-delay product, 14% lower EDP was achieved. This way benchmarks not benefiting from instruction level parallelism were run in RISC-V mode which lowered the energy consumption by 18% and increased run time only by 6% on average compared to a single-mode TTA processor.

The hardware overhead from instruction set modality and RISC-V ISA was negligible (3%), as was the impact to the clock frequency (2%) when compared to a single-mode TTA processor with similar datapath resources. This demonstrates that multi-issue TTA processors can be extended with RISC-V binary support at a low cost while providing the ability to minimize VLIW overhead in sequential programs with the serial execution mode.

In this paper, we used different instruction-set modes at a program granularity to optimize either performance or energy efficiency. In the future, we plan to investigate compiler support for switching of instruction-set modes and study at which granularity it is most beneficial to toggle modes. In addition to decreased instruction stream energy for the TTA, in-program mode switching would allow to share the local data in the caches and register files, which would be beneficial in terms of performance and latency compared to offloading tasks to a separate co-processor. In-program mode switching would be especially well suited for programs that have both control-oriented and parallel code regions.

Acknowledgments. The work for this publication was funded by European Union's Horizon 2020 research and innovation programme under Grant Agreement No 871738 (CPSoSaware) and Academy of Finland (decision #331344).

References

1. Albartus, N., Nasenberg, C., Stolz, F., Fyrbiak, M., Paar, C., Tessier, R.: On the design and misuse of microcoded (embedded) processors-a cautionary note. In: 30th USENIX Security Symposium (USENIX Security 21) (2021)
2. Boggs, D., Brown, G., Tuck, N., Venkatraman, K.: Denver: Nvidia's first 64-bit ARM processor. IEEE Micro **35**(2), 46–55 (2015)
3. Corporaal, H.: TTAs: missing the ILP complexity wall. J. Syst. Architect. **45**(12–13), 949–973 (1999)
4. Crepaldi, M., Merello, A., Di Salvo, M.: A multi-one instruction set computer for microcontroller applications. IEEE Access **9**, 113454–113474 (2021)
5. Guzma, V., Jääskeläinen, P., Kellomäki, P., Takala, J.: Impact of software bypassing on instruction level parallelism and register file traffic. In: Bereković, M., Dimopoulos, N., Wong, S. (eds.) SAMOS 2008. LNCS, vol. 5114, pp. 23–32. Springer, Heidelberg (2008). https://doi.org/10.1007/978-3-540-70550-5_4
6. Hara, Y., Tomiyama, H., Honda, S., Takada, H., Ishii, K.: CHStone: a benchmark program suite for practical C-based high-level synthesis. In: 2008 IEEE International Symposium on Circuits and Systems (ISCAS) (2008)
7. Hepola, K., Multanen, J., Jääskeläinen, P.: OpenASIP 2.0: co-design toolset for RISC-V application-specific instruction-set processors. In: IEEE 33rd International Conference on Application-specific Systems, Architectures and Processors (ASAP) (2022)
8. Hoogerbrugge, J., Corporaal, H.: Register file port requirements of transport triggered architectures. In: Proceedings of the 27th Annual International Symposium on Microarchitecture. MICRO 27, Association for Computing Machinery (1994)
9. Hoogerbrugge, J., Corporaal, H.: Transport-triggering vs. operation-triggering. In: Fritzson, P.A. (ed.) CC 1994. LNCS, vol. 786, pp. 435–449. Springer, Heidelberg (1994). https://doi.org/10.1007/3-540-57877-3_29
10. Horowitz, M., Indermaur, T., Gonzalez, R.: Low-power digital design. In: Proceedings of 1994 IEEE Symposium on Low Power Electronics (1994)
11. Hou, Y., et al.: FuMicro: a fused microarchitecture design integrating in-order superscalar and VLIW. VLSI Design (2016)
12. Jääskeläinen, P., Kultala, H., Viitanen, T., Takala, J.: Code density and energy efficiency of exposed datapath architectures. J. Sig. Process. Syst. **80**(1), 49–64 (2014). https://doi.org/10.1007/s11265-014-0924-x
13. Karaki, H., Akkary, H., Shahidzadeh, S.: X86-ARM binary hardware interpreter. In: 2011 18th IEEE International Conference on Electronics, Circuits, and Systems (2011)
14. Klaiber, A.: The technology behind Crusoe processors. Transmeta Techn. Brief (2000)
15. Klemmer, L., Große, D.: An exploration platform for microcoded RISC-V cores leveraging the one instruction set computer principle. In: 2022 IEEE Computer Society Annual Symposium on VLSI (ISVLSI) (2022)

16. Li, S., Chen, K., Ahn, J.H., Brockman, J.B., Jouppi, N.P.: CACTI-P: architecture-level modeling for SRAM-based structures with advanced leakage reduction techniques. In: 2011 IEEE/ACM International Conference on Computer-Aided Design (ICCAD) (2011)
17. Lin, T.J., et al.: A unified processor architecture for RISC & VLIW DSP. In: Proceedings of the 15th ACM Great Lakes Symposium on VLSI. Association for Computing Machinery (2005)
18. Taylor, M.B.: Is dark silicon useful? harnessing the four horsemen of the coming dark silicon apocalypse. In: DAC Design Automation Conference 2012 (2012)

Pasithea-1: An Energy-Efficient Self-contained CGRA with RISC-Like ISA

Tobias Kaiser(✉) and Friedel Gerfers

Technische Universität Berlin, Chair of Mixed Signal Circuit Design, Berlin, Germany
kaiser@tu-berlin.de

Abstract. This paper presents Pasithea-1, an energy-efficient coarse-grained reconfigurable array (CGRA) with RISC-like programming interface. In contrast to traditional RISC instruction sets, which are designed for centralized von Neumann architectures, it applies RISC principles to design an instruction set for energy-efficient CGRAs. Similar to dataflow and in-place processing architectures such as TRIPS and DiAG, Pasithea-1 can execute complex application code without external control. To demonstrate its programming, mechanisms and examples for dataflow, control flow, subroutine calls, coroutines and multi-threading are shown. A microarchitecture implementing the instruction set is presented. To reduce switching activity, its instructions, once fetched, remain in fabric, where they can be executed repeatedly without re-fetching. Pasithea-1 is compared against a minimal RISC system based on placed-and-routed designs. Using netlist simulation, energy and performance were compared. With a $10.1\times$ energy reduction in the memory hierarchy and a $3.1\times$ overall energy reduction, the described architecture surpasses the RISC system considerably in energy efficiency.

Keywords: Reconfigurable computing · Coarse-grained reconfigurable array · Instruction set architecture · Energy-efficient computing

1 Introduction

Energy-efficient computing enables future low-power applications. In addition, it is key to high performance under thermal constraints. Although technological scaling continues to increase logic densities, it no longer improves energy efficiency proportionally [1]. New approaches in computer architecture could provide ways forward [2]. This paper explores a reconfigurable array as general-purpose alternative to von Neumann architectures. Despite requiring more silicon area, this approach can improve energy efficiency by reducing switching activity.

1.1 Reconfigurable Computing

In von Neumann computers, a central processing unit (CPU) fetches, decodes and executes a continuous stream of instructions. Coarse-grained reconfigurable

© The Author(s), under exclusive license to Springer Nature Switzerland AG 2022
M. Schulz et al. (Eds.): ARCS 2022, LNCS 13642, pp. 33–47, 2022.
https://doi.org/10.1007/978-3-031-21867-5_3

arrays (CGRAs) break with this principle: Their machine code, also called configuration bitstream, is distributed to array elements and can remain largely stationary during execution. Array elements perform computations using local functional units and exchange data and control information to achieve complex behavior. CGRAs potentially require less energy than von Neumann architectures, as they do not require a sustained instruction stream.

Von Neumann processors execute instructions inherently in sequence. In CGRAs, spatial replication and coexistence of resources encourages parallel execution. While this inherent parallelism enables exceptional performance, it complicates their programming. General-purpose program code in high-level languages is founded upon an assumption of instruction (or statement) sequentiality. A shift away from this seems unlikely. This gap between software and CGRA hardware can be bridged by elaborate compiler techniques, as described by Cardoso et al. [3]. Despite successes, widespread replacement of von Neumann CPUs with CGRAs in general-purpose computing is currently seen as unlikely.

1.2   Related Work

The four-type classification shown in Table 1 covers pure von Neumann architectures, pure CGRA architectures and mixtures of both.

In Type II systems, CGRA configuration and von Neumann programming are separated in machine code. Thus, the programmer or compiler needs to divide programs into separate parts for the two sub-architectures. Examples for Type II systems are [9–12].

Type III systems are programmed using a von Neumann instruction set architecture (ISA) only. They execute some parts of the instruction stream natively on a von Neumann core; other parts are dynamically translated to CGRA configurations and offloaded to a CGRA. While this exposes a homogeneous ISA, the translation process limits the scope of CGRA execution and incurs additional hardware overhead. Examples for Type III systems are [13–16].

This paper focuses on Type IV systems: self-contained CGRAs that can run complex programs without supervising von Neumann CPU or a translation layer. Their homogeneous ISAs and microarchitectures make them compellingly simple. Table 2 compares Pasithea-1, which we propose in this paper, to four Type IV CGRAs and traditional RISC processors.

DiAG [4], a CGRA-like general-purpose processor, differs from the other approaches by implementing RISC-V, a von Neumann ISA, but spatially dis-

Table 1. Classification of processors based on integration and role of CGRA

	Type I	Type II	Type III	Type IV
Primary unit	von Neumann	von Neumann	von Neumann	**CGRA**
Subordinated unit	None	**CGRA**	**CGRA**	None
ISA	**homogeneous**	heterogeneous	**homogeneous**	**homogeneous**

Table 2. Qualitative comparison of classic RISC and Type IV CGRA architectures

	Classic RISC	DiAG [4]	Pasithea-1 (this work)	TRIPS [5] (EDGE [6])	Wavescalar [7]	PACT XPP [8]
Type	Type I (von Neumann)	Type IV (self-contained CGRA)				
ISA	RISC	custom, statically fragmented code				
	← RISC resemblance					
Local dataflow	central register file	register lanes	single shared bus	multiple regfiles	multiple shared buses + network	packet-oriented network
Local control flow	arbitrary			dataflow-driven		
				no internal loops	arbitrary	
Global dataflow	central register file		fragment-level msg. passing	central register file	instr.-level msg. passing	FIFO buffers
Self-reconfig.	N/A	implicit				explicit, low-level

tributing its instructions to PEs for *in-place execution*. Once loaded, instructions remain in PEs for extended time periods and can be executed several times. This instruction reuse distinguishes DiAG from earlier in-place processors [17,18].

Programming interfaces of TRIPS [5], Wavescalar [7] and PACT XPP [8] bear little resemblance to RISC. To allow running programs that exceed their fabric capacity, machine code of those architectures is statically divided into code fragments as smallest units of reconfiguration. In contrast to DiAG and RISC, their local control flow not explicitly encoded, but driven by dataflow.

1.3 This Work

To overcome challenges in CGRA programming and allow a wider range of applications to benefit from its merits, we propose rethinking instruction set design to bridge the gap between CGRA hardware and general-purpose software. We present Pasithea-1, an instruction set with a corresponding Type IV CGRA microarchitecture. Its two objectives are to allow easy programming and to surpass minimal RISC systems in energy efficiency by reducing instruction movement. Accordingly, the architecture is named Pasithea-1, after a mythical goddess of rest and relaxation.

RISC principles were used as guidance in the design process, leading to a simple and familiar programming interface. In establishing low-level instruction sequentiality, our ISA departs from typical CGRA programming. Being tailored for CGRA-based execution sets the Pasithea-1 ISA apart from other RISC instruction sets. Based on its hardware and software properties, Table 2 places Pasithea-1 between DiAG and TRIPS.

The Pasithea-1 ISA is laid out in Sect. 2. Its programming is explained in Sect. 3. The CGRA microarchitecture is presented in Sect. 4. Section 5 describes how the novel architecture was compared to a RISC system. Results are shown in Sect. 6. The paper finishes with a discussion in Sect. 7.

2   Instruction Set Architecture

Machine code for Pasithea-1 is structured in fragments, which are delimited by start and end markers shown in Fig. 1a. Each fragment consists of up to 64 instructions, which comprise a primary instruction word (formats D and W) and optional prefixes (formats S and I). Figure 1 gives an ISA overview.

Section 2.1 describes the fragment instance mechanism, a level of indirection that makes fragments reentrant. Section 2.2 introduces local dataflow and control flow mechanisms, which link instructions within a fragment. Section 2.3 describes creation and termination of fragment instances and communication between them. Section 2.4 relates the ISA to RISC principles.

2.1   Fragment Instances

A fragment is a group of up to 64 machine instructions that can be loaded into a contiguous CGRA sub-array. A fragment instance (FI) *attaches runtime data to a fragment* and thus represents execution state of a sub-array. Multiple FIs of a single fragment can coexist at runtime. This enables fragment reentrancy, i.e. independent coexisting function calls executing the same fragment code.

Such a code instantiation mechanism is not found in RISC processors, as they do not attach runtime data to machine code, but maintain execution state in the CPU register file and in memory using a call stack.

Coexisting FIs are concurrent, unless communication primitives (Sect. 2.3) constrain event ordering. Depending on microarchitecture capabilities, such coexisting FIs can be executed in sequence or in parallel. Section 3.2 demonstrates how fragments can be used as subroutines, coroutines and threads.

2.2   Local Interaction with Target Instruction Pointers (TIPs)

Pasithea-1 instructions are designed for decentral execution in a CGRA rather than a CPU. They are executed sequentially. Like in RISC, machine code order and explicitly encoded branches determine the sequence of execution.

Instantiation attaches two 32-bit **operand registers**, *opA* and *opB*, to each instruction. Their values are used by *local* instructions as ALU inputs; *memory* and *global* instructions use *opA* and *opB* as address or data words for memory access or communication operations, details of which are specified in Fig. 1b.

On instantiation, each instruction initializes the operand register selected by *immab* with an **immediate value** and the other operand register with zero. By default, immediates are limited to $[-32 .. 31]$. The I prefix extends this range to arbitrary 32-bit values.

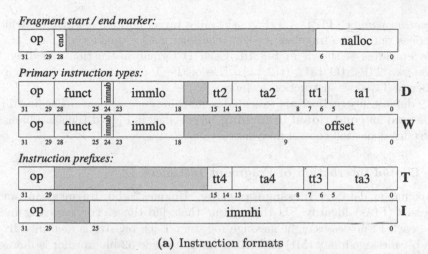

(a) Instruction formats

Group	Mnemonic	Fmt.	Operation
Local	or, and, xor, add, sub slt, sltu, sll, srl, sra	D	res := ALU(opA, opB)
Memory	lw, lh, lb, lhu, lbu	D	res := Mem [opA + opB]
	sw, sh, sb	W	Mem [opA + offset] := opB
Global	recv *(receive)*	D	res := Msg_{self} [MI] with $MI = (opA + opB)_{2:0}$
	send	W	Msg_{FIA} [MI] := opB with $FIA = (opA + offset)_{31:6}$, $MI = (opA + offset)_{2:0}$
	inv *(invoke)*	D	invokes fragment at *addr* using *RMI* as return MI with $addr_{31:3} = (opA + opB)_{31:3}$, $RMI = (opA + opB)_{2:0}$; res := new FIA
	term *(terminate)*	W	terminates current FI

(b) Operations encoded by mnemonics

op	funct									
	0000	0001	0010	0011	0100	0101	0110	0111	1000	1001
000	or	and	xor	add	sub	slt	sltu	sll	srl	sra
001	recv	lb	lh	lw	lbu	lhu	inv			
010	send	sb	sh	sw	term					
011	*T prefix*									
100	*I prefix*									
101	*fragment start / end marker*									

(c) Mnemonics by opcode and funct code

ttX	function	X
10	write opA	1,2,3,4
11	write opB	1,2,3,4
00	branch on zero	1
01	branch unless zero	1
0x	no operation	2,3,4

(d) Target type *ttX* (tt1, tt2, tt3, tt4) encoding

Fig. 1. Pasithea-1 ISA overview. Highlighted instructions are adopted from RISC-V.

All D format instructions produce a result word on execution. To achieve local **dataflow**, this result can be written to operand registers of other local instructions. The originating instruction encodes each such data transfer as *target* *instruction pointer* (TIP). A TIP consists of a target address field (taX), which references one of the fragment's 64 instructions, and a target type field (ttX), whose encoding is shown in Fig. 1d. Each D format instruction can directly encode two TIPs (tt1, ta1), (tt2, ta2). Use of the T prefix extends the possible number of TIPs per instruction to four.

By default, instructions are executed in machine code sequence. The first TIP can be used for **conditional branching**, as specified in Fig. 1d. This mechanism supersedes dedicated control flow instructions.

2.3 Global Interaction of Fragment Instances

FIs exchange data by **message passing**. Unique 26-bit fragment instance addresses (FIAs) identify FIs throughout their life times. For receiving messages, each FI possesses eight message registers. Each register is identified by a three-bit message index (MI) and either holds a single 32-bit word or is marked as empty. The *send* instruction, shown in Fig. 1b, sends *opB* to a message register of another FI. *opA* specifies FIA and MI of the target message register. Message registers already containing a value are overwritten. The *recv* instruction returns values received in local message registers. If a requested message register is empty, *recv* will block further FI execution and wait for message reception.

To **spawn new FIs**, fragments are invoked with *inv*, which takes a fragment address as input and returns the FIA of a newly created FI. The new FI automatically receives a *return handle* in message register 0. It can use this handle, which consists of the invoker FIA and a return MI (RMI) set by the invoker, to send return values to the invoker. The RMI can be used to assign return values of concurrent FIs to separate message registers. The *term* instruction terminates the current FI, invalidating its execution state and FIA.

2.4 What's the RISC?

Like RISC architectures, Pasithea-1 follows a scalar data model and sequential control flow model. Its adoption of RISC-V mnemonics [19] contributes to similarities in programming. It is furthermore influenced by key RISC concepts [20]:

1. Each instruction performs a simple operation, which can be executed easily without translating it to microinstructions.
2. Supporting concept 1, instructions only support one type of general-purpose operand by default: per-instruction operand registers.
3. Memory or message operands, less commonly needed than the general-purpose operand type, are only available through dedicated instructions.
4. The ISA is designed for hardware simplicity but leaves room for future hardware upscaling and optimizations that maintain ISA compatibility.

3 Programming

Sections 3.1 and 3.2 describe programming of individual fragments and programming patterns for interaction between fragments, respectively.

3.1 Local Programming

Within fragments, TIPs encode data and control flow. Defining them manually by labeling and cross-referencing instructions turned out infeasible for low-level programming by hand. Therefore, an intermediate assembly-like language (IAL) has been devised. It allows instructions to read and write local variables, which start with a $ sign and mimic RISC's general-purpose registers. The following syntax is used for IAL instructions:

[L:] [**goto** L (**if**|**ifnot**)] [$var =] **op**(opA, [offset,] opB)

The following steps translate an IAL fragment to machine code:

1. Compile-time expressions are resolved.
2. Unconditional jumps are transformed into conditionally branching *or* instructions with constant operands.
3. A control and data flow graph (CDFG) is constructed.
4. Ineffective data flow edges are removed from the graph. A data flow edge from instruction S to operand register opX of instruction T is ineffective, if there are no control flow paths from S to T that leave T.opX intact.
5. When instructions require more than four TIPs, excess TIPs are distributed to supplementarily inserted *or* instructions.
6. Machine code is generated. Dataflow edges and conditional branches are encoded as TIPs.

Table 3 shows an example fragment implementing Euclid's algorithm. Instructions 0 and 1 receive two input values, of which the greatest common divisor is to be calculated, from message registers 1 and 2. Instructions 2–5 form a loop, which is exited by a conditional jump from instruction 2 to instruction 6 once $p and $q are equal. Instructions 4 and 5 always branch to instruction 2

Table 3. Translation of IAL fragment *gcd*, which implements Euclid's algorithm, to Pasithea-1 machine code. Control flow: S = successor, C = conditional branch target, T = true (non-zero), F = false (zero); dataflow: A = write opA, B = write opB.

	↓ Source instruction	CDFG adjacency matrix									Fmt.	TIP 1	TIP 2	TIP 3	TIP 4
0	$p = **recv**(1, 0)	S	A						B		D	7.opB	2.opA	-	
1	$q = **recv**(2, 0)		SB								D	2.opB	-	-	
2	loop: goto end ifnot $diff = **sub**($p, $q)			SA	A	B	C				D	F→6	4.opA	5.opB	3.opA
3	goto p_lt_q if **slt**($diff, 0)				S	C					D	T→5	-	-	
4	goto loop if $p = **or**($diff, 0)		CA			S		B			D	T→2	7.opB	2.opA	-
5	p_lt_q: goto loop if $q = **sub**(0, $diff)		CB				S				D	T→2	2.opB	-	
6	end: $fia_ret = **recv**(0, 0)							SA			D	7.opA	-	-	
7	**send**($fia_ret, 0, $p)								S		W	-	-	-	
8	**term**()										W	-	-	-	
	Target instruction →	0	1	2	3	4	5	6	7	8					

because their results are never zero. Instruction 6 reads the return handle (see Sect. 2.3) and instruction 7 uses this handle to return the fragment's result value. Alongside the fragment's IAL source code, Table 3 shows the processed CDFG and resulting TIPs that will be encoded in machine code.

3.2   Global Programming

Typical programs comprise several hundred subroutines. Subroutines that are not too complex can be implemented using a single fragment. As programs commonly incur millions of subroutine calls per second [21], a streamlined calling mechanism is crucial for programmability and performance.

Figure 2a shows an example for subroutine calls. Like *gcd*, *gcd3* starts with receiving arguments and ends with returning a result. In between, it calculates the greatest common divisor of three numbers using two *gcd* subroutine calls: $\gcd3(p, q, r) = \gcd(\gcd(p, q), r)$. Subroutine calls are performed in three stages:

1. *Fragment invocation:* The requested subroutine fragment is invoked using *inv*. In addition to the fragment address, an RMI is specified and passed to the invoked fragment. Both calls in *gcd3* use an RMI of 1. *inv* returns a FIA, which will be used in the next two stages.
2. *Send arguments (optional):* The invoker sends argument values to the subroutine. By convention, the n-th argument is passed at $MI = n$.
3. *Receive return values & synchronize control flow:* The subroutine's return value is obtained using a receive instruction. As *recv* waits until the return value is written, it also provides synchronization. A subroutine without return value needs to return a blank message for synchronization.

Figure 2b shows recursive subroutine calls, making use of reentrancy.

As described in Sect. 2.1, coexisting FIs are concurrent by default. Figure 2c shows an example of two concurrent *gcd* calls, which can be considered separate threads. Depending on the microarchitecture's capabilities, they can be executed in parallel (**thread-level parallelism**).

Coroutines incorporate the full structural power of subroutines, but can pass control and data back and forth without relinquishing their local state [22]. Coroutine-like constructs are gaining popularity and are available in many modern programming languages such as Python, C++, Rust and Go. An example that implements coroutines in Pasithea-1 is shown in Fig. 2d: The iterator subroutine *lfsr_test* receives a stream of bits from the generator subroutine *lfsr*, which implements a Galois linear-feedback shift register (LFSR). *lfsr_test* prints all received bits through a subroutine call to *print_bit*.

4   Microarchitecture

The microarchitecture consists of 128 processing elements (PEs), grouped in 8 tiles of 16 PEs each. Figure 3a shows an overview. Section 4.1 describes the fragment instance manager (FIM), which manages creation and termination of FIs and transfers FIs between fabric and memory. Section 4.2 describes execution of FIs on fabric. Section 4.3 describes storage of dormant FIs in memory.

```
1  fragment gcd3
2  $p = recv(1, 0)        ⎫ Receive
3  $q = recv(2, 0)        ⎬ arguments
4  $r = recv(3, 0)        ⎭
5  $fia1 = inv(gcd+1, 0)  ⎫ Subroutine
6  send($fia1, 1, $p)     ⎬ call 1
7  send($fia1, 2, $q)     ⎭
8  $x = recv(1, 0)
9  $fia2 = inv(gcd+1, 0)  ⎫ Subroutine
10 send($fia2, 1, $x)     ⎬ call 2
11 send($fia2, 2, $r)     ⎭
12 $res = recv(1, 0)
13 $fia_r = recv(0, 0)    ⎫ Return result
14 send($fia_r, 0, $res)  ⎬ & terminate
15 term()                 ⎭
16 endfragment
```

(a) *gcd3:* subroutine call example

```
1  fragment qsort
2      $first = recv(1, 0)
3      $last = recv(2, 0)
4      goto end ifnot
                  slt($first, $last)
5      $piv = lbu($last, 0)
6      $p = sub($first, 1)
7      $j = or($first, 0)
8  loop: $mj = lbu($j, 0)
9      goto noswap if slt($piv, $mj)
10     $p = add($p, 1)
11     $mp = lbu($p, 0)
12     sb($p, 0, $mj)
13     sb($j, 0, $mp)
14 noswap: $j = add($j, 1)
15     goto loop ifnot slt($last, $j)
16     $p_minus_1 = sub($p, 1)
17     $p_plus_1 = add($p_minus_1, 2)
18     $fia_qs1 = inv(qsort+1, 0)
29     send($fia_qs1, 1, $first)
30     send($fia_qs1, 2, $p_minus_1)
31     recv(1, 0)
32     $fia_qs2 = inv(qsort+2, 0)
33     send($fia_qs2, 1, $p_plus_1)
34     send($fia_qs2, 2, $last)
35     recv(2, 0)
36 end: $fia_r = recv(0, 0)
37     send($fia_r, 0, 0)
38     term()
39 endfragment
```

(b) *qsort*: Quicksort implementation

```
1  fragment gcd4mt
2  $p = recv(1, 0)        ⎫ Receive
3  $q = recv(2, 0)        ⎬ arguments
4  $r = recv(3, 0)        ⎪
5  $s = recv(3, 0)        ⎭
6  $fia1 = inv(gcd+1, 0)  ⎫ Launch
7  send($fia1, 1, $p)     ⎬ thread 1
8  send($fia1, 2, $q)     ⎭
9  $fia2 = inv(gcd+2, 0)  ⎫ Launch
10 send($fia2, 1, $r)     ⎬ thread 2
11 send($fia2, 2, $s)     ⎭
12 $x = recv(1, 0)        ⎫ Join
13 $y = recv(2, 0)        ⎬ threads 1 & 2
14 $fia3 = inv(gcd+1, 0)  ⎫ Subroutine
15 send($fia3, 1, $x)     ⎬ call
16 send($fia3, 2, $y)     ⎪
17 $res = recv(1, 0)      ⎭
18 $fia_r = recv(0, 0)    ⎫ Return result
19 send($fia_r, 0, $res)  ⎬ & terminate
20 term()                 ⎭
21 endfragment
```

(c) *gcd4mt:* multi-threading example

```
1  fragment lfsr_test
2      $fia_lfsr = inv(lfsr + 1, 0)
3      $i = 20
4  loop: $bit = recv(1, 0)
5      $fia_print = inv(print_bit+1, 0)
6      send($fia_print, 1, $bit)
7      recv(1, 0)
8      send($fia_lfsr, 1, 1)
9      goto loop if $i = sub($i, 1)
10     term()
11 endfragment
12 fragment lfsr
13     $fia_r = recv(0,0)
14     $lfsr = 1
15 loop: $bit = and($lfsr, 1)
16     send($fia_r, 0, $bit)
17     $lfsr = srl($lfsr, 1)
18     goto skip ifnot or($bit, 0)
19     $lfsr = xor($lfsr, 46080)
20 skip: goto loop if recv(1,0)
21     term()
22 endfragment
```

(d) *lfsr:* coroutine example

Fig. 2. Example code for Pasithea-1

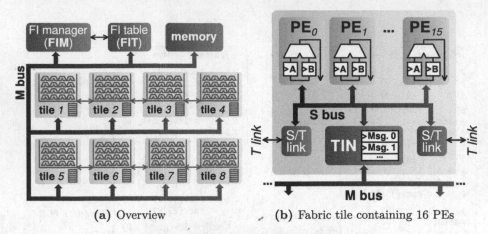

(a) Overview   (b) Fabric tile containing 16 PEs

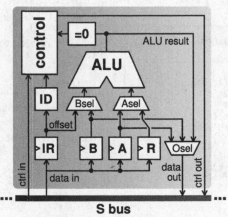

(c) Single processing element (PE)

Fig. 3. Pasithea-1 microarchitecture

4.1 Fragment Instance Management

The FIM allocates a fixed-size memory frame for every FI. It manages a pool of unused frames as linked list. Frame memory is only used when the corresponding FI is dormant, i.e. not present on fabric (see Sect. 4.3). Frame base addresses also serve as fragment instance addresses (FIAs).

When a FI is terminated, its machine code is retained in fabric as *residual fragment*. When a fragment is invoked and a matching residual fragment is available, the FIM reuses it, omitting instruction fetching.

By default, new FIs are created on fabric. If fabric occupancy of other FIs and residual fragments prevents this, new FIs are created in memory.

When all FIs on fabric are waiting for messages (*recv*) from dormant FIs, a stall is detected. This triggers the following **scheduling routine**: A dormant

FI from the ready queue (Sect. 4.3) is restored to fabric. To make space for the dormant FI, residual fragments are cleared. If this does not suffice, waiting FIs are evicted to memory. Least-recently used (LRU) policies are employed for clearing of residual fragments and eviction of waiting FIs.

4.2 Tiles and PEs: Fragment Instances on Fabric

Every PE can hold one instruction and its corresponding execution state. A variable number of tiles is required per FI: For FIs of 16 or fewer instructions, a single tile suffices. For FIs of up to 32 or 64 instructions, two or four tiles are linked together using the *T link*, which joins S buses of adjacent tiles. As FIs enter and leave fabric, tiles are linked and unlinked on-the-fly. A similar approach has previously been used in EDGE architectures [23].

FIs communicate with other FIs, the FIM and memory using tile interface nodes (TINs), which contain the message registers and connect to the global M bus. When messages are sent to FIs on fabric, target FIAs are translated to tile indices by the fragment instance table (FIT), which the FIM manages.

Figure 3b shows one tile. Within a tile or a group of T-linked tiles, the S bus connects all PEs and the TIN. The S bus is a shared 32-bit wide data bus with additional meta-data and control signals. It allows the active instruction to send output data to the TIN or up to two local PEs. Independent of this data flow capability, the S bus also features signals for passing control flow to a PE or the TIN.

Figure 3c shows the individual PE. Its instruction register (IR) can hold a primary instruction and optional prefixes. *opA* and *opB*, defined in the ISA, are held in the A and B registers. Results of memory and global operations are received by the TIN and forwarded through the R register of the initiating PE.

During FI loading, the memory unit sends the fragment's machine code to the TIN, which forwards it to local PEs through the S bus. If the FI was previously dormant, its memory representation is restored. The TIN starts execution once all instructions are fetched and their execution states are restored if necessary.

By default, local instructions (Fig. 1b) take one cycle to execute. Branches add no latency. An S prefix adds one additional cycle of latency. Global and memory instructions incur additional latencies.

4.3 Dormant Fragment Instances

When an FI waiting for a message is evicted from fabric, its execution state is transferred to its allocated memory frame. This includes all operand register values, message register values, the awaited MI, a marker for the currently active instruction and the fragment code address. Operand register values are stored using a compressed format, which encodes operand registers equal to zero or equal to their immediate value using compact four-bit codes.

Addresses of dormant FIs cannot be resolved by the FIT. Messages addressed to them are delivered through the FIM, which writes them to the frame memory of the targeted FI. If the delivered MI matches its awaited MI, the FI is tagged as ready and added to the ready queue, a linked list managed by the FIM.

4.4 Memory Subsystem

A 256-bit wide memory bus connects the system to main memory. For instruction fetching, a single 256-bit instruction buffer is used. Load/store accesses utilize a 4×256-bit fully associative data cache with LRU policy. The purpose of instruction buffer and data cache is not to increase latency and bandwidth but to increase energy efficiency by reducing the number of memory accesses.

5   Evaluation Methodology

We compared Pasithea-1 with a RISC-based reference system to evaluate energy efficiency, performance and area. Table 4 lists the used benchmark programs.

The open-source RISC-V core Ibex [24,25], configured for 32-bit integer and compressed instructions (RV32IC), was used as reference system CPU. The reference system integrates Ibex with the instruction buffer, data cache and memory of Pasithea-1. Instruction fetching using the instruction buffer and data cache hits require no wait cycles. Data cache misses incur one wait cycle.

SystemVerilog register-transfer-level models of Pasithea-1 and the RISC-V reference system were used as basis for physical implementation. Both systems use hierarchical clock gates to reduce switching activity. A 256 kB SRAM serves as main memory for both systems.

Both systems were synthesized, placed and routed in GlobalFoundries 22 nm FD-SOI CMOS [26]. For this purpose, Synopsys Design Compiler and IC Compiler II were used. Ultra-low-leakage standard cells based on high-V_T transistors were used to minimize the impact of static power.

Table 4. Benchmarks. (For Pasithea-1, all benchmarks were written in IAL.)

Name	Description	Data mem.	Subroutines	Recursion	Coroutines	Pasithea-1 Code Size	Pasithea-1 Instrs. / Frag.	RISC-V Code Size	RISC-V Impl. in
gcd	Euclid's algorithm					44	9	18	asm
mul	shift-and-add multiply					40	9	28	asm
lfsr	Galois LFSR & coroutines		✓		✓	132	10, 9, 7	104	asm
prime	primality test		✓			360	42, 9, 20	178	asm + C
md5	Message Digest 5	✓				448	30, 59	246	C
qsort	Quicksort	✓	✓	✓		204	27, 15	86	C

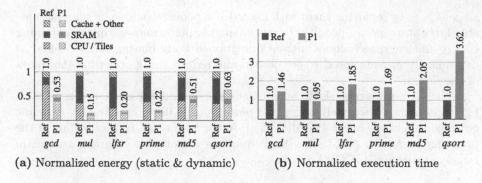

(a) Normalized energy (static & dynamic)   (b) Normalized execution time

Fig. 4. Benchmarking results for reference system (Ref) and Pasithea-1 (P1)

6 Results

Based on timing-annotated netlist simulation and vector-based power analysis of the placed-and-routed designs, Fig. 4b compares energy use of Pasithea-1 with that of the reference system. Static power accounted for 0.6 % and 4.4 % of total power for the reference system and Pasithea-1, respectively. Geometric means over the presented benchmarks reveal a 10.1× improvement of energy efficiency in the memory hierarchy and a 3.1× overall improvement.

Static timing analysis revealed maximum clock frequencies of 40 MHz for Pasithea-1 and 52 MHz for the reference system. Figure 4b compares execution times of the benchmarks at maximum clock speeds. In execution time, the reference system outperforms Pasithea-1 by a factor of 1.78. This can be attributed to latencies in global (FIM) and memory operations, which were not optimized during design.

Excluding SRAM, logic cell areas were $8932\,\mu m^2$ for the reference system and $244,121\,\mu m^2$ (27.3× larger) for Pasithea-1. This area disparity shrinks to 1.8× when the SRAM ($300,000\,\mu m^2$) is included.

7 Discussion

As shown in Sect. 6, Pasithea-1 achieves extraordinarily low switching rates and surpasses the RISC reference in energy efficiency considerably. Its easy low-level programming interface, demonstrated in Sect. 3, promises to make this energy efficiency available to a wide range of applications. A compiler backend for Pasithea-1 is currently under development and will enable further research into the viability and tradeoffs of using CGRA for general-purpose computing.

Clock frequency and per-cycle performance are weaknesses of the presented CGRA. Per-cycle performance was not optimized for in the presented microarchitecture and can likely be improved in future design iterations. To compete with general-purpose von Neumann processors in single-thread performance, higher clock frequencies must be supported using faster logic cells. Naively speeding up all cells, e.g. by replacing them with lower-V_T versions, would incur an unacceptably large static power penalty. To achieve higher performance while maintaining energy efficiency, techniques such as fine-grained body biasing could be used to dynamically provide speed where needed and reduce static power in other parts of the design.

With growing array sizes, we predict tile-tile and tile-memory data transfers to dominate energy efficiency and performance, likely encouraging dynamic optimization of tile and cache allocation. In the long term, further scaling of the presented approach could allow large fractions of complex programs to remain largely stationary in CGRA fabric.

Acknowledgements. We thank GlobalFoundries for access to their 22 nm FD-SOI technology and EUROPRACTICE for providing design tools.

References

1. Taylor, M.B.: A landscape of the new dark silicon design regime. IEEE Micro **33**(5), 8–19 (2013)
2. Patterson, D.: The future of computer architecture. In: A white paper prepared for the Computing Community Consortium Committee of the Computing Research Association (2008)
3. Cardoso, J.M.P., et al.: Compiling for reconfigurable computing. ACM Comput. Surv. **42**(4), 1–65 (2010)
4. Wang, D.K., and Kim, N.S.: DiAG: a dataflow-inspired architecture for general-purpose processors. In: Proceedings of the 26th ACM International Conference on Architectural Support for Programming Languages and Operating Systems. ACM (2021)
5. Sankaralingam, K., et al.: Exploiting ILP, TLP, and DLP with the polymorphous TRIPS architecture (2003)
6. Burger, D., et al.: Scaling to the end of silicon with EDGE architectures. Computer **37**(7), 44–55 (2004)
7. Swanson, S., et al.: The wavescalar architecture. ACM Trans. Comput. Syst. **25**(2), 1–54 (2007)
8. Baumgarte, V., et al.: PACT XPP – a self-reconfigurable data processing architecture. J. Supercomput. **26**(2), 167–184 (2003)
9. Gobieski, G., et al.: SNAFU: an ultra-low-power, energy-minimal CGRA-generation framework and architecture. In: 2021 ACM/IEEE 48th Annual International Symposium on Computer Architecture (ISCA). IEEE (2021)
10. Ozaki, N., et al.: Cool mega-arrays: ultralow-power reconfigurable accelerator chips. IEEE Micro **31**(6), 6–18 (2011)
11. Venkatesh, G., et al.: Conservation cores. ACM SIGPLAN Notices **45**(3), 205–218 (2010)
12. Mishra, M., et al.: Tartan: evaluating spatial computation for whole program execution. ACM SIGOPS Operating Syst. Rev. **40**(5), 163–174 (2006)
13. Lysecky, R., et al.: Warp processors. ACM Trans. Des. Autom. Electron. Syst. **11**(3), 659–681 (2006)
14. Watkins, M.A., et al.: Software transparent dynamic binary translation for coarse-grain reconfigurable architectures. In: 2016 IEEE International Symposium on High Performance Computer Architecture (HPCA). IEEE (2016)

15. Souza, J.D., et al.: A reconfigurable heterogeneous multicore with a homogeneous ISA. In: Proceedings of the 2016 Conference on Design, Automation & Test in Europe. DATE 2016, pp. 1598–1603. EDA Consortium, Dresden, Germany (2016)
16. Brandalero, M., et al.: Multi-target adaptive reconfigurable acceleration for low-power IoT processing. IEEE Trans. Comput. **70**(1), 83–98 (2021)
17. Henry, D., et al.: The Ultrascalar processor-an asymptotically scalable superscalar microarchitecture (1999)
18. Gunadi, E., Lipasti, M.H.: CRIB: consolidated rename, issue, and bypass. ACM SIGARCH Comput. Architect. News **39**(3), 23–32 (2011)
19. Waterman, A., and Asanović, K.: The RISC-V Instruction Set Manual, Volume I: User-Level ISA, Document Version 2019121. Technical report, RISCV Foundation (2019)
20. Séquin, C.H., Patterson, D.A.: Design and Implementation of RISC I. In: Proceedings of Advanced Course on VLSI Architecture (1982)
21. Spivey, J.M.: Fast, accurate call graph profiling. Softw.: Practi. Experience **34**(3), 249–264 (2004)
22. De Moura, A.L., Ierusalimschy, R.: Revisiting coroutines. ACM Trans. Program. Lang. Syst. **31**(2), 1–31 (2009)
23. Kim, C., et al.: Composable lightweight processors. In: 40th Annual IEEE/ACM International Symposium on Microarchitecture (MICRO 2007), pp. 381–394. IEEE (2007)
24. Schiavone, P.D., et al.: Slow and steady wins the race? A comparison of ultra-low-power RISC-V cores for Internet-of-Things applications (2017)
25. lowRISC Contributors: Ibex RISC-V Core (2022). https://github.com/lowrisc/ibex
26. Carter, R., et al.: 22nm FDSOI technology for emerging mobile, Internet-of-Things, and RF applications. In: 2016 IEEE International Electron Devices Meeting (IEDM). IEEE (2016)

Applied Machine Learning

Orchestrated Co-scheduling, Resource Partitioning, and Power Capping on CPU-GPU Heterogeneous Systems via Machine Learning

Issa Saba, Eishi Arima$^{(\boxtimes)}$, Dai Liu, and Martin Schulz

Technical University of Munich, Garching, Germany
{issa.saba,eishi.arima,dai.liu,martin.w.j.schulz}@tum.de

Abstract. CPU-GPU heterogeneous architectures are now commonly used in a wide variety of computing systems from mobile devices to supercomputers. Maximizing the throughput for multi-programmed workloads on such systems is indispensable as one single program typically cannot fully exploit all avaiable resources. At the same time, power consumption is a key issue and often requires optimizing power allocations to the CPU and GPU while enforcing a total power constraint, in particular when the power/thermal requirements are strict. The result is a system-wide optimization problem with several knobs. In particular we focus on (1) co-scheduling decisions, i.e., selecting programs to co-locate in a space sharing manner; (2) resource partitioning on both CPUs and GPUs; and (3) power capping on both CPUs and GPUs. We solve this problem using predictive performance modeling using machine learning in order to coordinately optimize the above knob setups. Our experiential results using a real system show that our approach achieves up to 67% of speedup compared to a time-sharing-based scheduling with a naive power capping that evenly distributes power budgets across components.

Keywords: Co-scheduling · Resource partitioning · Power capping · CPU-GPU heterogeneous systems · Machine learning

1 Introduction

Heterogeneous CPU-GPU architecture are now broadly used in a wide variety of computing systems, including mobile devices, PCs, datacenter servers, and HPC systems. For instance, over 160 out of the 500 top-class supercomputers are now GPU-accelerated systems (as of Jun 2022) [1]. This trend is driven by the end of Dennard scaling [14], i.e., the exponential growth of single-thread performance in microprocessors had ceased, and the industry rather shifted toward thread-level parallelism and heterogeneous computing using domain specific accelerators [15]. GPUs are one of the most commonly used accelerators due to their wide range of application areas, including image processing, scientific computing, artificial intelligence and data mining.

© The Author(s), under exclusive license to Springer Nature Switzerland AG 2022
M. Schulz et al. (Eds.): ARCS 2022, LNCS 13642, pp. 51–67, 2022.
https://doi.org/10.1007/978-3-031-21867-5_4

As computing systems are becoming more powerful and more heterogeneous using a wide variety of resources, it also becoming more difficult to fully utilize the entirety of compute resources by one single application. One reason behind the trend is that it is not always easy to identify a large enough fraction of a code that can be ported to GPUs (or any other accelerator) while balancing loads across all the processing units (CPU, GPU, or any accelerators). Further, the scalability of applications inside of a chip can be limited by various factors such as intensive memory accesses and shared resource contentions, which can induce a significant waste of compute resources.

Therefore, **co-scheduling**, i.e., co-locating multiple processes in a space sharing manner, is a key feature to mitigate resource wastes and to maximize throughput on such systems, if the processes are complimentary in their resource usage. To achieve the latter, a sophisticated mechanism to **partition resources** at each component and allocate them accordingly to co-scheduled processes is indispensable. Recent commercial CPUs and GPUs support such resource partitioning features: (1) one can designate physical core allocations to co-scheduled processes on CPUs; and (2) GPUs have begun to support hardware-level resource partitioning features for co-locating multiple processes—one example is NVIDIA's Multi-Instance GPU (or MIG) feature that is supported in the *most recent* high-end GPUs to enable co-locating multiple programs at the same chip while partitioning it at the granularity of GPC [21].

Meanwhile, as power (or energy) consumption is now a first-order concern in almost all the computing systems from embedded devices to HPC systems [10, 22,23], performance optimizations for modern computing systems, including co-scheduling, must consider power optimization and in most cases also hard power limits or constraints. Once a power constraint is set on a system, the power budgets must be distributed to components accordingly so as to maximize the performance while keeping the constraint. To realize such a mechanism, modern CPUs and GPUs now support **power capping** features that set a power limit at the granularity of chip (or even at a finer granularity for some hardware).

Driven by the above trends, this paper explicitly targets the combination of co-scheduling, resource partitioning, and power capping on CPU-GPU heterogeneous systems, and provides a systematic solution to co-optimize them using a machine-learning-based performance model as well as a graph-based scheduling algorithm. Our model takes both application profiles and hardware knob states into account as its inputs and returns the estimated performance of the co-located applications as the output. More specifically, the profiles are based on hardware performance counters, and the hardware knob states include resource partitioning and power capping on both the CPU and GPU. We use this performance model to estimate the best performance of different hardware setups for a given application pair, which is used to determine the best co-scheduling pairs in a graph-based algorithm, i.e., Edmonds' algorithm [13].

The followings are the major contributions of this paper:

1. We comprehensively and systematically optimize (1) co-scheduling pair selections, (2) resource partitioning at both CPU and GPU, and (3) power budget-

ing on both CPU and GPU, using a real CPU-GPU heterogeneous hardware platform.
2. We define an optimization problem and provide a systematic solution to select the best job pair and the best hardware setups including resource partitioning and power capping on CPU/GPU.
3. We develop a machine-learning-based performance model that takes both the characteristics of the co-located applications and the hardware states (including partitioning and power capping on CPU/GPU) into account.
4. We solve the optimization problem by using the above performance model building on the graph-based Edmonds' algorithm.
5. We quantify the benefits of our approach by using a real hardware, and show that we improve the system throughput by 67% compared to a time-sharing-based scheduling with a naive power capping that evenly distributes the power budgets across the CPU and GPU.

2 Related Work

Ever since multi-core processors appeared on the market, co-scheduling, resource partitioning, and power capping have been studied. However, ours is the first work that covers all of the following aspects simultaneously: (1) targeting CPU-GPU heterogeneous systems; (2) comprehensively co-optimizing co-scheduling pair selections, resource partitioning, and power capping, using machine-learning-based performance modeling and a graph-based algorithm; and (3) quantifying the benefits using a real hardware that is capable of both resource partitioning and power capping at both the CPU and the discrete GPU.

M. Bhadauria et al. explored co-scheduling multi-threaded programs in a space sharing manner using a multi-core processor [9]. S. Zhuravlev et al. focused on the shared resource contention across co-located programs on multi-core processors and proposed a scheduler-based solution to mitigate the interference [26]. R. Cochran et al. proposed Pack & Cap that optimizes the scale of multi-threaded applications via the thread packing technique while applying power capping [12]. Then, H. Sasaki et al. provided a sophisticated power-performance optimization method that coordinates the thread packing technique and DVFS for multi-programmed and multi-threaded environments [24]. These seminal studies provided insightful ideas, *however they did not target CPU-GPU heterogeneous systems.*

Few studies looked at the combination of co-scheduling and power capping on *CPU-GPU heterogeneous systems.* Q. Zhu et al. worked on the combination of job scheduling and power capping for integrated CPU-GPU systems [25], but they did not cover the following aspects: resource partitioning inside of CPU/GPU; and co-scheduling multiple processes on the GPU in a space sharing manner. R. Azimi et al. developed a framework called PowerCoord that allocates power budgets to components on CPU-GPU heterogeneous systems for co-scheduled workloads [5], but their work did not target adjusting the resource partitions as well. *Recent hardware advances (e.g., NVIDIA MIG feature [4,21]) made it possible to apply both the process co-location and resource partitioning on both CPUs and GPUs, which opened up new optimization opportunities.*

There have been several studies that utilize machine learning (including linear regression) for performance/power modeling in the literature. B. Lee et al. utilized the linear regression to predict performance for CPUs [18]. E. Ïpek et al. conducted microarchitectural design space explorations using a neural network [17]. B. Barnes et al. proposed a statistical approach to predict performance of parallel applications [7]. H. Nagasaka et al. constructed a power consumption model for GPUs that is based on the linear regression and hardware performance counters [19]. Beyond these pioneering studies, machine-learning-based approaches have been utilized also for more complicated system design and optimization purposes such as: clock frequency setups at both CPU and GPU at the same time on a CPU-GPU integrated chip [6]; power capping setups on CPU, DRAM, and NVRAM [3]; coordination of thread/page mapping and prefetcher configurations [8]; and CPU-GPU heterogeneous chip designs in the industry [16]. We follow the literature and utilize a neural network that is tailored to solve our new problem.

3   Motivation, Problem, and Solution Overview

3.1   Motivation: Technology Trends

Setting a power cap on a processor is a crucial feature and is now supported on a variety of commercial CPUs and GPUs. One prominent use case for this feature is to protect a chip from overheating and, instead of having to be conservative, to adjust the needed settings to the machine environment such as the cooling facility. Another prominent use case is enabling a hierarchical and cooperative power budgeting across components or compute nodes while keeping a total power constraint, which has been widely studied from standalone computers to large-scale systems, including datacenters and supercomputers [10,22,23]. In our work, we target CPU-GPU heterogeneous computing systems (or nodes) and optimize the power cap setups on both CPU and GPU in order to maximize performance under a total node power constraint.

As compute nodes are becoming fatter and systems more heterogeneous, it is also becoming more difficult to fully utilize an entire node's resources by one single process. For instance, compute resources are typically under utilized for memory-bound applications, while memory bandwidth is often wasted for compute-bound applications. Further, some applications are suitable for running on GPUs, but others are not. To improve resource utilization, mixing different kinds of processes and co-scheduling (or co-locating) them on the node at the same time while setting resource allocations accordingly at both the CPU and GPU is a desired feature.

3.2   Problem Definition

Figure 1 illustrates the overall problem we target in this paper. Here, we assume that we have one single job (or process) queue on the system (Q). We convert

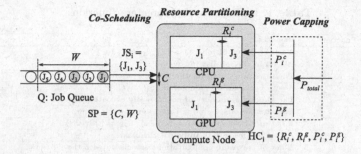

Fig. 1. Problem overview

the job queue into a list of job sets (or pairs) to co-schedule $(JS_1, JS_2, \cdots)$. Note these jobs are selected from inside of the window (W) on the queue. The concurrency, i.e., the maximum number of jobs launched at a time, is limited by a given parameter (C), and we particularly target $C = 2$ in this paper, meaning that no more than 2 CPU-GPU jobs will be co-scheduled at any given time. This value was chosen as for higher values no polynomial-time algorithms for job-set selection is known. We represent a set of these scheduling parameters as $SP = \{C, W\}$. When launching/co-locating the ith job set (JS_i), we optimize the hardware knob configurations (HC_i), i.e., resource partitioning on CPU/GPU (R_i^c/R_i^g) as well as the power cap setups on CPU/GPU (P_i^c/P_i^g). Note, the sum of the power caps must be less than or equal than the given total power constraint P_{total}.

The following is the mathematical formulation as an optimization problem:

$$inputs \ \ Q = \{J_1, J_2, \cdots, J_W\}, P_{total}, SP$$
$$outputs \ \ L_{JS} = \{JS_1, JS_2, \cdots\}, L_{HC} = \{HC_1, HC_2, \cdots\}$$
$$\min \ \ \sum_{i=1}^{|L_{JS}|} CoRunTime(JS_i, HC_i)$$
$$s.t. \ \ CoRunTime(JS_i, HC_i) \leq SoloRunTime(JS_i, P_{total})$$
$$P_i^c + P_i^g \leq P_{total}, \ \ 1 \leq |JS_i| \leq C$$
$$(\forall i : 1 \leq i \leq |L_{JS}|(= |L_{HC}|))$$
$$JS_1 \cup \cdots \cup JS_{|L_{JS}|} = Q, \ \ |JS_1| + \cdots + |JS_{|L_{JS}|}| = W$$

The inputs are the job queue, the total power cap setup, and the set of the scheduling parameters. The outputs are the lists of job sets (L_{JS}) and the associated hardware configurations (L_{HC}). The objective is to minimize the sum of the co-run execution time $(CoRunTime)$, each of which is a function of the co-located jobs as well as the hardware configurations.

We take several constraints for this optimization problem into count: the first is the requirement that the space-sharing co-run execution should take shorter time than the time-sharing execution with exclusive solo-runs under the power

Table 1. Definitions of parameters/functions

Parameter or Function	Remarks
Q	A list or queue of jobs: $Q = \{J_1, J_2, \cdots, J_W\}$
J_i	ith job in the job list (or queue)
P_{total}	The total power cap for the target computing node
SP	A set of scheduling parameters: $SP = \{C, W\}$
C	The maximum number of concurrently executed jobs
W	The number of scheduling targets on the job queue
L_{JS}	A list of job sets to be co-scheduled: $L_{JS} = \{JS_1, JS_2, \cdots\}$
JS_i	ith set of jobs in L_{JS} to be co-scheduled
L_{HC}	A list of hardware configurations associated with the job sets: $L_{HC} = \{HC_1, HC_2, \cdots\}$
HC_i	The hardware configurations for ith job set: $HC_i = \{R_i^c, R_i^g, P_i^c, P_i^g\}$
$R_i^* (* = c/g)$	The resource partitioning setup on CPU/GPU for ith job set
$P_i^* (* = c/g)$	The power cap set up on CPU/GPU for ith job set
$CoRunTime(JS_i, HC_i)$	The total execution time when co-locating JS_i with HC_i
$SoloRunTime(JS_i, P_{total})$	The total time when executing JS_i in a time-sharing manner under the total power cap (P_{total}); The power caps to CPU/GPU are optimized for each job execution

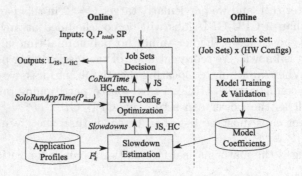

Fig. 2. Workflow of our solution

cap (*SoloRunTime*)—otherwise we should not co-schedule them. The second one is the power constraint, i.e., the sum of the CPU/GPU power caps must be less than or equal to the total node power cap. The next constraint regulates the concurrency on the system, i.e., the number of jobs in a set to be co-scheduled (JS_i) must be less than or equal to C. The last two constraints specify that the list of job sets (L_{JS}) must be created from the job queue (Q) in a mutually exclusive and collectively exhaustive manner. Note Table 1 summarizes the parameters/functions used.

3.3   Solution Overview

Figure 2 depicts the overall workflow of our approach. As shown in the figure, it consists of an offline (right) and an online part (left).

During the offline part, we train the coefficients of our performance model, which we describe later in the paper, by using a predetermined benchmark set. More specifically, by executing various job sets while changing the hardware configurations, we generate a large enough number of data sets, which are used as inputs for the model training.

During the online part, we solve the optimization problem described in Sect. 3.2. This solution process consists of three parts (from top to bottom), and they work in a cooperative manner. We first determine the list of co-scheduling job sets (L_{JS}) and return it with the associated list of optimal hardware configurations (L_{HC}) (top part in the left figure). This component then communicates with the next stage (middle part in the left figure), i.e., continuously sends a temporal job set (JS) and receives the estimated co-run execution time ($CoRunTime$) along with the optimal hardware configurations (HC) and the solo-run time ($SoloRunTime$), which are used for the scheduling decisions. The component in the middle optimizes the hardware configurations (HC) for the job set (JS) given by the previous component. More specifically, it continuously sends the job set (JS) and a temporal hardware configuration (HC) to the third part (bottom part in teh left figure) and receives the estimated slowdowns until finding the optimal hardware configuration. The latter component estimates the slowdowns for the given jobs (JS) with the given hardware configuration (HC) by using the associated job profiles as well as the model coefficients obtained in the offline model training. Here, we assume that the profile of a job is collected beforehand during its first run without co-scheduling nor power capping[1]. The details are described in the next section that provides also the definitions of $SoloRunAppTime(P_{max})$, F_k^j, and $Slowdown$ shown in the figure.

4 Modeling and Optimization

4.1 Slowdown Estimation for a Given Job Set and Hardware Setup

Metric Formulations: We first provide simple formulations for the metrics appeared in Sect. 3.2 as follows:

$$CoRunTime(\text{JS}, \text{HC}) = \max_{J_j \in \text{JS}} CoRunAppTime_j(\text{JS}, \text{HC})$$

$$SoloRunTime(\text{JS}, P_{total}) = \sum_{J_j \in \text{JS}} SoloRunAppTime_j(P_{total})$$

$$CoRunAppTime_j(\text{JS}, \text{HC}) = Slowdown_j(\text{JS}, \text{HC}) \cdot SoloRunAppTime_j(P_{max})$$

$$SoloRunAppTime_j(P_{total}) = Slowdown_j(\{J_j\}, \{R_{max}^c, R_{max}^g, OptP_j^c, OptP_j^g\})$$
$$\cdot SoloRunAppTime_j(P_{max})$$

The parameters and functions used to formulate them are summarized in Table 2. The first equation denotes that the total execution time when co-scheduling a job set (JS) is determined by the longest execution time in the set. The second

---

[1] In case no profile is available for a job, which we do not cover in the paper, we can exclude it from the co-scheduling candidates at the first stage in the diagram and execute it exclusively without power capping while obtaining the profile for the future references.

Table 2. Definitions of parameters or functions to formulate $CoRunTime()$/ $SoloRunTime()$

Parameter or Function	Remarks
$CoRunAppTime_j$(JS, HC)	The execution time of jth job in a given job set (JS) when co-scheduling JS under a given hardware setup (HC)
$SoloRunAppTime_j(P_{total})$	The execution time of jth job in a given job set (JS) when its exclusive solo run under a power cap (P_{total})
$Slowdown_j$(JS, HC)	The slowdown ratio of jth job in a given job set (JS) caused by co-scheduling JS under a given hardware setup (HC)
J_j	jth job in a given job set (JS)—JS = $\{J_1, J_2, \cdots\}$
$R^*_{max}(* = c/g)$	The maximum resource allocation on CPU/GPU to a given job
$OptP^*_j(* = c/g)$	The optimal power cap set up on CPU/GPU for jth job in a set when exclusive solo run ($OptP^c_j + OptP^g_j = P_{total}$)
P_{max}	The maximum total power cap or TDP ($P_{total} \leq P_{max}$)
F^j_k	kth parameter to characterize the features of J_j, given by hardware performance counters on both CPU and GPU

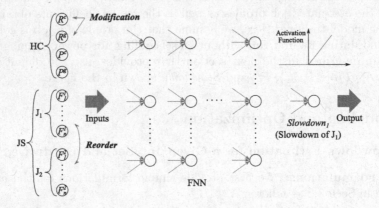

Fig. 3. General structure of our performance modeling ($C = 2$)

equation represents that the total execution time of time-shared scheduling is simply the sum of the solo-run execution time of the jobs in the set. The third equation shows that the execution time of a co-scheduled job ($CoRunAppTime_j$) is equal to the slowdown ($Slowdown_j$) multiplied by the solo-run execution time without power capping ($SoloRunAppTime_j(P_{max})$). In the fourth one, the performance degradation caused by power capping for a solo run can be described by using the same slowdown function used in the third equation. In this paper, the solo-run execution time without power capping is given by the associated profile, and we predict the slowdown part in those last two equations.

Performance Modeling: Figure 3 illustrates the general structure to model the slowdown function provided above. Here, we utilize a simple feedforward neural network (FNN) to estimate the slowdown for the first job (J_1) in the job set (JS) when co-scheduling. We regard the slowdown as a function of the job features (F_k^j) of all the co-located jobs as well as the hardware configuration (HC) to assess various factors such as scalability, interference, and resource allocations. The job features here are the hardware performance counters collected from both the CPU and GPU during the profile run described in Sect. 3.3. The exact definitions for the job features used in our evaluation are listed in Sect. 5.1. As for the slowdowns of the other co-located job(s), we simply reorder or replace the input locations (i.e., exchange the location between J_1 and J_j) and modify the resource allocation parameters (R_*) accordingly so that the allocations are associated with the new job order. Further, we also utilize the model to estimate the impact of power capping on solo-run performance. To do so, we simply designate HC = $\{R_{max}^c, R_{max}^g, OptP_j^c, OptP_j^g\}$ as previously mentioned and set all the job features other than the first job to zero in the model inputs. The detailed network configurations such as the exact inputs, the layer setups, the activation function, or the loss function are described in Sect. 5.1.

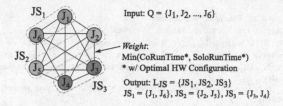

Input: Q = {J_1, J_2, ..., J_6}

Weight:
Min(CoRunTime*, SoloRunTime*)
* w/ Optimal HW Configuration

Output: L$_{JS}$ = {JS$_1$, JS$_2$, JS$_3$}
JS$_1$ = {J_1, J_6}, JS$_2$ = {J_2, J_5}, JS$_3$ = {J_3, J_4}

Fig. 4. Overview of graph-based job sets creation ($W = 6$, $C = 2$)

4.2   Hardware Setup Optimization for a Given Job Set

By using the performance model provided above, we optimize the hardware configuration parameters (HC) for a given job set (JS) when co-scheduling. Here, we attempt to pick up the best hardware configuration (HC) from all the possible configurations so as to minimize $CoRunTime$(JS, HC). In this study, we simply utilize the exhaustive search, i.e., testing all the possible HC for the model inputs and choosing one that minimizes $CoRunTime$ for the given job set (JS). This is because the number of all the possible setups for HC on our target platform (or other systems available today) is limited as described later in Sect. 5.1. If the configuration space would explode in future systems, applying heuristic algorithms (e.g., hill climbing) would be a promising option. In addition, we select the pair of ($OptP_j^c$, $OptP_j^g$) for each job (J_j) in a given job set so as to obtain $SoloRunTime$(JS, P_{total}), for which we also explore in an exhaustive manner under the constraint of $OptP_j^c + OptP_j^g = P_{total}$.

4.3   Job Sets Selection

We then make scheduling decisions using the above hardware setup optimization functionality based on the results of our performance model. We regard the job

---

Algorithm 1: Job Scheduling Procedure $(C = 2)$

Inputs: $Q = \{J_1, \cdots, J_W\}$, P_{total}, $SP = \{C = 2, W\}$
Outputs: $L_{JS} = \{JS_1, JS_2, \cdots\}$, $L_{HC} = \{HC_1, HC_2, \cdots\}$

```
    /* Initialization                                                        */
 1  LJS ← ∅; LHC ← ∅;
 2  Vortexes← Q; Edges← ∅; Weights← ∅; HWConfigs← ∅; CoRunFlags← ∅;
    /* Graph creation                                                        */
 3  for i = 1 → W do
 4  │   for j = i + 1 → W do
 5  │   │   Edges.push_back({Ji,Jj}); // Append this job set
 6  │   │   (HCco, CoRunTime) ← GetOptimalCoRunHWConfig(Ji,Jj);
 7  │   │   (HCsolo1, HCsolo2, SoloRunTime) ← GetOptimalSoloRunHWConfig(Ji,Jj);
    │   │   /* Append the weight and the HW config (incl. co-run or solo-runs) that
    │   │      minimizes time for this job set                               */
 8  │   │   if CoRunTime ≤ SoloRunTime then
 9  │   │   │   Weights.push_back(CoRunTime); CoRunFlags.push_back(1);
    │   │   │   HWConfigs.push_back({HCco});
10  │   │   else
11  │   │   │   Weights.push_back(SoloRunTime); CoRunFlags.push_back(0);
    │   │   │   HWConfigs.push_back({HCsolo1, HCsolo2});
12  │   │   end
13  │   end
14  end
    /* Job sets decision w/ Edmonds' Algorithm                               */
15  L'JS ← EdmondsAlgorithm(Vortexes, Edges, Weights);
16  L'HC ← PickupSets(HWConfigs, L'JS); // Pick the associated HW setups /w L'JS
17  LFlag ← PickupSets(CoRunFlags, L'JS); // Create a co-/solo-run flag list
    /* Divide sets in L'JS/L'HC if solo-run execution is better than co-scheduling */
18  while LFlag ≠ ∅ do
19  │   Flag ← LFlag.pop_front(); JS ← L'JS.pop_front(); HC ← L'HC.pop_front();
20  │   if Flag = 1 then
21  │   │   LJS.push_back(JS); LHC.push_back(HC);
22  │   else
23  │   │   while JS ≠ ∅ do
24  │   │   │   J ← JS.pop_front(); HCsolo ← HC.pop_front();
25  │   │   │   LJS.push_back({J}); LHC.push_back({HCsolo});
26  │   │   end
27  │   end
28  end
29  return (LJS, LHC);
```

---

co-scheduling problem as a minimum weight perfect matching problem and solve it using Edmonds' algorithm [13]. Figure 4 depicts the overview of the solution. In the figure, the vertices represent the jobs in the queue ($Q = \{J_1, \cdots, J_W\}$), and the weights represent the minimum execution time for the associated job sets. To obtain each weight, we estimate both of the best $CoRunTime$ and $SoloRunTime$ for each edge (or job pair) by using the model-based hardware configuration optimization described above, and choose one from them so that the execution time is minimized. Then, by using the graph, we create the list of job sets (L_{JS} = $\{JS_1, JS_2, \cdots\}$) that includes all jobs in the queue in a mutually exclusive and collectively exhaustive manner, while minimizing the sum of the weights of L_{JS}. This is a well-known minimum weight perfect matching problem and is identical to the optimization problem defined in Sect. 3.2 except that a job set can be executed in the time-sharing manner, which we can easily convert to meet the problem definition in Sect. 3.2 by simply dividing such a job set into multiple job sets, all of which include only one job. The Edmonds' algorithm provides the optimal solution with polynomial time complexity, particularly when the scheduling parameter set (SP) meets both of the following conditions: (1) W is an even number; and (2) C is equal to 2 [13]. For the former, we simply set the window size to an even number, and as for the latter, we focus on $C = 2$ to limit the complexity as described before. Note that a more precise version of the solution is described in Algorithm 1.

5 Evaluation

5.1 Evaluation Setup

Environment. For our evaluation, we use the platform summarized in Table 3. Our approach is applicable when both the CPU and GPU are capable of both resource partitioning and power capping. This is usually the case for most of the commercial CPUs today, and we utilize an NVIDIA A100 GPU card that supports the MIG feature and power capping [21].

Table 4 summarizes the resource partitioning and power capping settings we explore in this evaluation. We allocate CPU cores in a compact fashion, i.e., physically adjacent cores are assigned to the same program. We partition the GPU into 3GPCs/4GPCs or 4GPCs/3GPCs, on which low level memory hierarchies including L2 caches and memory modules are shared across all the GPCs[2]. To collect performance counter values when profiling, we utilize Linux perf [2] command for the CPU and NSight Compute [20] for the GPU. By using these profiling frameworks, we collect the performance counter values listed in Table 5. The definitions of these performance counters are the same as those shown in the tools (Table 5).

Benchmarks and Dataset. We use the Rodinia benchmarks [11], which is a well-known benchmark suite widely-used for various heterogeneous computing

Table 3. Evaluation system specifications

Name	Remarks
CPU	AMD Ryzen Threadripper 2990 WX, 32 cores
Main Memory	DDR4 2933 MT/s x4ch, 64 GB (Total)
GPU	NVIDIA A100 40 GB PCIe, 8GPCs
Operating system	Ubuntu 20.04.4 LTS, Kernel Version 5.4.0-120-generic
Compiler and drivers	GCC/G++ Version: 9.4.0, CUDA Version: 11.6, Driver Version: 510.73.08

---

[2] One GPC must be disabled when using MIG. Other partitioning options such as 1GPC/6GPCs or 2GPCs/5GPCs are not supported. We first create one GI with 7GPCs and then create CIs consisting of 3GPCs/4GPCs inside of it [4, 21].

Table 4. Power cap and partitioning setups

Variable	Selections
P_{total}/P_{max}	350, 400 [W]/500 [W]
P_*^c	100, 125, 150, 175, 200, 225, 250(max) [W]
P_*^g	150, 175, 200, 225, 250(max) [W]
R_*^c	(# of cores for J_1, # of cores for J_2): (2,30), (8,24), (16,16), (24,8), (30,2) (= co-runs), (32,0) (= solo-run, R_{max}^c)
R_*^g	(# of GPCs for J_1, # of GPCs for J_2): (3,4), (4,3) (= co-runs), (8,0) (= solo-run, R_{max}^g)

studies, as well as a synthetic compute-intensive dense matrix-vector multiplication program (`matvec`). In particular, from the Rodinia benchmark suite, we pick up seven programs that utilize both CPU and GPU extensively/cooperatively. Further, the `matvec` program uses both CPU and GPU in a cooperative manner, i.e., a part of the computation is offloaded to GPU and the rest is performed on CPU. We then create three different job queues (*JobMix1*, *JobMix2*, and *JobMix3*) with different window sizes (W) ranging from 4 to 8. The programs in the queues are selected mutually-exclusively (and randomly for *JobMix1* / *JobMix2*) from the eight benchmarks.

We then generate the training/validation/test datasets by using the benchmarks. More specifically, we randomly select $8 \times 2 = 16$ job pairs out of all the possible $_8C_2 = 28$ pairs and measure the co-scheduling slowdowns for each of them while testing 100 different hardware setups that is identical to all the co-run hardware setups that meet $P_{total} = 350$ or 400 [W] in Table 4. To validate the performance model, we divide the dataset in the following way: the first 12 pairs multiplied by 100 hardware configurations (= 2,400 data points) are used for the training and validation; and the rest of the 800 data are used for the inference testing. Note the above division process is based on random pair selections. The training and validation here are corresponding to the offline procedure shown in Fig. 2 in Sect. 3.3.

Neural Network Architecture and Training. Table 7 lists our neural network architecture and training setups based on the general structure described in Sect. 4.1. In our neural network, all the inputs are normalized between 0 and 1 (including the hardware configuration) in order to equalize the significance of them, which ultimately helps the convergence. To normalize the resource partitioning states (R_i^*), we simply pick the first element that represents the number of core or GPC allocation to the first job (J_1), and then divide it by the maximum number of the resource allocation (32 for cores and 8 for GPCs in our environment). We set up two hidden layers to well recognize the patterns in the input values, which is better than relying on one single hidden layer for this purpose. The rectified linear activation function is applied to all the layers except for the input layer, and all the neurons in both the hidden layers and the output have biases. The input layer is fully connected with the first hidden layer in order to use the model while re-ordering the job inputs (see also Sect. 4.1).

In our Python implementation, the training with the dataset described above takes only few minutes, and the slowdown estimations for all the jobs in a job set takes only 1.17 ms in total.

5.2   Experimental Results

Figure 5/6 demonstrate the total execution time comparisons across multiple different scheduling and resource management polices for different total power cap setup ($P_{total} = 350, 400$[W]). The vertical axis indicates the total execution time, while the horizontal axis lists job queues (*JobMix1-JobMix3*) in both the figures. The details of the compared policies listed in the legends are as follows: *Time Sharing + Naive Pow Cap* schedules jobs in the time-sharing manner while setting up the power caps to the CPU and GPU equally; *Time Sharing + Opt Pow Cap* also utilizes the time-shared scheduling but the power caps are set to the optimal; and *Our Co-scheduling* schedules jobs and configures the hardware using our proposed approach. As shown in these figures, we achieve significant speedups by up to 67.4% (= (108.8/65.0 − 1)*100) by using our approach compared with *Time Sharing + Naive Pow Cap*. Note the hardware partitioning is done only at the job launches, thus the overhead is negligible here. Table 8 presents the list of job sets created by our approach for each queue under different power capping. The job set selections can change depending on the total power cap setup, which implies our approach can flexibly deal with hardware environment changes, e.g., with changes in the power supply level.

We then compare the measured and estimated execution time (excluding online scheduling time) for different power cap setups in Fig. 7/8. The X-axis indicates the accumulated execution time of all the co-scheduled job sets created from *JobMix3* by using our approach. As shown in the figure, the estimated

Table 5. Collected performance counters (**F**)

Component	Counters and Definitions
CPU	$F_1^* =$ cpu-util, $F_2^* =$ context-switches, $F_3^* =$ page-faults, $F_4^* =$ IPC, $F_5^* =$ stalled-cycles, $F_6^* =$ branch-misses, $F_7^* =$ L1-dcache-load-misses, $F_8^* =$ L1-icache-load-misses, $F_9^* =$ dTLB-load-misses, $F_{10}^* =$ iTLB-load-misses
GPU	$F_{11}^* =$ Memory[%], $F_{12}^* =$ DRAM Throughput[%], $F_{13}^* =$ TEX cache Throughout[%], $F_{14}^* =$ LLC Throughput[%], $F_{15}^* =$ Compute[%], $F_{16}^* =$ Waves per SM, $F_{17}^* =$ Achieved Occupancy[%], and $F_{18}^* =$ Warps per SM

Table 6. Tested job mixes

Name	Job Mix
JobMix1	Q ={gaussian, lud, pathfinder, streamcluster}, $C = 2$, $W = 4$
JobMix2	Q ={gaussian, srad, hotspot, pathfinder, lavaMD, matvec}, $C = 2$, $W = 6$
JobMix3	Q ={gaussian, srad, hotspot, lud, pathfinder, lavaMD, streamcluster, matvec}, $C = 2$, $W = 8$

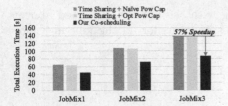

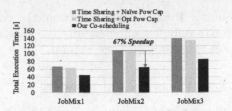

Fig. 5. Execution time comparison ($P_{total} = 350[W]$)

Fig. 6. Execution time comparison ($P_{total} = 400[W]$)

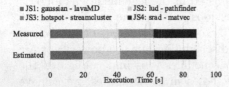

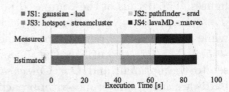

Fig. 7. Comparison of measured vs estimated time (*JobMix3*, $P_{total} = 350[W]$)

Fig. 8. Comparison of measured vs estimated time (*JobMix3*, $P_{total} = 400[W]$)

execution times are close to the measured ones, and the total estimation error is only 0.4% or 3.1% for $P_{total} = 350$ or 400, respectively. Note that our approach achieves closer performance to the optimal as the error becomes smaller. This is because the Edmonds' algorithm returns the optimal scheduling job sets if the performance estimation is 100% accurate.

Finally, we demonstrate the hardware setup decisions made by our scheduler in Figs. 9/10/11, in particular, for *JobMix3* under the total power cap of $P_{total} = 350[W]$. The X-axis indicates the job sets created from *JobMix3* by our approach, while the Y-axis represents the breakdown of power caps, core allocations, or GPC allocations in Figs. 9, 10, or 11, respectively. As shown in these figures, these hardware knobs are set very differently in accordance with the characteristics of co-located jobs, including the task size on CPU/GPU,

Table 7. Model and training setups

Type	Parameter List
Model	[**Input layer**]= 4 HW config states (HC) + 18 HW counters (J_1) + 18 HW counters (J_2); [**# of hidden layers**]= 2; [**# of neurons in each hidden layers**]= 18 (= # of HW counters); [**Layer connection**]= Fully connected; [**Activation function**]= Rectified Linear
Training	[**Learning rate**]= 0.001; [**Batch size**]= 4; [**Optimizer**]= Stochastic Gradient Descent; [**# of epochs**]= 200; [**Loss function**]= Mean Square Error

Table 8. Lists of job sets created by our approach

P_{total}	Lists of Job Sets (L_{JS})
350 W	(*JobMix1*): {gaussian-lud, pathfinder-streamcluster}, (*JobMix2*): {gaussian-hotspot, pathfinder-lavaMD, matvec-srad}, (*JobMix3*): {lavaMD-gaussian, lud-pathfinder, hotspot-streamcluster, matvec-srad}
400 W	(*JobMix1*): {gaussain-lud, pathfinder-streamcluster}, (*JobMix2*): {hotspot-lavaMD, srad-pathfinder, matvec-gaussian}, (*JobMix3*): {gaussian-lud, srad-pathfinder, hotspot-streamcluster, lavaMD-matvec}

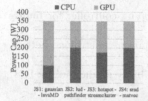 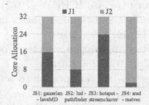 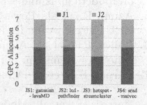

Fig. 9. Power cap setups (JobMix3, $P_{total} = 350[W]$) **Fig. 10.** Core allocation (JobMix3, $P_{total} = 350[W]$) **Fig. 11.** GPC allocation (JobMix3, $P_{total} = 350[W]$)

the compute/memory intensity, and the interference on shared resources. As our performance modeling can recognize these features well based on the corresponding hardware performance counters and the well-structured neural network, our approach achieves the significant performance improvement by up to 67%.

6   Conclusion

In this paper, we targeted co-scheduling, resource partitioning, and power capping comprehensively for CPU-GPU heterogeneous systems and proposed an approach to optimize them, which consists of performance modeling and a graph-based scheduling algorithm. We demonstrated how a machine learning model, namely a neural network, can successfully be used to predict the performance of co-scheduled applications, while using the application characteristics and partitioning/power states as inputs. We then moved on to the application pair selections where we successfully applied Edmond's algorithm to determine the mathematically optimal pairing. The experimental result using a real system shows that our approach improves the system throughput by up to 67% compared with a time-sharing-based scheduling with a naive power capping that evenly distributes power budgets on CPU/GPU.

Acknowledgements. This work has received funding under the European Commission's EuroHPC and H2020 programmes under grant agreement no. 956560 and was supported by the NVIDIA Academic Hardware Grant Program.

References

1. Top 500 list (2022). https://www.top500.org/lists. Accessed 24 July 2022
2. perf: Linux profiling with performance counters (2022). https://perf.wiki.kernel.org/index.php/Main_Page. Accessed 24 July 2022
3. Arima, E., Hanawa, T., Trinitis, C., Schulz, M.: Footprint-aware power capping for hybrid memory based systems. In: Sadayappan, P., Chamberlain, B.L., Juckeland, G., Ltaief, H. (eds.) ISC High Performance 2020. LNCS, vol. 12151, pp. 347–369. Springer, Cham (2020). https://doi.org/10.1007/978-3-030-50743-5_18
4. Arima, E., et al.: Optimizing hardware resource partitioning and job allocations on modern gpus under power caps. In: ICPPW (2022)
5. Azimi, R., et al.: PowerCoord: a coordinated power capping controller for multi-CPU/GPU servers. In: IGSC, pp. 1–9 (2018)
6. Bailey, P.E., et al.: Adaptive configuration selection for power-constrained heterogeneous systems. In: ICPP, pp. 371–380 (2014)
7. Barnes, B.J., et al.: A regression-based approach to scalability prediction. In: ICS, pp. 368–377 (2008)
8. Barrera, S., et al.: Modeling and optimizing NUMA effects and prefetching with machine learning. In: ICS, no. 34 (2020)
9. Bhadauria, M., et al.: An approach to resource-aware co-scheduling for CMPs. In: ICS, pp. 189–199 (2010)
10. Cao, T., et al.: Demand-aware power management for power-constrained HPC systems. In: CCGrid, pp. 21–31 (2016)
11. Che, S., et al.: Rodinia: a benchmark suite for heterogeneous computing. In: IISWC, pp. 44–54 (2009)
12. Cochran, R., et al.: Pack & cap: adaptive DVFs and thread packing under power caps. In: MICRO, pp. 175–185 (2011)
13. Cook, W., et al.: Computing minimum-weight perfect matchings. In: INFORMS Journal on Computing, vol. 11 (1999)
14. Dennard, R.H., et al.: Design of ion-implanted MOSFET's with very small physical dimensions. IEEE J. Solid-State Circ. 9(5), 256–268 (1974)
15. Eeckhout, L.: Heterogeneity in response to the power wall. IEEE Micro 35(04), 2–3 (2015)
16. Greathouse, J.L., et al.: Machine learning for performance and power modeling of heterogeneous systems. In: ICCAD, pp. 1–6 (2018)
17. ïpek, E., et al.: Efficiently exploring architectural design spaces via predictive modeling. In: ASPLOS, pp. 195–206 (2006)
18. Lee, B.C., et al.: Accurate and efficient regression modeling for microarchitectural performance and power prediction. In: ASPLOS, pp. 185–194 (2006)
19. Nagasaka, H., et al.: Statistical power modeling of GPU kernels using performance counters. In: International Conference on Green Computing, pp. 115–122 (2010)
20. NVIDIA: Nsight compute (2022). https://developer.nvidia.com/nsight-compute. Accessed 24 July 2022
21. Nvidia: Nvidia multi-instance GPU (2022). https://www.nvidia.com/en-us/technologies/multi-instance-gpu/. Accessed 24 July 2022
22. Patki, T., et al.: Exploring hardware overprovisioning in power-constrained, high performance computing. In: ICS, pp. 173–182 (2013)
23. Sarood, O., et al.: Maximizing throughput of overprovisioned HPC data centers under a strict power budget. In: SC, pp. 807–818 (2014)

24. Sasaki, H., et al.: Coordinated power-performance optimization in manycores. In: PACT, pp. 51–61 (2013)
25. Zhu, Q., et al.: Co-run scheduling with power cap on integrated CPU-GPU systems. In: IPDPS, pp. 967–977 (2017)
26. Zhuravlev, S., et al.: Addressing shared resource contention in multicore processors via scheduling. In: ASPLOS, pp. 129–142 (2010)

FPGA-Based Dynamic Deep Learning Acceleration for Real-Time Video Analytics

Yufan Lu, Cong Gao[✉], Rappy Saha, Sangeet Saha,
Klaus D. McDonald-Maier, and Xiaojun Zhai

University of Essex, Colchester, UK
{yl19888,cg21670,sangeet.saha,kdm,xzhai}@essex.ac.uk

Abstract. Deep neural networks (DNNs) are a key technique in modern artificial intelligence that has provided state-of-the-art accuracy on many applications, and they have received significant interest. The requirements for ubiquity of smart devices and autonomous robot systems are placing heavy demands on DNNs-inference hardware, with high requirement for energy and computing efficiencies, along with the rapid development of AI techniques. The high energy efficiency, computing capabilities, and reconfigurability of FPGAs make these a promising platform for hardware acceleration of such computing tasks. This paper primarily addresses this challenge and proposes a new flexible hardware accelerator framework to enable adaptive support for various DL algorithms on an FPGA-based edge computing platform. This framework allows run-time reconfiguration to increase power and computing efficiency of both DNN model/software and hardware, to meet the requirements of dedicated application specifications and operating environments. The achieved results show that with the proposed framework is capable to reduce energy consumption and processing time up to 53.8% and 36.5% respectively by switching to a smaller model. In addition, the time and energy consumption are further elaborated with a benchmark test set, which shows that how input data in each frame and size of a model can affect the performance of the system.

Keywords: Deep neural networks · Hardware accelerator · Edge computing · Real-time video analytics · FPGAs

1 Introduction

Due to the recent advancement of digital technologies, deep neural networks (DNNs) have emerged as a key technique in modern artificial intelligence (AI), that provides state-of-the-art accuracy for many applications [1]. Generally speaking, DNN models inference technique can be adopted wide range of devices, i.e. CPU, ASIC, FPGA, GPU, Microcontroller. While for CPU and GPU implementation, these techniques are available for a wide range of DNN models.

M. Schulz et al. (Eds.): ARCS 2022, LNCS 13642, pp. 68–82, 2022.
https://doi.org/10.1007/978-3-031-21867-5_5

For ASIC and FPGA implementation, although they are commonly applied in embedded fields [2], the techniques and tools supported in DNNs applications are relatively new. Different hardware platforms have different advantages, depending on the applications and user requirements. For our paper, we focus on FPGA based heterogeneous platform. FPGA based DNN model implementation can deliver better performance and energy efficiency compare to CPU and GPU [3]. We conclude this statement from the previous researches, proposed different kinds of FPGA based accelerators [3–6] to improve overall performance.

Although it is important to choose a hardware, it is also important to understand the application, implementation technique and tool's availability. Usually, we focus to solve a problem by applying single model. But it may not seem to be the best solution. In [7], it is showed that for image classification purpose switching between different models based on the input increases overall performance. They demonstrated their idea in a GPU-based environment. In [8], authors focused on available resource monitoring in run-time to switch between the pre-defined models in a CPU-GPU environment. To be able to switch between different models, it must be necessary to generate multiple models based on the necessity. Here comes the idea of neural architectural search (NAS) [9]. Multiple model generation, model switching to improve performance, model switching to improve resource usability, these three aspects drive our motivation to propose a new framework for the FPGA based heterogeneous environment where we will be able to switch between the models in order to improve performance and resource usability.

In this paper, we present an improved flexible hardware accelerator framework, that can provide a significant level of adaptability support for various DL algorithms on an FPGA-based edge computing platforms. The platform can dynamically configure hardware and software processing pipelines to achieve better cost, power, and processing efficiency for the dedicated application requirements at run-time. To demonstrate the effectiveness of the proposed solution, we implement our framework for a DNNs based real-time video processing pipeline on a Xilinx ZCU104 platform, where we carry out a set of comprehensive experiment tests to evaluate the performance of the proposed scheme.

The achieved results show that with the proposed framework is capable to reduce energy consumption and processing time up to 53.8% and 36.5% respectively by switching a smaller model. With a further discussion on time and power cost of the framework, a algorithm could be developed to define a strategy to control the switching behavior to achieve the optimised system performance. In summary, we make the following novel contributions in this paper:

– We propose an improved flexible DNN hardware accelerator framework that can dynamically configure the hardware and software processing pipelines to achieve improved power consumption and latency performance metrics.
– We have carried out comprehensive evaluations of DNN model sizes and inference performance, when using Xilinx DPUs in video analytic applications.
– We build a complete DNNs based real-time video processing pipeline and evaluate the effectiveness of the proposed framework.

- We designed a benchmark tool set to further analysis time and energy consumption of the framework.

The paper is organized as follows: Sect. 2 introduces the overall system. Section 3 briefly explains the DNN model optimisation strategy. Section 4 details the hardware and software pipeline setups. Section 5 details the experiments carried out under different scenarios and evaluates, compares, and discusses the results, Sect. 6 details the time and energy consumption of the proposed framework, and Sect. 7 draws conclusions and future plans.

2   Overview of the Proposed System

The proposed scheme can support one to n implementations and can offer a great level of flexibility and run-time efficiency for run-time video analytics applications. The proposed system consists of three main software components: 1) Neural network architecture search algorithms, that can generate different sub-networks with given constraints, 2) Neural network model compilation that can convert sub-networks into FPGA focused executing formats, and 3) Run-time management that can support dynamic execution of sub-networks on heterogeneous devices. A high-level overview diagram is presented in Fig. 1.

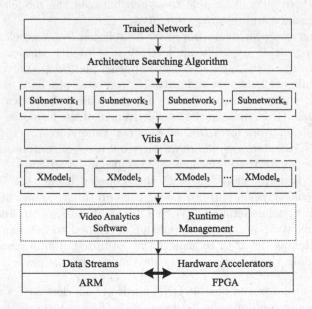

Fig. 1. The system architecture of the proposed scheme.

2.1   Neural Network Architecture Search

Neural network architecture search (NAS) is a popular technologies to reduce the size of the neural networks. Generally, the NAS algorithm does not consider the target hardware architecture and run-time conditions directly because it lacks accurate cost information to feedback to the NAS algorithm. For example, one to one NAS optimisation is able to generate a network architecture Net_1 that meets the design requirements of accuracy $a_1 > A$, power consumption $p_1 < P$, and latency $l_1 < L$. However, during run-time inference, the input data might be challenging. The accuracy does not meet the designed parameters, e.g. $a_1 < A$.

Consequently, the power consumption and latency could increase accordingly due to longer processing time required. Recent work proposed by [10] introduced an interesting NAS method, OFA that can produce a variety of network architectures based on the constraints of latency and accuracy. In this paper, we integrate OFA into a joint optimisation tool-chain, that can take advantage of this approach to produce a one to n inference model to meet various needs at run-time. The details of this optimisation approach are introduced in Sect. 3.

2.2   Neural Network Model Compilation

Network models developed in the mainstream frameworks needs to be mapped into a high-efficient instruction set and data flow for the targeted hardware platform. In this work, we use Vitis-AI to generate complied network model, where 32-bit floating-point weights and activations are converted 8-bit fixed-point [11]. Ultimately, the AI model is mapped into a high-efficient instruction set and data flow along with sophisticated optimisations, such as layer fusion, instruction scheduling, and reuses on-chip memory as much as possible by Vitis-AI.

2.3   Software and Hardware Run-Time Management

The run-time management of this system is implemented using Vitis AI Run-time (VART), which enables the applications to use the unified high-level run-time API. VART offers asynchronous submission and collection of jobs to the accelerator and supports multi-threading, and multi-process execution [12].

3   DNN Model Optimisation

3.1   Brief Introduction of OFA

OFA [10] consists mainly of 5 blocks, and in each block (i.e. convolution layers unit), depth, width and weight kernel size can be varied as per the following example: depth $D = \{2, 3, 4\}$, width $W = \{3, 4, 6\}$, kernel size $K = \{3, 5, 7\}$, where D, W and K represents the number of convolution layers and channels, size of filters in a single block respectively. It is assumed that each variable is independent to each other, so, number of subnetworks will be $((3 \times 3)^2 + (3 \times$

$3)^3 + (3 \times 3)^4)^5 \approx 2 \times 10^9$. In OFA, any model like Resnet [13] and Mobilenet [14] can be utilised and trained progressively, while maintaining the variability in depth, width, or kernel size. To identify a subnetwork from this vast number of subnetworks, they used latency and accuracy as a constraint in the random search and evolutionary search algorithms.

3.2   Model Generation and Optimisation

We use the OFA trained network as a super network and its searching algorithms to generate multiple subnetworks according to our requirements. The latency is firstly used as an input parameter in the search algorithm. Figure 2 describes the model generation technique, where the model is optimised in terms of latency and accuracy. In the OFA framework, random search is first used to determine a set of subnetworks (Subnet N) that are close to the defined latency. Evolutionary search is then used to identify the subnetworks (Subnet K) with the highest accuracy among the previously selected subnetworks.

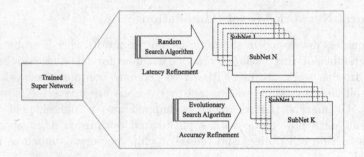

Fig. 2. The model generation and optimisation technique.

4   System Hardware/Software Co-design

4.1   Hardware Architecture

A real-time DNN based video analytic system typically includes four parts: 1) *video decoding*, 2) *preprocessing* (e.g. resize and normalisation), 3) *DNN inference* and 4) *post-processing*. Because both DNN, inference and other processes, require significant computational resources, the acceleration design should consider DNN inference and other processing tasks. Therefore, in addition, to deploying the DNN inference, hardware accelerators for video decoding and preprocessing should also be deployed. However, as the requirements of post-processing algorithms vary in different DNN models, the post-processing tasks are implemented in software.

The overall system architecture is shown in Fig. 3. There are mainly three types of accelerators: 1) *Xilinx H.264/H.265 video Codec unit (VCU)* [15], which is a hardware IP used for video coding and decoding tasks; 2) *Preprocessing module*, which is a high level synthesis (HLS) implemented hardware module and dedicated for resizing and normalisation tasks; and 3) *Deep learning processing units (DPUs)*, used for deep learning inference tasks, which can be reconfigured in different scenarios at run-time.

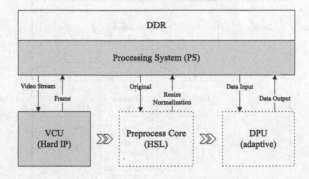

Fig. 3. The hardware architecture of the proposed platform.

To process video streams in real-time, the input video stream will be firstly decompressed by the VCU, so that the video stream is converted into separate frames. Secondly, the preprocessing core will carry out resize and pixel value normalisation on each frame. Both the VCU and preprocessing modules in this system can process up to 3840×2160 pixels at 60 frames per second, which has been set to 1080p video streams in our experimental scenarios. Therefore, the system's bottleneck should not be the VCU or preprocessing modules. Instead, the system performance will most likely be limited by the DPUs and other processes. Hence our ultimate goal is to reconfigure them at run-time to achieve the optimal performance for the entire system.

4.2 Software Implementation

For the software part, we developed video analytic applications using Vitis Video Analytics SDK (VVAS) [12], a GStreamer-based plugin development framework. The Gstreamer runs video processing pipelines in multi-threads. Hence, we can precisely control the DNN inference processes by introducing several customised plugins for multiple video analytic applications.

Figure 4 shows two types of pipelines representing different video analytic applications. 'Pipeline (a)' represents a typical one-stage video analytic application (e.g. object detection and segmentation), where only one DNN model is used to conduct an inference once per frame. 'Pipeline (b)' represents a two-stage video analytic application (e.g. tracking, Re-Identification, and car plates detection), where two DNN models are executing simultaneously, and the second one may execute multiple times, due to detection results of the first one.

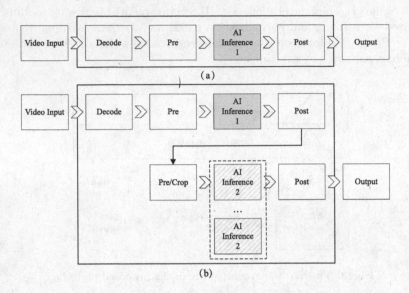

Fig. 4. Video processing pipelines in the proposed system. (a) represents an application with one stage AI inference task. (b) represents an application with two-stage AI inference task.

4.3   Communication Between Processes

We design a pair of communication interfaces (e.g., read and write communications) in DNN inference plugins, to report DNN inference information and control its run-time DNN model process. While the pipeline is running, the execution time of the DNN model, processing time of pipeline and the power consumption of the entire system will be simultaneously sent to a separate system management thread. According to the real-time performance metrics from the system, the processing pipeline can be reconfigured accordingly. In our previous work, [16], it is concluded that power and computing efficiency of the proposed system can be further improved by hardware reconfiguration, when workloads of the system are increased.

The design of the communication framework is shown in Fig. 5. There are three software layers, including 1) Python management interfaces for user control, 2) Gstreamer applications to run AI inference and 3) system info (e.g., hardware temperature and power consumption). In the work, the system info is recorded in Proc file system (a virtual file system in Linux). During run-time, Gstreamer applications continuously read the virtual via file IO interfaces. Each time when a virtual file is read, a function will be triggered to read sensor data.

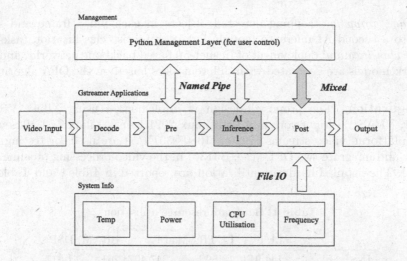

Fig. 5. Design of the communication framework.

The history data points are stored in applications. If necessary, the data can also be passed to the Python management program via the name pipe interface. The named pipe interface is the main method to transfer data between applications and management programs. Applications can send real-time status to or get commands from the management program. The "post" plugin in Gstreamer applications is a key module to collect system info (e.g., power) and running status (e.g., FPS). It is also responsible for transferring inference results. If the output result contains massive data (e.g., semantic segmentation), it will use file IO to store output results.

5 Experiments

In this section, experimental setup and results are comprehensively reported. A typical real-time video processing pipeline is implemented on a Xilinx ZCU104 (XCZU7EV) for both car and pedestrian detection and classification via analytic applications.

5.1 Overall System Setup

We implement the proposed video analytics framework on a Xilinx ZCU104 (XCZU7EV-2FFVC1156 MPSoC) development platform, where each frame follows the architecture of the pipeline described below:

1) *The input*: the video streams are loaded to the pipeline; 2) *Pre-processing unit*: carries out resizing and normalisation functions to allow the processed video data streams to meet the input requirements of DNN models; 3) *Object detection DNN inference*: deployment of object-detect DNN model on DPUs (e.g. YOLOv3 for cars and Refinet for pedestrians detection respectively [17,18]);

4) *Image cropping*: cropping detected objects in each video frame and send them to a second AI inference module for more precise classification tasks; 5) *Object classification*: deployment of Resnet-50 based backbone networks, and the network models are generated with different sizes based on the OFA algorithm.

Configuration. The proposed design is implemented using Xilinx Vivado 2021.1, VVAS 1.0 framework and PetaLinux 2021.1 on a Xilinx ZCU104 evaluation platform, video streams ($1920 \times 1080@30FPS$) are used for testing. We deploy and integrate two DPUs (i.e. B3136) in the video processing pipeline (i.e. Fig. 3). The detailed hardware utilization are reported in Table 1 and Table 2.

Table 1. Hardware resource utilisation

	LUT	LUTRAM	FF	BRAM	DSP
Used	144,913	13,599	247,407	261	1,217
Available	230,400	101,760	460,800	312	1,728
Utilisation (%)	62.9	13.4	53.7	83.5	70.4

Table 2. Sub-module resource utilisation

Sub module	LUT	Register	BRAM	DSP
DPU	47667	85778	210	436
VPU	105	24	0	0
Pre-processing unit	13147	17390	12	40

5.2   DNN Model Management

We use Xilinx Vitis-AI 1.4.1 tool-chain to convert Pytorch DNN models into xmodel files. By scaling DNN models based on the OFA searching strategy, we obtain three different sizes of OFA-resnet-50 models: OFA700, OFA1000 and OFA2000. The number after each OFA model represents million floating-point operations per second (MFLOPs), which is used as the threshold of the subnet searching in the OFA algorithm. Because 700 is the lowest value from all selected sub-networks and when value above 2000 the model size will increase with less accuracy improved, and we select 700 and 2000 to represent a large model and a small model separately and select 1000 as a medium one. Table 3 summarises a list of models used in our experiments, which includes a number of sub-networks generated by using the OFA network. The communication interfaces introduced in Sect. 4. C are implemented to update the DNN models at frame level dynamically.

Table 3. Parameters of the used DNN models

Model	Parameter size (MB)	Workload (MOPS)	Accuracy (Top1/Top5 ImageNet-1k)
OFA700	10.75	1340.61	74.9%/92.4%
OFA1000	18.02	1905.48	77.0%/92.8%
OFA2000	32.88	3805.47	79.7%/94.7%
ResNet-50	26.22	7360.32	83.2%/96.5%

In our experiment, we have verified the effectiveness of this management scheme using a DNN powered car/pedestrian re-identification application, where a two-stage DNN pipeline is implemented. The first stage of the DNN pipeline uses Yolov3/Refinet for car/pedestrian detection, respectively, and the second stage of the pipeline uses Resnet-50 as a backbone network for car/pedestrian classification.

5.3 Results and Analysis

As shown in Fig. 6, we have tested our framework for two different video analytic applications: car and pedestrian Re-Identification. The proposed framework shows the capability to handle the videos and identify objects correctly through tests in both scenarios.

(a)   (b)

Fig. 6. Testing scenarios. (a) Car re-identification; (b) Pedestrian re-identification

In our experiment, we use the same video processing pipeline to handle different video input streams, and continuously monitoring system's performance metrics, such as frame rate (FPS), energy consumption and DPU latency, via the proposed customised communication interference plugin. In the proposed work, we measure real-time on-board power from ZCU104 registers when using different sizes of DNN models. The total energy consumption can be calculated using the following equation:

$$E = \sum_{i=1}^{n} P_i/f \tag{1}$$

where E denotes the total energy consumption in Joules (J), P denotes power consumption in Watt (W) at time i, f denotes sampling frequency in Hz. From Fig. 7, the total energy consumption is reduced by 18.9%, 38.4% and 53.8% in the car scenarios respectively, and similarly reduced by 25.4%, 41.1% and 61.6% respectively in the pedestrian scenarios.

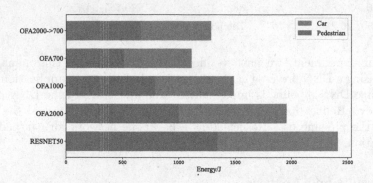

Fig. 7. Total energy consumption for running different models

In general, smaller size DNN models achieve better DPU inference latency due to less operations required, as the result of this, the entire video pipeline will finish quicker than deploying a larger model. Therefore, we can implement a dynamic model-switch strategy to select a suitable DNN model based on the real-time performance metrics to improve performance of the entire system. By comparing the original model, the proposed system can reduce the latency of DPUs for the whole video pipeline by 12.9%, 23.9%, and 36.5%, 14.0%, 25.9%, and 38.6% in car and pedestrian scenarios respectively.

The detailed DPU inference latencies for each OFA network model are summarised in Fig. 8.

Figure 9.(a) and (c) show FPS results of OFA700, OFA1000, OFA2000 and Resnet-50 on the car and pedestrian scenarios respectively. By comparing the FPS of Resnet-50, the overall FPS is increased by 26.3%, 65.6% and 113.0% in car scenarios by using OFA700, OFA1000, and OFA2000 models respectively; Similarly, it is also increased 27.1%, 65.7% and 132.1% FPS in pedestrian scenarios respectively.

In certain running environments (e.g. simple scenarios but with varying amounts of objects), we can dynamically switch the DNN models by monitoring the run-time performance metrics. Thus it could further increase overall power and computing efficiency with an acceptable loss of classification accuracy (Table 3). For example, as shown in Fig. 9(b) and (d), by switching the DNN model to a smaller one at run-time, the average frame rates are increased from 17.04 FPS to 29.4 FPS in the car scenarios and from 16.9 FPS to 30.8 FPS in the pedestrian scenarios respectively. Meanwhile the energy consumption is also dropped by 34.2% and 34.0% respectively for the two scenarios (see Fig 7).

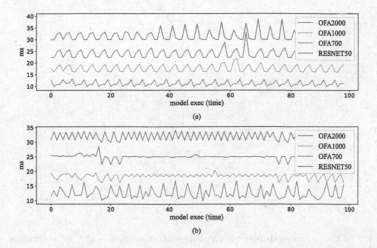

Fig. 8. Latency in different scenarios. (a) represents Latency in car scenarios. (b) represents Latency in pedestrian scenarios

6 Time and Power Consumption

In this sections, we will discuss and elaborate consumption (e.g. Time and power) for the proposed framework.

6.1 Impact Factors

Data Volume: In Sect. 5, each detected object will be cropped and sent to the second stage of the pipeline (e.g. Resnet-50 or OFA-Resnet-50 networks) for the classification work. The workloads will be significantly varied in the second stage of the pipeline with the number of objects were detected in the first stage. **Size of models:** Additional time consumption is majorly needed for rewriting the bitstream and updating software drivers, and the time for rewriting bitstream is varied by the sizes of the reconfiguration stream. On the other hand, the extra power consumption maybe caused by rewriting the RAMs. Scale/size of a model may influence time consumption of a single object classification job as well.

6.2 Benchmark

In order to analysis these factors, we create 7 different scene videos contain different number of cars, and test them for 2 different modes. The first mode is normal display mode, in which it just displays videos using VVAS. In the second mode, there are some model switch behaviors added with same time interval. We record both time and energy consumption and attempt to analyse how these factors influence the system performance.

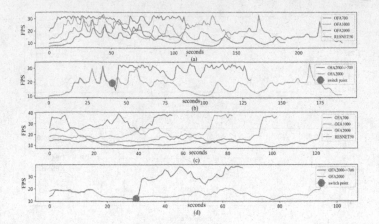

Fig. 9. FPS of the proposed system in different scenarios. (a) Car scenarios without model switch. (b) Car scenarios with model switch. (c) Pedestrian scenarios without model switch. (d) Pedestrian scenarios with model switch

Time Consumption: We can calculate a single switch time cost by comparing the time consumption between two modes, and through multi-set of data, we find that time cost of model switching behavior is irrelevant to the sizes of the models. It is varied between 30 ms to 300 ms. It may because the bandwidth of DDR is large enough for small data exchanges in the benchmark. From Fig. 10, it is easily to conclude that the cost in a full process will increase if either the sizes of the models or the target number increases, and there is a linear relationship between data volume and total time consumption, which is a factor of 12 ms per object for using OFA700 model. Models with larger size (e.g. OFA1000 and OFA2000) will spend 64.4% and 112.5% more time respectively compared to OFA700 model.

Power Consumption: As shown in Fig. 11, the energy consumption will be increased by 24.6%, 111.8%, 289.0%, 636.2% and 1345.4% for detecting 2, 4, 8, 16, 32 objects respectively when comparing to only 1 object is detected. With the same object number, the energy consumption will be increased by 3% and 9% for OFA1000 and OFA2000 respectively when comparing to OFA700.

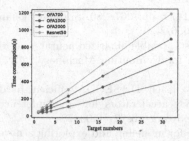

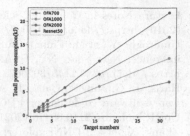

Fig. 10. Time consumption with different target numbers

Fig. 11. Power consumption with different target numbers

7   Conclusion

In this work, we proposed designing a new flexible hardware accelerator framework to enable adaptive support for various DNN algorithms on a FPGA-based edge computing platform. The achieved results show that with the proposed framework is capable to reduce energy consumption and processing time up to 53.8% and 36.5% respectively by switching to a smaller model. While using a dynamical model-switch strategy, the frame rates are increased immediately at the switching point. The average frame rates are increased from 17.04 FPS to 29.4 FPS in the car scenarios and from 16.9 FPS to 30.8 FPS in the pedestrian scenarios, respectively. Two major impact factors, data volumes and size of model, have been further discussed with a designed benchmark and the statistical data shows that both factors have the positive impact on the energy and time consumption of the framework. By further combining a dynamic-reconfiguration strategy in hardware modules, the proposed system could offer an unprecedented opportunity to create new adaptable architectures and algorithm models using the hybrid-computing units and resources. It is anticipated that it will greatly impact increasing energy efficiency, performance, and flexibility.

Acknowledgment. This work is supported by the UK Engineering and Physical Sciences Research Council through grants EP/R02572X/1, EP/P017487/1, EP/V034111/1, EP/X015955/1 and EP/V000462/1.

References

1. Shawahna, A., Sait, S.M., El-Maleh, A.: FPGA-based accelerators of deep learning networks for learning and classification: a review. IEEE Access **7**, 7823–7859 (2019)
2. Lu, Y., Zhai, X., Saha, S., Ehsan, S., McDonald-Maier, K.D.: A self-adaptive SEU mitigation scheme for embedded systems in extreme radiation environments. IEEE Syst. J. **16**(1), 1436–1447 (2022)
3. Lübeck, K., Bringmann, O.: A heterogeneous and reconfigurable embedded architecture for energy-efficient execution of convolutional neural networks. In: Schoeberl, M., Hochberger, C., Uhrig, S., Brehm, J., Pionteck, T. (eds.) ARCS 2019.

Lecture Notes in Computer Science(), vol. 11479, pp. 267–280. Springer, Cham (2019). https://doi.org/10.1007/978-3-030-18656-2_20

4. Umuroglu, Y., et al.: Finn: a framework for fast, scalable binarized neural network inference. New York, NY, USA: Association for Computing Machinery (2017). https://doi.org/10.1145/3020078.3021744

5. Haris, J., Gibson, P., Cano, J., Agostini, N.B., Kaeli, D.: SECDA: efficient hardware/software co-design of FPGA-based DNN accelerators for edge inference, CoRR, vol. abs/2110.00478 (2021). https://arxiv.org/abs/2110.00478

6. Zhang, X., et al.: DNNExplorer: a framework for modeling and exploring a novel paradigm of FPGA-based DNN accelerator. In: Proceedings of the 39th International Conference on Computer-Aided Design, ser. ICCAD 2020. New York, NY, USA. Association for Computing Machinery (2020). https://doi.org/10.1145/3400302.3415609

7. Taylor, B., Marco, V.S., Wolff, W., Elkhatib, Y., Wang, Z.: Adaptive deep learning model selection on embedded systems. In: SIGPLAN Notices, vol. 53, no. 6, p. 31–43 (2018). https://doi.org/10.1145/3299710.3211336

8. Lou, W., Xun, L., Sabet, A., Bi, J., Hare, J., Merrett, G.V.: Dynamic-OFA: runtime DNN architecture switching for performance scaling on heterogeneous embedded platforms. In: IEEE/CVF Conference on Computer Vision and Pattern Recognition Workshops (CVPRW), vol. 2021, pp. 3104–3112 (2021)

9. Elsken, T., Metzen, J.H., Hutter, F.: Neural architecture search: a survey. J. Mach. Learn. Res. **20**(55), 1–21 (2019). http://jmlr.org/papers/v20/18-598.html

10. Cai, H., Gan, C., Wang, T., Zhang, Z., Han, S.: Once for all: train one network and specialize it for efficient deployment. In: International Conference on Learning Representations (2020). https://arxiv.org/pdf/1908.09791.pdf

11. Kathail, V.: Xilinx vitis unified software platform. In: Proceedings of the 2020 ACM/SIGDA International Symposium on Field-Programmable Gate Arrays, pp. 173–174 (2020)

12. Xilinx vitis-ai 1.4 release (2011). https://github.com/Xilinx/Vitis-AI

13. He, K., Zhang, X., Ren, S., Sun, J.: Deep residual learning for image recognition. In: 2016 IEEE Conference on Computer Vision and Pattern Recognition (CVPR). Los Alamitos, CA, USA: IEEE Computer Society, pp. 770–778 (2016). https://doi.ieeecomputersociety.org/10.1109/CVPR.2016.90

14. Howard, A.G., et al.: Mobilenets: efficient convolutional neural networks for mobile vision applications (2017)

15. Xilinx, H.264/H.265 Video Codec Unit v1.2, Technical report (2021). https://www.xilinx.com/support/documentation/ip_documentation/vcu/v1_2/pg252-vcu.pdf

16. Lu, Y., Zhai, X., Saha, S., Ehsan, S., McDonald-Maier, K.D.: FPGA based adaptive hardware acceleration for multiple deep learning tasks. In: 2021 IEEE 14th International Symposium on Embedded Multicore (2021)

17. Redmon, J., Farhadi, A.: YOLOv3: an incremental improvement (2018). https://arxiv.org/abs/1804.02767v1

18. Fu, K., Zhao, Q., Gu, I.Y.-H.: Refinet: a deep segmentation assisted refinement network for salient object detection. IEEE Trans. Multimedia **21**(2), 457–469 (2018)

Advanced Computing Techniques

Effects of Approximate Computing on Workload Characteristics

Daniel Maier[(⊠)], Stefan Schirmeister, and Ben Juurlink

Technische Universität Berlin, Berlin, Germany
`daniel.maier@tu-berlin.de`

Abstract. In recent years, many new approaches in approximate computing have been presented. These techniques have shown great opportunities to improve performance or energy consumption of applications while trading often a negligible decrease in accuracy. Many different techniques have been invented, ranging from hardware techniques to approaches purely implemented in software, compilers, and frameworks. Research has shown that applications often have very specific demands on hardware and usually suffer from specific bottlenecks such as memory bandwidth or compute capabilities. Developers optimize applications employing advanced techniques to optimally exploit hardware capabilities. We study how the workload character of the applications is affected when they are optimized using approximate computing techniques. We analyze the detailed micro-architectural application character using 55 characteristics. We evaluate four approximate computing techniques on all 37 applications from PolyBench/C and AxBench. We show how the optimization using the different approximation techniques influences both the properties of individual applications and groups of similar applications' characters. We find results that contradict general expectations, such as an increasing number of instructions executed when the opposite is expected. Furthermore, some applications are slowed down when approximated, which is confirmed by the number of executed instructions. These results show that the approximation of an application changes the core of its characteristics and that a detailed analysis of approximated applications is required. Interference between traditional optimizations and approximation requires a holistic approach.

1 Introduction

In many applications, there is a gap between the accuracy provided by a platform and the accuracy required by an application to provide *good enough* results. Exploiting this gap purposely to gain performance or to save energy describes the emerging paradigm of Approximate Computing. Approximate computing has been a hot topic and many works have been published in recent years presenting approaches that range from hardware-based techniques implementing approximate adders [23], lossy memory compression [9], or approximating function units to techniques implemented purely in software using compiler-based approaches [3,22], libraries or frameworks [2,6,14].

M. Schulz et al. (Eds.): ARCS 2022, LNCS 13642, pp. 85–99, 2022.
https://doi.org/10.1007/978-3-031-21867-5_6

We argue that approximate computing techniques should be understood as optimization techniques. Traditional optimization techniques involve many tools such as compilers and profilers; manual optimization using detailed knowledge about the hardware and domain-specific expertise about the applications; and hardware-based optimizations such as SIMD and parallelization. These approaches interfere with each other. All involved parts in the process from theoretical algorithm to retrieval of the result have to be aware of each other and work cooperatively to minimize negative effects. Developers have to be aware of where the bottlenecks in the problem being solved are; what kind of specific properties the hardware system has; and how the compiler is optimizing the code. Many scientific and other computationally demanding applications have a long history of optimizations to make the best possible use of hardware. By making use of approximate computing techniques to optimize these applications with many involved and interlocked parts, unforeseen and unwanted complications may occur.

We give an example to illustrate the problem. Consider an application with a compute-intense loop nest, that has been optimized to be unrolled by the compiler to better exploit branch predictors and to allow the compiler to make use of SIMD. Furthermore, to optimally utilize the memory hierarchy and memory bandwidth, the layout of data structures was optimized. Now, the application should be further accelerated using loop perforation, a general-purpose approximate computing technique where some iterations of loops are skipped to lower the execution time. This interferes with the aforementioned steps in multiple ways: 1) After loop perforation is applied, the compiler finds a different situation and chooses a different loop optimization strategy. 2) Loop perforation also affects the way data is accessed, resulting in sparse data structures, which leads to a waste of memory bandwidth and cache capacity. 3) Using SIMD for data-parallel computations is complicated as data accesses are sparse, leading to inefficient computations.

It is evident that assumptions that were used to optimize applications based on workload characteristics of accurate applications do not hold and need a close consideration of how approximate computing techniques affect the situation on different optimization levels. We use micro-architecture independent workload characteristics, a metric that has been proven valuable in characterizing workloads [7]. We show how approximation techniques affect the workload characteristics of applications. To summarize, our contributions are:

1. We revisit four approximate computing techniques (loop perforation, memoization, precision tuning, and neural approximation) and study their effects on 37 applications from PolyBench/C and AxBench.
2. We evaluate 55 characteristics in five categories. In our study, we perform a detailed analysis of changes in applications' workload characteristics.
3. We analyze the effects of approximation on individual applications and groups of similar characterized applications. We observe strong changes in characteristics, in some cases counteracting the optimization goals.

In the next section, we discuss related work. The details of our study are given in Sect. 3. We evaluate and analyze our results in Sect. 4. In Sect. 5 we conclude our work and discuss the impact on future work.

2   Related Work and Background

In many applications, the compute-intense part is located in loops. Consequently, loops are the target of many optimizations. One of these optimizations is loop perforation, where only a subset of all loop iterations is actually executed and, therefore, the performance is improved. Loop perforation [24] is a general-purpose technique, where iterations in loops are skipped and the loop is *perforated*. The technique has been refined to allow for dynamic patterns [11] and to take different phases during program execution into account [11,15]. The approach has been proven to work on parallel loops and threads [10,12,21]. Loop perforation was integrated into the OpenACC parallel programming model [10].

Precision tuning is a technique that reduces the number of bits to store information, e.g., using single-precision 32-bit instead of double-precision 64-bit floating-point numbers, or using fixed-point data representations instead. While higher precision provides more accurate storage and operations, the costs are also higher, e.g., latency, cache occupancy, chip area or energy/power. Precimonious is a tuning assistant for floating-point point precision [20]. Chiang et al. [4] present FPTuner, a tool that automatically generates a precision-annotated version of real expressions. TAFFO [3] is a framework for precision tuning that has recently been adapted for dynamic precision autotuning.

Memoization is a technique to dynamically save the result of expensive functions and later *reuse* the result instead of recomputing the result using the expensive function. The results can be also reused for similar arguments yielding an approximating memoization. Clava [1] is a framework for memoization implemented as a source-to-source compiler. It provides approximation for functions with floating-point arguments, where a user-definable number of the least significant bits are masked from the mantissa. Approximate Task Memoization [2] is a runtime system for dynamic and approximate memoization of tasks. Temporal approximate function memoization [25] has been shown to be able to exploit temporal output locality similar to output approximation [12].

Neural networks can be trained to approximate functions and even rather complex applications such as object detection or image classification. During training, given a number of inputs and expected outputs, the network parameters are continuously adjusted to minimize the approximation error. Approximation of general purpose functions was studied before [6,16]. Parrot [6] is a framework to automatize the process of approximating parts of general-purpose programs using neural networks. In the learning phase, a network is trained to mimic a selected part of a program. Then, a compiler replaces this part with the invocation of a neural accelerator. SSNAP [16] is an FPGA-based accelerator that promises low development costs similar to high-level synthesis tools. The approach targets low-cost SOCs with built-in FPGAs.

HPC-MixPBench [18] is a benchmark suite specifically for Mixed-Precision Analysis in the HPC context. PolyBench/C [19] is a collection of benchmarks originally designed to develop and assess Polyhedral compilation techniques. PolyBench/C contains 30 C programs that solve mathematical problems. Poly-Bench/C has been proven to be useful for benchmarking HPC systems [8] and Automatic Loop Perforation [13]. AxBench [26] is a benchmark suite curated for Approximate Computing. Hoste and Eeckhout perform an in-detail analysis of micro-architectural independent workload characteristics [7]. Chippa et al. study applications' inherent resilience towards approximation [5]. The concept of different phases during program execution each with a different sensitivity towards approximation is explored by Mitra et al. [15]

3   Our Study

In this section, we detail how we conduct our study. First, we discuss the four techniques that we study. We briefly introduce the tools that we use and we give visual examples of the results of approximated applications. Then we discuss the workloads and we explain how we acquire our results.

Loop Perforation. We use ACCEPT [22] to approximate applications using loop perforation. This framework tries to find the best possible speedup while staying within a given error budget. We specify two different error budgets of 10% and 50%. The result of an application optimized using loop perforation with 50% error budget is shown in Fig. 1. Figure 1a shows the output of the accurate SOBEL application. Figure 1b shows the approximation with visible distortion due to every other column being completely black.

Precision Tuning. We use TAFFO [3] as a framework for precision tuning. TAFFO was recently published and is one of the state-of-the-art tools for precision tuning. Compared to other approaches such as Precimonious [20] and HiFP-Tuner [4], TAFFO dynamically observes and evaluates the current situation and generates a new code version if required. The output of the SOBEL application is shown in Fig. 2. Figure 2a shows the accurate output and Fig. 2b shows the output when approximated using precision tuning. Some artifacts between both figures can be identified, however, they do not follow a specific pattern.

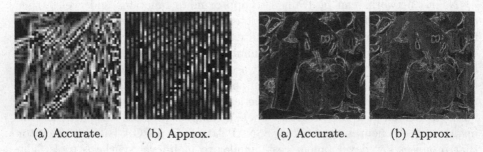

(a) Accurate.   (b) Approx.   (a) Accurate.   (b) Approx.

Fig. 1. Loop perforation example.   **Fig. 2.** Precision tuning example.

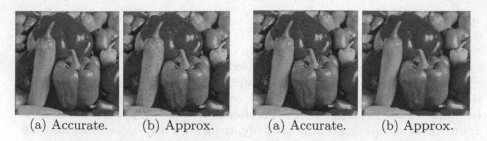

(a) Accurate.   (b) Approx.   (a) Accurate.   (b) Approx.

Fig. 3. Memoization example.   **Fig. 4.** Neural Approx. example.

Memoization. As none of the available memoization frameworks fit our needs, we chose to implement memoization manually. We implement memoization after close consideration for all seven applications from AxBench. PolyBench/C applications are loop nests, that do not use functions expensive enough for memoization. We show in Fig. 3 the output of the JPEG application. Figure 3a shows the accurate output and Fig. 3b shows the output of the approximation using memoization. Memoization introduces a distinct pattern of artifacts that align with the block-based compression of JPEG.

Neural Approximation. We use parrot [6] for neural approximation. Parrot is designed to be used in conjunction with a neural accelerator. As we have no access to such a device, we use the following approach to measure the performance: We remove the NPU invocation code completely and assume a zero-runtime NPU. Therefore, our measurements are the lower bound of the runtime. Figure 4 depicts exemplary output for the accurate (Fig. 4a) and approximated (Fig. 4b) JPEG application. The approximated output is blurry and on some edges there are artifacts.

For our study, we use 37 applications from PolyBench/C and AxBench. We study the effects of four approximation techniques. For PolyBench/C we apply loop perforation (10% and 50% error budget) and precision tuning. As memoization and neural approximation are not suitable for algebraic math kernels that PolyBench/C's applications implement, we do not apply these techniques. For AxBench, we implement loop perforation (10% and 50% error budget), precision tuning, memoization, and neural approximation. PolyBench/C is not equipped with built-in error measurement. Therefore, we implement error calculation using the true and approximate results. We calculate the element-wise relative error and aggregate it as the mean relative error. AxBench applications provide error assessment functionality and we rely on the built-in functionality. Related work [12] has shown that the accuracy of some applications is sensitive to input data. We use the supplied input data for all applications.

We conduct our study on an Intel Core i3-350M CPU clocked at 2.3 GHz and 4 GB RAM using a single CPU thread. All applications are compiled using the optimization level O3, and we use the Clang/llvm compiler toolchain. We measure run time of the applications by recording the time that passes from application start to application finish, i.e., including setup, memory transfers, etc. By repeating our measurements 50× and calculating the average of the run time we get a stable result. We then compare the run time of the accurate application to the run time of the approximated application and calculate the speedup. To be able to measure the accuracy of the approximation, we compare the result of the accurate application (known as true result) to the result of the approximated application. For PolyBench/C, which is not curated to be an approximate computing benchmark suite, there is no built-in accuracy measurement. All PolyBench/C applications operate on array data and their result is also an array. Therefore, we save the output of each application run and compare outputs generated by approximated applications element-wise to the known-good output. Then we calculate the *mean relative error* (MRE).

We use Valgrind [17] to profile the execution of applications and to record workload characteristics. Valgrind is a set of tools for dynamic binary instrumentation. The binary is on the fly translated to an intermediate representation (IR). The IR is then executed on a virtual machine. Valgrind tools can transform the IR to accomplish various tasks, e.g., profiling for possible memory leaks. We use a proprietary Valgrind tool to collect the data. We profile 55 characteristics. Each characteristic belongs to one of five groups: *1. Program flow* contains the number of executed blocks, average number of instructions per basic block, and the total number of executed instructions. *2. Registers* is the number of average registers accessed by instructions and the number of instructions between writing to and reading from a specific register. *3. Instruction mix* is the ratio of instruction categories (loads, stores, simple arithmetic operations, integer multiplications, divisions, comparisons, conversions, FP, SIMD) executed. *4. Working set size* represents the number of unique addresses accessed by data and instruction stream. *5. Data stream strides* is the distribution of temporally adjacent memory accesses, across instructions and for the same instruction.

4   Evaluation

Our evaluation section covers two main aspects. First, we show our analysis of how micro-architecture independent characteristics are affected by approximate computing techniques. We limit our evaluation to characteristics that are not constant. In the second part, we report speedup and error for the different techniques.

4.1   Workload Characteristics

As an application is usually optimized for one or more goals, specific knowledge about the character of the application is important to optimally exploit the application's properties and platform-specific properties. In this section, we analyze how the character of the applications unexpectedly changes when applying approximate computing techniques, thereby, invalidating assumptions based on knowledge about the accurate applications.

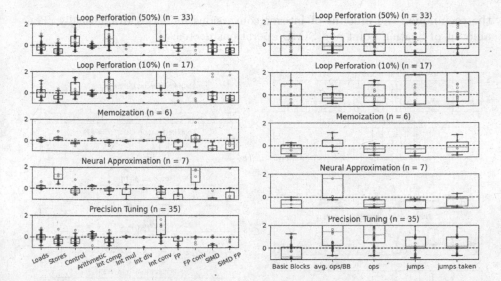

Fig. 5. Change in instruction mix.

Fig. 6. Change in instruction-related characteristics.

Instruction Mix is a high-level characteristic. We use the difference in the instruction mix of approximated and accurate programs. The instruction mix describes the relative amount of instructions executed from different categories of instructions. We use the following categories: load, store, control transfer, arithmetic operation, integer comparison, integer multiplication, integer division, integer conversion, floating-point operation, floating-point conversion, SIMD operation, and SIMD floating-point operation. We compare relative changes of the instruction mix: if the same set of instructions is executed a different number of times, the instruction mix is the same. In Fig. 5, a box plot shows the relative change in the instruction mix of all applications for a given approximation technique. For loop perforation, the amount of loads and stores decreases, as does the amount of floating-point operations and SIMD operations. This is expected, as the loops are perforated to perform less work. The amount of control flow operations, integer comparisons, and integer conversions increases, which can be explained by the overhead due to checking if a loop iteration should be perforated. The instruction mix for memoization shows the smallest changes compared to all other techniques. There is a significantly smaller amount of floating-point operations, which is expected, as memoization caches the result of expensive, often floating-point, operations. Neural approximation shows very distinct instruction mix changes. The amount of stores and floating-point conversions increase dramatically, while there is only a moderate increase in the amount of loads and arithmetic operations. The amount of control flow operations, integer and floating-point operations decreases. These observations are consistent with the way an NPU accelerator is accessed through memory transfers. The instruction mix changes for precision scaling, clearly identifying the technique. The amount of integer conversions increases dramatically. The amount of floating-point and SIMD operations decreases.

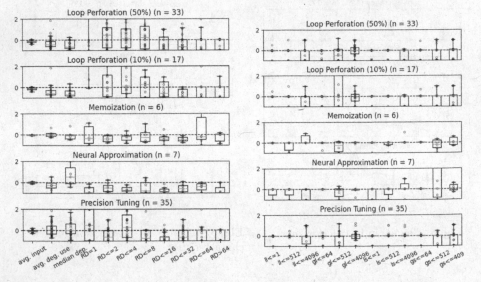

Fig. 7. Change in register-related characteristics.

Fig. 8. Change in memory access pattern (ll = local load, gl = global load, ls = local store, gs = global store).

Basic Blocks characteristics are related to changes in program flow, they are shown in Fig. 6. Loop perforation shows an interesting result. The median number of basic blocks does not change and the average number of instructions per block decreases. However, the total number of instructions executed is slightly increasing. A detailed look at our data shows that these numbers correlate with our performance result: for applications with a speedup, a smaller number of instructions is executed, while for applications with no speedup, the number of instructions executed increases. The number of jumps and jumps taken increased. Applications approximated using memoization have a smaller number of basic blocks. The average number of instructions per basic block shows a large variation, but on average it shows no change. The total number of executed instructions decreases significantly, as expected by the use of cached approximate results. The number of jumps and jumps taken decreases along with the total number of instructions. Neural approximation shows a decreased number of basic blocks, which can be attributed to a large part of the program being off-loaded to the accelerator. Similarly, the total number of instructions, jumps, and jumps taken are decreased. The average number of instructions per basic block increases. For precision tuning, the number of basic blocks decreases while the average number of instructions per basic block, the total number of instructions executed, jumps, and jumps taken increase. We assume that this is the result of unexpected cross interference of the compiler.

Register characteristic changes are shown in Fig. 7. Overall, we see only slight changes for average input meaning that the complexity of the code is constant, when measured by the number of input registers. For loop perforation, we observe an increase in register dependency = 1 (RD=1). This is the result of a register value being read as soon as it is written, which is a common pattern for loop counters. For loop perforation and neural approximation, the intermediate results are used less often which can be seen in a decreasing average degree of use value. The median register dependency decreases for loop perforation and memoization, which translates to faster reuse of registers. For neural approximation, the register dependency increases as a result of transferring data to and from the accelerator.

Memory Access Pattern characteristic changes are shown in Fig. 8. For loop perforation, we observe that loads of smaller sizes, both local and global, are not affected. Larger local and global loads decrease. The same pattern can be seen for stores. We see that a performance gain very likely is not based on perforated computations only but also on a smaller number of memory transfers. Memoization shows a distinct pattern: the number of small local loads decreases while the number of larger loads increases. Global loads, regardless of size, do not change, or decrease. Global stores show the same behavior. For neural approximation, on average the number of memory accesses does not change. Some applications show a lower number of local loads and a higher number of larger local or global stores. For precision scaling, the numbers show no change on average.

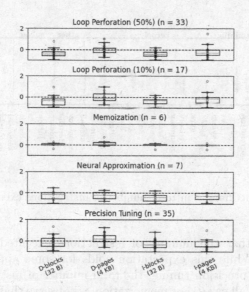

Fig. 9. Change in data and instruction stream.

Data and Instruction Stream accesses are shown in Fig. 9. These characteristics map to page accesses and have strong influence on caches. For loop perforation, we observe a decrease of block accesses in data and instruction space, independent of block size. Memoization shows almost no change in the data and instruction stream, which is expected, as the technique only adds a small wrapper function. A small increase in accesses data blocks can be attributed to the lookup of cached results. Neural approximation shows a strong decrease in the number of accessed memory blocks. This is obvious, as a large part of the applications' code is removed and offloaded to the NPU. The data upload to the NPU and the download from the NPU is accomplished over memory. Apparently, these additional transfers do not compensate for the decrease due to code removal.

4.2 Details on Application-Level

In this section, we have a look at individual applications' changes in selected characteristics. We show the changes in the total number of instructions executed in Fig. 10. On the y-axis we show the change in the specific characteristics when compared to the accurate program, e.g., a value of 1 represents an increase of 100% and a value of −0.5 represents a decrease of 50%. If there is no bar visible, there is no change in the characteristic. On the x-axis, we show a group of bars for each application. Each bar represents an approximation for this application. We sort the bars by categories of applications and label the groups on top.

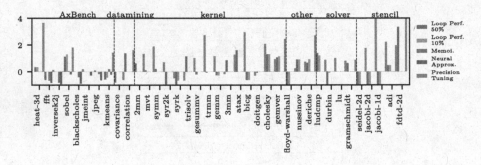

Fig. 10. Changes in total number of instructions executed.

We do expect that the number of instructions executed is decreasing or does not change. While this expectation holds for some applications, it does not for others. For precision tuning, the total number of instructions executed increases for almost all cases. For memoization, we observe that the total number of instructions executed is decreasing for all applications except for KMEANS.

In Fig. 11, we show the changes in characteristics for the number of stores. For the majority of applications and approximation techniques the total number of stores decreases. A notable exemption is precision tuning, where the total

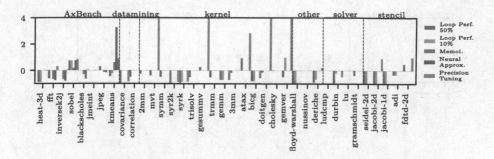

Fig. 11. Changes in total number of stores.

number of instructions executed increases by a large factor for some kernel applications. There are two applications from AxBench that show a different picture: for SOBEL, there are more stores observed for all approximation methods. For KMEANS, loop perforation yields a smaller number of loads while all other techniques show more loads. A particularly interesting situation can be observed for GEMVER: for loop perforation with 10% error budget, the number of stores increases; while it decreases for a larger error budget.

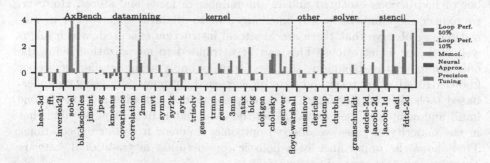

Fig. 12. Changes in total number of loads.

The changes in the number of loads is shown in Fig. 12. The situation is different from that for the number of stores. Again, precision tuning shows an increase. However, we also observe that the number increases for loop perforation for some applications (SOBEL, CHOLESKY, GEMVER, ADI).

The impact on data accesses when viewed from an architectural perspective is shown in Fig. 13 where we show changes in 32 Byte data stream block accesses. For most applications, the data stream block accesses are diminishing. However, there are notable exemptions: SOBEL shows a strong increasing number, independent of the approximation technique employed. The same observation can be made for KMEANS and NUSSINOV.

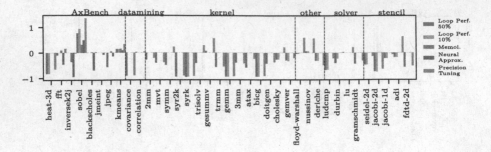

Fig. 13. Changes in 32 byte data stream block accesses.

4.3   Expectations and Observations

In this section, we briefly summarize our expectations on how the characteristics are supposed to change when a specific approximation technique is applied. Then, we show how our observations contradict our expectations. For loop perforation, we expect the number of instructions executed, loads, and stores to *decrease*. However, we observe that the number actually *increases* for roughly half of the cases. We observe a lot of unexpected changes in characteristics for precision tuning. Some applications show a dramatic increase in the number of instructions executed and in the number of loads and stores. However, we expect the numbers to stay unchanged or to diminish slightly. For memoization, we observe that there are less total instruction executed, which aligns well with our expectations. This can be attributed to memoization being the only approximation technique that we manually apply using detailed developer knowledge. All other techniques are implemented automatically using compiler-based tools that are not aware of developer intended optimizations on the one hand and compiler-based decisions on the other hand. In general, we find that in the majority of cases we observe outcomes different from our expectations. This shows the importance of a holistic consideration of traditional software optimizations and approximation.

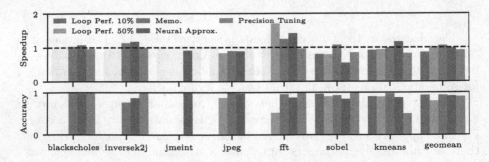

Fig. 14. Speedup and accuracy of AxBench applications.

4.4   Speedup and Accuracy

The results for speedup and accuracy are shown in Fig. 14 (AxBench) and Fig. 15 (PolyBench/C). On top, we report speedup and in the lower part, we report accuracy. We show results for loop perforation with 10% error budget (blue) and 50% error budget (orange) and precision tuning (green). Opaque speedup bars indicate that, given the aforementioned error budget, no solution could be found. We report the geometrical mean for the speedup and the arithmetic mean for the accuracy.

PolyBench/C. Using loop perforation, 7 PolyBench/C applications can be accelerated up to 2.21× when given a 10% error budget. When the error budget is increased to 50%, there are 17 applications with up to 2.55× speedup. We observe that, given a larger error budget, the speedup is usually higher. The geometrical mean of the speedup of both techniques is very close. These findings can be explained by assuming that perforating loops results in both faster execution and less accuracy. For most of the applications, loop perforation utilizes the full error budget it is given. Precision tuning is always able to find a solution and can accelerate 4 applications with speedups of up to 1.46×. Overall, there is a very small decline in the accuracy of precision tuning. For 27 out 30 applications, the accuracy is higher than 99% while the average is more than 95%. The high accuracy can be explained by the rationale that PolyBench/C applications are not exploiting the full floating-point accuracy and range.

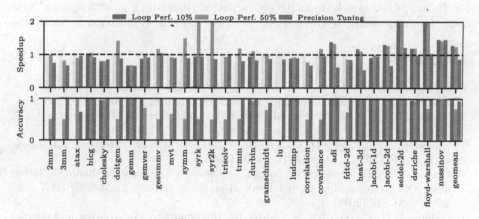

Fig. 15. Speedup and accuracy of PolyBench/C applications. (Color figure online)

AxBench. Three out of seven AxBench applications can be accelerated using loop perforation with 50% error budget. Speedups are up to 1.7×. Acceleration using approximate memoization is successful for four applications and the geometrical mean is 1.02. Neural approximation is beneficial in four cases and delivers a speedup of up to 1.42×. For none of the AxBench applications, precision tuning is able to lower the execution time.

5   Conclusions

We study how different Approximate Computing techniques affect workload characteristics. We evaluate four approximation techniques: loop perforation, memoization, neural approximation and precision tuning on 37 applications from PolyBench/C and AxBench. We use 55 micro-architecture independent characteristics to analyze workload characteristics. We observe that approximated applications show a significantly different workload characteristic when compared to their accurate counterparts. For some applications, we observe that more instructions are executed when we expect fewer instructions being executed. For loop perforation, we can deduce that performance gains originate from a smaller number of memory transfers and not from a smaller number of instructions executed. The workload characteristics depend on both the approximation technique and the application. When using approximate computing techniques to optimize applications for execution time or energy consumption, it is strongly advisable to consider the changes in workload characteristics when further optimizing applications, as original applications were developed considering constraints that changed dramatically by approximation.

Given our findings, we strongly propose to consider approximation as a regular optimization technique that is to be integrated into compiler toolchains. We propose to aim for a holistic approach that is aware of side effects between traditional optimization techniques and approximation approaches. Secondly, there is clearly a need for more sophisticated benchmark suites curated for approximation techniques that take multiple scenarios into account, e.g., different realistic input data to investigate the leverage of input data on application accuracy.

References

1. Besnard, L., Pinto, P., Lasri, I., Bispo, J., Rohou, E., Cardoso, J.M.: A framework for automatic and parameterizable memoization. SoftwareX **10**, 100322 (2019)
2. Brumar, I., Casas, M., Moreto, M., Valero, M., Sohi, G.S.: ATM: approximate task memoization in the runtime system. In: IPDPS. IEEE (2017)
3. Cherubin, S., Cattaneo, D., Chiari, M., Agosta, G.: Dynamic precision autotuning with TAFFO. ACM TACO **17**(2), 1–26 (2020)
4. Chiang, W.F., Baranowski, M., Briggs, I., Solovyev, A., Gopalakrishnan, G., Rakamarić, Z.: Rigorous floating-point mixed-precision tuning. ACM SIGPLAN Not. **52**(1), 300–315 (2017)
5. Chippa, V.K., Chakradhar, S.T., Roy, K., Raghunathan, A.: Analysis and characterization of inherent application resilience for approximate computing. In: DAC (2013)
6. Esmaeilzadeh, H., Sampson, A., Ceze, L., Burger, D.: Neural acceleration for general-purpose approximate programs. In: MICRO. IEEE (2012)
7. Hoste, K., Eeckhout, L.: Comparing benchmarks using key microarchitecture-independent characteristics. In: IISWC. IEEE (2006)
8. Lal, S., et al.: SYCL-bench: a versatile cross-platform benchmark suite for heterogeneous computing. In: Malawski, M., Rzadca, K. (eds.) Euro-Par 2020. LNCS, vol. 12247, pp. 629–644. Springer, Cham (2020). https://doi.org/10.1007/978-3-030-57675-2_39

9. Lal, S., Lucas, J., Juurlink, B.: SLC: memory access granularity aware selective lossy compression for GPUs. In: DATE. IEEE (2019)
10. Lashgar, A., Atoofian, E., Baniasadi, A.: Loop perforation in OpenACC. In: ISPA/IUCC/BDCloud/SocialCom/SustainCom. IEEE (2018)
11. Li, S., Park, S., Mahlke, S.: Sculptor: flexible approximation with selective dynamic loop perforation. In: ICS (2018)
12. Maier, D., Cosenza, B., Juurlink, B.: Local memory-aware kernel perforation. In: CGO (2018)
13. Maier, D., Cosenza, B., Juurlink, B.: ALONA: automatic loop nest approximation with reconstruction and space pruning. In: Sousa, L., Roma, N., Tomás, P. (eds.) Euro-Par 2021. LNCS, vol. 12820, pp. 3–18. Springer, Cham (2021). https://doi.org/10.1007/978-3-030-85665-6_1
14. Misailovic, S., Carbin, M., Achour, S., Qi, Z., Rinard, M.C.: Chisel: reliability- and accuracy-aware optimization of approximate computational kernels. ACM Sigplan Not. 49(10), 309–328 (2014)
15. Mitra, S., Gupta, M.K., Misailovic, S., Bagchi, S.: Phase-aware optimization in approximate computing. In: CGO. IEEE (2017)
16. Moreau, T., et al.: SNNAP: approximate computing on programmable SOCs via neural acceleration. In: HPCA. IEEE (2015)
17. Nethercote, N., Seward, J.: Valgrind: a framework for heavyweight dynamic binary instrumentation. ACM Sigplan Not. 42(6), 89–100 (2007)
18. Parasyris, K., et al.: HPC-MixPBench: an HPC benchmark suite for mixed-precision analysis. In: IISWC (2020)
19. Pouchet, L.N.: PolyBench/C 3.2. http://www.cse.ohio-state.edu/pouchet/software/polybench/
20. Rubio-González, C., et al.: Precimonious: tuning assistant for floating-point precision. In: SC. IEEE (2013)
21. Samadi, M., Jamshidi, D.A., Lee, J., Mahlke, S.: Paraprox: pattern-based approximation for data parallel applications. In: ASPLOS (2014)
22. Sampson, A., et al.: Accept: a programmer-guided compiler framework for practical approximate computing. University of Washington Technical Report UW-CSE-15-01 (2015)
23. Shafique, M., Ahmad, W., Hafiz, R., Henkel, J.: A low latency generic accuracy configurable adder. In: DAC. IEEE (2015)
24. Sidiroglou-Douskos, S., Misailovic, S., Hoffmann, H., Rinard, M.: Managing performance vs. ESEC/FSE, accuracy trade-offs with loop perforation (2011)
25. Tziantzioulis, G., Hardavellas, N., Campanoni, S.: Temporal approximate function memoization. MICRO 38(4), 60–70 (2018)
26. Yazdanbakhsh, A., Mahajan, D., Esmaeilzadeh, H., Lotfi-Kamran, P.: AxBench: a multiplatform benchmark suite for approximate computing. IEEE Des. Test 34(2), 60–68 (2016)

QPU-System Co-design for Quantum HPC Accelerators

Karen Wintersperger[1]([envelope])[ID], Hila Safi[1,2], and Wolfgang Mauerer[1,2][ID]

[1] Siemens AG, Corporate Technology, Otto-Hahn-Ring 6, 81739 München, Germany
{karen.wintersperger,hila.safi}@siemens.com
[2] Technical University of Applied Sciences Regensburg, Galgenbergstraße 32,
93053 Regensburg, Germany
wolfgang.mauerer@othr.de

Abstract. The use of quantum processing units (QPUs) promises speed-ups for solving computational problems, but the quantum devices currently available possess only a very limited number of qubits and suffer from considerable imperfections. One possibility to progress towards practical utility is to use a co-design approach: Problem formulation and algorithm, but also the physical QPU properties are tailored to the specific application. Since QPUs will likely be used as accelerators for classical computers, details of systemic integration into existing architectures are another lever to influence and improve the practical utility of QPUs.

In this work, we investigate the influence of different parameters on the runtime of quantum programs on tailored hybrid CPU-QPU-systems. We study the influence of communication times between CPU and QPU, how adapting QPU designs influences quantum and overall execution performance, and how these factors interact. Using a simple model that allows for estimating which design choices should be subjected to optimisation for a given task, we provide an intuition to the HPC community on potentials and limitations of co-design approaches. We also discuss physical limitations for implementing the proposed changes on real quantum hardware devices.

1 Introduction

Quantum computers available today are restricted in their performance by relatively small ($\approx$ 50–100) number of quantum bits (qubits), and suffer from various imperfections. Since they cannot yet implement error correction routinely, they classify as NISQ (Noisy Intermediate Scale Quantum) hardware [1], whose capabilities are subject to ongoing exploration. Nevertheless, there is a growing interest to deploy NISQ devices in high-performance computing (HPC) scenarios [2].

All authors acknowledge funding from the German Federal Ministry of Education and Research within the funding program quantum technologies—from basic research to market, contract number 13N16093.

M. Schulz et al. (Eds.): ARCS 2022, LNCS 13642, pp. 100–114, 2022.
https://doi.org/10.1007/978-3-031-21867-5_7

Fitting complex problems to NISQ devices usually requires many simplifications. Also, the mapping of the problem to a quantum model and the algorithm can be optimised to reduce both, the number of necessary qubits, and the number of quantum operations [3]. Properties of quantum algorithms strongly depend on specific QPUs. Many factors, size (number of qubits), the geometric arrangement of and number of connections between the qubits, as well as the specific errors and execution times of quantum operations, influence quantum circuit execution. Prior to running a quantum circuit on a quantum device, the circuit structure must be adjusted to its requirements, which usually increases the number of quantum operations, and thus the circuit depth. Co-designing QPUs by adapting them to specific problem classes is therefore a promising approach.

QPUs will likely be used as accelerators for classical computers, and require integration with classical hardware. Moreover, hybrid algorithms that combine classical and quantum operations are a commonly occurring pattern. Thus, the interaction between quantum and classical devices needs to be taken into account to estimate the performance of a quantum program in practice.

In this work, we investigate optimisation potentials for the co-design of such CPU-QPU-systems, exemplified by a hybrid quantum algorithm used to solve the maximum cut (Max-Cut) problem. In detail, our contributions are as follows:

- We analyse the properties of compiled quantum circuits for various instances of the Max-Cut problem when modifying geometric properties of the QPU, namely the connectivity between qubits and the number of qubits.
- We estimate the runtime on real quantum hardware based on simulations, and investigate the overall runtime on QPU-systems including the communication between classical and quantum machines, and other classical calculations required to execute and evaluate quantum circuits.
- Based on these results, we give recommendations for the design of quantum hardware adapted to applications.
- We provide a self-contained replication package [4] for the simulations that is available at https://github.com/lfd/arcs2022.git.

The Max-Cut problem is an optimisation problem with applications in network design, clustering or statistical physics. Considering an undirected graph with a set of nodes V and a set of edges E, a cut is defined as a partition of the node set into two subsets. The Max-Cut problem seeks to find a partition such that the number of edges connecting the two subsets is maximised. Many applications for this primitive can be found in all areas of computing; for us, it suffices to state that Max-Cut serves as typical representative for hard problems that we will further motivate in Sect. 2.2.

There are different, yet equivalent models for quantum computation, such as gate-based [5,6], measurement-based [7], adiabatic [8], or topological quantum computing. In this work, we focus on gate-based quantum computation. The Max-Cut problem is solved using the Quantum Approximate Optimisation Algorithm (QAOA) [9], which is a widely used variational hybrid quantum algorithm for solving combinatorial optimisation problems on NISQ hardware.

As a starting point for the investigation of quantum hardware designs, IBM-Q devices are used, which are based on superconducting qubit technology [10,11]. Superconducting qubits are one of the most common and advanced quantum hardware platforms, used by many vendors such as IBM, Google and Rigetti. Since superconducting qubits are artificial quantum systems, they can in principle be designed at will. By now, several different types of superconducting qubits exist, and the technology is continuously developed. However, this also means that no two qubits are completely identical, and properties such as the gate fidelity, which is a measure for the quality of a quantum operation, differ for each qubit. The superconducting quantum devices of different vendors usually differ by the geometric arrangement of qubits, and the number and structure of connections between them. The IBM-Q topology that we use as basis for our considerations is described in detail in Sect. 2.4.

2   Quantum Max-Cut with QAOA

Before we discuss co-design optimisation possibilities, we need to set the stage for the considered problem, and illustrate the solution algorithm.

2.1   The Quantum Approximate Optimisation Algorithm

QAOA implements a quantum circuit consisting of $p \in \mathbb{N}$ layers of unitary operators (the elementary type of operation a quantum computer can effect on qubits) whose properties are specified by a set of $2p$ parameters $\vec{\beta}, \vec{\gamma} \in \mathbb{R}^p$. The algorithm can determine minima of objective functions specified in quadratic, unconstrained binary form; these are specified such that the minimum solution corresponds to a solution of a specific problem of interest. Using well-known techniques from computer science, all problems in **NP** can be reduced to *Quadratic Unconstrained Binary Optimisation* (QUBO) form [12]. Speedups of QAOA compared to classical approaches are not yet fully understood [13]; yet the existence of a classical algorithm that efficiently samples the output distribution of QAOA even for $p = 1$ is impossible, given reasonable complexity-theoretic assumptions [14]. This is seen as likely indicator for quantum advantage, but theoretical or experimental progress is required to find utility on practical problems.

Figure 1 sketches the structure of the QAOA circuit for $p = 2$: After applying the operators to a well-defined initial state, the expectation value of H_P, which encodes the objective function, is measured in the final state. Using a classical optimiser, the parameters of the circuit are changed with the goal of minimising the expectation value of H_P. Each layer i consists of two different kinds of unitaries: First, $U(\beta_i) = e^{-i\beta H_B}$ is applied, implementing the evolution under a so-called mixer Hamiltonian H_B. The mixer Hamiltonian is commonly chosen as a superposition of X-rotations applied to each qubit, thus consisting of a series of rotation gates $R_X(\beta_i)$. The second part of each layer comprises $U(\gamma_i) = e^{-i\gamma H_P}$ consisting of single-qubit Z-rotations $R_Z(\gamma_i)$ and two-qubit

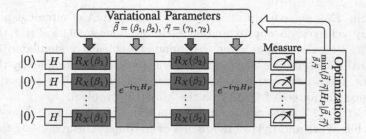

Fig. 1. Sketch of the QAOA-circuit for $p = 2$.

rotation gates $R_{ZZ}(\gamma_i)$. The repeated application of several QAOA layers corresponds to the discretised time evolution governed by the Hamiltonians H_P and H_B. It is known that the quality of the approximation increases for a larger number of layers [9]. The initial state of the QAOA algorithm is usually chosen as the ground state of H_B, in which each qubit is in an equal superposition of $|0\rangle$ and $|1\rangle$, prepared using a layer of Hadamard gates H.

To characterise the probability distribution of the final state depending on $\vec{\beta}, \vec{\gamma}$ after each iteration of the optimiser, the quantum circuit is executed several times (known as *sampling*), and the qubits are measured in the computational basis $\{|0\rangle, |1\rangle\}$. The mean of the expectation values of H_P for each measurement outcome is used as the objective function minimised by the classical optimiser. The optimal solution is then given by the state (or bit string) with the lowest energy expectation value taken from the probability distribution obtained for the final set of parameters.

2.2 Background on Max-Cut and QAOA

Given a graph $G = (V, E)$ consisting of a set of vertices V and a set of edges $E \subseteq V \times V$, the Max-Cut problem is a seminal graph-theoretic task that seeks two subsets $V_0, V_1 \subseteq V$ such that $V_0 \cup V_1 = V$ and $V_0 \cap V_1 = \varnothing$, and maximises the size $|C|$ of the cut set $C = \{(u, v) \in E : u \in V_0, v \in V_1\}$ (as a decision problem, the k-Cut variant seeks a cut with $|C| = k$). While the Max-Cut problem is very simple to formulate, it counts among the hardest optimisation problems to solve [15]. It is textbook knowledge that the decision variant lies in complexity class **NP**, while the optimisation variant is **APX**-hard, which essentially means that any polynomial-time approximation algorithm can at best find solutions whose approximation ratio (*i.e.*, the size of the found cut size divided by the optimal cut size) is bounded by a constant for general graphs.

Classical approximation algorithms and heuristics for Max-Cut, including formulations adapted to graphs with specific properties, have been studied in the literature, and polynomial-time approximation algorithms with non-trivial performance guarantees are known. In particular, the seminal algorithm of Goemans and Williamson [16] achieves an approximation ratio of 87.86% on generic graphs, while Khot *et al.* discuss the optimality of inapproximability results for the problem. Ever since Farhi *et al.* [9] found that QAOA at circuit depth $p = 1$ (a) already achieves an approximation ratio of at least 69.25% (for the class of uniform, 3-regular graphs), yet (b) cannot be efficiently simulated by classical algorithms, assuming the validity of widely accepted complexity-theoretic hypotheses, there has been a steady interest in understanding properties and performance guarantees of QAOA on the Max-Cut problem.

Fuchs *et al.* [17] present an efficient encoding of (weighted) Max-Cut for QAOA, while Wurz and Lykov [18] discuss open conjectures regarding the quantum performance of the problem. On the negative side from the QPU point of view, Marwaha [19] showed that classical algorithms outperform QAOA with $p = 2$ with a certain type of graphs. On the positive side for quantum algorithms, Wurtz and Love [20] give performance guarantees for QAOA-Max-Cut for $p > 1$ in terms of an approximation ratio of 75.59%. Recent approaches solve Max-Cut with coherent networks [21], and also go beyond standard quantum hardware. A comprehensive evaluation of quantum annealing performance on different QPUs for the Max-Cut problem is provided by Willsch *et al.* [22].

More general investigations of QAOA are plentiful; Barthi *et al.* [13] summarise many of them. For instance, Xue *et al.* [23] consider the effect of noise on QAOA performance, while Yu *et al.* [24] provide an automatic depth optimisation technique. At present, a widely accepted and empirically observed, yet not fully understood hypothesis claims a concentration of the optimisation parameters $\vec{\beta}, \vec{\gamma}$ on relatively low-dimensional sub-manifolds of the possible search space. Akshay *et al.* [25] report positive results in this directions, and Zhou *et al.* [26] give a concrete construction to benefit from this concentration to improve the algorithmic performance of the classical component of the hybrid algorithm (their FOURIER construction is numerically conjectured to produce quasi-optima in time $\mathcal{O}(\text{poly}(p))$ instead of $2^{\mathcal{O}(p)}$ for the standard QAOA algorithm). Additionally, several extensions to the QAOA algorithm have been proposed, for instance for quantum alternating operator ansatz by Hadfield *et al.* [27], or the mixer-phaser ansätze by LaRose *et al.* [28].

However, to the best of our knowledge, we are not aware of any discussion on how to improve performance and feasibility of Max-Cut on quantum computers (QCs) using co-design, and how to holistically evaluate potential performance benefits including the overhead by unavoidable classical computing components beyond the optimisation algorithms employed in the hybrid approach. We discuss these issues in this paper, and believe they hold potential for more general insights on how to achieve first practical speedups for quantum algorithms given realistic systemic constraints and boundary conditions.

2.3   Modelling Max-Cut as QUBO

Following the seminal collection of transformations provided by Lucas [12], the Max-Cut problem can be cast as a QUBO using binary variables x_i with $x_i = 1$ if node i lies within the first subset, and $x_i = 0$ if it lies in the second subset. If an edge connecting the nodes i and j is part of the cut, thus connecting the two subsets, exactly one of x_i and x_j is equal to zero and the other one is equal to one. In this case, $H_{i,j} = (x_i + x_j - 2x_ix_j)$ equals one and in the cases where $x_i = x_j$ it equals zero. Finding the maximum cut corresponds to maximising the sum of $H_{i,j}$ over all edges of the underlying graph, or, equivalently, minimising the sum over $-H_{i,j}$. In the following, the latter approach will be used. Thus, the optimal solution of the Max-Cut problem can be encoded as the ground state of the Hamiltonian $H_P = \sum_{i,j\in E}(2x_ix_j - x_i - x_j)$, which is passed to the generic QAOA algorithm as objective function to determine a minimum solution.

2.4   Setup

The problem graphs $G = (V, E)$ subjected to Max-Cut are characterised by the number of nodes, $N = |V|$, and the graph density defined as $d = |E|/|E_{max}| \in [0,1]$, where $|E|$ is the number of edges of G, and $|E_{max}| = n(n-1)/2$ is the number of edges of a clique comprising $|V|$ nodes, which upper bounds the possible number of edges in G. Each node is represented by one qubit.

To run a quantum circuit on a QPU, it has to be compiled to meet the requirements of the hardware. The process of compilation consists of several steps and accounts for the limited connectivity between the qubits as well as for the native gate set, which describes the set of gates that can be executed on the specific hardware. Both properties depend on the chosen technology. For instance, quantum devices such as ion traps exhibit all-to-all connectivity, whereas others do not. If the circuit contains gates which are not part of the native gate set, they are decomposed accordingly. Missing connections between qubits are countered by adding so-called SWAP-gates, which themselves often need to be decomposed again into $C-X$ gates, for instance when using the IBM-Q gate set considered here. All of these steps increase the depth of the circuit. Within this work, creation, compilation and simulation of quantum circuits was implemented using Qiskit. For compilation (which is called transpilation in Qiskit), we use a predefined routine of Qiskit. It consists of the following steps:

1. Virtual circuit optimisation, for instance, parallelisation of gates
2. Decomposition of gates containing three qubits or more into two-qubit gates
3. Placement of the virtual qubits on the physical qubits
4. Routing on coupling map, introduction of necessary SWAP gates
5. Translation to native gate set
6. Optimisation of the resulting physical circuit

Circuit optimisation can be executed at different levels. For all investigations in this work, the optimisation level was set to the maximal value of 3, which describes heavy optimisation, including also re-synthesis of two-qubit blocks. The placement of the SWAP gates is performed using a stochastic method, called stochastic SWAP, which leads to different compilation results for the same initial circuit. Therefore, we repeat the compilation process 20 times for each parameter set and consider the mean of the circuit depth over these values.

The base coupling map is derived from the IBM-Q Washington backend with 127 qubits by adding two connections which are missing in the original hardware.

The qubits are arranged in the so-called heavy-hex lattice geometry illustrated in Fig. 6a. The native gate set of IBM-Q hardware is used: Rotation R_Z, phase shift S_X, Pauli (Not) X, and controlled X (C$-X$).

NISQ QPUs suffer from limited gate fidelities and noise. These effects could also be included when simulating and compiling quantum circuits. Within the compilation process, the placement of the virtual qubits could be adapted to the differences in noise characteristics between the qubits, which occur for super-conducting quantum devices, minimising the overall effect of noise. However, the limited available space does not allow us to consider these aspects.

3   Hardware-System Co-design

3.1   Optimisation Potentials

QPUs require integration with classical computers to solve problems [29], regard-less if hybrid or "pure" quantum algorithms are used. This, invariably, induces temporal overheads that are usually ignored when studying the complexity-theoretic performance of quantum algorithms. However, especially for NISQ devices that are unlikely to produce exponential speedups, such details cannot be ignored to judge potential gains by quantum technology [30]. The time required to execute an algorithm on a QPU that interacts with a CPU comprises several contributions: (a) Circuit execution time t_{circ} on the QPU (also considering the number n_{samp} of samples required to obtain accurate statistics), (b) time t_{meas} for performing measurements of quantum states, (c) classical parameter opti-misation time t_{opt} on the CPU, (d) the amount of optimisation iterations n_{iter}, and (e) time for passing input parameters and output results between QPU and CPU t_{comm}. A straightforward model to describe the execution time required for hybrid algorithms like QAOA is therefore given by

$$T = n_{iter} \cdot [n_{samp} \cdot (t_{circ} + t_{meas}) + t_{opt} + t_{comm}]. \tag{1}$$

3.2   Parameter Estimation on IBM-Q Hardware

To evaluate optimisation potentials using the model in Eq. (1), we need to deter-mine performance values on QPUs. Obviously, these parameters not only depend on size and possibly structure of the input instance, but also on the underlying execution platform. To illustrate the *relative* influence of the factors for a typ-ically sized instance, it suffices to consider one set of parameters, for which we chose a graph with 20 nodes (amounting to 20 qubits) and a graph density of 0.5 solved using QAOA with a single layer.

In the following, we estimate the runtime of such a QAOA circuit using a custom routine that pre-compiles the logical circuit to the gate set provided by IBM-Q hardware, and then executes the result on a simulator. We deliberately do not resort to physical hardware to avoid any degradation by noise, as our goal is to find optimisation potentials for QPU-system co-design, not to evaluate limitations of current NISQ devices. The QAOA circuit is parameterised by $\vec{\beta}$

107

and $\vec{\gamma}$, which are optimised using the COBYLA routine provided by Qiskit. As an objective function, we compute the mean expectation value of H_P, as described in Sect. 2.3. (see the replication package for details). We sample the quantum circuit using $n_{samp} = 1,024$ shots in each iteration. We find $t_{opt} = 159\,\mu s$, $t_{meas} = 28.6\,\mu s$, and $n_{iter} = 25$.

A quantum circuit comprises different gates, and the time it takes each gate to operate is denoted as *gate time*. To obtain an estimate of the distribution of classical and quantum contributions to the total algorithmic runtime, we estimate the quantum circuit execution time t_{circ} from the (known) hardware gate times and the structure of the circuit.

Approximate values for the gate times as provided by the Qiskit *mock backend* FakeBrooklyn are used. In case of $C-X$ gates, different values arise for different possible qubit pairs, and we consider the average value. The execution times for the single qubit gates are identical for all qubits. Table 1 lists the concrete gate times. The execution time of the circuit calculated from the gate times is $t_{circ} = 120 \pm 20\,\mu s$, averaged over 20 circuit transpilation runs.

Table 1. Gate times from backend FakeBrooklyn.

Gate	Exec^n time [ns]	Std Dev.
R_Z	0	0
S_X	35.56	0
X	35.56	0
$C-X$	370	80

The CPU-QPU communication time t_{comm} depends on how QPUs are deployed, and may vary over several orders of magnitude. We consider three different scenarios in Table 2: (a) access to a QPU via cloud services, with a communication round-trip time of about 50 ms; (b) a QPU with direct attachment to the local CPU (for instance via direct LAN connection), for which we expect $t_{comm} \approx 1\,ms$, and an integrated system comprising a QPU and CPU that communicate via an internal system bus with $t_{comm} \approx 25\,\mu s$.[1] Assume that, as in many scenarios of practical interest, we deal with a "typically" sized problem instance, for which we can assume that n_{iter}, n_{samp} and t_{opt} are approximately independent of the specific input. This leaves the communication time t_{comm} and the circuit time t_{circ} as candidates for optimisation. With n_{iter}, n_{samp} and t_{opt} constant, they linearly contribute to the growth of the total execution time T, and the corresponding slopes are 25 for t_{comm} and 25,600 for t_{circ}. The magnitude of the latter slope would seem to indicate that reducing communication times holds greater optimisation potential than decreasing circuit execution times. Alas, as Table 2 indicates, moving

[1] The given communication times are rough estimates supposed to *illustrate* optimisation potentials and relative parameter influence. We obtained the numbers by measuring typical `ping` durations in cloud and local network scenarios, and estimate QPU-CPU communication time by the round-trip time of an inter-processor-interrupt in a RiscV-system, given the assumptions that a QPU-CPU SoC design will likely be based on modifiable classical architectures, and that communication times between QPU and CPU are similar to inter-core communication times.

Owing to the restricted space, we do not provide more fine-grained and realistic estimates of and models for these quantities, but remark that they would very likely not substantially change our findings and conclusions.

from a local QPU deployment to on-chip integration is much less beneficial than moving from a cloud deployment to local operation of QPUs.[2]

Table 2. Communication and total execution time T for QPU deployment scenarios.

Scenario	t_{comm}	T
Cloud	50 ms	5.07 s
Local Bus	1 ms	3.84 s
SoC[3]	25 μs	3.82 s

However, when we consider the "Local Bus" scenario and assume that the circuit execution time can be reduced from $120\,\mu s$ to $30\,\mu s$ (see Fig. 3 and later explanations for a rationale), the overall execution time reduces from $T = 3.84\,s$ to $T = 1.28\,s$, which indicates substantial potential for optimisation using hardware adaption. Comparing the baseline scenario (cloud + standard topology) with the co-design results (local communication, adapted topology), we find a total execution time reduction of $1 - 1.28/5.07 \approx 75\%$, which may substantially impact practical scenarios, especially given that accelerators often solve the same primitive repeatedly in inner loops.

3.3   Physical Possibilities and Limitations

Different properties of QPUs can be considered to reduce circuit execution times. On the one hand, there is the geometric layout of the qubits and their connectivity. On the other hand, the native gate set, as well as the fidelities and execution times of the gates influence the performance of algorithms, as well as the effects of noise. Depending on the hardware platform, the gate times and fidelities can differ for each individual (pair of) qubit(s), as it is the case for superconducting qubits. In this work, we focus on the effects of the qubit connectivity and the number of qubits available on the device compared to the problem size.

Changing the qubit connectivity for superconducting devices necessitates to physically re-wire qubits. Moreover, issues such as cross-talk can occur if the connectivity increases too much. This is reflected in the heavy-hex lattice design of IBM-Q, which features reduced connectivity compared to previous layouts.

In contrast, trapped ion quantum computers feature all-to-all connectivity [31], but are currently limited to few qubits (≈ 20). QCs based on neutral atom technology do not feature all-to-all connectivity, but their connectivity is usually higher than nearest-neighbour, and can be further increased.

3.4   Variation of the Coupling Density

The connectivity between qubits is described by the coupling density c given by $c = N_C/N_{C,\max}$, where N_C denotes the number of connections between pairs of qubits (that is, the possible interactions), and $N_{C,\max}$ gives the maximal *possible* number of connections, which is obviously reached for a clique connectivity with $N_{C,\max} = n(n-1)/2$ for n available qubits. Thus, $c = 1$ describes a quantum device with all-to-all connectivity. The base topology of the IBM-Q devices has

---

[2] Moving from locally connected components to on-chip integration might be beneficial for latency-critical embedded systems with quantum acceleration, but is likely not overly relevant for many HPC use-cases.

a coupling density of $c \approx 0.0139$. For the simulations in this subsection, the size of the backend is kept constant at 127 qubits. The coupling density is increased by randomly adding connections between the qubits.[4] Each data point shown in this section is an average over 20 compilation runs, using again the standard transpilation process of Qiskit with optimisation level 3.

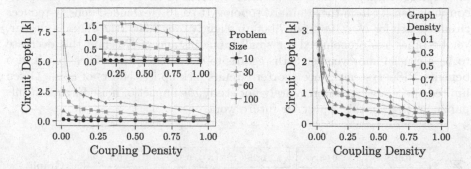

Fig. 2. Mean circuit depth vs. coupling density for $p = 1$ (127 qubit backend), varying problem size (lhs) for $d = 0.5$ and graph density (rhs) for $N = 60$.

We investigate the effect of increasing coupling density for different problem sizes, graph densities, and QAOA layers. In general, a higher coupling density reduces the number of SWAP gates needed to realise the desired two-qubit interactions, and decreases circuit depth. This is evident in the left panel of Fig. 2, where the resulting circuit depth is plotted vs. coupling density for different problem sizes and $d = 0.5$. The circuit depth saturates for higher coupling densities. The saturation density c_{sat} as well as the saturation value of the circuit depth increase with the problem size, which can also be seen in the inset of the plot. Solving larger problem instances requires more qubits and thus also more two-qubit gates, which leads to deeper circuits in general.

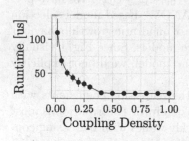

Fig. 3. Circuit runtime for $N = 20, d = 0.5, p = 1$.

Modifying the graph density for a fixed problem size does not change c_{sat}, as illustrated by the data in the right panel of Fig. 2 for $N = 60$, where the circuit depth remains constant for $c > 0.8$. The overall circuit depth and its saturation value increase with graph density. This can be traced back to an increased density of the QUBO resulting from an increasing amount of edges that necessitate more two-qubit gates. For larger number of QAOA layers, the circuit depth increases linearly, whereas the saturation density c_{sat}

---

[4] The placement of new connection favours augmenting regions with existing high connectivity density, following the assumption that adding extra connections is easier for regions that are already well connected. Given the lack of space, we refer readers to the replication package for the exact details.

remains unchanged. The decrease in circuit depth for higher coupling densities results in shorter runtimes as illustrated in Fig. 3. Since a relatively small problem instance with 20 qubits is considered, the runtime saturates for moderate coupling densities, similar as the circuit depth (see Fig. 2).

Both graphs in Fig. 2 show an important trend: Even a moderate increase in coupling density causes a substantial decrease in circuit depth - growing the coupling density from the standard topology to a 10% extended density reduces circuit depth for $N = 100$ from 7,000 to slightly over 2,000 (the effect is similar, yet becomes less pronounced for small input instances). We find this decrease to be a crucial improvement with regards to circuit execution times, but it also benefits NISQ systems, since shorter circuits pick up less effects of noise. Given limited space, we can unfortunately not study the impact of noise further in this paper, but retain this aspect for future work.

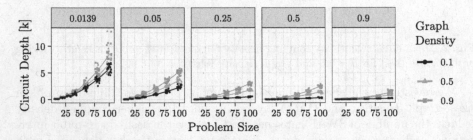

Fig. 4. Circuit depth growth behaviour over problem size for different coupling densities in the panels. Solid lines represent regression models for varying input graph dependencies.

To quantify the growth of the circuit depth with problem size, we construct a univariate regression model[5] of the form $f(x) = c_0 + c_1 x + c_2 x^2$. We have performed the usual regression diagnostics, and an ANOVA based model selection procedure unambiguously confirms that the choice of quadratic growth behaviour is preferable to linear and exponential alternative models. Since Fig. 4 visually demonstrates an excellent match between data and model, we do not explicitly spell out details of these diagnostics.

It is interesting to observe the behaviour of the regression coefficients with increasing connectivity map density in Fig. 5: The quadratic contribution is most pronounced for the unmodified topology, but quickly wanes with increasing connectivity map densities, and saturates in the connectivity density map range $[0.25, 0.75]$. Regardless of input problem structure (graph density), any quadratic contribution to growth vanishes for fully connected topologies. In general, more effort in implementing physical connections pays off with more favourable QPU scaling behaviour.

---

[5] Technically, we employ a robust quantile regression approach [32] because the stochastic circuit generation process produces pronounced outliers.

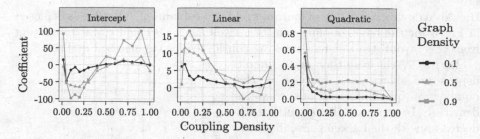

Fig. 5. Coefficients of the quadratic quantile regression model depending on graph and coupling density.

3.5 Variation of the Backend Size

The properties of the compiled circuit also depend on the size of the quantum device, namely the number of available qubits relative to the problem size. If the backend has more qubits available than needed, there are more possibilities for routing the virtual to physical qubits. In general, a more efficient placement of the circuit on the hardware can be found, for

Table 3. Backend sizes used for the data in Fig. 7, characterised by the number of unit cell rows N_{rows}, unit cell columns N_{cols} and number of qubits.

N_{rows}	N_{cols}	N_{qubits}	N_{rows}	N_{cols}	N_{qubits}
4	2	65	5	3	108
3	3	70	4	4	113
5	2	79	6	3	127
4	3	89	5	4	137
6	2	93	6	4	161

instance, by assigning more of the virtual qubit pairs that share two-qubit gates to physical qubits which are directly connected.

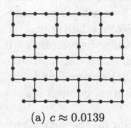

(a) $c \approx 0.0139$

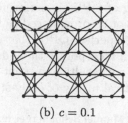

(b) $c = 0.1$

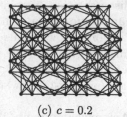

(c) $c = 0.2$

Fig. 6. Sketch of the heavy-hex lattice coupling map for 65 qubits with base (a) and extended (b, c) coupling density.

To examine the influence of the backend size on the circuit depth, the circuit for a Max-Cut problem with $N = 60$, $d = 0.5$ and $p = 1$ is compiled on backends of different sizes between 65 and 161 qubits. The qubits are arranged in the heavy-hex lattice geometry and the size is increased by successively adding unit cells below or on the right. The smallest backend corresponds to the IBM-Q

Brooklyn device, consisting of four rows and two columns of unit cells, as depicted in Fig. 6 for the base coupling density as well as $c = 0.1$ and $c = 0.2$. Starting from this layout, ten different sizes are considered, as summarised in Table 3.

In Fig. 7, the resulting mean circuit depths are shown as a function of the number of qubits for various coupling densities. In general, the circuit depth decreases with the backend size, illustrating the effects of a more efficient placement of the circuit described above. These effects become less pronounced for higher coupling densities, since the backend then exhibits more qubit pairs that are directly connected. Consequently, for a backend with all-to-all connectivity ($c = 1$), the backend size has no influence on the depth of the compiled circuit.

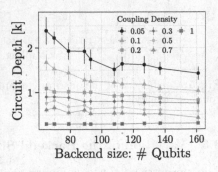

Fig. 7. Mean depth vs. backend size for $N = 60$, $d = 0.5$ and $p = 1$.

4   Conclusion and Outlook

In this paper, we have investigated integration and co-design possibilities for QPUs that are supposed to act as computational accelerators in high performance computing systems. Our results show that designing purpose-specific QPUs with adapted topologies holds promises in terms of computational capabilities. We have also shown that circuit depth is reduced by increasing the connectivity map density, but already saturates at values $c \ll 1$, with a slight dependency on the problem size. Thus, all-to-all connectivity is not needed in all cases, relaxing the requirements on the quantum hardware devices. We have also discussed that how integration of QPUs is performed can have effects on their capabilities, even if these are not as pronounced as for topology adaptations.

For now, we have focused on perfect QPUs that do not suffer from noise and imperfections. Future work will incorporate these deficiencies into our analysis, which is important to transfer our results to present-day NISQ systems, and will help progressing towards practical utility of early-stage quantum computers.

Acknowledgement. We thank Manuel Schönberger for providing his topology adaptation simulation code as starting point for our efforts.

References

1. Preskill, J.: Quantum computing in the NISQ era and beyond, Quantum, 2, 79 (2018). https://doi.org/10.48550/arXiv.1801.00862
2. Quantum technology and application consortium-QUTAC: industry quantum computing applications. EPJ Quant. Technol. **8**(1), 25 (2021)

3. Krüger, T., Mauerer, W.: Quantum annealing-based software components: an experimental case study with SAT solving, pp. 445–450 (2020). https://doi.org/10.1145/3387940.3391472

4. Mauerer, W., Scherzinger, S.: 1-2-3 reproducibility for quantum software experiments. In: Q-SANER@IEEE International Conference on Software Analysis, Evolution and Reengineering (2022)

5. Deutsch, D.E.: Quantum computational networks. Proc. R. Soc. A **425**, 73–90 (1989). https://doi.org/10.1098/rspa.1989.0099

6. Barenco, A., et al.: Elementary gates for quantum computation. Phys. Rev. A **52**, 3457–3467 (1995). https://doi.org/10.1103/PhysRevA.52.3457

7. Raussendorf, R., Browne, D.E., Briegel, H.J.: Measurement-based quantum computation on cluster states. Nat. Phys. **68**, 022312 (2003). https://doi.org/10.1103/PhysRevA.68.022312

8. Farhi, E., Goldstone, J., Gutmann, S., Lapan, J., Lundgren, A., Preda, D.: A quantum adiabatic evolution algorithm applied to random instances of an NP-complete problem. Science **292**, 472–475 (2001). https://doi.org/10.1126%2Fscience.1057726

9. Farhi, E., Goldstone, J., Gutmann, S.: A quantum approximate optimization algorithm. arXiv:1411.4028 (2014). https://doi.org/10.48550/arXiv.1411.4028

10. Huang, H.-L., Wu, D., Fan, D., Zhu, X.: Superconducting quantum computing: a review," arXiv:2006.10433 (2020). https://doi.org/10.48550/arxiv.2006.10433

11. Kjaergaard, M., et al.: Superconducting qubits: current state of play. Ann. Rev. Condens. Matter Phys. **11**, 369–395 (2020). https://doi.org/10.1146%2Fannurev-conmatphys-031119-050605

12. Lucas, A.: Ising formulations of many NP problems, vol. 2 (2014). https://doi.org/10.48550/arXiv.1302.5843

13. Bharti, K., et al.: Noisy intermediate-scale quantum algorithms. Rev. Mod. Phys. 94, 015004 (2022). https://doi.org/10.1103/RevModPhys.94.015004

14. Farhi, E., Harrow, A.W.: Quantum supremacy through the quantum approximate optimization algorithm. arXiv:1602.07674 (2016)

15. C.W. Commander, Maximum cut problem, MAX-CUT Maximum Cut Problem, MAX-CUT. In: Floudas, C., Pardalos, P. (eds.) Encyclopedia of Optimization. Springer, Boston, pp. 1991–1999 (2009). https://doi.org/10.1007/978-0-387-74759-0_358

16. Goemans, M.X., Williamson, D.P.: Improved approximation algorithms for maximum cut and satisfiability problems using semidefinite programming. J. ACM **42**(6), 1115–1145 (1995). https://doi.org/10.1145/227683.227684

17. Fuchs, F.G., Kolden, H.Ø., Aase, N.H., Sartor, G.: Efficient encoding of the weighted MAX k-CUT on a quantum computer using QAOA. SN Comput. Sci. **2**(2), 1–14 (2021). https://doi.org/10.1007/s42979-020-00437-z

18. Wurtz, J., Lykov, D.: Fixed-angle conjectures for the quantum approximate optimization algorithm on regular maxcut graphs. Phys. Rev. A, 104, 052419 (2021). https://doi.org/10.1103/PhysRevA.104.052419

19. Marwaha, K.: Local classical MAX-CUT algorithm outperforms $p = 2$ QAOA on high-girth regular graphs. Quantum, 5, 437 (2021). https://doi.org/10.22331/q-2021-04-20-437

20. Wurtz, J., Love, P.: Maxcut quantum approximate optimization algorithm performance guarantees for $p > 1$. Phys. Rev. A, 103, 042612 (2021). https://doi.org/10.1103/PhysRevA.103.042612

21. Harrison, S., Sigurdsson, H., Alyatkin, S., Töpfer, J., Lagoudakis, P.: Solving the max-3-cut problem with coherent networks. Phys. Rev. Appl. 17, 024063 (2022). https://doi.org/10.1103/PhysRevApplied.17.024063

22. Willsch, M., Willsch, D., Jin, F., De Raedt, H., Michielsen, K.: Benchmarking the quantum approximate optimization algorithm. Quantum Inf. Process. **19**(7), 1–24 (2020). https://doi.org/10.1007/s11128-020-02692-8

23. Xue, C., Chen, Z.-Y., Wu, Y.-C., Guo, G.-P.: Effects of quantum noise on quantum approximate optimization algorithm. Chinese Phys. Lett. 38(3) (2021). https://doi.org/10.1088/0256-307x/38/3/030302

24. Pan, Y., Tong, Y., Yang, Y.: Automatic depth optimization for a quantum approximate ptimization algorithm. Phys. Rev. A, 105, 032433 (2022). https://doi.org/10.1103/PhysRevA.105.032433

25. Akshay, V., Rabinovich, D., Campos, E., Biamonte, J.: Parameter concentrations in quantum approximate optimization. Phys. Rev. A, 104, L010401 (2021). https://doi.org/10.1103/PhysRevA.104.L010401

26. Zhou, L., Wang, S.-T., Choi, S., Pichler, H., Lukin, M.D.: Quantum approximate optimization algorithm: performance, mechanism, and implementation on near-term devices. Phys. Rev. X, 10, 021067 (2020). https://link.aps.org/doi/10.1103/PhysRevX.10.021067

27. Hadfield, S., Wang, Z., O'Gorman, B., Rieffel, E., Venturelli, D., Biswas, R.: From the quantum approximate optimization algorithm to a quantum alternating operator ansatz. Algorithms, 12(2), 34 (2019). https://doi.org/10.3390%2Fa12020034

28. LaRose, R. Rieffel, E., Venturelli, D.: Mixer-phaser ansätze for quantum optimization with hard constraints. Quantum Mach. Intell. 4(2), 17 (2022). https://doi.org/10.1007/s42484-022-00069-x

29. Schönberger, M., Franz, M., Scherzinger, S., Mauerer, W.: Peel | Pile? Cross-framework portability of quantum software. In: 2022 IEEE 19th International Conference on Software Architecture Companion (ICSA-C), pp. 164–169 (2022)

30. Franz, M., et al.: Uncovering instabilities in variational-quantum deep q-networks. J. Franklin Inst. (2022). https://doi.org/10.1016/j.jfranklin.2022.08.021

31. Bruzewicz, C.D., Chiaverini, J., McConnell, R., Sage, J.M.: Trapped-ion quantum computing: progress and challenges. Appl. Phys. Rev. 6, 021314 (2019). https://doi.org/10.1063%2F1.5088164

32. Koenker, R.: quantreg: quantile regression, 2022, r package version 5.88 (2022). https://doi.org/10.1201/9781315120256

Hardware and Software System Security

Protected Functions: User Space Privileged Function Calls

Nafiseh Moti[(✉)] [iD], Reza Salkhordeh [iD], and André Brinkmann [iD]

Johannes Gutenberg University Mainz, Mainz, Germany
{moti,rsalkhor,brinkman}@uni-mainz.de

Abstract. The operating system's traditional design controls and manages all system resources, which comes at the cost of performance and scalability overhead. The scalability overhead results from the kernel's internal metadata structures and locks primarily designed for sequential access. Additionally, implementing software services and resource management requires compliance with the strict kernel abstractions and programming paradigms that can result in semantic bugs. Although plausible, decoupling from the strict kernel control path and code stack comes at the penalty of losing a higher trust entity to enforce protection separation and protection of user code and data. This paper offers a hardware-assisted method to run confined user-space functions at a higher privilege level. Our method allows the implementation of fined-grained user-level services and protocols without modifying the operating system's protection scheme. This is done by introducing two high-level instructions to the x86 ISA. Our simulation shows that user-level functions that leverage our instructions run in the same order as standard function calls, while the real benefit lies in the flexibility and ability to decouple the protected code from the kernel limitations.

Keywords: Operating system · Protection rings · Privilege separation · User space protection

1 Introduction

The sub-microsecond latency of new storage technologies and network interfaces accentuates the cost of software overhead previously masked by the cost of slow I/O [23]. The monolithic kernel software stack and its scalability limit are among the main contributors to the software overhead in traditional storage and network services [21,22]. The cost of kernel software stack stems from its role in applications' control and data path as a centralized resource management entity and, accordingly, the overhead of synchronization, context switch, and data copies [22]. Kernel code contains general-purpose abstractions and sequential data structures containing internal locks that limit the scalability of ever-increasing parallel codes. As a result, Kernel-bypass and decentralized, ad-hoc user-level services have gained popularity to mitigate these costs [23].

© The Author(s), under exclusive license to Springer Nature Switzerland AG 2022
M. Schulz et al. (Eds.): ARCS 2022, LNCS 13642, pp. 117–131, 2022.
https://doi.org/10.1007/978-3-031-21867-5_8

Although bypassing monolithic kernel abstraction for data and control path seems plausible, any implemented resource management needs to enforce permissions and isolation between user processes accessing the data. As a result, control plane management still requires a higher trust entity to ensure protection protocols. The previous kernel-bypass proposals either kept the control plane inside the kernel or radically changed the process isolation schemes of the OS. The former limits the scalability and flexibility of user-level code design, and the latter requires forgoing compatibility with the previous libraries and services.

To implement a secure user-space code in conventional operating systems, many user-level data services such as memcached [12] and in-memory file systems [8,17] leverage Intel's memory protection keys (MPK) to decouple their control plane from the kernel. Intel MPK offers a set of instructions and register and provides a mechanism for enforcing page-based protections without modification of the page tables and by using unused bits as encryption keys [17]. However, MPK is unaware of the user code and relies on page-level protection, making developing fine-grained protocols complicated. Additionally, access control change in MPK is costly and only supports a maximum of 16 protection domains. In Simurgh [15], we took a different approach and provided hardware-assisted function level protection in a user-level NVMM (non-volatile main memory) file system and showed how enabling lightweight, safe user-level functions and, as a result decoupling from the kernel virtual file system led to scalability and performance benefits. However, the Simurgh approach did not consider control transfer cases in the CPU, which limits the generality of the approach.

This paper offers a general-purpose hardware-assisted solution that enables running user-enforced protocols and software services implemented as protected functions at a higher CPU privilege level.

Implementing protected functions is enabled through introducing two instructions JMPP (protected jump) and RETP (protected return) and one microinstruction RDEP. These instructions provide the means to execute a confined user-level set of functions with higher privilege under special circumstances. Similar to Simurgh, we use predefined page offsets as entries to the protected code pages. Our proposal removes the need for switching to kernel code stack through system calls for protection. Protected functions ease the design of decentralized protocols, conditional data sharing, and permission enforcement tailored to the needs of applications. Our solution requires minimal changes to the kernel and page table entries and is compatible with both SMEP and SMAP (Supervisor Mode Execution Prevention and Supervisor Mode Access Prevention [9]).

The key challenges of providing a solution to run privileged instructions in the user space are preserving the integrity of the operating system kernel and the system's stability. We address these challenges by proposing changes to the memory and interrupt management of the system and by offering suggestions for the code linking and compilation so that it minimizes the system vulnerability.

Our simulation analysis on Gem5 [3] shows that the protected functions run at the order of regular function calls. However, the actual performance benefit of protected functions lies in the possibility of running decentralized and user-level implemented protocols at a higher privilege level in the context of monolithic kernels while avoiding internal kernel locks and abstractions. This can help with the performance-critical software services that require microsecond latency.

The next section discusses the background and related work. Section 3 describes the protected functions architecture and how we manage control transfer cases in the CPU. In Sect. 4 we evaluate the protected functions and finally, Sect. 5 concludes the paper.

2 Background and Related Work

Many research proposals tried to address the limitation of context switches between kernel and user code in data and control path of the system by either defining new protection schemes and blurring the line between kernel and user space or by improving context switch overhead through different methods such as a batching system calls or removing unnecessary checks. However, these methods either need extensive operating system change or do not offer the flexibility and scalability of user-level code [11].

Aside from the scalability penalty, implementing the control path of the application in the kernel restricts the flexibility of the implementation, complicates the code debugging, and might even come at a vulnerability cost due to semantic mismatch and concurrency control. For example, in 2018, a ten years analysis of syscall-specific commits to the Linux kernel showed that 35% of these commits were bug fixes, mostly rising from semantic and concurrency control bugs in memory management [1]. Another study in file system design showed that data structure inconsistencies between the kernel virtual file system (VFS) and file system code in metadata management compose more than 70% of the file system vulnerabilities [5]. These data services, therefore, often take years to enter the Linux kernel upstream path since they need to gain a general user audience and go through the verification process to prevent compromising system's security.

Our goal is to provide a method for developing safe user-level services and to enable running privileged instructions from the user space without affecting the system's stability or changing operating system paradigms. This section first explains the CPU and operating system's privilege level, protection mechanism, and inter-privilege control transfer mechanism. Later we discuss the related work and how our solution can be compared to them.

2.1 Protection Rings and Paging

CPU protection rings are the legacy of segmentation in the system's memory. Before the introduction of virtual memory, paging, and flat memory model, segmentation was the default method to provide memory and inter-process isolation [6,9]. Each segment has a size of 64 KB. Accessing a segment requires that a 16-bit segment selector be loaded into a segment register. The segment selector contains the Requested Privilege Level (RPL) and is used to make requests

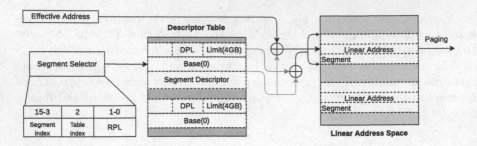

Fig. 1. Segmentation in 64-bit Long mode

from a high privilege level on behalf of a lower one [6,9]. Figure 1 shows how segmentation is being implemented in the X86 processors.

Four protection rings define the system's running state and privilege level. Ring 0 is the highest privilege level used to define the kernel mode. The operating system uses code and data segments to switch between different rings. The minimum access level for these segments is defined by their Descriptor Privilege Level (DPL), while the current privilege level (CPL) defines the privilege level the processor is running in. CPL is changed by setting the DPL value of the code segment (CS). The processor keeps a cached CPL value stored inside the lower two bits of the %cs register. The equations $RPL \geq CPL$ and $DPL \geq CPL$ need to be satisfied to access a segment.

Although X86 supports four protection rings, most operating systems only support rings 0 and 3. Ring 0 provides privilege instructions that protect writes to %cs, memory read and writes, I/O port access and control registers, and allows running privilege instructions in CPU. The operating systems' addressing and memory access control methods depend on the CPU's running mode. Most operating systems use the 64-bit protected mode of the x86 architecture. This mode uses a flat memory space, and all segments create the same flat 64-bit linear address space. It supports only flat address spaces with a single code, data, and stack space. In this mode, memory segmentation is mostly disabled; however, it is still used to change between different privilege rings.

For efficiency and to prevent TLB flushes upon system calls and traps, the Linux kernel places the kernel code and data into the address space of every running process. Every x86 page table entry(PTE) contains a user/supervisor (U/S) bit to define kernel pages and prevent unprivileged memory access. For 64-Bit Long mode, there are four levels of page tables used to translate an address. Setting the U/S bit in each PTE level marks all the pages below that level as supervisor. These pages are only accessible in rings 0–2, and any unprivileged access to them results in a general protection exception (#GP).

2.2   System Call and Control Transfer Mechanisms

There are various x86 instructions to pass control over to the kernel (ring 0) and to request services from it. This service interface is implemented inside the kernel by providing different system calls. Each system call is uniquely identified by a number and is used to expose kernel functionalities such as managing inter-process communication and shared resource management.

Control transfer instructions such as SYSCALL/SYSRET, CALL/JMP/RET and INTn/IRET causes the processor to perform privilege check. Fast system call instruction pairs SYSENTER/SYSEXIT and SYSCALL/SYSRET eliminate unnecessary checks and load pre-determined values inside CS and SS registers [6]. These instructions can enter and exit the kernel code on predefined locations specified by special purpose registers [6,9] and only after the necessary checks are they allowed to change the privilege level.

2.3   Related Work

The previous kernel bypass research focus on overcoming the performance and scalability limitation of user/level context switch by moving all or part of the data or control path to the user space. In these systems, protection in user space is offered through new hardware-assisted methods or special CPU instructions.

Data-centric [2,4,16] operating systems and capability-based designs [18,20] are two approaches proposed in previous studies to offer complete user space designs and to address the protection and isolation requirements. In these systems, data often carries its permission through universal pointers, and the data access control is checked using hardware-assisted capability design or programming language level bound checks. However, using new operating systems means compromising the compatibility of the existing libraries and applications.

Intel memory protection keys (MPK) offer user-space protection, and it has been used by several user-level services to protect their code and data pages [10,17]. However, MPK-based protection lacks flexibility and the protection granularity of general-purpose microservices. Additionally, executing privilege instructions is impossible due to the inability to share user/supervisor pages.

Since system calls are an integral part of an operating system to allow user mode to interact with the kernel, there has been a vast body of research on improving them. System calls must constantly change to meet current security requirements as new vulnerabilities are discovered. These changes often come with a performance penalty [1]. Different approaches focus on improving security or performance by providing alternatives to the syscall. LOTRx86 is a response to the HeartBleed vulnerability [14]. It introduces an additional privilege level at ring one and exports these functions using a new call interface. This approach takes 1000–1500 cycles since it affects caching mechanism. FlexSC [19] proposes exception-less system calls by asynchronously handling them. Finally, Privbox [13] runs the syscall-heavy parts of the code in a privileged sandbox. These approaches, however, only focus on solving the overhead of system calls. Simurgh [15] proposed a hardware-assisted method to provide fine-grained security to their user-level NVMM file system. File system functions were implemented in confined protected code pages, and they showed how they could improve the performance and scalability of the file system design. In this paper we take a similar approach to Simurgh, and extend the protected functions to cover different control mechanisms.

3 Protected Functions

Executing protected functions and allowing the user space process to elevate its privilege level without going through the standard kernel entry points requires some measures to ensure that they comply with operating system security and do not affect the system's stability. These system stability measures need to be guaranteed: 1) prevent normal functions from accessing the protected data, 2) disallow normal functions to change protected code, and 3) provide a safe means for transitioning privilege from normal to supervised mode. A user application can access the protected data pages exclusively through the protected functions. These functions are exported in a one-time bootstrapping process via a kernel module to the user address space and act as a cross-privilege trampoline. Upon the library's initialization, this module is invoked, and the application, as a result, can continue its protected execution in the user space.

3.1 Protected Pages

Allowing arbitrary code to be executed with an elevated privilege level causes security risks. An attacker could execute malicious code with an elevated privilege level, thereby compromising the whole system's security. Privilege elevation can only be performed upon jumping to code locations that are stored in protected pages to disallow arbitrary and malicious code to be executed with a higher privilege level. These pages are marked with a special execute protected bit (ep-bit). Changing the execute protected bit or the page's content is only possible from within the kernel. We have modified existing page table entries (PTE), and translation lookaside buffer (TLB) check policies to guarantee these protections. Figure 2b shows the view of protected pages. Each protected page is divided into four evenly sized sections, resulting in four entry points. Given a page size of 4096 bytes, a page can only be entered on byte 0 (0×000), 1024 (0×400), 2048 (0×800) and 3072 ($0 \times C00$). If the virtual address of the destination corresponds to one of them, the code is allowed to be executed with a higher privilege level. Otherwise, a general protection fault will occur and aborts the execution.

3.2 Privilege Escalation/De-escalation

To enable ring elevation and to jump to the protected user space function, we have introduced two new instructions:

- Jump protected (JMPP): This instruction allows to jump through protected functions on protected page entry points, change the call stack pointer to protected pages and continue the execution.

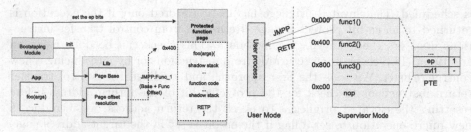

(a) Application code running process   (b) View of JMPP/RETP instructoins

Fig. 2. Protected jump layout

- Return protected (RETP): This instruction returns from the protected execution function and restores the privilege level if required.

Unlike the system call mechanism mentioned in Sect. 2.1, JMPP does not change the existing user code segment and does not exchange and load the segments. It runs in the context of the user process. Similar to the absolute indirect JMP/CALL mechanism, the JMPP instruction jumps to a specific code location and saves the next instruction pointer onto the stack. When running an application in user mode, it has a privilege level of 3. JMPP instructions elevate the current privilege level of the running process, so a jump to a predefined user-specific address can be performed. The code continues its execution from this address until a RETP instruction is encountered. This instruction will revert the privilege level to the user level and return the program flow to the next instruction after JMPP. Figure 2a shows the execution mechanism of a protected function.

Nesting JMPP calls is enabled by popping the return addresses from the stack on RETP. In case of a nested JMPP/RETP call, RETP must not reset the privilege level. Otherwise, the parent JMPP operation would resume execution with a privilege level of 3 instead of 0. Therefore resetting the privilege level is skipped if the ep-bit for the corresponding return page is set.

Executing JMPP At Intermediate Rings. If protected functions do not need privilege instructions and only require the safe execution of the user code in a higher privilege level, they can be implemented in the intermediate rings 1 or 2 alternatively. In this case, the control path still needs to pass the CPU segmentation check, and any attempt to execute privileged instructions will result in a general protection fault. The design and overhead of JMPP and RETP will remain the same in this case.

3.3 Control Transfer Management

The JMPP instruction changes the privilege level without handing over control to the kernel. The current process can therefore be interrupted or run a control transfer instruction. To guarantee system stability in case of an external interrupt, it is necessary to ensure the privilege level is reverted if another process is scheduled. The elevated privilege has to be restored only if the execution is returned to an ep-bit protected page. Returning from control transfer instructions does not check any paging metadata. This check can be done using an additional TLB check upon returning from instructions or by introducing a new control register. We took the first approach and modified the control transfer return instructions to check for the protected bit of the return address before resetting the elevated privilege. To check the return address, we introduce a new micro-operation to set a flag if the ep-bit is set in the target address page. This instruction is necessary if we want to restore the elevated privilege while an interrupt or system call occurs in the middle of the protected function execution.

Handling Timer Interrupts. When an interrupt occurs, the main process information is stored on the stack in an interrupt frame. This interrupt frame includes a copy of the current code segment register, which in turn contains the RPL value of the code segment. When IRET is executed, the CPL value is restored using the RPL value inside this interrupt frame. We have changed the IRET instruction to check whether the return address is inside a protected page. In this case, the CPL value of 0 is loaded instead of the RPL value.

Handling Interrupts. The kernel is not involved in the execution path of the protected functions. Therefore CPU is responsible for handling interrupts. If an interrupt happens while a protected function with elevated privilege is running, the privilege level has to revert to the user level before another process is scheduled. Otherwise, a newly scheduled process could run with supervisor privilege.

Handling System Calls. On SYSENTER/SYSCALL the kernel software stack and page tables will be loaded before elevating the privilege; therefore, it is safe to enter the kernel space using kernel entry points in the system call. Upon returning from the system call, we need to check and restore the elevated privilege to the protected execution mode. This can be done by checking the return address of the caller process in the call stack. Consider the scenario that two processes, A and B, should be scheduled. Assuming process A is executing code with an elevated privilege level using JMPP. Process B becomes active, and A waits for the execution to resume. If B forces a scheduled event by calling the corresponding syscall, the kernel might return the execution to process A using the SYSRET instruction instead of IRET. SYSRET always restores the user code segment with a DPL value of 3, discarding the elevated privilege level that A held previously. It is necessary to modify SYSRET similar to IRET to consider this case and restore the privilege level if required. Before loading the user code segment attributes, the instruction must check if the ep-bit is set. If this is the case, it loads a DPL value of 0 instead of 3. Writing the attributes will cause the CPL value to be set to the code segment DPL value.

SMAP/SMEP. Supervisor Mode Access Prevention (SMAP) is an Intel CPU feature that prevents supervisor mode (Ring 0–2) from accessing user pages.

Similarly, if Supervisor mode execution prevention (SMEP) is enabled, the operating system will not be allowed to directly execute application code, even speculatively.

SMEP does not affect protected function since protected function does not execute any code in user pages. Protected functions are also compatible with SMAP as protected, and supervisor data pages are only accessible and modifiable from within the protected functions.

3.4   Security Consideration

Protected functions provide a way to run privileged instructions from the user space. We guarantee that normal users cannot access the privileged code or the protected data, and we guarantee a protected control transfer between different privilege modes. In addition, we guarantee that a user cannot execute or jump to arbitrary locations inside the kernel. However, our work does not guarantee the security of the user code. Developers need to verify and trust their code shared by different processes.

When executing code using JMPP, no branch instructions pointing outside of an ep-bit protected page should be performed since the privilege level is not reset in this case. For E.g., while executing privileged code with JMPP, a call instruction to a standard user page is performed. In this case, the privilege level is not reset. The code executed by the call instruction is therefore executed with a privilege level of 0. It is the responsibility of the user to prevent this case.

To prevent return-oriented programming (ROP) attack, the return address and the stack must be placed inside protected pages. Storing the stack in a normal user page could enable another thread of the same process to change the return addresses on the stack. In this case, RETP would return to the compromised return address and execute the altered program flow. If the return address does not point to an ep-bit protected page, RETP will reset the privilege level to user level. This minimizes the risk of an unintended privilege escalation but does not solve the problem of the altered program flow. Therefore changing the stack pointer is still necessary. Since JMPP to a protected page elevates the privilege, Time Of Check To Time Of Use (TOCTTOU) does not happen between the JMPP and the beginning of the function.

3.5   Bootstrapping Process

For an application to be able to access the protected functions, a one-time bootstrapping process is being enforced that marks the supervisor bit in the protected pages. Bootstrapping module creates a mapping between the user and protected code pages and returns the base address of the protected pages.

3.6   Implementation

We have implemented and prototyped the new instructions in Gem5 [3] simulator. Table 1 lists the micro-ops and symbols used in this section.

Table 1. micro-op symbols used in the code snippets

micro-op	param1	param2	param3	Description
limm	dest	lmm		Stores the 64 bit immediate lmm into the integer register dest
rdip	dest			Set the dest register to the current value of rip
wrattr	dest	src1		Writes the selector in src1 to the register dest
subi	dest	src1	lmm	Substracts the contents of lmm from src1 and pushes to dest
wrip	src1	src2		Set the rip to the sum of src1 and src2, this causes a macroop branch
addi	dest	src1	lmm	Adds src1 and the immediate lmm and puts the result in dest

Execute Protected Bit. To mark a page as executed protected, the ep bit on all four levels of page table entries needs to be set. However, for setting the supervisor bit, only the last level needs to check the bit as the CPU extends supervisor mode to all pages below a page level [6,9]. To implement ep-bit, we have repurposed the bit 10 in the page table entry. This bit is one of the bits available to the user. We have modified the TLB check to disallow normal users to change the ep-bit. Additionally, we have implemented a new micro-op called **rdep**. This instruction reads the ep-bit value and sets the EZF flag. JMPP utilizes this flag to check the protected jump condition.

Implementing JMPP and RETP. Figure 3 shows the implementation of JMPP. At the beginning, it is checked whether the jump address is a valid offset in a page. This is done by checking whether the lower 12-bits of the address are divisible by 1024 and subsequently sets the EZF flag. The instruction will next check the execute protected bit. This is done through *rdep* micro-operation. If all the checks pass successfully, the instruction needs to save the return address on top of the stack. Nesting JMPP calls is, therefore, possible by popping the return addresses from the stack on the RETP. Before performing the jump, the instruction loads new attributes with a DPL value of 0 for the current user code segment. By applying these attributes using **wrattr**, the current privilege level is elevated from 3 to 0. At the end of this macro-operation, a branch happens by writing the new instruction pointer. However, in our real hardware test, it seems that Intel processors does not bother to check DPL and RPL selector and only rely on CPL and paging protection mechanism.

The RETP instruction does not need any input parameters. Figure 4 shows the Gem5 implementation of the return instruction. The CPU reads the return address from the top of the stack and loads it into t1.

Interrupt Return Handling. As explained in Sect. 3.3 to restore the privilege level in case of a return from control transfer instructions, we have to modify the interrupt return instruction. We have used the **rdep** micro-op to check whether the ep-bit is set for the return address, and in this case, we can safely return to the code execution using elevated privilege. Figure 5 shows the micro-op code that needs to be inserted into the IRET instruction. Register t5 stores the temporary value that will be used to restore the CPL. If the ep-bit is set for the return location, the default behavior of loading the RPL value into t5 (line 4) is skipped.

Register t5 will still hold the value of 0 set in line 2. If the ep-bit is not set, line 4 will be executed and override the temporary CPL value of 0 with the cached RPL value. This approach causes an additional performance overhead to the IRET instruction. The slowest part of this modification lies within the fact, that the page of the return address has to be loaded into the TLB to check the ep-bit. To resume the code execution, this step has to be performed anyways. The time spent on the TLB load operation is therefore negligible.

```
1   limm t1 , 0x3FF ; checking the entry points
2   and t0 , reg , t1 , EZF<-1
3   IF EZF=0 THEN #GP(0)
4   ...
5   limm t1 , 0x3FF ; checking the ep-bit
6   and t0 , reg , t1, EZF<-1
7   IF EZF=0 THEN #GP(0) ; issue general protection fault
8   ...
9   rdip t1 ;saving the return address
10  stis t1 , ss , [0 , t0 , rsp ] ; store t1 on the stack
11  subi rsp , rsp , ssz ; subtract the stacksize from rsp
12  ...
13  limm t4 , 4GB ; changing the privilege level and jump
14  wrattr cs , t4
15  wripi reg , 0
```

Fig. 3. Jumping to a protected page

```
1   ld t1 , ss , [1 , t0 , rsp ]
2   addi rsp , rsp , dsz ; check for return to an ep-bit protected page
3   rdep t1 , flags =( EZF,) , atCPL0=True
4   br RETURN , flags =( CEZF,)
5   limm t4 , 4GB ; reset the privilege level
6   wrattr cs , t4 ; changing the CPl.
7   RETURN:
8   wripi t1 , 0 ; jump to the return address .
9
```

Fig. 4. Returning from JMPP

```
1   rdep t1 , flags =( EZF,) , atCPL0=True
2   limm t5 , 0
3   br SKIP , flags =( CEZF,)
4   andi t5 , t2 , 0x3
5   SKIP: ...
6
```

Fig. 5. IRET instruction modification

Linking the Library and Alignment Check. The protected function code should be compiled as position independent without any external library dependency. Additionally, no branch to the outside of the pages like exception handling should be allowed. All needed functions need to be implemented inside the protected pages. The entry of functions needs to be placed in the predefined page offsets of the .text section as jumping is only allowed to those offsets. In GCC, this can be done in the application link script by telling the compiler to put each function in a separate section and by adding section attributes to the functions.

4   Evaluation

This section describes the simulation infrastructure, experimental setup, and results. As mentioned in Sect. 3.6 we have implemented our new instructions in Gem5 [3] simulator. We have measured the overhead of the JMPP/RETP instruction and compared it with the Linux system call and Linux fast system call (vDSO call) on the Gem5 simulator using a 1 GB DerivO3CPU, 512 MB memory. vDSO (virtual dynamic shared library) is a small shared library provided by the kernel and mapped into the address space of the user application. This enables the fast execution of frequent system calls that do not need additional security measures without mode and stack change [7]. Additionally, we measured the overhead of the Linux system call and fast system call on an Intel Xeon Gold 5212 processor running at 2.5 GHz. Next, we show the breakdown measurement of protected function and system call on Gem5.

The simulator runs a Gentoo distribution on top of the Linux kernel 5.4.55. The kernel module and PTEditor[1] were loaded to the image. The goal of the simulation is to show that the JMPP overhead is low compared to a system call.

4.1   Measurements

To measure the overhead of syscall, we have added an empty system call and vDSO call to the kernel. We modified the syscall entries, used m5_reset_stats and m5_dump_stats pseudo instructions, and hardcoded the *rdi* and *rsi* registers to minimize the measurement overhead. Each measurement was performed 100 times to account for caching and speculation execution effects. The overhead of the vDSO call and protected function were measured between the function calls.

Figure 6 shows the baseline measurements. On Gem5, JMPP/RETP call performs close to vDSO call. Table 2 shows the instructions' breakdown and their overhead on Gem5 for protected jump compared to system calls. The Gem5 overhead of a vDSO routine, including its return, is 30 cycles. On Xeon CPU, this call takes less than two cycles.

The gem5 implementation JMPP checks the ep bit in the page table, modifies the CPL value of the CPU, and performs the call routine to the predefined

---

[1] https://github.com/misc0110/PTEditor.

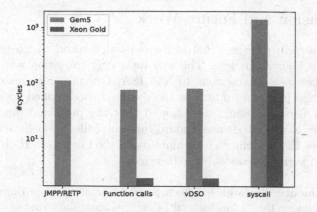

Fig. 6. Cycle count measurement

Table 2. The breakdown of instruction measurements on Gem5 simulator

JMPP/RETP		System call	
Instruction	Time(cycles)	Instruction	Time(cycles)
Checking entries	6	syscall wrapper	241
PTE check	6	swapgs	22
Saving return address	9	Switch to CR3	214
Change CPL	32	construct pt_regs	248
Write instruction pointer	6	do_syscall	226
Read Return Address	6	find return path	10
PTE check	6	sysret	45
Revert CPL	32	USERGS_SYSRET64	400
Write Instruction pointer	6		
Total: 111 cycles		Total: 1432 cycles	

protected function page. The JMPP and RETP combined overhead is 111 cycles and, therefore, in the same order as a standard function call on Gem5.

The syscall overhead is induced not only by the call itself but also by setting up the registers and copying parameters to memory, switching to the kernel context, and locating the corresponding function for the syscall through the dispatching table. In contrast, JMPP employs the same technique as a normal function call for passing parameters and does not require a context switch. The user code calls protected functions by their addresses and not by a number; hence, JMPP does not need a dispatching table. Changing the CPL value and writing the return address in the protected stacks are the subset of the syscalls' operations also needed by JMPP and take 30 cycles. Additionally, checking the ep bit and entry points can be made in 6 cycles.

5   Conclusion and Future Work

This paper introduced a new hardware-assisted method to execute user-level functions in a higher privilege. The safe inter-ring transition was provided by introducing two new instructions to X86 ISA. Our proposed instructions provide a protected jump and return to the confined user-verified code pages. Our prototype on the Gem5 simulator showed that the protected functions run at the same order of magnitude as standard function calls. We believe that our proposal improves the flexibility and scalability in the implementation of protected user-level and kernel-bypass software services.

Acknowledgment. This work has been partially funded by the European Union's Horizon 2020 under the "Adaptive multi-tier intelligent data manager for Exascale (ADMIRE)" project; Grant Agreement No: 956748-ADMIRE-H2020-JTI-EuroHPC-2019-1 and the IO-SEA project, supported by the European High-Performance Computing Joint Undertaking (JU) and from BMBF/DLR under grant agreement No 955811.

References

1. Bagherzadeh, M., Kahani, N., Bezemer, C., Hassan, A.E., Dingel, J., Cordy, J.R.: Analyzing a decade of Linux system calls. Empir. Softw. Eng. **23**(3), 1519–1551 (2018)
2. Baumann, A., et al.: The multikernel: a new OS architecture for scalable multicore systems. In: Proceedings of the 22nd ACM Symposium on Operating Systems Principles, SOSP (2009)
3. Binkert, N.L., et al.: The gem5 simulator. SIGARCH Comput. Archit. News **39**(2), 1–7 (2011)
4. Bittman, D., Alvaro, P., Mehra, P., Long, D.D.E., Miller, E.L.: Twizzler: a data-centric OS for non-volatile memory. In: USENIX Annual Technical Conference (ATC) (2020)
5. Cai, M., Huang, H., Huang, J.: Understanding security vulnerabilities in file systems. In: Proceedings of the 10th ACM SIGOPS Asia-Pacific Workshop on Systems, APSys 2019, Hangzhou, China, 19–20 August 2019, pp. 8–15. ACM (2019)
6. Corporation, A.: Amd64 architecture programmer's manual (2021)
7. Davis, M.: Creating a vDSO: the colonel's other chicken (2012). https://dl.acm.org/doi/fullHtml/10.5555/2073763.2073769
8. Dong, M., Bu, H., Yi, J., Dong, B., Chen, H.: Performance and protection in the ZoFS user-space NVM file system. In: Proceedings of the 27th ACM Symposium on Operating Systems Principles, SOSP (2019)
9. Guide, P.: Intel® 64 and IA-32 architectures software developer's manual, vol. 4 (2022)
10. Hedayati, M., et al.: Hodor: intra-process isolation for high-throughput data plane libraries. In: USENIX Annual Technical ConferenceATC (2019)
11. Kim, T., Peinado, M., Mainar-Ruiz, G.: STEALTHMEM: system-level protection against cache-based side channel attacks in the cloud. In: Kohno, T. (ed.) Proceedings of the 21th USENIX Security Symposium. USENIX Association (2012)
12. Kjellqvist, C., Hedayati, M., Scott, M.L.: Safe, fast sharing of memcached as a protected library. In: 49th International Conference on Parallel Processing (2020)

13. Kuznetsov, D., Morrison, A.: Privbox: faster system calls through sandboxed privileged execution. In: USENIX Annual Technical Conference (USENIX ATC) (2022)
14. Lee, H., Song, C., Kang, B.B.: Lord of the x86 rings: a portable user mode privilege separation architecture on x86. In: Lie, D., Mannan, M., Backes, M., Wang, X. (eds.) Proceedings of the ACM SIGSAC Conference on Computer and Communications Security, CCS (2018)
15. Moti, N., et al.: Simurgh: a fully decentralized and secure NVMM user space file system. In: SC 2021: The International Conference for High Performance Computing, Networking, Storage and Analysis (2021)
16. Narayanan, V., et al.: Redleaf: isolation and communication in a safe operating system. In: 14th USENIX Symposium on Operating Systems Design and Implementation, OSDI 2020, Virtual Event, 4–6 November 2020, pp. 21–39. USENIX Association (2020)
17. Park, S., Lee, S., Xu, W., Moon, H., Kim, T.: libmpk: software abstraction for intel memory protection keys (intel MPK). In: 2019 USENIX Annual Technical Conference, USENIX ATC 2019, Renton, WA, USA, 10–12 July 2019, pp. 241–254. USENIX Association (2019)
18. Shapiro, J.S., Smith, J.M., Farber, D.J.: EROS: a fast capability system. In: Proceedings of the 17th ACM Symposium on Operating System Principles (SOSP), 12–15 December, pp. 170–185 (1999)
19. Song, C., et al.: HDFI: hardware-assisted data-flow isolation. In: IEEE Symposium on Security and Privacy (SP), San Jose, CA, USA, 22–26 May, pp. 1–17 (2016)
20. Watson, R.N.M., et al.: CHERI: a hybrid capability-system architecture for scalable software compartmentalization. In: IEEE Symposium on Security and Privacy (SP), San Jose, CA, USA, 17–21 May, pp. 20–37 (2015)
21. Wippel, H.: DPDK-based implementation of application-tailored networks on end user nodes. In: International Conference and Workshop on the Network of the Future, NOF (2014)
22. Yang, Z., et al.: SPDK: a development kit to build high performance storage applications. In: IEEE International Conference on Cloud Computing Technology and Science, CloudCom (2017)
23. Zhang, I., et al.: The demikernel datapath OS architecture for microsecond-scale datacenter systems. In: SOSP: ACM SIGOPS 28th Symposium on Operating Systems Principles (2021)

Using Look Up Table Content as Signatures to Identify IP Cores in Modern FPGAs

Ali Asghar[1(✉)], Amanda Katherine Robillard[1], Ilya Tuzov[2], Andreas Becher[1], and Daniel Ziener[1]

[1] Technische Universität Ilmenau, Ilmenau, Germany
{ali.asghar,amanda-katherine.robillard,
andreas.becher,daniel.ziener}@tu-ilmenau.de
[2] Universitat Politècnica de València, València, Spain
tuil@disca.upv.es

Abstract. The increasing amount of logic resources in FPGA architectures has enabled the realization of larger and more complex designs. Today, most of the large-scale designs rely heavily on off-the-shelf *Intellectual Property Cores* (IP Cores) to ease their development. This dependency raises an important issue: the unlicensed use of IP Cores. In this paper, we utilize LUT contents, which represent the functionality of an IP Core, as a signature to determine if a core might be part of an accused design. For this, we present a technique to reconstruct the contained LUT contents from modern FPGA configurations which not only contain 6-input one-output LUTs but also 5-input two-output LUTs. By making use of LUT decomposition together with a fast Boolean matching algorithm, we consolidate the work for commercial architectures. The proposed method is evaluated using 8 IP Cores to find in 4 different designs using two different architectures. Our findings show a 100% identification rate with no false-positives or false-negatives for all experiments carried out. Especially the presence of larger cores can be established with a difference of at least 10% between true and false positives.

Keywords: IP Core · FGPA architecture · Bitstream

1 Introduction

The world semiconductor business stood at around \$440 billion in 2020 – an increase of 6.5% from the year 2019 [1]. For almost three decades now, the worldwide semiconductor revenues have seen a perpetual rise. Even after the slowing of Moore's Law [7], the global demand for semiconductors continues to increase.

Naturally, in a market with such high stakes competitiveness is at its peak. For two rival companies selling the same product, time to market is everything. A delay in the release of a product by few weeks can significantly impact the overall sales. Consequently, the design lifecycle of integrated circuits has decreased significantly. To keep pace with the challenging deadlines, designers switched to a

M. Schulz et al. (Eds.): ARCS 2022, LNCS 13642, pp. 132–147, 2022.
https://doi.org/10.1007/978-3-031-21867-5_9

modular approach utilizing *Intellectual Property Cores* (IP Cores) [10]. IP Cores alleviate the requirement to design every module from scratch. If needed, the designers can choose from a wide range of IP Cores from specialized developers. These off-the-shelf cores can then be stitched to the main design, resulting in a shorter development cycle.

The ubiquitous use of IP Cores results in an undesired behavior: their unlicensed usage. The distribution and licensing of IP Cores is similar to that of software. While software distributions come with a license or a key to limit the use to a particular user(s), IP Cores, once sold, cannot be tracked for usage and as a result, can be copied or sold illegally. To counter this issue, several security measures have been proposed for IP Core identification.

Various IP protection methods work at different abstraction levels. At the algorithmic level, encryption of HDL or netlists can prevent unlicensed usage or modification of the core. A problem with this method is the lack of an industrial standard for the encryption of IP Cores [8]. Hence, an IP Core encrypted with an EDA tool may not be decryptable by the tool from the FPGA vendor. Then at the synthesis/implementation level, a unique signature in the form of watermarks can be embedded into the design. In some cases, the watermark can be removed by an attacker or unintentionally by the CAD tool during optimizations. Therefore, it is desirable to have an intrinsic attribute of the design as a signature alleviating the need for any additional circuitry or constraints and the removal of which would result in loss of functionality.

In this work, we utilize the LUT contents of an IP Core as the signature. Since the main functionality of a core is determined by its LUT contents, they can, therefore, be used as a unique identifier. If all or a large percentage of the LUT values of the claimant's IP are found in an accused design, then it could be ascertained that the IP Core was used without a proper license.

The remainder of the work is organized as follows. In Sect. 2, we discuss the existing methods for IP Core identification followed by the concept of our approach in Sect. 3. Section 4 covers the implementation details, extraction of LUT values from bitstreams and our fine-grained mapping approach to obtain the exact representation for each function present in the bitstream. In Sect. 5, we present the results of our approach and conclude our findings with possible future research directions in Sect. 6.

2 Background and Previous Work

Numerous methods have been proposed to safeguard the confidentiality and integrity of IP Cores. In this section, we review the existing techniques, which prevent or can be used to prevent the breach of confidentiality resulting from unlicensed usage of IP Cores. In Sect. 1, we briefly mentioned two protection methods, namely encryption and watermarking. Encryption can be a useful tool to hide the details of a design. Most of the commercial EDA tools, such as Cadence's *ncprotect* and *Calibre* by Mentor Graphics, provide en/decryption of design files using public-key cryptography. For FPGAs, both vendors Xilinx [20] and Altera [2] allow bitstream encryption, while a dedicated hardware core is embedded in the fabric for decryption. A major limitation of the encryption-based countermeasure is the incompatibility between different tools in the CAD flow due to unavailability of an industrial standard for the encryption of cores. Encryption could also be vulnerable to side-channel attacks as shown by Moradi et al [14]. More recently, the bitstream encryption of Xilinx 7-series was successfully broken [9] by exploiting a design flaw which leaks the decrypted bitstream.

Watermarking is another popular approach preventing the unlicensed usage of IP Cores. In simple words, watermarking is the process of hiding a unique signature in user data. For IP Cores, watermarking can be divided into two categories: *additive* and *constraint-based watermarking*. The additive methods, as the name suggests, add a signature to the core design. In [16], utilization of unused LUT entries was proposed to store the signature. The work in [26] exploits the power side-channel leakages to hide the signature in power traces. Upon the execution of a shift-register containing the watermark, unique power traces are generated. Some constraint-based watermarking techniques include: placement constraints for CLBs [12] and routing constraints [12].

All of these watermarking techniques have their drawbacks. The additive-based watermarks increase the resource consumption or require specialized hardware and additional files for verification. Moreover, there is always a possibility for an attacker to either remove or modify these watermarks, such as by reverse-engineering the bitfile. For the constraint-based watermarks, additional watermarks can be created by adding further constraints, making it impossible to identify the original author.

More recently, some papers [5,13] have demonstrated the use of machine learning for identifying IP Cores. The work in [13] employs convolutional neural networks to identify certain hardware modules or fragments of an IP. However, the circuits used for testing, such as adders, subtractors, and multipliers, are relatively small compared to modern IP Cores. The authors in [5] perform the identification of cryptographic operators for different encryption algorithms using deep neural networks (DNNs). They propose the conversion of a bitstream into images, which are then fed to a DNN for classification. A major limitation for both works is the generation of training and test sets. For example, for the identification of a particular functional block, a large number of circuits implementing the same or similar functionality are needed to train the network. When searching for a particular core in a design, in most cases, it would be extremely difficult to find a large number of such cores.

This work makes use of LUT contents as signatures for IP Core identification. The initial idea was first introduced in [25] for the then used 4-input LUT (LUT4) architectures. The presented method extracts the LUT contents directly from the bitfile and then performs brute-force Boolean matching to account for LUTs whose inputs get permuted by the CAD tool for better routing and critical path (further discussed in Sect. 4). If a large percentage of functions present in the netlist are also found inside the bitstream, then it can be established with a degree of certainty that the core has been utilized in the design. For a more robust assessment, the authors utilized the locations of matching LUTs, which can also be extracted from the bitstream. It is assumed that the LUTs belonging to the same core should be placed close to each other and as a result, the mean distance between the found LUTs should also be low. If this is the case, then the probability that the LUTs belong to the searched core is high and vice versa. However, this approach has difficulties on bigger designs where IP Cores can get fragmented or in the case where more than one illegal IP Core is included.

From a developer's perspective, the countermeasures to prevent illegal IP copying should be low-cost (in terms of area, delay, and power), easy to implement, and require minimal resources for verification. The LUT-based IP identification meets all these requirements as no additional resources are needed for creating signatures or their verification. This basic idea was introduced by Ziener et al. [25]. While showing promising results, modern devices such as Xilinx 7 Series devices cannot be addressed with the original method. In this paper, we propose the utilization of recent advances in the fields of bitstream reverse-engineering for FPGAs [3,15,19] and the development of Boolean matching algorithms [11,24]. These can find equivalence classes for functions with input sizes ≥ 6 at an extremely fast rate, with a high degree of accuracy. We present fine-grained mapping of bitstream contents to LUT values to extract the exact INIT (LUT's logic function) values and a technique to recover the LUTs lost to recombination during CAD optimizations. Furthermore, we generate a template containing signature classes which are essential to the functionality of a core, along with a new ratio metric to improve the robustness of our proposed algorithm.

3 Concept

To explain the workings of the method presented, we assume a scenario in which an attacker attempts the illegal use of an IP Core. Meanwhile, a defendant tries to prevent this usage or pursue legal action by proving ownership of the core. In the assumed scenario, the attacker has the capability to obtain a copy of the IP Core in a legal manner. They then perform illegal copying or utilize the core in a way that violates the agreed terms of usage. The defendant can make a claim and ask the accused party for the bitstream. If this is not possible, a simpler way could be to purchase a copy of the design suspected to be using the stolen IP. The bitstream can then be wiretapped [23,25] (using a logic analyzer) during reconfiguration and if needed, decrypted using one of the known methods such as [9,14,17]. Afterwards, the contents of the LUTs and their positions can be read from the bitstream and then compared with the netlist of the original core. Figure 1 further illustrates this idea.

In this work, the identification of an IP Core is done using:

1. DAVOS toolkit [19]: To extract the content of LUT cells from the bitstream.
2. LUT Decomposition: To obtain LUTs that have been combined during synthesis and/or implementation.
3. Boolean Matching: To account for LUT values which may have been changed due to the permutation of inputs resulting from routing.

4. Core Identification: To compare the equivalence classes obtained from the netlist and bitstream in such a way that it is less prone to the influence of synthesis parameters of an IP Core and synthesis and implementation optimizations.

More details on these steps will be provided in the following section.

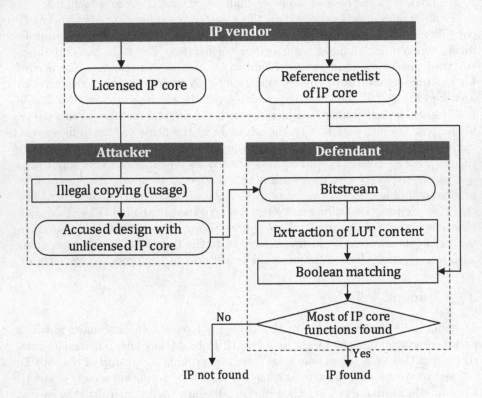

Fig. 1. Identification process for the unlicensed usage of an IP Core

4   Implementation

This section describes the steps involved in determining whether the accused design contains the licensed IP Core. First, the contents of the LUTs are extracted from the bitfile (provided by the accused party) and post-processed to obtain the LUTs logic functions (INIT attributes). Second, the INIT values of the LUT cells are extracted from the reference netlist (provided by the IP vendor). Third, the identification process. The INIT values extracted from both the bitstream and the netlist are translated into a set of equivalence classes through a Boolean matching algorithm. Obtained equivalence classes are subsequently

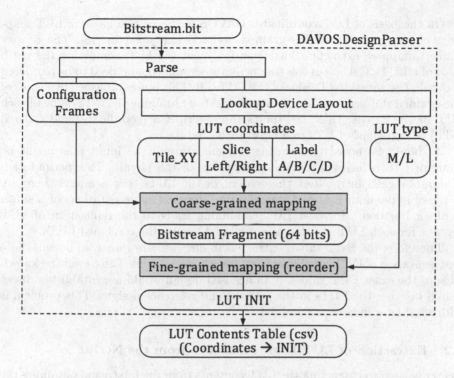

Fig. 2. Extraction of LUT content from the bitstream by means of DAVOS toolkit

supplied to the core identification process to calculate a percentage of classes that match across the bitstream and the netlist. This percentage is interpreted as a probability that a given IP Core is present in the accused bitstream.

4.1   Extraction of LUT Logic Functions from the Bitstream

The content of used LUTs is extracted from the accused bitstream by means of the *DesignParser* tool of the DAVOS toolkit [18, 19]. An overview of the LUT extraction procedure is depicted in Fig. 2. The tool is invoked with a target bitfile as the input. DAVOS parses the bitstream into a set of *configuration memory* (CM) Frames of the used device part. After that, DAVOS calculates the coordinates of each LUT in the layout of the target device part and determines their types: type-L (logic only), or type-M (logic or distributed memory). These LUT coordinates are defined in terms of:

- X (column) and Y (row) coordinates of a Configurable Logic Block (CLB) Tile;
- Slice label (Left or Right) within a Tile;
- LUT label (A, B, C, or D) within a Slice.

On the basis of LUT coordinates DAVOS performs two levels of LUT mapping: coarse-grained and fine-grained, as it is explained in [18]. The coarse-grained mapping extracts a bitstream fragment (64 bits) containing the truth table of a LUT. The bits of this fragment are scrambled, and need to be reordered to obtain the actual INIT value of the LUT cell. This is accomplished by means of fine-grained (bit-accurate) LUT mapping. After obtaining the INIT value of each LUT in the FPGA, DAVOS exports the description (coordinates and ordered INIT) of non-empty LUTs to a CSV-formatted file.

It should be noted that during implementation, the input pins might be remapped to reduce the critical path delay of the circuit. This permutation of inputs significantly alters the content of the LUTs. For n inputs there are n! possible permutations and, therefore, n! different representations of a single Boolean function. Moreover LUT combining leads to the replication of LUT content for each LUT pin that is not shared among the combined LUTs.

Therefore, the INIT values extracted in our case are rather an intermediate representation of INIT attributes from the accused design. Thus, even the knowledge of the exact INIT values of an accused design would not establish a direct match between the LUTs in the accused and reference designs. This problem is addressed later in Sect. 4.3 and 4.4.

4.2   Extraction of LUT Logic Functions from the Netlist

In comparison to extracting the LUT contents from the bitstream, obtaining the INIT values from the netlist is considerably simpler. INIT attributes of LUT cells can be extracted from an EDIF (or Verilog) netlist by means of third-party netlist parsers. Alternatively, attributes of LUT cells can be extracted directly from the Vivado design (or its post-implementation checkpoint) by means of TCL scripting [22]. Unlike the LUT contents from the bitstream, the LUT contents in the netlist aren't necessarily presented as a 64-bit value, since depending on the function a LUT implements, it might have less than 6 inputs. Therefore, to facilitate the LUT matching between the bitstream and the netlist, we can simplify the INIT values extracted from the bitstream, by removing the don't care LUT inputs. Such don't care inputs can be detected by checking for the replicated bits of the INIT attribute.

4.3   LUT Decomposition

Modern FPGAs offer the possibility of mapping two functions (input size < 6) on a LUT6_2 primitive with 6 inputs, 2 outputs, and input 6 set to '1' [21]. This optimization is known as 'LUT Recombining' and results in area-delay savings for functions with shared inputs. Since there is often no information available about recombining at the synthesized netlist level, the optimization becomes a nuisance for the identification of an IP Core using netlist contents. The higher the number of combined LUTs, the lower the percentage of netlist LUTs found in the bitstream. From our evaluation with different designs, we observed a significant influence of LUT recombining on core detection, as the distinction between the true/false positive was not possible with a certain degree of confidence. To circumvent this problem, we try to recover the functions lost to recombining by decomposing all the 6-input LUT (LUT6) functions found in the bitstream. First, we test if input 6 of LUT6 primitives is a don't care by comparing the upper and lower half of the 64-bit INIT value for equality. If input 6 is not a don't care, then the LUT either implements one 6-input LUT (input 6 has influence on the output) or two LUTs with less than 6 inputs each (input 6 is hardwired to a '1'). Unfortunately, we can't be sure which case is actually true without reconstruction of the routing in the FPGA. Therefore, we split the 64-bit (6-input) INIT value into a lower and upper half and remove any don't cares from the two resulting functions. Any remaining function is afterwards added to the set of found functions of the bitstream.

In summary, for each 6-input LUT in the bitstream, we generate up to 3 possible INIT values. While this can increase the number of false-positives during matching due to falsely added decomposed INIT values, it ensures more functions present in the netlist are also found in the bitstream. Due to aggressive LUT recombining in modern synthesis and implementation tools, the decomposition is necessary in order to be able to match synthesis level INIT values with the INIT values extracted from the bitstream.

4.4 Boolean Matching

To account for changing LUT contents (caused by input swapping) during routing optimizations, we make use of Boolean matching. Boolean matching is a method to check if two functions are identical under specific transformations (e.g., permutation or negation of inputs/outputs). Functions that are equal in respect to these transformations belong to an equivalence class. For the case of safely identifying remapped LUT contents, the *Permutation* (P) equivalence class is of interest. This class covers all functions which are equal under permutation of inputs. Similar to LUT recombining, without the use of equivalence classes, the presence of a core couldn't be established with any degree of certainty. For this work, we utilized a Boolean matching algorithm [11], embedded in the system ABC [4]. For the remainder of this paper, we refer to equivalence classes as classes.

4.5 Core Identification

In order to establish if a specific IP Core is used in an FPGA, we have to determine whether the functions (F) of the IP Core netlist are a subset of the functions of the accused FPGA design.

Let F_n be the set of functions contained in the netlist n of the IP Core and F_d the set of functions extracted and decomposed (see Sect. 4.3) from the bitstream of design d. Then C_n is the set of classes contained in F_n and C_d is the set of classes contained in F_d. Furthermore, $cnt_{n,c}$ is the number of occurrences of a class cin the netlist nand $cnt_{d,c}$ is the number of occurrences of class cin the design d.

Unlike the approach in [25], which searches for the classes contained in the netlist of a reference IP Core, our algorithm makes use of an architecture/design agnostic approach. Instead of using functions only from a single netlist, we synthesize v variations of the searched IP Core across different architectures and designs including small variations in the synthesis time generics[1]. From the resulting netlists $(n_1, \ldots, n_v)$ we generate a *template* by using the intersection of the classes contained in each netlist variant.

Therefore, the classes of a template and the occurrence of each class are defined as follows:

$$C_t = \bigcap_{i=1}^{v} C_{n_i} \qquad (1)$$

$$cnt_{t,c} = min(cnt_{n_i,c} | i \in \{1, 2, \ldots, v\}) \qquad (2)$$

In a straight-forward approach, we would assume that an IP Core is present in a design if the occurrence of every class in it is greater or equal to the occurrence in the template.

$$\forall\, c \in C_t | cnt_{d,c} \geq cnt_{t,c} \qquad (3)$$

Yet, optimizations during the implementation of a netlist can alter functions (including their classes) or even remove them completely by merging them into multiplexers or latches [21]. From our experiments, this metric was found to be very inefficient in confirming the presence of an IP. For some IP Cores, which were present in the design (*true-case*), the percentage of found LUTs was relatively low and at times, even less than when an IP Core was not included (*false-case*).

To account for these optimizations and improve the results, we relax the condition by which we determine if a class is contained in the design. This is achieved by introducing the ratio $r \in [0, 1]$ as a variable leading to:

$$\forall\, c \in C_t | \frac{cnt_{d,c}}{cnt_{t,c}} \geq r \qquad (4)$$

Finally we determine the percentage of matched, *i.e.* $\frac{cnt_{d,c}}{cnt_{t,c}} \geq r$, classes in relation to the number of classes in the template as the metric to decide if an IP Core is included in a design or not[2].

$$cov_{t,d} = \frac{\left| \left\{ c \mid c \in C_t, \frac{cnt_{d,c}}{cnt_{t,c}} \geq r \right\} \right|}{|C_t|} \qquad (5)$$

5   Evaluation

Searching for an IP Core in industrial scale designs can be challenging as several parameters can influence the eventual outcome of identification. Therefore,

---

[1] An example of such a variation is the change of bus-width or address space of peripheral IP Cores.
[2] We denote $|s|$ as the amount of elements within a set s.

Table 1. The 8 IP Core templates used for the evaluation together with the information on their contained amount of classes and LUTs (b) as well as in which designs each core is originally present (a).

	LEON5 VC707	LEON3 Arty-A7	NOELV Arty-A7	NOELV VC707
jtag	X	X	X	X
uart	X	X	X	X
i2c	X	X		
ethc	X	X	X	X
sgmii	X			X
leon3		X		
leon5	X			
noelv			X	X

(a)

Template	classes	LUTs	LUT6s
jtag	34	250	8
uart	59	341	216
i2c	44	114	23
ethc	271	1,229	426
sgmii	278	1,176	249
leon3	359	5,248	1,768
leon5	3,443	41,661	23,603
noelv	3,020	51,151	27,864

(b)

to validate our proposed approach, we have performed extensive testing on a number of different scenarios which may arise when a search is carried out in large-scale designs. In this section, we evaluate our matching algorithm and present the influence of the ratio variable r.

For our evaluation, we have created 4 designs, with each design including one of the 3 processor cores (LEON3, LEON5, and NOELV) from the Gaisler IP library [6], mapped on two different targets (Arty-A7 and VC707). The targets have a considerable difference in the available logic resources. Each processor has a list of peripherals and embedded cores. We selected 5 of such cores, making a total of 8 cores. It should be noted that the 5 additional cores are part of some/all processor cores and were not simply stitched to the processors by adding pins to the top-level module. Each design was synthesized globally (instead of out-of-context mode) to incorporate cross-boundary optimizations. The selection of cores was made to create multiple search scenarios. For example, i2c is not part of both NOELV designs. Therefore, searching for i2c in NOELV would constitute a test for a false-positive. Similarly, the rationale behind selecting IP cores of different sizes is to carry out searches for a small/large IP in a small/large design.

Table 1a lists all cores and designs, as well as where each core is included. The symbol (X) represents the presence of the respective IP Core in the corresponding design architecture pair. For example, the core jtag is present in all 4 designs but i2c is available only in LEON3 and LEON5. All designs have been synthesised and implemented using Xilinx Vivado 2020.1. The default parameters for the synthesis and implementation have been used. These include optimizations such as LUT combining and shift-register extraction to evaluate our proposed IP identification method under real-word conditions.

The resource utilization and the number of classes of the selected cores differ greatly (see Table 1b) in order to evaluate our algorithm for various scenarios.

In the ideal case, the proposed method would find 100% of all classes if a core is included in the design and 0% if it is not. However, due to optimizations during the implementation and variations in the cores using synthesis time generics, not all classes of a template can be found exactly as often as present in the template. In order to determine if our approach can identify a contained core (true-case) and won't identify one if it's not present (false-case) we use a metric called min_diff. It is the worst-case difference between the true-cases and false-cases for all possible experiments and provides an indication whether our approach is able to find all selected IP Cores without false-positives or false-negatives. min_diff is defined as the difference between all true-case results (T) and all false-case results ($\mathcal{F}$)[3]:

$$T = \{ cov_{t,d} | d \in D, t \in T, \Xi_{t,d} \} \tag{6}$$

$$\mathcal{F} = \{ cov_{t,d} | d \in D, t \in T, \neg\Xi_{t,d} \} \tag{7}$$

$$min\_diff = min(T) - max(\mathcal{F}) \tag{8}$$

with D being the set of designs ($\{LEON5\ VC707, LEON3\ Arty\text{-}A7, ...\}$). and T being the set of templates generated for the IP Cores ($\{$jtag, uart, ...$\}$). To further evaluate the resistance to false-positives, we include additional results. They are obtained by removing the respective IP Core from the design before using the above mentioned algorithm. These results are included in the set $\mathcal{F}$.

Similarly, a second metric called $mean\_diff$ can be calculated as:

$$mean\_diff = mean(T) - mean(\mathcal{F}) \tag{9}$$

It is the average difference between the true-cases and false-cases of the results for all possible experiments and is an indicator of how far apart the result values are on average.

While a positive min_diff value (>0) is critical to be able to use the above mentioned algorithm for IP Core detection, a high $mean\_diff$ allows to infer feasibility of our approach in the average case.

5.1   Revisiting the Ratio Variable

As mentioned earlier, for successful identification of an IP Core the value of r has to be picked carefully. Therefore, it should come as no surprise that both min_diff and $mean\_diff$ are influenced by this variable. Figure 3 illustrates the effect of ratio r on the metrics min_diff and $mean\_diff$.

The value of r determines whether a matched class can be considered as found or not (see Eq. 4). Therefore, for low values of r, the selection criterion is relaxed. As a result, most of the matched classes are classified as found. With this high-level of flexibility, many classes are also included in the list of found classes as false-positives, increasing cov in the case of no IP Core included in the design. This accounts for a lower min_diff and $mean\_diff$. Upon increasing the

---

[3] $\Xi_{t,d}$ is true if the template t of a core is present in the design d.

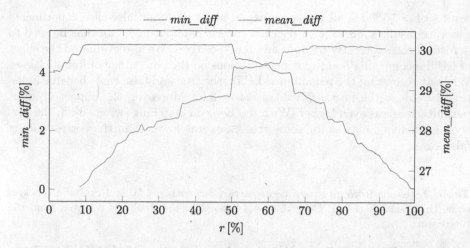

Fig. 3. Influence of *ratio r* on *min_diff* and *mean_diff* over all experiments.

ratio value, the identification algorithm becomes more selective. Consequently, the probability of including false-positives also decreases, which in turn increases *min_diff* and *mean_diff*.

However, a further increase of $r (r > 50\%)$ leads to a decline of *min_diff* due to an increasing selectivity of Eq. (4). This is dominated by small cores such as jtag, i2c, and uart, e.g. jtag has a total of only 34 classes (see Table 1b) of which more and more will be discarded with an increasing r. This has a significant effect on the percentage of classes meeting the ratio criteria. On one hand, a ratio of 100% leads to *min_diff* of almost zero which in turn means the proposed algorithm would not be a good candidate to robustly identify cores. On the other hand, *mean_diff* benefits from higher r values as it eliminates false-positives in the average case. A high difference on average allows to gain confidence in the proposed approach as the difference between when an IP Core is included in the design and when it is not is around 28% points on average. In conclusion, we find $r = 50\%$ to be the best choice as it has the maximum *min_diff* value while providing an elevated *mean_diff* compared to a lower r.

5.2   Experimental Results

As mentioned earlier, we have performed experiments on 8 IP Cores across 4 different designs. Based on the evaluation presented in previous section, the value of the ratio is fixed to $r = 50\%$ for all the experiments. The decision on the presence of a core is made on the basis of the percentage of found classes, which has been calculated using Eq. 5. Table 2 lists the percentages of found classes for all the mentioned experiments. The emboldened values represent the results if the core was present in the design. The values in brackets show the results for the experiments where the core was intentionally removed to test for potential false-positives. As can be seen, our proposed IP identification method generates results of $> 93\%$ for all true-case experiments while all false-case experiments generate results $< 88.23\%$. A decision criteria of about 91% can thus be used to detect all cores correctly without any false-positives. We also evaluated the effect of LUT recombining and input permutations on the percentage of found classes. Without recovering the recombined LUTs, the true and false cases became indistinguishable as the min_diff value fell to -3.62. Moreover, the impact of input permutations was even higher. With the Boolean matching switched-off, the percentage of found classes for some true-cases was lower than the corresponding false-cases.

Table 2. Results from all experiments carried out with $r = 50\%$. Results in brackets show the results if the IP Core that was present in the design is removed from the bitstream.

	LEON5 VC707	LEON3 Arty-A7	NOELV Arty-A7	NOELV VC707
jtag	**97.06** (85.29)	**97.06** (82.35)	**100.00** (88.24)	**100.00** (85.29)
uart	**96.61** (84.75)	**96.61** (79.66)	**98.31** (79.66)	**98.31** (88.14)
i2c	**97.73** (79.55)	**93.18** (75.00)	81.82	77.27
ethc	**97.42** (66.42)	**94.46** (57.56)	**97.42** (66.79)	**97.05** (67.16)
sgmii	**97.84** (80.94)	75.54	79.86	**97.48** (81.29)
leon3	84.96	**96.66** (67.97)	83.29	83.01
leon5	**96.31** (31.16)	31.28	49.67	48.91
noelv	48.71	31.29	**97.25** (30.73)	**95.33** (30.13)

It can be observed that larger cores (i.e. more classes) yield even higher differences in results. This is also true for IP Cores containing more 6-input LUTs. By excluding the relatively smaller cores (jtag, uart, and i2c), the min_diff value increases to 10% and the decision threshold can be increased to 94.46%. Even though the larger IP cores allow for more stable results, the proposed method successfully identified even small cores with only 100 LUTs, or 34 classes, even in larger design.

Among the larger cores, a very interesting case of a potential false-positive was discovered. When searching for LEON3 in LEON5, a high match-rate of 84.96% was observed. LEON3 is the predecessor of LEON5, both are 32-bit processors compliant with the SPARC V8 architecture. LEON5 is backward compatible with LEON3 and therefore inherits a lot of features from LEON3 with some enhancements in the pipeline and cache. All these similarities create a large function overlap which results in a high percentage of matched classes between the two cores. Despite of this overlap, our algorithm can still distinguish betweeen the two cores using a threshold of 91%.

Another interesting search scenario which could result in a potential false-positive, involves the identification of a core when the design includes functionally similar core(s). For this particular scenario, we would like to highlight the uart identification case. All the designs except LEON3 on Arty-A7, have two instances of UART: Console UART and Debug UART [6]. For experimentation, we selected the Console UART. Therefore, the numbers seen for uart in Table 2 are for Console UART. As can be seen, searching for uart in LEON3 Arty-A7, when the core was excluded from the design (value in brackets), resulted in a match rate of 79.66%. Despite the presence of a functionally similar core, our algorithm was able to distinguish between the two uart cores with a high-degree of confidence.

6   Conclusion and Future Work

In this paper, we have presented an approach for the identification of IP Cores using LUT contents. Since the functionality of an FPGA-based design depends on LUT contents, the values are used as a robust signature, which cannot be tampered with. The proposed method searches for the presence of an IP Core by extracting LUT contents from the bitfile and then comparing the obtained values with the INIT values of the functions present in the netlist.

A Boolean matching algorithm addresses the issue of LUT input permutations (resulting from routing optimizations) making this approach scalable for modern LUT6 FPGA devices. The proposed algorithm presents a new *ratio* metric which defines the selectivity level for matched classes. The value of this metric has been determined after comprehensive evaluation and proves to be robust in varying search scenarios. The proposed approach has been validated by performing experimentation with 8 IP Cores in 4 different designs. The conducted experiments involved varying search scenarios depending upon the relative sizes of the searched core and design. Promising results were obtained for all the cores, with all of the true-cases found with a confidence of ($> 93\%$), while all the false-cases stayed below ($< 88.23\%$). Smaller cores such as jtag and uart were also detected with a high-degree of certainty in large designs such as NOELV, which proves the robustness of the proposed algorithm.

A possible future research direction could be the integration of this work with recently proposed machine learning approaches for functional block identification such as [5]. The proposed method in this paper could be used as a fast precheck for the presence of an IP Core and later, functional block identification could be utilized to complement the findings. Furthermore, we would like to explore the locality of the found LUT contents in the bitstream to improve the reliability of the proposed approach.

Acknowledgements. This work has been funded by Thuringian Ministry for Economics, Science and Digital Society, under grant 2021FGI0008. We are indebted to their support.

References

1. Global semiconductor sales increase 6.5% to $439 billion in 2020 (2021). https://www.semiconductors.org/global-semiconductor-sales-increase-6-5-to-439-billion-in-2020/

2. Protecting the FPGA design from common threats. Altera (2009)
3. Bozzoli, L., Sterpone, L.: Comet: a configuration memory tool to analyze, visualize and manipulate FPGAs bitstream. In: ARCS Workshop 2018; 31th International Conference on Architecture of Computing Systems. VDE (2018)
4. Brayton, R., et al.: Berkeley logic synthesis and verification group, ABC: a system for sequential synthesis and verification
5. Chen, M., Liu, P.: A deep learning-based FPGA function block detection method with bitstream to image transformation, vol. 9. IEEE (2021)
6. Cobham Gaisler AB: GRLIB IP core user manual, 2022.1 (2022)
7. Courtland, R.: Transistors will stop shrinking in 2021, Moore's law roadmap - predicts the last itrs report forecasts an end to traditional 2D scaling. IEEE Spectrum (2016)
8. Dauman, A.: An open IP encryption flow permits industry-wide interoperability. In: White Paper. Synopsys, Inc. (2006)
9. Ender, M., Moradi, A., Paar, C.: The unpatchable silicon: a full break of the bitstream encryption of xilinx 7-series {FPGAs}. In: 29th USENIX Security Symposium (USENIX Security 20) (2020)
10. Gupta, R.K., Zorian, Y.: Introducing core-based system design. IEEE Des. Test Comput. **14**(4), 15–25 (1997)
11. Huang, Z., Wang, L., Nasikovskiy, Y., Mishchenko, A.: Fast Boolean matching based on NPN classification. In: 2013 International Conference on Field-Programmable Technology (FPT). IEEE (2013)
12. Kahng, A.B., et al.: Constraint-based watermarking techniques for design IP protection. vol. 20. IEEE (2001)
13. Mahmood, S., Rettkowski, J., Shallufa, A., Hübner, M., Göhringer, D.: IP core identification in FPGA configuration files using machine learning techniques. In: 2019 IEEE 9th International Conference on Consumer Electronics (ICCE-Berlin). IEEE (2019)
14. Moradi, A., Schneider, T.: Improved side-channel analysis attacks on Xilinx bitstream encryption of 5, 6, and 7 series. In: Standaert, F.-X., Oswald, E. (eds.) COSADE 2016. LNCS, vol. 9689, pp. 71–87. Springer, Cham (2016). https://doi.org/10.1007/978-3-319-43283-0_5
15. Pham, K.D., Horta, E., Koch, D.: BITMAN: a tool and API for FPGA bitstream manipulations. In: Design, Automation & Test in Europe Conference & Exhibition (DATE), 2017. IEEE (2017)
16. Schmid, M., Ziener, D., Teich, J.: Netlist-level IP protection by watermarking for LUT-based FPGAs. In: 2008 International Conference on Field-Programmable Technology. IEEE (2008)
17. Tajik, S., Lohrke, H., Seifert, J.P., Boit, C.: On the power of optical contactless probing: attacking bitstream encryption of FPGAs. In: Proceedings of the 2017 ACM SIGSAC Conference on Computer and Communications Security (2017)
18. Tuzov, I.: Dependability-driven strategies to improve the design and verification of safety-critical HDL-based embedded systems. Ph.D. thesis, Universitat Politècnica de València (2020)
19. Tuzov, I., de Andrés, D., Ruiz, J.C.: DAVOS: EDA toolkit for dependability assessment, verification, optimisation and selection of hardware models. In: 2018 48th Annual IEEE/IFIP International Conference on Dependable Systems and Networks (DSN). IEEE (2018)
20. Wilkinson, K.: Using encryption to secure a 7 series FPGA bitstream, technical report. Technical report, Xilinx (2015)

21. Xilinx Inc.: 7 Series FPGAs Configurable Logic Block. UG474 (2017)
22. Xilinx Inc.: Vivado Design Suite TCL Command Reference Guide UG835 (v2019.2) (2019)
23. Yu, Y., Moraitis, M., Dubrova, E.: Can deep learning break a true random number generator? vol. 68. IEEE (2021)
24. Zhou, X., Wang, L., Mishchenko, A.: Fast exact NPN classification by co-designing canonical form and its computation algorithm, vol. 69. IEEE (2020)
25. Ziener, D., Aßmus, S., Teich, J.: Identifying FPGA IP-cores based on lookup table content analysis. In: 2006 International Conference on Field Programmable Logic and Applications. IEEE (2006)
26. Ziener, D., Teich, J.: Power signature watermarking of IP cores for FPGAs. J. Sig. Process. Syst. **51**(1), 123–136 (2008)

Hardware Isolation Support for Low-Cost SoC-FPGAs

Daniele Passaretti[(✉)], Felix Boehm, Martin Wilhelm, and Thilo Pionteck

Institut für Informations- und Kommunikationstechnik, Fakultät für Elektrotechnik und Informationstechnik, Otto-von-Guericke-Universität Magdeburg, Magdeburg, Germany
{daniele.passaretti,felix.boehm,martin.wilhelm,thilo.pionteck}@ovgu.de

Abstract. In the last years, System-on-Chip (SoC)-FPGAs have been widely used in Mixed-Criticality Systems, where multiple applications with different criticality domains are executed. In these systems, it is essential to guarantee isolation between the associated memory regions and peripherals of different application domains. Most high-performance SoC-FPGAs already provide hardware components for supporting isolation. By contrast, low-cost SoC-FPGAs usually don't have any mechanism for guaranteeing isolation. In this paper, we investigate the problem of hardware spatial isolation in low-cost SoC-FPGAs. First, we point out the issues and the limitations given by the fixed components in the Processing System and show how to address them. Second, we propose a Protection Unit, which is a lightweight hardware architecture for AXI communication that ensures memory and peripheral isolation between masters of different protection domains. The proposed architecture can be instantiated either on the master or on the slave side of an AXI interconnection. In addition, it is scalable from 1 to 16 memory regions, and application domains and policies are set up at run-time. We implement our architecture on the SoC-FPGA XC7Z020, where a Microblaze soft-core and the Arm Cortex-A9 are used simultaneously for different application domains. In the proposed implementation, the Protection Unit is implemented in combinatorial logic, and its execution does not contribute to the critical path. Therefore, it adds zero latency for the single communication transaction and uses only 0,5% lookup tables and 0,1% flip-flops of the target SoC-FPGA.

Keywords: Hypervisor · Mixed-criticality systems · Hardware/software co-design · Edge computing · Confidential computing

1 Introduction

With the advent of Industry 4.0 and new computational paradigms, such as Internet-of-Things and Edge Computing, the focus of real-time processing is shifting from the cloud to sensors, creating the demand for small, scalable and energy-efficient processing devices [5, 17]. These challenges are frequently tackled through the utilization of System-on-Chips (SoCs) that integrate a Field Programmable Gate Array (FPGA). In many fields, e.g. driver assistance [7], medical [18,19], railway, or avionic systems, these must adhere to various security and dependability requirements. At the same time, the same component should often be used for the execution of different applications. When multiple tasks of different application domains must coexist in a system, it is essential to guarantee spatial and temporal isolation between them, such that they cannot interfere with each other. This is especially important in Mixed-Criticality Systems (MCS), where tasks with different criticalities are run together in one system [6].

Spatial isolation protects shared peripherals or memory regions so that tasks can access only a part of them freely, or only a subset of existing tasks can access them [22]. Temporal isolation protects shared peripherals or memory regions so that only a subset of tasks can access them in a given time [22].

In a SoC-FPGA, the FPGA is also referred to as the Programmable Logic (PL), whereas the hardwired part, which contains the Application Processing Unit (APU), the fixed communication infrastructure, hardwired peripherals, and all other fixed components, is called the Processing System (PS). For high-performance SoC-FPGAs, vendors usually provide proprietary solutions for the isolation problem as part of the PS [8,15,23] through protection units. In contrast, low-cost SoC-FPGAs, which are mostly used close to sensors for Internet-of-Things applications, do not have such solutions provided for isolation. In addition, they have strict limitations in terms of available resources. Hence, the realization of a robust and flexible isolation mechanism on low-cost SoC-FPGAs is still an open challenge.

Various solutions have been proposed in literature for generic SoC-FPGAs [10,13,14]. While these solutions can be adapted for low-cost systems, most of them use protection units that rely on external memory to implement the mechanisms to check access policies. Due to the resource limitation of low-cost SoC-FPGAs and the usage of external memory, these solutions can lead to resource problems and severe timing issues. In our work, we point out the isolation challenges caused by the PS in modern low-cost FPGAs and propose a new isolation method to resolve these issues.

In our method, we statically associate the masters of the different application domains with one or more protection domains (PDs) and the available memory/peripheral space addresses with memory regions (MRs). Then, at run-time, dynamic access policies (APs) are set in order to spatially and temporally isolate masters associated with different PDs and/or MRs, similar to a white list. With this separation, it is possible to implement the whole decision path for granting AXI transactions completely with combinatorial logic and to guarantee isolation through a lightweight Protection Unit (PU). Using this approach, the proposed PU has an execution time that does not contribute to the critical path and can be added to the system between two AXI-Interfaces without additional latency.

The PU is described in SystemVerilog and is implemented to support up to 16 PDs and 16 MRs per instance. In addition, it is highly flexible in the sense that it can be instantiated in various parts of the communication infrastructure and deployed on any SoC-FPGA where the communication infrastructure uses the

AXI-Interface. This flexibility enables a degree of optimization that is essential for low-cost SoC-FPGAs. We validate the design using a simulation environment together with a test design running on the SoC-FPGA XC7Z020 at an AXI clock speed of 100 MHz.

The rest of the paper is structured as follows: Sect. 2 describes related works from Industry and Academia, and Sect. 3 discusses the isolation limitations in low-cost SoC-FPGAs. Sect. 4 describes the proposed isolation method and the lightweight PU with its micro-architecture, a functional example, and validation. Sec. 5 presents the implementation and integration of the PU in the target low-cost SoC-FPGA. Section 6 discusses the advantages of the proposed method and compares it to related works.

2   Related Work

Supporting isolation is a well know problem in both academia [10,13,14,21] and industry [8,15,20,23]. As mentioned above, most of the proposed methods are designed for high-performance SoC-FPGAs. In this paper, we mainly consider related works, where enough information is given to compare them with our work in terms of functionality and performance.

In industry, one of the most used mechanisms to guarantee isolation in SoC-FPGAs is the Arm TrustZone [20]. It's a system-wide security extension, which provides two execution contexts, *secure* and *non-secure*. Memory regions and peripherals can be configured to allow access to only the secure context. On the downside, the Arm TrustZone considers only two domains and cannot be extended. Furthermore, several vulnerabilities and weaknesses have been investigated in [20], which are the consequence of the lack of robust Trusted Execution Environments (TEE) runtime implementations, and microarchitectural defects.

Due to these limitations, Xilinx proposed two types of protection units for high-performance SoC-FPGAs: the Xilinx Peripheral Protection Unit (XPPU), and the Xilinx Memory Protection Unit (XMPU) [23]. Both protection units are hardwired and implemented in the Processing System (PS) of Ultrascale+ MPSoC chips. They check the master ID and the accessing address for each AXI transaction inside the PS and between PS and PL to guarantee spatial isolation. If the transaction is allowed, then it proceeds normally; otherwise, it's invalidated and won't reach its intended destination. XMPU and XPPU have two different implementations because they are optimized for memory read/write and for device control, respectively. These protection units are not implemented in low-cost SoC-FPGAs.

Sensaoui et al. [21] propose a hardware architecture for isolation in low-cost SoCs, which is for ASIC. It is compatible with RISC-V and Arm CPUs and considers the bus communication between the different masters and memories, for which different policies are defined. The hardware architecture is mainly composed of a master "look-side buffer" and their "uCode" block that implements the logic responsible for checking the communication transactions.

Kumar Saha and Bobda [11] propose a security framework for isolation, which uses Mandatory Access Control (MAC) based authentication policies. It considers a fixed subpart of the device ID and the memory address for defining different application domains and memory regions. This solution can be used to protect the different peripherals in the PL. It consists of software and hardware management modules; therefore, it is suitable only for SoC-FPGAs. The software manages the policy server that is implemented on the PS, and sets up the Hardware IP management module (HIMM). These are implemented on the PL in front of each peripheral (slaves in the communication protocol). This method requires a Linux OS to run the software module, and the policies are read at run-time from the PS. Due to the delay in reading the policies, this solution adds to the transaction a delay of 35 µs if a new entry has to be fetched.

LeMay et al. [14] propose a hardware-based Network-on-Chip Firewall (NoCF) that also uses a software and a hardware module. The software configures NoCF and specifies the policies to enforce isolation between the cores. The policies are maintained by an integrity kernel that runs on a dedicated integrity core which is implemented in hardware. The software module can be controlled by a hypervisor, but the overall NoCF is mainly optimized for NoC communication infrastructure and uses a big amount of FPGA resources, and it is not suitable for Low-Cost SoC-FPGAs in most of the cases.

Kornaros et al. [10] propose a memory partition protection unit that isolates physical memory regions by applying access rules. This unit is implemented in the PL and is set up by a software driver running on the PS. The driver runs on Linux. The Memory Partition Protection Unit (MPPU) supports a maximum of 16 application domains. This solution can also be used for Low-Cost SoC-FPGAs but with a lack of performance, as we will discuss in Sect. 6.

All analyzed works consider different methods for implementing the policy rules and policy checking. Yet, they are not flexible for deploying them in different parts of the system design, e.g., close to the master side or to the slave side. We will compare them with the proposed isolation method and the proposed PU, in Sect. 6.

3   Isolation Limitations in Low-Cost SoC-FPGAs

In this section, we describe the micro-architecture of low-cost SoC-FPGAs, analyze their limitations in terms of spatial isolation, and propose our solution for isolating the peripherals on the PS.

As mentioned in Sect. 1, SoC-FPGAs generally consist of the PS, containing hardwired processing units, input/output peripherals and communication infrastructure, and the PL, comprising programmable look-up tables, memory, and digital signal processing components. To describe the micro-architecture of low-cost SoC-FPGAs, we analyzed the Xilinx Zynq-7000 [3] and Intel Cyclone V SoC [9], which are the low-cost SoC-FPGAs of the two biggest FPGA vendors in the world. As shown in Fig. 1, these two FPGAs have a similar micro-architecture at the system level and use the same PS interconnection core link, which is the Arm NIC-301 [4]. To highlight the similarity between the two chips, we use the AMD-Xilinx nomenclature in Fig. 1, even though AMD-Xilinx and Intel-Altera use different names in their reference manuals.

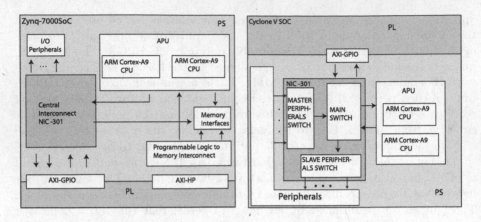

Fig. 1. Micro-architecture of Zynq-7000 SoC and Cyclone V SoC

As shown in Fig. 1, the Application Processing Unit (APU) is connected to the PS peripherals through the NIC-301, and there are no hardware protection mechanisms between them. Hence, malicious applications running on the APU that try to access PS peripherals can not be blocked, and spatial isolation can not be guaranteed. Due to the fact that PS components are dedicated physical components with a fixed implementation, it is not possible to add any protection units between the APU and PS peripherals. As shown by the red arrow in Fig. 2a the APU has direct access to PS peripherals without any checks. For this reason, the PS peripherals usually are exclusively used by the APU, and the connection between PS peripherals and the PL is not initialized. In addition, if a peripheral should be shared between the APU and a PL master (e.g. a Microblaze), it has to be instantiated on the PL where can be protected by a protection unit. This design is shown in Fig. 2a, where $UART_0$ has exclusive access to the APU and $UART_1$ is shared between the APU and the Soft CPU.

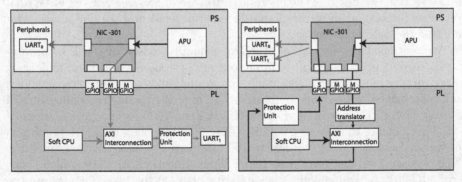

(a) Default communication pattern   (b) Proposed communication pattern

Fig. 2. State-of-the-art and proposed communication pattern between APU, PL and PS peripherals in low-cost SoC-FPGAs

The design solution in Fig. 2a guarantees the isolation of $UART_1$, with the additional cost of implementing the UART peripheral on the PL.

In this work, we propose a communication pattern that allows sharing of PS peripherals between PS and PL masters while guaranteeing their isolation through a protection unit. In the proposed communication pattern, the APU's direct access to PS peripherals over the NIC-301 is disabled. Instead, PS peripherals are mapped into the APU address space in the same way that GPIO peripherals are mapped into the PL address space, as shown in Fig. 2b. By this, the NIC-301 forwards the AXI transactions from the APU to the PL through the PS-to-PL Master interface. The transactions cross the AXI interconnect bus which forwards them to the PS peripheral through the protection unit and the PL-to-PS interface, which is connected to the NiC-301. By sending all transactions between APU and PS peripheral over the PL, we can instantiate a protection unit that guarantees spatial isolation of the PS peripherals and can also be accessed from multiple masters, as shown in Fig. 2b. In this way, we have guaranteed isolation and also reduced the PL resources' utilization.

To correctly forward AXI transactions from APU to PL and back from PL to PS peripherals, the following assumptions must be fulfilled:

- PS peripherals can be accessed with their physical addresses only from the PL. To guarantee that the APU can not access to PS peripherals, they are not enabled in the PS. They are mapped only to the PL GPIO master interface instead.
- The PS peripherals are mapped to the APU as GPIO peripherals. In this way, the GPIO space address represents the virtual address of the PS peripherals, and the NIC-301 will forward all AXI transactions from APU to PL over the PS-to-PL interface.
- The AXI transaction coming from the PS that has the GPIO base address must be translated to the physical address of the PS peripherals and forwarded to the AXI interconnect component. For that, an AXI address translator is required.
- The AXI interconnect, which is connected to the AXI address translator, has to be connected to the PS peripherals through the PS-to-PL GPIO interface. In this way, the transactions can be forwarded to the PS peripherals
- A protection unit has to be instantiated between the AXI Interconnect and the PS-to-PL GPIO interface. In this way, the instantiated protection unit checks all transactions and guarantees isolation of the PS peripherals.

For the best of our knowledge, the proposed communication pattern has not been discussed in other related works that simply assume that PS peripherals are accessible only by the APU. But reserving PS peripherals only for APU accesses can lead to an under-utilization of the PS peripherals and an over-utilization of the PL, where additional peripherals have to be instantiated, instead. In low-cost FPGAs the distribution of resources is essential, therefore this peripheral distribution can limit the overall system design. We tested the utilization of PS peripherals from the PL side with a soft-processor as master and the protection unit without sharing the peripherals with the APU. The details on the proposed isolation method, the protection unit, and its features and configuration will be presented in detail in the following section.

4   Proposed Method

This section clarifies our terminology, presents our proposed method for supporting isolation based on Protection Domains, Memory Regions, and Access Policies, and describes the architecture and validation of the introduced Protection Unit.

In our work, a **Protection Domain** (PD) consists of a set of master components of the same application domain. A master component can be part of multiple PDs at the same time. A PD is defined by a *domain ID* and a *domain mask*. These two parameters are used to derive the association of its master with one or more PDs in the AXI transaction. This is possible because each AXI transaction contains an AXI ID, which is related to the master that generates the transaction.

Table 1. Example of domains and AXI ID relations

	Domain mask	Domain ID	Exemplary IDs
Domain 0	1100	1000	1011, 1000
Domain 1	1110	1000	1000
Domain 2	1110	1010	1011

The matching between an AXI ID and its PDs is done by comparing the bits of the available domain IDs, which are selected by the mask, to the corresponding bits of the transaction's AXI ID. If all of the bits are equal, the transaction belongs to the current PD. Table 1 shows a simple example, where the master ID *1011* is part of the domains 0 and 2. To associate multiple masters with one of the PDs, the designer has to extract the common subpart of the master IDs to determine the domain ID. To make this step easy and to determine a domain ID, when there are no common subparts between different master IDs, we propose an ID-manipulating component, which adds or modifies the AXI-ID. It will be described in Sect. 5. The main advantage of this solution is that its implementation requires only few resources to match the master component ID with the domain IDs at run-time. In particular, it is possible to determine the domain associations of each AXI transaction with simple combinatorial logic.

A **Memory Region** (MR) is an aligned address space. A peripheral and a memory address can be part of multiple MRs, in the same way that masters can be part of multiple PDs. We define a MR by using a starting address and its most significant bits, which contain the addresses of the whole MR. Consequently, a MR always consists of continuous addresses. To optimize the execution time and resource utilization of the MR matching component, we use the position of the Least Significant Bit (LSB) of the MR as a parameter. The LSB position determines the size of the memory region that is equal to $2^{LSB\ pos.}$. By using it as a parameter, the PU has to check only the range of bits between the MSB and the LSB per input address. An example of MR matching is given in Sect. 4.1.

An **Access Policy** (AP) describes which protection domain may access which memory region, i.e., it consists of a set of "PD_X may read/write MR_Y" rules. A transaction may pass if any of these rules gives it permission to do so. If there is no rule for a master because it is not associated with any PD or MR, all its requests will be denied. In this work, each protection unit has their own dedicated APs for read and write access.

PDs, MRs and their parameters are set at design time, while APs are defined at run-time. In this way, it is possible to optimize each PU instance at synthesis time and implement the whole decision path as a fixed combinatorial logic component, where the input is the AXI-transaction and the rules of the AP. Only the APs are set at run-time; otherwise, temporal isolation can not be guaranteed.

4.1 Protection Unit Architecture

The Protection Unit (PU) restricts traffic through an AXI connection based on the given policy. An overview of the architecture is shown in Fig. 3. A PU has three AXI instances. The two red interfaces are complementary, pass-through, full AXI interfaces and identically parameterized. These are transparent for all allowed transactions. The orange AXI-Lite interface provides access to status, control, and policy configuration registers.

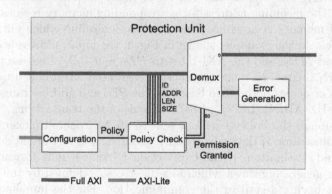

Fig. 3. Architecture of the protection unit

The APs are stored in a configuration module in the PU. Each PU contains its own APs, one for reading and one for writing transactions. This module forwards the policies as signals to the Policy Check module that is the core of the PU. In this way, every clock cycle, all current APs are read from the Policy Check. This last component is responsible for matching the master ID (AXI-ID)

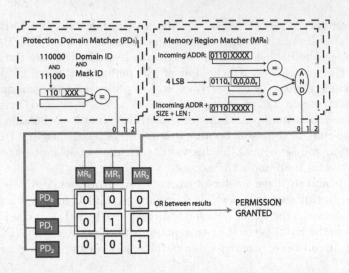

Fig. 4. Policy check functionality

and the incoming memory address with the PDs and the MRs available. Then it checks the defined policy and the signal's permission to read/write. In each PU, there are two instances of the Policy Check module, one for the read channel and the other for the write channel.

As shown in Fig. 4, the Policy Check contains PD matching and MR matching components. These two components are instantiated once for each PD and MR, respectively. They check the AXI ID of the transaction for corresponding domains and the incoming address for corresponding memory regions. Matched domains and memory regions are then used to determine which entries in the policy to check. In the example, shown in Fig. 4, the input address is associated with MR_0 and MR_1, and the AXI-ID with PD_0 and PD_1. Because the AP for PD_1 and MR_1 is equal to 1, the transaction is granted. To sum it up, the Policy Check grants or denies permission based on the PDs and address ranges, current APs and the ID, ADDR, LEN and SIZE signals of the transactions.

The decision of the Policy Check is sent to an AXI demultiplexer which forwards the transaction. If the transaction is granted, it is forwarded downstream to its intended destination. If the transaction is denied, it is forwarded to an internal error-generating slave, which asserts errors as defined by the AXI standard without having a stall in the communication. For the implementation of the prototype, both the AXI demultiplexer and the error generator are taken from the PULP-platform AXI library [12].

4.2 Example

Here, we describe a concrete example of an Access Policy to give a better idea of what they look like and how a decision is inferred. For simplicity, a system with two masters, two slaves, and a single PU is considered.

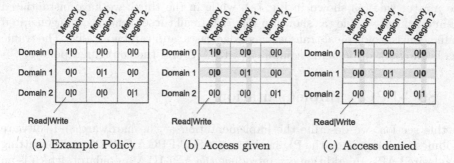

(a) Example Policy   (b) Access given   (c) Access denied

Fig. 5. Exemplary policy configuration and decision

The first master is included in the PD_1 and the second one in the PD_2. PD_0 includes both. Analogously, the first slave is associated with MR_1, the second one with MR_2, and both are part of MR_0. For access to slaves, masters must be included in PDs, and slaves must associate their memory space address to MRs. These parameters have to be set before synthesis. During run-time, read access is given to PD_0 for the MR_0, in this way both masters can read from to both slaves. Instead, write access is given to PD_1 for the MR_1 and PD_2 for the MR_2. This results in the APs shown in Fig. 5a.

If the first master tries to write on the first slave, PD_0 and PD_1 are matched as well as MR_0 and MR_1 are matched as shown by green boxes in Fig. 5b. The matched PDs and MRs represent the eligible PDs and MRs that are considered for making the decision. These entries are marked red in Fig. 5b. In this specific case, the access is given because the policy states that PD_1 has write access to MR_1, indicated by the red 1. If the first master tries to obtain write access on the second slave, MR_0 and MR_2 are matched instead of MR_0 and MR_1, as shown in Fig. 5c, but in the AP there is no value equal to 1, so the access is denied. No access is given if none of the rules in the policy allows it.

4.3   Validation

Before integrating the PU with a running design, it has been tested in simulation, using Xilinx Vivado 2020.2 and the AXI Verification IP (VIP) [2]. The VIP is used for generating traffic on master and slave sides as well as for checking the AXI protocol compliance.

Three scenarios have been considered. In the first one, two masters, one PU, and one slave have been instantiated. The first master has been used for the run-time configuration of the PU, and the other master communicates to the slave through the PU itself. In this way, we have tested the correct functionality of the PU, when correct and illegal transactions are generated from the master to the slave. In the other two cases, we increase the masters, the PUs, and the slave to validate the behavior of the system when multiple requests arrive from different masters. In the second configuration, we have instantiated the PU on the master side (as shown in Fig. 7a), while in the third, we have instantiated them on the slave side (as shown in Fig. 7b). In all these scenarios, the generated traffic consists of typical transactions, edge cases, and random traffic. The traffic has been checked for being compliant with AXI and the configured policy.

5   SoC-FPGA Implementation

In this section, we describe the implementation of the hardware and software modules for integrating the PU in the target SoC-FPGA C7Z020 and for setting the desired APs. In addition, we introduce the AXI-ID Manipulator, which is an additional hardware component required for supporting masters/slaves that do not have defined AXI-IDs.

The PU and the AXI-ID Manipulator, as well as the internal modules, which are taken from the PULP-platform AXI library [12] are implemented in SystemVerilog. To simplify the integration of these components in a system design, we pack them as IP Core modules compatible with any Xilinx FPGAs of the 7 series family [1]. The designer can add them to the IP repository and instantiate them either in HDL entities or into a block design. As explained in Sect. 4, each PU has an AXI-Lite interface used for setting up the policies. In the system design, the AXI-Lite interface of all PUs is connected to a dedicated control bus as a slave peripheral. The master that starts up the whole system (setting up the PS and programming the PL) and manages the temporal domains at run-time is the only master which is physically connected to this control bus.

For evaluating the PU, we implemented the use case shown in Fig. 7a, which resulted in the block design shown in Fig. 6. This block design has two masters: the Cortex-A9 and a Microblaze. The Cortex-A9 is the APU of the target SoC-FPGA, and the Microblaze is a soft processor, which is instantiated in the PL. In addition, two slaves in the PL are instantiated, and the Microblaze can also access the slaves that are on the PS part. For this design, where there are two masters and multiple slaves, we instantiate the PUs on the master side. By this,

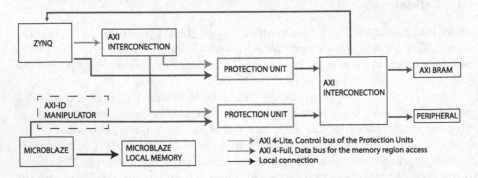

Fig. 6. Implemented system design. Two Protection Units on the master side. The AXI-ID Manipulator is not required with Microblaze, but is inserted for demonstration purpose.

we only require two PUs, as shown in Fig. 6; other possible configurations are explained in Sect. 6.

In our design, the APU is responsible for starting up the system. When the FPGA is turned on, the Cortex-A9 runs the First Stage Boot Loader (FSBL), a bare-metal program responsible for loading the bitstream from memory and programming the PL. When the PL is running, the FSBL program sets up the PUs and runs the APU and Microblaze applications. It is essential that the PUs are set up before any other applications. By this, the applications can run either as bare-metal source code or through an operating system, and the PU is set up in a secure way. In order to provide temporal isolation, the APs have to be properly updated at run-time with the support of a hypervisor. In addition, to guarantee the security of the PUs and of the whole system, the FSBL should be run with a secure boot, or the PUs should be set with the support of a hypervisor. In this paper, we focus on the proposed isolation methodology and the PUs, therefore we do not explain all security aspects that involve the whole system.

During the implementation, the designer should know all AXI-IDs of masters and slaves. If an AXI-ID is not provided, or a master/slave has no AXI-ID, the designer can use the AXI-Manipulator between the master/slave module and the AXI interconnection bus as shown in Fig. 6. The AXI-ID Manipulator adds or overwrites specific bits of the AXI-ID for the AXI requests and restores the old AXI-ID for the related responses. This component is essential for defining the various AXI-IDs used for recognizing the different PD.

6   Results and Discussion

In this section, we report and discuss the results of our work. We consider various implications related to the deployment step. In addition, we analyze the results of the testing design and different PU configurations used for comparing our work with the related works. In the end, we point out possible improvements and potential future works.

The proposed isolation method aims for low-cost SoC-FPGAs, so it has been conceived to be flexible and lightweight. The presented PU can be deployed on every SoC-FPGA that uses AXI as communicating interface protocol. As shown in Fig. 7, it can be instantiated on the master side, slave side, and between two AXI interconnects. This allows the PUs to be deployed at the points in the system where they are most effective. These points may differ between different systems.

A system design, where masters are much more than slaves can save resources if the PUs are deployed on the slave side, or the other way around. When the PU is instantiated on the master side, it manages only the transaction coming from this master component; in this case (shown in Fig. 7a), each master component has its PU, where only the MRs have to be checked. This configuration can also have the advantage of blocking unwanted transactions before they could cause contention in the downstream interconnect.

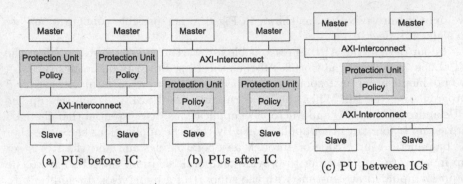

(a) PUs before IC   (b) PUs after IC   (c) PU between ICs

Fig. 7. Exemplary deployment of protection units

In contrast, if the PU is instantiated on the slave side, each slave has its own PU, which is only responsible for the MRs of the related slave. The last configuration is shown in Fig. 7c, where there is only one PU. In this case, two interconnect busses are used, where the first groups all master connections and the second groups all slave connections. In this case, all PDs and MRs are managed by a single PU. This solution can be advantageous when there is a similar number of masters and slaves in the system and they are few, because it will use less resources than using multiple PUs.

To analyze the performance of our PU, we have implemented it with Vivado 2020.2 on the target SoC-FPGA XC7Z020 using different configurations. First, we run it in the test design shown in Fig. 6. In this design, we use two PUs and we set the AXI Clock to a frequency of 100 MHz. Each PU has one PD and two MRs.

Table 2. Resource utilization for the test design

	LUTs	FFs	LUTRAM	Block	DSP
PU: axi demux	53	22	0	0	0
PU: configuration block	58	109	0	0	0
PU: policy check write	35	0	0	0	0
PU: policy check read	34	0	0	0	0
PU: axi error	22	15	0	0	0
PU Microblaze	202	146	0	0	0
Test Design	4470	4449	299	3	3

As shown in Table 2, the PU in front of the Microblaze uses only 202 LUTs and 146 FFs. In fact, in relation to the resource utilization of the test design, it uses only 4.51% of the LUTs and 3.28% of the FFs. Also, in relation to the available resources of the target FPGA, it uses only 0.37% of LUTs and 0.13%

of FFs. This low utilization of resources is essential for low-cost SoC-FPGAs
with limited resources. Table 2 also shows the resources used by the internal
components. As expected, the policy check components do not use any FFs,
because it has been designed with combinatorial logic in the Register-Transfer
Level (RTL). This is an important result because this component determines the
decision path and the delay of the granted transaction, which is combinatorial
and does not contribute to the critical clock path. Since we set the clock frequency at 100 MHz, it means that the PU processes a single transaction in less
than 10 ns. Most of the FFs are used in the configuration block that contains
the control/status register and APs of the PU.

Table 3. Resources' utilization and execution time (c.c. means clock's cycle)

Work	LUTs	FFs	LUTRAMs	Execution time
PU, 1PD/16MR	339	198	0	<10 ns (<1 c.c.)
PU, 16PD/1MR	191	198	0	<10 ns (<1 c.c.)
PU, 16PD/16MR	950	678	0	<10 ns (<1 c.c.)
PU, 1PD/1MR	164	168	0	<10 ns (< 1 c.c.)
MPPU [10]	655	1082	12	(4 c.c) only the decision
HIMM [11]	86	75	6	220–35000 ns

In Table 3 we compare the resource utilization of our PU to the MPPU of
Kornaros et al. [10] and the Hardware IP management module (HIMM) of Kumar
Saha and Bobda [11].

Our PU's resource usage is listed for different numbers of PDs and MRs. Since
the resource usage is optimized at design time based on the set parameters, we
can see how the PU scales by changing the number of PDs and MRs. The MPPU
has similar functionality as the PU with 1PD/16MR configuration as it is also
able to differentiate 16 memory regions. Because we define PDs and MRs at
design time and implement the policy check only with LUTs, we reached better
performance in terms of resource optimization and execution time. The HIMM
has similar functionality to the 16PD/1MR configuration as they protect a single
slave by 16 different application contexts (application contexts have the same
functionality as our PDs). They use less resources as most of their processing is
done outside the HIMM. They manage and store the policy in the PS and hold
local copies in the HIMM. If a rule is not present locally, it has to be fetched
first leading to delays of up to 35000 ns.

In the future, additional optimization can be done by substituting the library
components with specialized components that are optimized for the PU. In addition, this PU can be used as a foundation to integrate a basic hypervisor in the
SoC-FPGA that will manage the temporal isolation properly. Finally, the combinatorial path of the PU can be pipelined in the case that it can not be executed
in one clock cycle on a given target FPGA.

7 Conclusion

In this work, we have analyzed the isolation limitations of low-cost SoC-FPGAs and we have proposed an isolation method that results in a lightweight Protection Unit that uses combinatorial logic for the decision path. We also implemented and integrated the PU in a test design, where we confirmed that a single transaction is processed with no additional latency. The key to this result is that the decision path is combinatorial, so no FFs are used in the policy check and it does not contribute to the critical path of the system design. Compared to the state of the art, where external memory is the bottleneck, the presented isolation method and the PU implementation result in a much faster execution. In addition, its deployment flexibility, configurability and scalability makes it especially well-suited for the integration with low-cost SoC-FPGAs. The presented Protection Unit can be found as SystemVerilog component and/or IP Core block on our website [16].

References

1. AMD-Xilinx: 7 Series FPGAs Data Sheet: Overview (DS180)
2. AMD-Xilinx: AXI Verification IP LogiCORE IP Product Guide (PG267)
3. AMD-Xilinx: Zynq-7000 SoC Technical Reference Manual (UG585)
4. ARM: CoreLink Network Interconnect NIC-301 Technical Reference Manual
5. De Donno, M., Tange, K., Dragoni, N.: Foundations and evolution of modern computing paradigms: Cloud, iot, edge, and fog. IEEE Access (2019)
6. Gracioli, G., et al.: Designing mixed criticality applications on modern heterogeneous mpsoc platforms. In: ECRTS 2019 (2019)
7. Hassan, M.: Heterogeneous mpsocs for mixed-criticality systems: challenges and opportunities. IEEE Design Test **35**(4), 47–55 (2018). https://doi.org/10.1109/MDAT.2017.2771447
8. Intel: External Memory Interface Handbook Volume 3: Reference Material. https://www.intel.com/content/www/us/en/docs/programmable/683841/17-0/memory-protection.html. Accessed 13 July 2022
9. Intel-Altera: Cyclone V Hard Processor System Technical Reference Manual
10. Kornaros, G., et al.: Hardware support for cost-effective system-level protection in multi-core socs. In: 2015 Euromicro Conference on Digital System Design (2015)
11. Kumar Saha, S., Bobda, C.: FPGA accelerated embedded system security through hardware isolation. In: 2020 Asian Hardware Oriented Security and Trust Symposium (AsianHOST), pp. 1–6 (2020)
12. Kurth, A., Cavalcante, M., Zaruba, F.: PULP platform. https://github.com/pulp-platform/axi (2022)
13. Kurth, A., et al.: An open-source platform for high-performance non-coherent on-chip communication. IEEE Trans. Comput. **71**(8), 1794–1809 (2022)
14. LeMay, M., Gunter, C.A.: Network-on-chip firewall: countering defective and malicious system-on-chip hardware. In: Martí-Oliet, N., Ölveczky, P.C., Talcott, C. (eds.) Logic, Rewriting, and Concurrency. LNCS, vol. 9200, pp. 404–426. Springer, Cham (2015). https://doi.org/10.1007/978-3-319-23165-5_19
15. Microchip: Polarfireŏ soc mss technical reference manual

16. Passaretti, D., Böhm, F., Pionteck, T.: Isolation-support for low-cost soc-fpgas. https://github.com/pasdani/Isolation-Support-for-Low-Cost-SoC-FPGAs
17. Passaretti, D., Ghosh, M., Abdurahman, S., Egito, M.L., Pionteck, T.: Hardware optimizations of the x-ray pre-processing for interventional computed tomography using the FPGA. Appl. Sci. **12**(11), 5659 (2022)
18. Passaretti, D., Pionteck, T.: Configurable pipelined datapath for data acquisition in interventional computed tomography. In: 2021 IEEE 29th Annual International Symposium on Field-Programmable Custom Computing Machines (FCCM)
19. Passaretti, D., Pionteck, T.: Hardware/software co-design of a control and data acquisition system for computed tomography. In: 2020 9th International Conference on Modern Circuits and Systems Technologies (MOCAST), pp. 1–4 (2020). https://doi.org/10.1109/MOCAST49295.2020.9200273
20. Pinto, S., Santos, N.: Demystifying arm trustzone: a comprehensive survey. ACM Comput. Surv. **51**(6), 1–36 (2019)
21. Sensaoui, A., Hely, D., et al.: Toubkal: a flexible and efficient hardware isolation module for secure lightweight devices. In: 2019 15th European Dependable Computing Conference (EDCC), pp. 31–38. IEEE (2019)
22. Valente, G., Giammatteo, P., Muttillo, V., Pomante, L., Di Mascio, T.: A lightweight, hardware-based support for isolation in mixed-criticality network-on-chip architectures. ASTES (2019)
23. Xilinx Inc: Isolation methods in zynq ultrascale+ mpsocs application note

Reliable and Fault-Tolerant Systems

Memristor Based FPGAs: Understanding the Effect of Configuration Memory Faults

Tobias Schwarz[✉][iD] and Christian Hochberger[iD]

Computer Systems Group, Technische Universität Darmstadt,
Merckstr. 25, 64283 Darmstadt, Germany
{schladt,hochberger}@rs.tu-darmstadt.de

Abstract. Memristors are receiving a growing attention for many different application areas in computer engineering. Besides replacement for main memory and storage class memory they can also be used as configuration memory in FPGAs. Unfortunately, memristors will not be 100% defect free. This paper first categorizes the different types of errors that memristors can exhibit. Then it is shown how configuration memory can be built in FPGAs using memristors. Using these defect types and configuration memory implementations, the influence of these defects on the operation of FPGAs is analyzed. We carry out this novel analysis with respect to logic implementation and with respect to the routing architecture. It turns out that the respective choices of current FPGAs are not well suited for memristor based configuration memory since even 1% defect rate among the memristors prevents successful implementation of any of our benchmarks.

Keywords: Memristor · Configuration memory · FPGA · Defect Rate

1 Introduction

Over the last decade memory technology has evolved dramatically. Particularly, memristors are causing a lot of attraction. Besides main memory or storage class memory, memristors can also be used as configuration memory for FPGAs. This approach has multiple benefits. 1) The configuration is non volatile, such that after powering on the FPGA it can immediately start to work. 2) Typical memristors are built on top of the active CMOS area in $2\frac{1}{2}$ or 3D structure as back end of line (BEOL) process. As configuration storage consumes the biggest share of chip area such 3D structures will save considerably chip area and thus will reduce the cost for FPGAs dramatically.

Unfortunately, producing memristors is not as reliable as producing CMOS transistors. Thus, defects in the configuration memory are to be expected if they are used in FPGAs. As current architecture of FPGAs was developed with the assumption of a 100% defect free configuration memory it is unclear how good the current architecture works with memristors.

M. Schulz et al. (Eds.): ARCS 2022, LNCS 13642, pp. 167–180, 2022.
https://doi.org/10.1007/978-3-031-21867-5_11

In this paper, the effects of defects in the configuration memory are investigated. To this end, we first give an overview of circuit architectures used to store the configuration and then categorize the different types of defects that can appear in these use cases. Based on this categorization it is analyzed how many defects can be tolerated in the logic realization with look-up tables (LUTs) and how defects influence the routing abilities of FPGAs. This is a new point of view.

The remainder of this contribution is structured like follows: Sect. 2 discusses related work, explains memristor defects and how memristors can be turned into configuration memory. Additionally, it gives an overview of an open source FPGA tool flow. Section 3 discusses the impact of defects on LUT realizations and shows some experimental results for different defect rates. It is followed by a discussion of effects of defects in the routing in Sect. 4. Here, also the experimental setup and analysis of how many defects can be tolerated with current routing architectures are described. Finally, in Sect. 5 we give a conclusion and an outline which further steps have to be taken to make memristors a better choice for configuration memory.

2   Technical Background

2.1   Related Work

The impact of single event upsets (SEUs) in configuration memory cells of FPGAs has been examined in [8]. The effects of these errors are similar to the ones assumed in this work except the fact that SEUs occur spontaneously during up-time. They do not lead to an undefined state of memory cells and thus do not cause uncontrolled switches in SRAM based FPGAs. It has been shown that especially SEUs in the routing network impact the performance of FPGAs. Nonetheless, the work is limited by a missing in-depth examination of error modes of routing multiplexers which are rather only examined on the logical level.

The sensitivity of routing multiplexers used in commercial FPGAs has been examined with respect to SEUs in [2]. The findings show that current routing element architecture is highly sensitive to configuration errors due to error propagation through shorted paths and failure of connections due to open paths.

A mapping approach similar to the one used by us to evaluate the effect of defects in logic elements in Chap. 3 is presented in [14]. In this work, Stuck-At-0 and Stuck-At-1 errors occurring in LUTs based on carbon nanotube switches are mitigated by adapting the input order and output polarity of the mapped functions.

2.2   Memristor Types and Typical Defects

Memristors can be built using different effects and materials. Currently, two memristor types receive the widest attention: resistive RAM (RRAM) and spin-transfer-torque MRAM (STT-MRAM). In RRAM an insulator is placed between two metal contacts. Through applying a forming voltage a filament can be created between the two contacts. This filament can be changed by applying programming current to it. Thus it will change its resistance. In this work, typically only two states are used: the high resistive state (HRS) and the low resistive state (LRS). Depending on the material used as contact and insulator very different ranges exist for HRS and LRS. AlO_2 based memristors can reach HRS of $G\Omega$ and LRS values of $M\Omega$. $Hf0_x$ based memristors achieve HRS values of $100\,K\Omega$ and LRS values of 1–$10\,K\Omega$.

Defects can occur during the forming. Then, the memristor can be in an unknown state with resistance even lower than LRS or higher than HRS. Defects can also be caused during programming again with an unknown resulting resistance. A discussion of defect densities and types can be found in [4,6]. Here, a fault rate of up to 17% has been measured for an RRAM-Array.

STT-MRAM uses a magnetic tunnel junction. It is placed between to magnetized layers. One layer has a permanent orientation of the magnetic field whereas the other layer can be changed. Depending on this second layer the resistance changes. LRS values of 1–$10\,K\Omega$ can be achieved and HRS values are 2 to 3 times higher. In STT-MRAM defects can be caused by contact problems during manufacturing causing either a short circuit at the tunnel junction or an open contact leading to very high resistance values. Additionally, the free magnetic layer can be stuck at one orientation and a write current would be needed to change the orientation which exceeds the on-chip drivers capabilities. Thus, such a memristor would be permanently in the HRS or LRS. A more thorough discussion of these defects can be found in [11,16].

Given the high expected endurance of RRAM and STT-MRAM [18] compared to other non volatile memory technologies it is unlikely that defects appear after manufacturing during the lifetime of a device. It is therefore probably not necessary to continuously monitor cells. For the further discussion of defects in this paper a more abstract view of defects is used. They are categorized as

S@L Stuck at LRS. This refers to the case where the memristor permanently stays in the LRS.
S@H Stuck at HRS. Here, the memristor permanently stays in the HRS.
S@U Stuck at unknown. In this case, the memristor remains in any possible state and does not change its value.

In all three cases it is assumed that the state of the memristor cannot be changed.

2.3   Configuration Memory with Memristors

Memristors can be used in different ways to implement configuration memory. Common for all these ways is the fact that memristors are used in a voltage divider to detect the state of the memristor.

1T2R Cell. In this configuration two memristors are connected in series and the supply voltage is applied. The voltage at the middle contact now depends on the resistances of both memristors. Only two constellations are useful where both memristors are in opposite state. Now the voltage is close to VDD or GND. In this application the HRS value should be very high to minimize the quiescent current. The transistor is needed to program the memristors (Fig. 1a).

1T1R Cell. In LUTs, where only one out of many bits needs to be read, either the pull-up or pull-down path of the different configuration bits can be unified as shown in Fig. 1c. All memristors are connected to GND on one side while the other side is connected to a multiplexer tree. At the output of the multiplexer tree a sense amplifier including the pull-up evaluates the resistance state of the chosen memristor. This way, the quiescent current only flows through one out of 2^n memristors. Thus, also SOT-MRAM memristors can be used in this circuit variant. Again, the transistor is needed to apply the programming voltage to the memristor.

2T2R Cell. Sometimes in literature also a 2T2R cell is referenced (Fig. 1b). It should be noted that it is very similar to the 1T2R cell. The additional transistor is controlled by the stored value and basically operates as a programmable switch. Thus, this type of cell typically appears in the routing architecture.

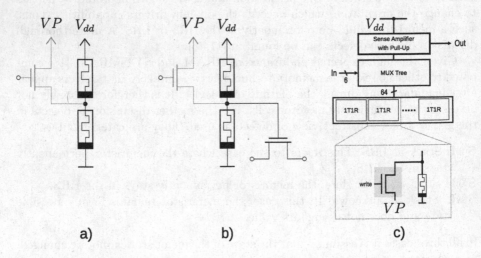

Fig. 1. Usage of memristors in memory cells *a)* 1T2R cell *b)* 2T2R cell *c)* LUT architecture based on 1T1R cells (on the basis of [12])

Cell Defects. Defect memristors translate to defects on the cell level. For example, if the memristor in the pull-up path of a 1T2R cell exhibits a S@H behavior the cell can only be programmed to contain a logical 0 by setting the pull-down memristor to LRS. Thus, the effect is that of a Stuck-At-0 (S@0) error of the cell. The same holds if the pull-down memristor exhibits a S@L behavior. In the reversed case, i.e. if the pull-up memristor exhibits a S@L and/or the pull-down memristor exhibits a S@H the cell is fixed to a logical 1 (S@1). If at least one of the memristors exhibits a S@U behavior or both memristors feature a Stuck-At-fault of the same type the cell features an undefined logic state (S@U).

2.4   Tool Flow of VTR

To evaluate the impact of defect configuration memory cells on the synthesis process for FPGAs, the tool flow of Verilog-to-Routing (VTR) [13] is modified. VTR uses Odin II to parse HDL input and generate a BLIF netlist which is then mapped by ABC to LUTs of the size given by the device description. The following steps of packing, placement and routing are especially relevant for the integration of defect handling, all of which are carried out by VPR (Versatile Place and Route). VPR uses the AAPack algorithm [9] to create clusters of LUTs of size corresponding to the logic block architecture of the given device. To this end, AAPack utilizes an affinity metric for functions to leverage the intra-block routing. In the placement phase VPR positions the packed clusters on logic blocks of the device with the well known Simulated Annealing (SA) [1] heuristic optimization scheme. First, a valid initial solution is generated by mapping each cluster on a fitting logic block. Then, positions of clusters are swapped iteratively, representing a new solution to the placement problem. Each solution is then scored by a heuristic routing cost metric and accepted based on SA's acceptance probability. In the routing phase an initial and potentially invalid solution is generated by a Breadth First Search that is allowed to overuse routing channels. The overusage is then iteratively eliminated by the PathFinder routing algorithm [10].

3   Lookup Tables

First, the effect of defect configuration memory cells of LUTs, the main logic elements of FPGAs is investigated. After examining the effects on a LUT local level a modified tool flow for VPR to map designs on faulty devices is presented. By this, the impact of defect memory cells of LUTs on the synthesis process for FPGAs is evaluated.

3.1   Impact of Memory Defects

For a single LUT the effect of a defect configuration memory cell depends strongly on its precise error characteristic. If a cell features an S@U the undefined logic state would be propagated to the output of the LUT, leading to an undefined behavior of the whole circuit. To avoid this, the input combination leading to the output of the corresponding erroneous value may not be reached. This can be achieved by deactivating one input signal by tying it to a constant value and thus deactivating half of the LUT. S@0 and S@1 errors on the other hand are not necessarily as impactful. In this case, affected cells represent valid logic values. That enables the usage of configuration level techniques such as mapping functions on affected LUTs that match the value of the fixed valued cells for the given input combination. Furthermore, a match at the corresponding positions may be established by permuting the input signals of the LUT in a proper way.

3.2 Modified Tool Flow

As VPR does not natively support the consideration of defect memory cells in its flow it is first necessary to define the errors existing in a device. To this end, the number and size of LUTs present in a device from VTR's architecture description are read and a supplementary file containing the error type of each memory cell of every LUT is generated. The errors themselves are distributed randomly according to a given error rate.

We integrated the consideration of defect cells into VPR's SA placement process. Note that technology mapping and placement do not represent strictly separate phases of the synthesis process anymore as soon as erroneous logic blocks are considered. This is because configurable elements with defects do not represent a library of uniform, but instead of individual technological elements. By considering faulty elements the placement process also becomes part of the technology mapping process. The core of the modification represents the compatibility check of clusters of functions and logic blocks of the device. First, the compatibility of every function of a cluster with every LUT inside a logic block is checked. This is done by first naively checking whether there are any defects in the LUT that prevent it from implementing the function. This is always the case for S@U errors unless the function features less inputs than the LUT and it is possible to mask the errors by omitting specific inputs of the LUT. The same holds for Stuck-At errors of wrong polarity, i.e. a S@1 where the function requires a Boolean 0 and a S@0 where the function requires a Boolean 1, respectively. If the naive check fails, the inputs of the function are permuted heuristically to find a possible permutation where the errors of the LUT match the required values of the function. After performing this check for all functions in the cluster it is known which function is compatible to which LUT. A greedy approach is then applied to find a compatible mapping of functions to LUTs of the logic block. This is done by mapping the functions one after another starting with the function that is compatible to the least LUTs. Finally, the check is integrated into VPR's SA placer. In every iteration of the scheme a mapping of a cluster on a specific logic element is swapped with another randomly chosen cluster. Thus, it has to be checked whether both clusters to be swapped are compatible with the logic block at their corresponding destinations. Due to the stochastic nature of the SA process it is possible that checks for the same elements are repeatedly carried out during the placement. To avoid the repetition of the associated calculations the compatibility information is stored in a buffer which is first queried.

3.3   Experimental Setup

We compiled a set of 35 benchmark designs, 25 of which are taken from the MCNC20 benchmark suite covering the complete range of sizes available in this suite. The other 10 designs are taken from VPR's set of benchmark designs. All tests have been carried out with the same device containing logic blocks with four LUTs each and a grid size of 48 * 50. This size has been chosen to reach a device utilization of 95 % with the biggest design in the set. Cell-error distributions for the device ranging from 1 % to 10 % in steps of 1 % where then generated assuming an equal ratio of S@0, S@1 and S@U faults. Finally, we ran the modified flow of VTR with all designs.

3.4   Experimental Results

While at an error rate of 1 % still 34 of 35 designs could be mapped on the device, at 10 % only 1 design could be mapped naively, i.e. without permuting the inputs of LUTs (see Fig. 2). With the permutation heuristic this number rises to 7 designs.

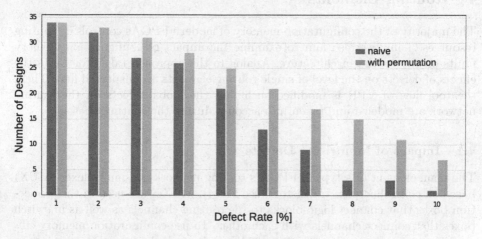

Fig. 2. Number of the 35 benchmark designs implementable with rising defect rate naively and with permutation of LUT inputs.

Figure 3 shows the maximum error ratio up to which designs could be mapped with respect to their device utilization. Accordingly, designs that feature a lower utilization tolerate more defects on the device, while designs in the range of 80 % – 90 % utilization only tolerate a defect rate of maximally 2 %. Additionally, we measured the impact of the defect rate on the timing of the mapped designs. For an error rate of 1 % a mean timing degradation of approx. 2 % has been measured, while the observed worst case is a degradation of 15 % at an error rate of 9 %.

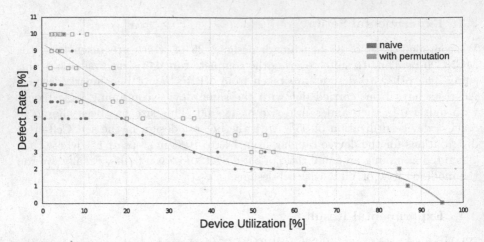

Fig. 3. Highest defect rate for which every benchmark design was implementable with respect to the device utilization. Additionally, a polynomial interpolation is shown.

4   Routing Elements

The majority of the configuration memory of modern FPGAs controls its routing resources. Thus, we also aim to examine the impact of configuration memory faults on the routing architecture. Analog to the approach taken for LUTs the effects of defects on the level of single routing elements are inspected first. Then, the tool flow of VPR is modified such that the global effects on the routing network are modeled and taken into account during the routing phase.

4.1   Impact of Memristor Defects

The main element of a typical FPGA's routing network is a multiplexer (MUX) based on controlled pass transistors (see Fig. 4). MUXes are used in the connection boxes that connect logic blocks to the routing channels as well as in switch boxes that connect channels with each other. To use configuration memory efficiently a two stage implementation of MUXes is applied where the second stage selects a block of input signals and the first stage selects a specific input signal in every block.

Based on the architecture shown in Fig. 4 it is possible to examine the effects of different types of memory errors on the MUX as a whole. If any of the two memory cells controlling the transistors on a path from input to output exhibits a S@0 error the path is not usable anymore, as at least one of the transistors is always switched off. Nonetheless, this type of defect does not influence other paths of the MUX. If there is a single S@1 defect present in the MUX the set of routable input signals is reduced, as either one signal of every block or one block of signals is hardwired to the output. Multiple S@1 defect can lead to shorted signals or one hardwired path from input to output based on their distribution.

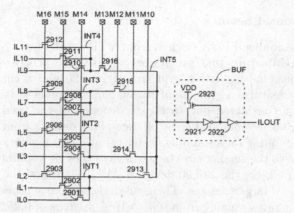

Fig. 4. Assumed two stage architecture of routing MUXes [17]

S@U defects always render the whole MUX defective as the signal propagation characteristic of an affected transistor is also undefined. These error phenomena would also be present if memristors were not used in memory cells controlling a transistor, but directly in-path as a switch.

4.2   Modified Tool Flow

To evaluate the global effects of cell errors on the routing network the tool flow of VPR is modified. VPR uses a routing resource graph that contains all point-to-point connections of the device and their type, e.g. MUX switchable or buffer, i.e. hardwired. It natively supports writing the graph of a given device and reading it prior to the routing step, making the graph an ideal vehicle for entering changes to the network. The routing resource graph from VPR is written out, modified as follows according to the assumed defects and read back into VPR which then carries out the routing based on the modified graph. The graph and the XML file containing it grow approx. quadratically with respect to the grid size of the FPGA device. Thus, the efficiency of the used XML parser poses a restriction to the sizes practically processable.

As the routing resource graph only contains point-to-point connections it is first necessary to infer which connections are part of a common routing MUX. All edges of the graph ending in a common sink node are collected and it is assumed that they belong to one MUX. For every MUX inferred in this way a graph is built representing the two-stage architecture from Fig. 4. Then, defects are distributed randomly for all configuration memory cells present in all MUXes according to a given defect rate and their local effects are determined for every MUX. Possible outcomes of this evaluation are that a MUX is fault free, has unusable paths or is completely defective due to shorts or undefined errors according to Sect. 4.1. These effects are then reflected on the routing resource graph by deleting edges that represent defective paths of routing MUXes.

4.3 Experimental Setup

We derived two smaller FPGA devices from VTR's »k6_frac_N10_mem32K-_40nm.xml« architecture that are processable by the proposed tool flow in appropriate time. One features a grid size of 20 ∗ 20 and a channel width of 60 and the other features a grid size of 30 ∗ 30 and a channel width of 80. Larger devices were not considered due to the inefficiency of the used XML parser. Analog to Sect. 3.3 we compiled a set of exemplary designs from the MCNC20 benchmark suite and VTR's example designs that cause a wide range of device utilizations. Due to the smaller sizes of the devices they fit a subset of the designs selected in Sect. 3.3, i.e. the 20 ∗ 20 device fits 17 designs and the 30 ∗ 30 device additionally fits 10 larger designs. Then, all designs were synthesized assuming memristor defect rates ranging from 0 % to 10 % in steps of 0.25 %. In a second run the range of 0 % to 3 % has been covered with more fine grained steps due to the strong observed degradation of the routing network for higher defect rates.

4.4 Experimental Results

Figure 5 shows the ratio of defect memory cells and routing graph edges with respect to the memristor defect rate. Even at a moderate defect rate of 2 %, approx. 8 % of the memory cells and 30 % of the routing resources are unusable. For higher rates the routing network is quickly rendered nearly completely defect.

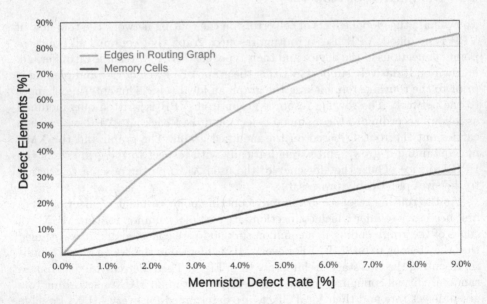

Fig. 5. Ratio of defect memory cells and routing graph edges with respect to the memristor defect rate.

Figure 6 depicts the synthesis results for the small 20 ∗ 20 device and the 17 designs fitting on it in the fault free case. Even at a defect rate of 0.003 % one of the designs is not routable, depending on the random distribution of the defects. At a rate of 0.06 %, merely 7 out of 17 designs can be routed and it becomes impossible to implement any design at a rate of 1.5 %. A worst case timing deterioration of 12 % has been measured in these runs.

A similar observation can be made for the synthesis runs of the 10 largest designs using the 30 ∗ 30 device (see Fig. 7). Here, the routability degradation is

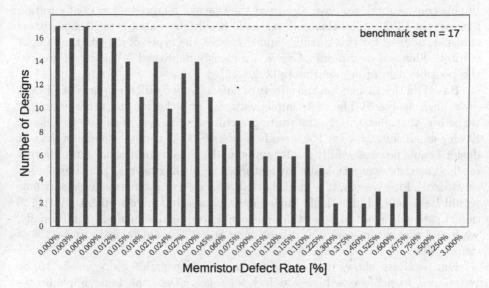

Fig. 6. Number of designs routable in the smaller 20 ∗ 20 device with respect to the memristor error rate.

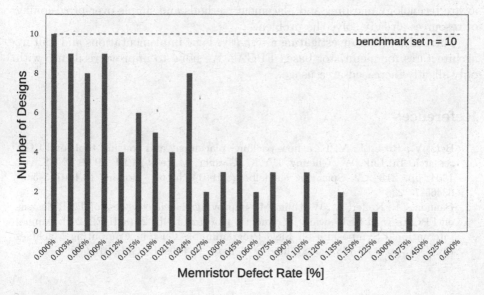

Fig. 7. Number of designs routable in the bigger 30 ∗ 30 device with respect to the memristor defect rate.

even stronger and for the specific defect distribution in the case of a defect rate of 0.12 %, none of the designs could be implemented.

5   Conclusion

In this contribution, we have discussed the usage of memristors as configuration memory in FPGAs. To this end, we have briefly presented typical memristors that can be used for this purpose and discussed the types of defects they might exhibit. This is a new point of view. Previously published NV-FPGAs ignored the possible defects in memristors [3,5,7,15].

Based on this discussion the effects of defects in two different parts of FPGAs have been analyzed: The logic implementation and the routing architecture. It turns out that particularly the routing architecture is very sensitive to defects. Even a small defect rate of 1 % already renders FPGAs useless as none of the test designs could be successfully implemented under these conditions. As the routing method used for evaluation already features a highly flexible resource usage based on Breadth First search, it is unlikely that refined error aware routing algorithms would be beneficial. The logic implementation is a bit more resilient: With 1 % defect rate only 1 out of 35 test designs could not be implemented. Additionally, we found that designs with a utilization of 80–90 % could tolerate up to 2 % of defect rate.

Our analysis shows that at least the routing architecture needs to be redesigned to achieve a higher defect tolerance. Also, the logic implementation could benefit from alternative circuit architectures. Yet, in this area the pressure is not as high as in the routing architecture since it seems that error aware technology mapping and placement methods and simple over-provisioning of resources already solve the problem.

Currently, we are investigating alternative logic implementations and routing architectures for memristor based FPGAs. We hope to improve resilience with only slightly increased area usage.

References

1. Betz, V., Rose, J.: VPR: a new packing, placement and routing tool for FPGA research. In: Luk, W., Cheung, P.Y.K., Glesner, M. (eds.) FPL 1997. LNCS, vol. 1304, pp. 213–222. Springer, Heidelberg (1997). https://doi.org/10.1007/3-540-63465-7_226
2. Cannon, M., Keller, A., Wirthlin, M.: Improving the effectiveness of TMR designs on FPGAs with SEU-aware incremental placement. In: 2018 IEEE 26th Annual International Symposium on Field-Programmable Custom Computing Machines (FCCM), pp. 141–148 (2018). https://doi.org/10.1109/FCCM.2018.00031

3. Chee, H.L., Kumar, T.N., Almurib, H.A., Kang, D.W.H.: Analysis of a novel non-volatile look-up table (NV LUT) controller design with resistive random-access memories (RRAM) for field-programmable gate arrays (FPGA). In: 2019 IEEE Regional Symposium on Micro and Nanoelectronics (RSM), pp. 87–90 (2019). https://doi.org/10.1109/RSM46715.2019.8943560

4. Chen, C.Y., et al.: RRAM defect modeling and failure analysis based on march test and a novel squeeze-search scheme. IEEE Trans. Comput. **64**(1), 180–190 (2015). https://doi.org/10.1109/TC.2014.12

5. Chen, Y.C., Wang, W., Li, H., Zhang, W.: Non-volatile 3d stacking rram-based fpga. In: 22nd International Conference on Field Programmable Logic and Applications (FPL), pp. 367–372 (2012). https://doi.org/10.1109/FPL.2012.6339206

6. Chen, Y.X., Li, J.F.: Fault modeling and testing of 1T1R memristor memories. In: 2015 IEEE 33rd VLSI Test Symposium (VTS), pp. 1–6 (2015). https://doi.org/10.1109/VTS.2015.7116247

7. Huang, K., Zhao, R., He, W., Lian, Y.: High-density and high-reliability nonvolatile field-programmable gate array with stacked 1d2r rram array. IEEE Trans. Very Large Scale Integr. (VLSI) Systems, **24**(1), 139–150 (2016). https://doi.org/10.1109/TVLSI.2015.2389260

8. Jing, N., Lee, J.Y., Feng, Z., He, W., Mao, Z., He, L.: SEU fault evaluation and characteristics for SRAM-based FPGA architectures and synthesis algorithms. ACM Trans. Des. Autom. Electron. Syst. **18**(1), 1–18 (2013). https://doi.org/10.1145/2390191.2390204

9. Luu, J., Anderson, J.H., Rose, J.S.: architecture description and packing for logic blocks with hierarchy, modes and complex interconnect. In: Proceedings of the 19th ACM/SIGDA International Symposium on Field Programmable Gate Arrays, pp. 227–236. FPGA '11, Association for Computing Machinery, New York, NY, USA (2011). https://doi.org/10.1145/1950413.1950457

10. McMurchie, L., Ebeling, C.: Chapter 17 - Pathfinder: a negotiation-based performance-driven router for FPGAs. In: Hauck, S., Dehon, A. (eds.) Reconfigurable Computing, pp. 365–381. Systems on Silicon, Morgan Kaufmann, Burlington (2008). https://doi.org/10.1016/B978-012370522-8.50024-8

11. Nair, S.M., etal.: Defect injection, fault modeling and test algorithm generation methodology for STT-MRAM. In: 2018 IEEE International Test Conference (ITC), pp. 1–10 (2018). https://doi.org/10.1109/TEST.2018.8624725

12. Natsui, M., et al.: A 47. 14-uW 200-MHz MOS/MTJ-hybrid nonvolatile microcontroller unit embedding STT-MRAM and FPGA for IoT applications. IEEE Journal of Solid-State Circuits **54**(11), 2991–3004 (2019). https://doi.org/10.1109/JSSC.2019.2930910

13. Rose, J., et al.: The VTR project: architecture and CAD for FPGAs from verilog to routing. In: Proceedings of the ACM/SIGDA international symposium on Field Programmable Gate Arrays - FPGA '12, pp. 77–86 (2012). https://doi.org/10.1145/2145694.2145708

14. Chakraborty, R.S., Paul, S., Zhou, Y., Bhunia, S.: Low-power hybrid complementary metal-oxide-semiconductor-nano-electro-mechanical systems field programmable gate array: circuit level analysis and defect-aware mapping. IET Comput. Digital Tech. **3**, 609–624(15) (2009). https://digital-library.theiet.org/content/journals/10.1049/iet-cdt.2008.0135

15. Tanachutiwat, S., Liu, M., Wang, W.: FPGA based on integration of CMOS and RRAM. IEEE Trans. Very Large Scale Integr. (VLSI) Syst. 19(11), 2023–2032 (2011). https://doi.org/10.1109/TVLSI.2010.2063444

16. Wu, L., Taouil, M., Rao, S., Marinissen, E.J., Hamdioui, S.: Survey on STT-MRAM testing: failure mechanisms, fault models, and tests. CoRR abs/2001.05463 (2020). https://arxiv.org/abs/2001.05463
17. Young, S.P.: Integrated circuit having fast interconnect paths between memory elements and carry logic (2007). (US Patent 7 218 143 B12007)
18. Yu, S., Chen, P.Y.: Emerging memory technologies: Recent trends and prospects. IEEE Solid-State Circ. Mag. 8(2), 43–56 (2016). https://doi.org/10.1109/MSSC.2016.2546199

On the Reliability of Real-Time Operating System on Embedded Soft Processor for Space Applications

Andrea Portaluri, Sarah Azimi[✉], Corrado De Sio, Daniele Rizzieri,
and Luca Sterpone

Politecnico di Torino, Torino, Italy
{andrea.portaluri,sarah.azimi,corrado.desio,daniele.rizzieri,
luca.sterpone}@polito.it

Abstract. The interest of the space industry in Real-Time Operating Systems for achieving stringent real-time requirement is drastically increasing. Among the different available hardware architectures, the solution of RTOS implemented on soft processors embedded in programmable devices is one of the most efficient and flexible solution for the mission deployment. However, radiation-induced failures are a severe concern affecting the reliability of electronic systems in space applications. In this paper, we investigate the impact of radiation-induced architectural faults affecting the reliability of application running on a Xilinx Microblaze embedded soft-processor within FreeRTOS Operating System. We developed a fault model through a proton radiation test, while the effects of the faults are evaluated in terms of Mean Time To Failure and Mean Executions To Failure, by a fault injection campaign using detected fault models. Finally, the occurrence and contribution to the error rate of specific MBUs events based on different shapes and sizes are evaluated through dedicated fault injection campaigns.

1 Introduction

The usage of Field Programmable Gate Arrays (FPGA) has been tremendously increasing recently, especially for space applications. With satellite lifetimes increased far beyond 10 years, hardware reconfigurability in flight has become a demanded requirement [1]. Soft-core processors are one of the cores commonly implemented using the programmable logic of the FPGAs [2]. Among the available solutions, Microblaze is an industry leader in FPGA-based soft processing solutions. Due to the flexible architecture and configuration options, it became highly suitable for embedded applications. Moreover, it requires few resources for implementation on programmable hardware. The increasing task complexity required for embedded systems led to the decrease of bare-metal applications and the migration toward the adoption of Real-Time Operating Systems (RTOSs) which provide an efficient solution for meeting stringent real-time requirements [3], especially in safety-critical applications to manage the execution of multiple applications sharing resources.

FreeRTOS is an excellent choice when there are multiple tasks to be executed in an organized and predictable fashion. It is a real-time operating system with deterministic

© The Author(s), under exclusive license to Springer Nature Switzerland AG 2022
M. Schulz et al. (Eds.): ARCS 2022, LNCS 13642, pp. 181–193, 2022.
https://doi.org/10.1007/978-3-031-21867-5_12

and predictable task scheduling which allows the important task to meet hard deadlines for executions. FreeRTOS allows to schedule tasks by priority and time slicing which is designed to run on small microprocessors which need to perform multiple tasks deterministically.

Nowadays, due to the transistors scaling and increasing of the number of available resources in a device, radiation-induced failure is becoming an important challenge to overcome [4, 5], especially focusing on mission-critical space applications. To show the significant impact of these effects, it is worth to mention the user-observable Mean Time To Failure (MTTF) of an Apple iPhone 3 operating at commercial aircraft altitude can reduce to 1 year [6].

Therefore, when using an operating system running on a soft microprocessor in mission-critical applications, the reliability issues deriving from the exposure of the devices to ionizing radiation, such as Single Event Upsets (SEUs), should be considered [7–10]. Differently from hardwired microprocessors, the netlist of soft microprocessors such as Microblaze is implemented in the programmable hardware relying on the configuration memory (CRAM) of the FPGA. This memory can be corrupted by SEU [9, 11], leading to the hardware micro-architectural faults which can propagate to the application layer and, in the case of the usage of a microprocessor supporting an operating system, it can lead to catastrophic results, especially in mission-critical applications [12].

The main contribution of this work is oriented toward the reliability evaluation of a Real-time Operating System on the Microblaze embedded soft processor for space application. To do so, we performed a detailed evaluation of the impact of radiation-induced architectural faults affecting the application benchmarks running on the FreeRTOS of the Microblaze embedded soft processor. The analysis has been performed through a fault injection campaign while an accurate fault model consisting of different clusters patterns of Multiple Bit Upset (MBU) has been identified through proton radiation performed at Paul Scherrer Institute (PSI) radiation facility. We evaluated the effect of faults during the execution of different software applications on FreeRTOS supported by Microblaze implemented on Zynq-7020 FPGA while we performed a deep investigation on the outcome of the software application, reporting the system reliability in terms of calculated Mean Time To Failure and Mean Executions to Failure as an impact of radiation-induced errors.

Please notice that the developed platform is not targeting the software-level fault injections but targeting the hardware faults and their impact on the execution of the software running in the operating system.

2 Related Works

Recently, reliability has become one of the main challenges of embedded systems applied to mission-critical applications. Several works elaborate on the software-level techniques for evaluating the sensitivity to Single Event Upsets (SEUs) of the embedded operating system. Commonly, these approaches are based on modifying the original kernel of the embedded operating system or altering either the memory that the OS uses or the parameters of system calls.

In [15], the vulnerability of FreeRTOS has been evaluated through a software-based fault injection methodology that targets the most relevant variables and data structures of the OS. An automatic method for fault injection into program and data memory is presented in [16]. The authors of [17] proposed a detailed analysis and hardening architecture based on lockstep synchronization supporting FreeRTOS. The heavy ion irradiation test presented in [18] targets the SRAM and the special purpose registers of an ARM microcontroller to evaluate the impact of the radiation-induced SEU. However, software application-level methods do not take into account the impact of faults occurring at the architectural level of the soft-core processor on the functionality of the operating system.

Other approaches are based on the simulation of HDL description of microprocessors [19]. The advantage of these methods is the feasibility of injecting upsets into any CPU register and structure at any time however, these methods are time expensive.

3 Background on Radiation-Induced Effect on Reconfigurable Logic

Modern programmable hardware devices, such as Field Programmable Gate Arrays (FPGAs), are reconfigurable integrated circuits that can be programmed to implement any digital hardware circuit. FPGA consists of configurable logic blocks that can be connected via prefabricated programmable interconnects. The functionality of all the FPGA's programmable blocks and interconnections are controlled using millions of static random access memory (SRAM) cells that are programmed to realize a specific function. The user describes the desired function of the hardware in one of the hardware languages such as VHDL, Verilog, or recently high-level synthesis (HLS). Utilizing the commercial FPGA computer-aided design (CAD) flow, the hardware design is compiled into a bitstream file which is used to program all the FPGA's configuration SRAM cells [20].

Bitstream is a configuration array of binary data. Each bit of the bitstream file is responsible to configure logic blocks such as Look-Up Tables (LUTs), Flip-Flops (FFs), configuration Logic Block (CLB), and interconnections among them.

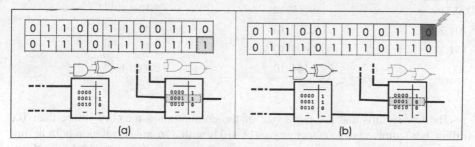

Fig. 1. The radiation particle creating an seu on the configuration memory of FPGA.

The SRAM cell representing the bitstream of the implemented hardware consists of millions of transistors. When a high-energy particle is interacting within the silicon of the device and releases its energy in these transistors, it can lead to the modification of the content of the memory cell (SRAM cell). This phenomenon is known as Single Event Upset (SEU) which corrupts the information stored in the memory cell, producing a fault that can lead to error and eventual malfunction of the system implemented on the FPGA. For example, as is represented in Fig. 1, an SEU in the bitstream can change the configuration of a LUT from NAND to NOR and therefore, change the functionality of the circuit and eventual failure.

In order to consider an accurate fault model affecting the hardware under the study to evaluate the reliability of FreeRTOS on soft-core Microblaze, we have performed a radiation test as the closest scenario to the space application one. The performed test and extracted fault models are described in the following section.

4   Proton Radiation Test-Based Reliability Fault Model

In order to achieve accurate reliability analysis, we have performed a proton radiation test at the Paul Scherrer Institute (PSI) Proton Facility in Switzerland. From this experiment, we have identified an accurate fault model for performing fault injection campaigns.

A Zynq-7020 device has been irradiated with a proton beam with energies between 29 and 200 meV. The value of energies and fluxes used during the radiation test experiment is represented in Table 1. During the experiment, the configuration memory of the device has been continuously monitored through a periodic reading of the content every 5 s. The snapshots of the configuration memory content have been then analyzed for detecting the occurrence of Multiple Bit Upsets (MBUs). The flux of the particles has been tuned to keep a few bitflips in configuration memory in each snapshot.

Table 1. Radiation test conditions: energy, flux and fluence

Energy [MeV]	Flux $[\mathrm{cm}^{-2}\mathrm{s}^{-1}]$	Fluence $[\mathrm{cm}^{-2}]$
29.31	$4.124 \cdot 10^7$	$9.173 \cdot 10^{10}$
50.80	$4.024 \cdot 10^7$	$6.064 \cdot 10^{10}$
69.71	$4.110 \cdot 10^7$	$2.124 \cdot 10^{10}$
101.34	$4.319 \cdot 10^7$	$2.415 \cdot 10^{10}$
151.18	$4.094 \cdot 10^7$	$1.226 \cdot 10^{10}$
200	$4.144 \cdot 10^7$	$3.942 \cdot 10^{10}$

The few bitflips and the large size of the configuration memory (more than 100 million bits) allowed us to detect groups of SEUs with a strong correlation both in time and space. Therefore, it has been possible to select a group of bits with a high probability to have occurred as a result of a Single Event Multiple Upsets (SEMUs).

Figure 2 illustrates the observed pattern for MBUs resulting from the radiation test experiment while Table 2 shows the cross-section per particle of each cluster size observed during the whole radiation test. It can be noticed how the contribution of SEMUs is not negligible compared to SEUs. Indeed, more than 40% of the detected

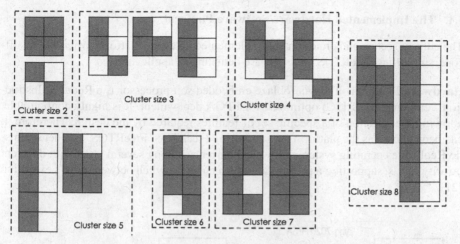

Fig. 2. Detected cluster sizes and shapes during the Zynq-7020 proton test.

Table 2. Cross-section of different cluster sizes

Cluster size	Cross section per Particle [cm^2]
1	$1.87 \cdot 10^{-8}$
2	$1.11 \cdot 10^{-8}$
3	$1.70 \cdot 10^{-9}$
4	$5.99 \cdot 10^{-10}$
5	$1.73 \cdot 10^{-10}$
6	$1.02 \cdot 10^{-10}$
7	$5.65 \cdot 10^{-11}$
8	$2.64 \cdot 10^{-11}$

events have been SEMUs. The proposed cluster of faults has been used as the fault model in the fault injection campaign. In order to obtain an analysis as closest as possible to reality, the occurrence rate of the different clusters during the fault emulation has been weighted on the cross-section reported in Table 2. Since the high occurrence rate of SEMUs, evaluating only an SEU fault model will result in a loose approximation of the observed events.

5 The Reliability Analysis Workflow

The fault model collected through the proton test has been used to perform an accurate radiation analysis on the impact of radiation-induced faults on the Microblaze embedded soft processor porting FreeRTOS through fault injection campaigns.

5.1   The Implemented Hardware/Software Platform

The current section elaborates on the implemented hardware platform, Microblaze soft-core, supporting FreeRTOS and software benchmarks applications.

Hardware Platform. The Microblaze embedded soft processor is a Reduced Instruction Set Computer (RISC) optimized for FPGA deployment. It is highly configurable, allowing the selection of a specific set of features required by the design. Therefore, it has been chosen as the platform for supporting FreeRTOS. FreeRTOS, as a deterministic Real-time operating system, allows concurrency among several tasks with different priority levels, supporting a preemption mechanism to switch between task's execution [21].

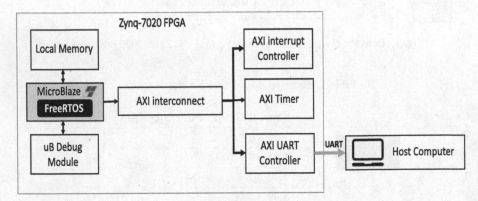

Fig. 3. The implemented hardware platform.

Another important feature that characterizes the Microblaze porting of FreeRTOS is the possibility to instantiate exception handlers to cope with the standard exception conditions defined by Microblaze soft-core [22].

A Xilinx 28 nm CMOS Zynq-7020 FPGA is chosen as a target hardware device.

Figure 3 represents the implemented hardware while Table 3 reports the device utilization when implementing a Microblaze porting FreeRTOS. As it is can be observed from the table, the implemented design used few resources of the FPGA. Therefore, fault injection campaigns are performed selectively to target only a subset of the whole configuration memory of the FPGA where the circuit is implemented.

Software Platform. As a software application suite, a set of software benchmarks has been chosen to run on FreeRTOS while exploiting its main functionalities. To exploit the capability of FreeRTOS to schedule the execution of different tasks, for each software application, three different tasks (software benchmark) with the same priority have been instantiated. Therefore, three tasks running on FreeRTOS have the same instruction code, however, they are operating on different input data while sharing the processor execution time. The three selected software benchmarks are:

Table 3. Resource utilization of the hardware platform

Resources	Used [#]	Available [#]	Usage [%]
LUTs	2,596	53,200	4.88
Logic slices	966	13,300	7.26
Flip-flops	2,998	106,400	2.51
BRAM	32	140	22.86

– matmul: matrix multiplication between large matrices of integers.
– matconv: matrix convolution between large matrices of integers.
– dijkstra: computation of shortest path between nodes in a large graph using the Dijkstra algorithm.

5.2 Fault Injection Analysis

Reliability analysis of the applications under test against radiation-induced hardware architectural faults in soft microprocessors has been performed by fault injection campaigns. The PyXEL platform has been used as a supporting fault injection framework [23]. PyXEL is an open-source Python-based platform easing the execution of FPGA fault injection campaigns. The platform has been instrumented to inject MBU patterns identified during the proton radiation test in the configuration memory of the FPGA. The device under test is connected to the host computer running the PyXEL experiment manager through a serial connection allowing to run the experiments on the platform and collecting results. A timeout mechanism is used to handle the halt and loop of the processor due to the injected faults.

Two fault injection campaigns have been performed. The former has been carried out based on the distribution of SEUs and MBUs represented in Fig. 2 and Table 2. In the latter, each detected cluster has been extensively tested in order to estimate the impact of the different MBU clusters on the application failures. As it has been mentioned before, during the fault injection campaigns, only the part of the whole configuration memory implementing the circuit under test is targeted by the fault injection task in order to reduce the injection space to the resources used by the implemented netlist.

6 Experimental Analysis and Results

Results of the two fault injection campaigns based on fault models collected through a proton radiation test campaign targeting the Zynq-7020 device have been collected, categorized, and discussed.

Error Classification. Four categories have been identified. They are defined as follows:

– *Correct*: the FreeRTOS succeeded in executing the application and produced an output that matches the golden one.

- *Silent Data Corruption*: the task execution on FreeRTOS terminates but the produced output data does not match with the golden one.
- *Halt*: the FreeRTOS does not complete the task. It can be due to different causes, such as infinite loops and application timeout.
- *Raising Exceptions:* an exception is generated in the FreeRTOS (i.e., at the software level) as a result of a fault affecting Microblaze architecture (i.e., netlist modification due to configuration memory corruption).

Moreover, we have performed a detailed investigation on the cause of each raised exception and classified them as follows:

- *FSL_EXCEPTION*: data bus error exception.
- *UNALIGNED_ACCESS*: attempt to perform unsupported unaligned access to memory.
- *ILLEGAL_OPCODE*: attempt to execute an illegal opcode.
- *AXI_D_EXCEPTION*: data system bus timeout.

Experimental Results. For the first fault injection campaign, we injected and singularly evaluated 10,000 faults, generated considering the cluster distribution represented in Table 2 and Fig. 2. As these data show, the occurrence rate of different MBU cluster sizes is not constant, so this first campaign has been done to evaluate the robustness of the different applications in a real-world effects scenario. The error rates observed with the described fault configuration are reported in Fig. 4.

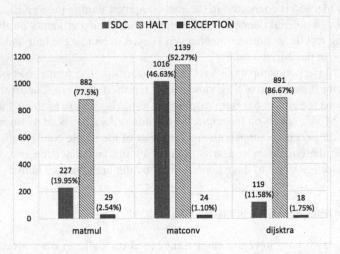

Fig. 4. Error Rates for each application with distributed MBU injection

As it can be observed in Fig. 4, most of the errors cause the HALT of the system while errors resulting in SDC and rising EXCEPTION are observed less. This information can be used to identify critical scenarios such as HALT in order to provide sufficient and efficient mitigation techniques.

Moving forward, for the second campaign of fault injection, we focused on performing a deep analysis of the criticality of the MBU occurrences with respect to SEU in terms of corruption in the system. Therefore, the second campaign is performed considering 5,000 fault injections for each cluster size (40,000 fault injections in total) without considering the distribution, aiming to estimate the impact that the different MBU cluster sizes – considered one at a time – have on the three applications. The obtained results are presented in Fig. 5.

Results Discussion. Data show that the three applications have been impacted differently. In particular, the *matconv* has registered the highest number of total errors (including all the four categories) with 2,179 corruptions over 10,000 injections while *matmul* and *dijkstra* collected 1,028 and 1,026 errors, respectively. It can be noticed that the highest value always belongs to the *Halt* label for all the software applications, most likely due to the corruption of communication modules (e.g. UART controller) within the design.

As can be seen in Fig. 5, the cluster size has a marginal effect on the error rate. It may be related to the fact that bits associated with a specific hardware resource are located closely in the configuration memory. If that part of configuration memory is selected as a fault location, the size of the injected cluster will only marginally increase the corruption of the used logic resource.

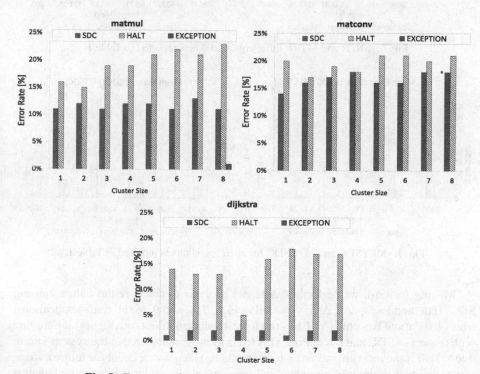

Fig. 5. Error rates for each application with fixed MBU injection

To clarify further the sensitivity of the analyzed software and platform, the mean-time-to-failure (MTTF) and the mean-executions-to-failure (METF) have been evaluated for the various applications, based on the cross-sections of different cluster sizes at different energies, and the error rate of the applications against the specific clusters resulting from the second fault injection campaign. The MTTF is the mean time between two faulty outcomes of the application. The MTTF is reported in Fig. 6 based on energies and the fluxes reported in Table 1. The METF has been computed using the average execution time of the software applications. As is expected, for the particles with lower energies, the Mean Execution To Failure as well as Mean Time to Failure is higher which means that fewer errors or failures have been observed. By the particles moving toward the one with higher energies, the failure rate increases which leads to a smaller value for MTTF and METF.

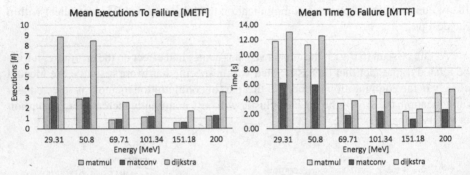

Fig. 6. METf and MTTF for energies ad fluxes reported in Table 1.

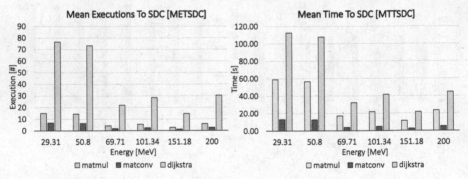

Fig. 7. METSDC and MTTSDC for energies ad fluxes reported in Table 1.

Moving forward, we performed a deeper analysis to compare the failure causing SDC, Halt, and Exception. As is reported in Figs. 7, 8, and 9, for all three applications, Mean Execution/Time to HALT has the lowest value and therefore highest failure rate with respect to SDC and Exception. This leads to the conclusion that the system failure due to Halt is the most critical one which should be taken into account for future mitigation techniques in order to provide a real-time operating system that is tolerant against radiation-induced failure and therefore suitable for space applications.

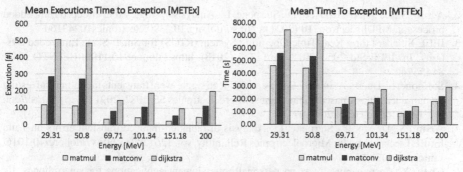

Fig. 8. METEx and MTTEx for energies ad fluxes reported in Table 1.

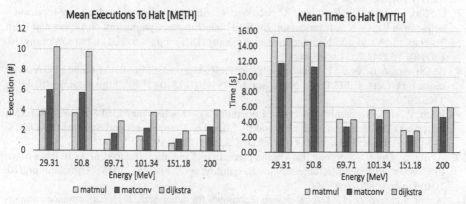

Fig. 9. METH and MTTH for energies ad fluxes reported in Table 1.

7   Conclusions and Future Works

In this paper, we provided an evaluation of the reliability of the software applications running on Soft Core Microblaze running FreeRTOS. The impact of radiation-induced architectural failures identified through a proton radiation test, affecting different applications has been evaluated. The occurrence and contribution to the error rate of specific MBUs events based on different shapes and sizes have been evaluated in detail. Moreover, we performed a deep reliability analysis in order to classify the radiation-induced errors causing the failure of the running software application in terms of Mean Time/Execution To Failure. In the future, we plan to consider both software and hardware approaches for mitigating radiation-induced errors on applications running within FreeRTOS.

References

1. Hofmann, et al.: An FPGA based on-board processor platform for space application. In: NASA/ESA Conference on Adaptive Hardware and Systems (AHS), pp. 17–22, 2012. https://doi.org/10.1109/AHS.2012.6268653

2. Azimi, S., De Sio, C., Rizzieri, D., Sterpone, L.: Analysis of single event effects on embedded processor. MPDI Electron. **10** (2021). https://doi.org/10.3390/electronics10243160
3. IEEE Standard for a Real-Time Operating System (RTOS) for Small-Scale Embedded Systems. In: IEEE Std 2050–2018, pp.1–333 (2018). https://doi.org/10.1109/IEEESTD.2018.8445674
4. Sterpone, L., Du, B., Azimi, S.: Radiation-induced single event transients modeling and testing on nanometric flash-based technologies. Microelectronics **55**, 2087–2091 (2015). https://doi.org/10.1016/j.microrel.2015.07.035
5. Azimi, S., De Sio, C., Sterpone, L.: Analysis of radiation-induced transient errors on 7 nm FinFET technology. In: Microelectronics Reliability, vol. 126 (2021). https://doi.org/10.1016/j.microrel.2021.114319
6. Chen, Y.: Cosmic ray effects on personal entertainment applications for smartphones. In: IEEE Radiation Effects Data Workshop (REDW) (2013), pp. 1–4. https://doi.org/10.1109/REDW.2013.6658194
7. De Sio, C., Azimi, S., Portaluri, A., Sterpone, L.: SEU evaluation of hardened-by-replication software in RISC- V soft processor. In: IEEE International Symposium on Defect and Fault Tolerance in VLSI and Nanotechnology Systems (DFT), pp. 1–6 (2021). https://doi.org/10.1109/DFT52944.2021.9568342
8. de Oliveira, Á.B., et al.: Evaluating soft core RISC-V processor in SRAM-based FPGA under radiation effects. IEEE Trans. Nucl. Sci. **67**(7), 1503–1510 (2020). https://doi.org/10.1109/TNS.2020.2995729
9. Rech, P., et al.: Reliability analysis of operating systems for embedded SoC. In: 2015 15th European Conference on Radiation and Its Effects on Components and Systems (RADECS) 1–5 (2015). https://doi.org/10.1109/RADECS.2015.7365659
10. Azimi, S., Du, B., Sterpone, L.: On the prediction of radiation-induced SETs in flash-based FPGAs. In: Elsevier Microelectronics Reliability, pp. 230–234. (2016). https://doi.org/10.1016/j.microrel.2016.07.106
11. Azimi, S., Sterpone, L.: Digital design techniques for dependable high performance computing. IEEE Int. Test Conf. (ITC) **2020**, 1 (2020). https://doi.org/10.1109/ITC44778.2020.9325281
12. Du, B., Azimi, S., et al.: Ultrahigh energy heavy ion test beam on Xilinx Kintex-7 SRAM-based FPGA. IEEE Trans. Nucl. Sci. **66**(7), 1813–1819 (2019). https://doi.org/10.1109/TNS.2019.2915207
13. Azimi, S., De Sio, C., Sterpone, L., A radiation-hardened CMOS full-adder based on layout selective transistor duplication. In: IEEE Transactions on Very Large Scale Integration (VLSI) Systems, vol. 29, no. 8, pp. 1596–1600 (2021).https://doi.org/10.1109/TVLSI.2021.3086897
14. Nekrasov, P.V., et al.: Investigation of single event functional interrupts in microcontroller with PIC17 architecture. In: 2015 15th European Conference on Radiation and Its Effects on Components and Systems (RADECS), pp. 1–4 (2015) https://doi.org/10.1109/TNS.2019.2915207
15. Mamone, D., et al.: On the analysis of real-time operating system reliability in embedded systems. In: IEEE International Symposium on Defect and Fault Tolerance in VLSI and Nanotechnology Systems (DFT), pp. 1–6 (2020) https://doi.org/10.1109/DFT50435.2020.9250861
16. Loskutov, I.O., et al.: Investigation of operating system influence on single event functional interrupts using fault injection and hardware error detection in ARM microcontroller. In: International Siberian Conference on Control and Communications (SIBCON), pp. 1–4 (2021) https://doi.org/10.1109/SIBCON50419.2021.9438916
17. Aviles, P.M., et al.: Radiation testing of a multiprocessor macrosynchronized lockstep architecture with FreeRTOS. IEEE Trans. Nucl. Sci. **69**(3), 462–469 (2022). https://doi.org/10.1109/TNS.2021.3129164

18. Loskutov, I.O., et al.: SEFI cross-section evaluation by fault injection software approach and hardware detection. In: IEEE 30th International Conference on Microelectronics (MIEL), pp. 251–254 (2017) https://doi.org/10.1109/MIEL.2017.8190114
19. Mansour, W., Velazco, R.: SEU fault-injection in VHDL-based processors: a case study. J. Electron. Testing: Theory Appl. (JETTA) **29**(1), 87–94 (2013). https://doi.org/10.1109/LATW.2012.6261258
20. Boutros, A., Betz, V.: FPGA architecture: principles and progression. In: IEEE Circuits and Systems Magazine, vol. 21, no. 2, pp. 4–29, Secondquarter (2021). https://doi.org/10.1109/MCAS.2021.3071607
21. FreeRTOS. "Xilinx Microblaze Port" informative. https://bit.ly/3r5Y3ph. Accessed 06 April 2022
22. Xilinx. MicroBlaze Processor Reference Guide. UG984 v2021.2, 27 Oct 2021, pp. 80–89
23. Bozzoli, L., et al.: PyXEL: an integrated environment for the analysis of fault effects in SRAM-based FPGA routing. In: International Symposium on Rapid System Prototyping (RSP), pp. 70–75 (2018). https://doi.org/10.1109/RSP.2018.8632000

Special Track: Organic Computing

NDNET: A Unified Framework
for Anomaly and Novelty Detection

Jens Decke[1]([✉])(iD), Jörn Schmeißing[1], Diego Botache[1](iD), Maarten Bieshaar[2](iD),
Bernhard Sick[1](iD), and Christian Gruhl[1](iD)

[1] Department of Electrical Engineering and Computer Science, University of Kassel,
Kassel, Germany
{jens.decke,jschmeissing,diego.botache,bsick,cgruhl}@uni-kassel.de
[2] Bosch Center for Artificial Intelligence, Hildesheim, Germany
maarten.bieshaar@de.bosch.com
https://www.uni-kassel.de/eecs/ies/, https://www.bosch-ai.com/

Abstract. We introduce NDNET (https://novelty-detection.net/p/
ndnet), an anomaly and novelty detection library that implements various detection algorithms adjusted for online processing of data streams.
The intention of this library is threefold: 1) Make experimentation with
different anomaly and novelty detection algorithms simple. 2) Support
the development of new novelty detection approaches by providing the
mCANDIES framework. 3) Provide fundamentals to analyze and evaluate novelty detection algorithms on data streams. The library is freely
available and developed as open-source software.

Keywords: Novelty detection · Library · Machine learning ·
Unsupervised learning · Anomaly detection

1 Introduction

Technical systems that require the monitoring of their environment use the
information acquired by sensors or different data sources to establish the current status and health of the processes in the system. However, changes in the
environment and the underlying process can cause a discrepancy in the data
distribution. For example, they must be detected to update the parameters of
probabilistic models describing the system's behaviour. Detection of emerging
changes in the system, which require adaptation of model parameters, is essential
because knowledge about all possible situations in a time-variant environment is
not available at design time. Therefore, the novelty detection task corresponds
to distinguishing whether the unseen samples belong to a normal pattern or are
different from the previously observed normal data. This task is closely related
to *anomaly detection* and *outlier detection*, but these tasks are often confused
and do not have a clear definitional boundary [1].

Some works model the normal behaviour and precisely define "normal" areas
in the input space of the data, then describe the accumulation of observations

M. Schulz et al. (Eds.): ARCS 2022, LNCS 13642, pp. 197–210, 2022.
https://doi.org/10.1007/978-3-031-21867-5_13

outside this "normal" space as novelties [2–6]. However, the challenges lie in defining and modelling the normal behaviour of a system, which is strongly dependent on the area and type of application. Moreover, the concept of an anomaly is context-dependent, meaning that it can refer to either small or significant deviations from normal behaviour [7]. Novelty detection techniques require specific assumptions, which allows the definition of normal and anomalous behavior. In the case of *data streams*, which refer to a continuous flow of data, normal behaviour is not a static state, but can change over time [8]. Noisy data, for example, triggered by sensors, can sometimes hardly be distinguished from anomalies. Examples of data streams include those found in web applications [9], sensor networks [10], and hardware component monitoring [11].

In this work, NDNET[1] is introduced, an open source library for novelty detection algorithms written in Python. NDNET plays a crucial role in detecting novelties in the described scenarios, i.e. by combining several eminent novelty detection algorithms to identify novel processes that are highly relevant, especially in applications with data streams. The NDNET library consists of multiple novelty and anomaly detection algorithms, which are either re-implementations of known procedures or novel algorithms such as the Combined Approach to Novelty Detection in Intelligent Embedded System (CANDIES) methodology [4,12]. The library is fully open source and can be used similar to the sklearn library [13].

Many of the algorithms are explicitly designed for online applications, as anomalies are to be detected fast to ensure a quick response of the system considering limitations on systems imposed by processor and memory capacities. Additionally, NDNET presents multiple methods for data processing. To demonstrate the advantages of using this framework, we present two examples of unrelated applications that present multiple challenges in the solution of predetermined tasks. Compared to classification algorithms, no manual annotations are required for this process. Novelty detection is thus explicitly suitable for areas where it is difficult or costly to generate examples of abnormal behaviour. The two discussed use cases show the library's versatility. The first problem is not typically encountered using novelty or anomaly detection. In a design optimization process an anomaly detector is used to select interesting designs and efficiently explore the solution space to reduce the number of time consuming numerical simulations. Due to the ease of applicability of NDNET, it is demonstrated that using these algorithms can generate an additional benefit in solving problems in other use cases. The second application corresponds to a motor test bench to optimize the extensive and vulnerable experimental evaluation of electric motors. NDNET allows the analysis of the high dimensional heterogeneous time series data to detect abnormal instances without the explicit use of labels or annotations.

The remainder of this work is organized as follows: In Sect. 2, the related work is presented. Section 3 presents a description of the library with an overview of the implemented algorithms in NDNET. The use cases, demonstrating the

---

[1] https://novelty-detection.net/p/ndnet.

versatility of the presented library, are presented in Sect. 4 with a corresponding results discussion. Section 5 concludes the article and gives a brief outlook on future work.

2 Related Work

Anomaly and novelty detection have been around for years. The terminology anomaly, novelty and outlier are frequently used synonymously. In this article, we consider novelties to be agglomerations of anomalies. Observations that represent the normal behaviour of a system are called regulars and are usually affiliated with a normal model. Anomalies and outliers are distinguished in the sense that outliers are regulars with a small probability of being observed, and anomalies are observations that are not affiliated with the expected normal model [4,5,12].

Quite a few frameworks provide implementations of anomaly and novelty detectors. For instance, a small set of detectors is available in sklearn [13], and a collection of outlier detectors is also available in PyOD [14]. However, both frameworks are only considered with offline data. That is, the detectors are aimed to detect anomalies in a static data set that can be evaluated at once. In contrast, NDNET is oriented towards the online detection of novelties in data streams and provides a collection of detectors that bring this capability. An overview of related detectors (together with references to their respective research articles) is given in Table 1.

Research is also carried out to provide meaningful (static) reference data sets, e.g., [15]. In this regard, NDNET offers a data stream synthesiser that can generate different scenarios with multiple novelties.

3 The Library NDNET

The NDNET library (its name is derived from novelty-detection.net) provides implementations of different anomaly and novelty detection algorithms in Python that offer a common interface. One of its core parts is the provision of the **mCANDIES** subpackage (a framework in itself) that implements the CANDIES Methodology [4,5], a modular approach to prototype application-specific novelty detectors rapidly. An overview of the implemented detectors is given in Sect. 3.3. Its intention is to be used in scientific research, especially in the field of data streams and novelty detection. Besides implementing different detectors, another goal is to support a meaningful evaluation methodology. The interfaces are roughly oriented to be compatible with *sklearn* [13]. NDNET is freely available under https://novelty-detection.net/p/ndnet.

3.1 Overview

The library consists of multiple sub-packages; an overview is given in Fig. 1. The mCANDIES framework and the detector packages provide various anomaly and novelty detection approaches and are discussed in more detail in their respective subsections.

The **distribution** sub-package contains implementations of machine learning algorithms to infer Gaussian Mixture Models (GMM), which are frequently used in the implemented detection algorithms. Grouped as other in Fig. 1, the library also provides tools to visualise the detectors.

The **generator** sub-package provides tools to synthesise multivariate data streams to evaluate novelty detection algorithms. It allows the generation of so-called scenarios, which the user configures (i.e. number and type of the novelties in the data stream). While the user configures the general properties of the novelties, the generator samples them at random (i.e. the time instance of their appearance, location, and duration) but in a reproducible way. Thus providing a large amount of available test data.

Currently, the library mainly focuses on statistical models and does not incorporate detectors based on artificial neural networks.

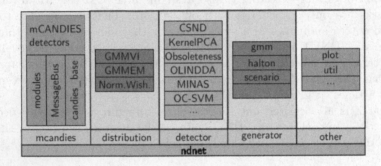

Fig. 1. NDNET sub-packages and modules. The *mCANDIES* sub-package implements the CANDIES methodology and contains several sub-modules for rapid prototyping. The *detector* sub-packages contains various anomaly and novelty detection approaches with a commin interface. Figure taken from [12].

3.2   mCANDIES

The modular implementation of the CANDIES methodology is one of the core parts of NDNET; refer to [4,5,12] for a detailed discussion.

The central aspect of the CANDIES is to combine different anomaly and novelty detectors and use them in different regions of the input space. Here, the main separation is into high-density regions (HDR) and low-density regions (LDR). Regular observations are expected to be observed in HDR (where most of the density mass is located), while everything that resides in LDR is considered suspicious. In NDNET, novelties are considered to be on a more abstract level than anomalies in the sense that novelties are agglomerations of anomalies that share some relations (either in time or in space).

The **mCANDIES** sub-package provides various modules which can be combined to implement new novelty detectors. The starting point for every new detector is the *BaseCANDIES* class (see Fig. 2). The *BaseCANDIES* class provides the scaffolding structure that the user can augment with the available modules or by implementing new ones. For instance, the GlobalBuffer implements a *sliding window* that makes the currently processed observations from a data stream available to all modules. Likewise, all modules are loosely coupled through a *MessageBus* (based on a publish/subscribe scheme) that allows the passing of messages between any module. Currently, NDNET has two pre-defined mCANDIES based detectors, **NDTDet** and **NDTCDDet**.

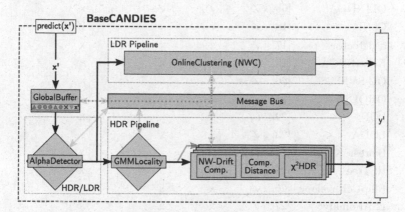

Fig. 2. The fundamental mCANDIES architecture as implemented in **mcandies**. Structural components provided by *BaseCANDIES* are coloured in blue and orange. Augmented *modules* (selected by the user) are represented as green boxes. The *MessageBus* allows all modules to exchange messages with each other, allowing a significant amount of flexibility in developing new modules. Figure from [12]. (Color figure online)

3.3 Detectors

While implementations of different anomaly and novelty detectors are already available, their implementations are often not suitable to be directly compared, either because they are written in other languages, their interfaces and assumptions differ, or simply due to a lack of performance (especially if an extensive hyper-parameter optimization is conducted). The detector sub-package offers a selection of anomaly and novelty detection algorithms. Table 1 contains an overview of the currently implemented detectors. The selection is based on a structured literature study conducted in [12], with the intention to compare them against *mCANDIES* based detectors.

Table 1. Overview of the algorithms implemented in NDNET and their properties; *Online*: can the algorithm process data streams, *Novelty*: does the algorithm detect novelties, *Concept Drift*: is a drift compensation available, *Obliviation*: is the forgetting of model components available. ✓ = yes, x = no, () = partially. The first part of the table contains novelty detectors, while the second part consists of anomaly detectors.

Method	Ref.	Online	Novelty	Concept drift	Obliviation
MINAS	[16]	✓	✓	✓	x
NDTCDDet	[12]	✓	✓	✓	(✓)
NDTDet	[12]	✓	✓	x	(✓)
2SNDR	[17]	✓	✓	x	✓
OLINDDA	[6]	✓	✓	✓	x
CSND	[18]	✓	✓	x	✓
α-detector	[17]	✓	x	x	x
Kernel-PCA	[19]	✓	x	x	x
OC-SVM	[20]	✓	x	x	x
OHODIN	[21]	✓	x	x	x
LOF	[22]	(✓)	x	x	x
LODA	[23]	✓	x	x	x
IForest	[24]	(✓)	x	x	x
HSTree	[25]	✓	x	x	x
EllipticEnvelope	[26]	✓	x	x	x
LSAnomaly	[27]	✓	x	x	x

4   Use Cases

In this Section, two use cases are discussed that take advantage of the NDNET library. The first use-case uses the **mCANDIES** framework (i.e. the subpackage) to develop an anomaly detector that is used to guide the optimization process of a U-bend design. In the second use case, the NDNET library is used to investigate if a proposed motor test bench problem is an anomaly or a novelty detection problem, by comparing the results of various detectors.

4.1   Anomaly Detection in Design Optimization

Shape and topology design optimizations of technical components are particularly computationally demanding operations since the Navier-Stokes equations are applied with the help of Computational Fluid Dynamics (CFD) using e.g., the Finite Volume Method for every design instance. Computation times for industrial applications that last from weeks to months are common [28]. Therefore, an exhaustive or random search in conjunction with prior knowledge is often used to find a design parameter set that satisfies the requirements of the technical system. For complex and high-dimensional problems from industrial

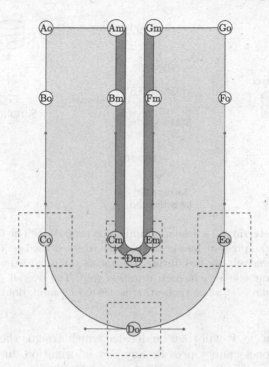

Fig. 3. Design optimization of a U-bend flow. Parameterized initial design with boundary points (green) and curve parameters (red). The Green filled circles represent the boundary points of the design and can vary within the dashed boxes. These boxes are the limits of the design parameters of the respective boundary point. The boundary points are connected using cubic Bézier curves. Each curve is controlled by two curve design parameters, which are represented by the red dots. (Color figure online)

applications, however, it is often not possible to consider prior knowledge in optimization. Hence design optimization processes should operate without using prior knowledge. With the help of anomaly detection, we are now trying to make the process of identifying suitable designs more intelligent.

Experimental Setup. A data set was generated on the basis of the VKI benchmark case of a U-bend flow [29]. The data set contains 6000 randomly generated designs and each of them contains a total of 28 parameters describing the shape of a design and target value which is determined using CFD. The target value is the pressure loss in the U-bend, which is the difference of the pressure between the inlet and outlet of the channel. The pressure loss is proportional to the power that must be consumed to pump the fluid through the channel. The parameter space of the initial design is shown in Fig. 3. The goal is to find suitable or the best designs within the database with as few evaluations as possible. The method presented in this work is depicted in Fig. 4 and aims to develop a meta model that categorizes a design parameter set as either novel or already known. Based

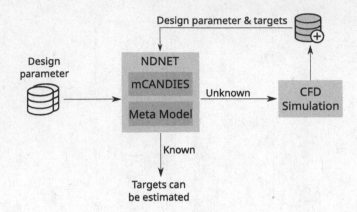

Fig. 4. Anomaly detection in a design optimization procedure. The CFD Simulation is used to determine the pressure loss in the channel which is used as a target value. The Meta Model is successively trained during the process and provided with new randomly selected design parameter sets in each iteration step. The overall goal is to find the best design in the data set while requesting as few CFD simulations as possible.

on this categorization, it will then be decided which designs should be solved by CFD and which ones cannot provide any new information due to similarity to already known (evaluated) designs. This approach aims to make the exploration of the high-dimensional parameter space more efficient and save computationally expensive evaluations. Therefore, even with little or no prior physical knowledge of the system, it is possible to limit the design parameter space in such a way that an optimization algorithm using gradient descent does not get stuck in its first local minima. In the first iteration, the Meta Model gets assigned 100 random designs, of which none can already be known, and therefore the target value will be assigned from the CFD-Simulation. It can be assumed that in the following iterations designs are increasingly recognized as known and less novel designs are discovered in every iteration step. Since similar but possibly better designs would be discarded by the anomaly detection, it is only possible to explore but not exploit the solution space with the method presented here. To face the exploration-exploitation trade-off, the most promising designs can be further investigated using a gradient-based optimization method [30]. This allows finding better local minima in a complex parameter and solution space computationally more efficiently. mCANDIES is used in this experiment but could be replaced by another anomaly detector.

Results. The results can be seen in Table 2. The experiments are performed for different hyperparameters α. Varying α, the anomaly detection selects different numbers of candidates for evaluation, i.e. simulation. For α values <0.08, the best design is identified overall 6000 available designs, evaluating only 7.13% of the available design parameter sets. Nevertheless, by increasing α, the number of evaluated design parameter sets decreases, and from a value of $\alpha \geq 0.09$, the best design instance of the data set is no longer found. It can be concluded that the problem can be solved with only a small subset of the total data set. It should be noted that CANDIES only selects design candidates in the exploratory domain. The sampling is shown in the t-Distributed Stochastic Neighbor Embedding (t-SNE) representation in Fig. 5. For the t-SNE representation, we reduce the dimensionality of the 28 design parameters and their corresponding target value to two dimensions [31]. The entire data set with 6000 designs and their corresponding target values are shown using colour gradients. The grey crosses represent the subset of designs selected by CANDIES. It can be seen that the design space, in terms of designs and performance, is sampled almost uniformly.

Table 2. Experiment results. $|Simulated|$ is the number of simulated observations selected by CANDIES with $Simulated(\%)$ being the percentage. $\Delta best$ is the difference in the performance between the best simulated shape and the best shape in the data set. $Best(\%)$ describes the percentage of better shapes in the data set compared to the best simulated shape. The arrows in the column headers indicate whether a high ↑ or low ↓ value is favourable.

α	$|Simulated|$ ↓	$Simulated(\%)$ ↓	$\Delta best$ ↓	$best(\%)$ ↓
0.070	598	9.97	0.0000	0.00
0.080	428	7.13	0.0000	0.00
0.090	319	5.32	6.8674	2.52
0.100	264	4.40	6.8674	2.52
0.110	232	3.87	7.8728	3.78
0.120	219	3.65	10.8946	8.67

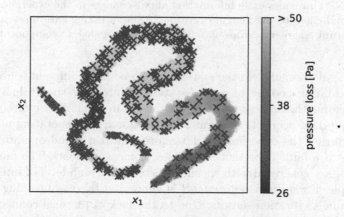

Fig. 5. t-SNE representation of the 28 design parameters including the target value. The colour of the circles indicates the performance; the Grey crosses are the selected topology parameters with $\alpha = 0.08$. (Color figure online)

4.2   Novelty-, Anomaly-Detection in a Motor Test Bench

In our next use-case, we investigate the application of our novelty detection library within the monitoring of motor test benches. A motor test bench produces vast amounts of heterogeneous time series data, consisting of physical quantities, discrete state variables, CAN-bus (Controller Area Network) based communication messages, and other signals. The multitude of factors influencing the motor performance and the complexity of the acquired data can affect the experimental process. The early identification of novelties and abnormal instances in the test bench is essential for avoiding emergency stops and reducing the risk of damage to the devices [32]. A scheme of the setup is shown in Fig. 6. The potential in the application of NDNET algorithms is exceptionally high because it optimizes the development cycle of new electric drives, i.e., when a faulty condition is detected, human operators can quickly correct it before a shutdown of the test bench occurs.

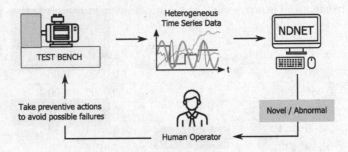

Fig. 6. Visual schematic of the NDNET application in the monitoring of an engine test bench. NDNET provides early information about changes in the experimental process and abnormal cases to the human operator. It allows taking early preventive actions to avoid abrupt emergency stops and avoid possible damage to components.

Errors and anomalies in the system can come from different sources, caused by sensor failure, cooling or power system failure. For the evaluation of this case we assume that the types of faults present in the data are unknown. However, during data acquisition, event logs are stored for annotating malfunctions or faults during the experiments. Therefore, the test stand operator manually determines if a fault is present in a series of measurements. The faults present in the data are generated with specific sensors for a high level of interpretation. For example, a *vibration sensor fault* is generated by disconnecting one of the load machine's vibration sensors. Due to the lack of physical connection of the sensor to the machine, the sensor values are not plausible with the corresponding operating modes. Another example is the *cooling fault*, which is induced by closing one valve of the liquid cooling system. Temperatures during experiments will rise more quickly during load and experiments. A more detailed description of generated fault cases is presented in a monitoring concept for motor test benches [32].

Table 3. Results of novelty and anomaly detection algorithms in the monitoring task of a motor test bench.

Predictor	MCC [%] ↓	F1 [%] ↑	Accuracy [%] ↑
MINAS	7.59 ± 13.68	29.65 ± 21.15	63.07 ± 20.30
NDTDet	8.71 ± 10.16	38.77 ± 18.62	33.71 ± 9.38
OLINDDA	2.20 ± 3.12	0.54 ± 0.76	**75.70** ± 15.80
CSND	11.54 ± 26.79	21.72 ± 23.71	70.67 ± 5.05
α-detector	**40.46** ± 15.17	**49.94** ± 18.67	66.18 ± 14.32
OC-SVM	4.90 ± 22.43	23.68 ± 17.42	53.55 ± 2.97
OHODIN	11.39 ± 8.46	37.87 ± 20.93	27.68 ± 17.80
LOF	17.87 ± 11.79	39.69 ± 22.04	34.26 ± 18.54
LODA-offline	26.91 ± 10.54	36.74 ± 13.20	49.81 ± 13.86
LODA-on-line	3.38 ± 1.62	36.84 ± 19.92	25.17 ± 15.82
IForest	15.95 ± 23.25	23.59 ± 14.38	68.22 ± 7.07
HSTrees	10.97 ± 23.02	34.71 ± 24.73	54.93 ± 7.33
EllipticEnvelope	10.73 ± 29.42	25.38 ± 22.13	56.11 ± 9.84
LSAnomaly	28.84 ± 14.46	43.62 ± 23.08	44.08 ± 18.14

Experimental Setup and Preprocessing. The data used in this experiment correspond to 31 series of measurements with 48 features. Each series of measurements varies highly, from 20 s to almost 35 min. The entire length of the data available is around 6 h, with a sampling rate 100 Hz. The sample rate is reduced 10 Hz by applying a sliding-window sub-sampling strategy to reduce the amount of data and therefore computation time. The data is preprocessed by applying a standardization and a principal-component-analysis (PCA) reduction with five dimensions. The data is split into a training set and a test set with a ratio of 60% to 40%. A hyperparameter optimization (HPO), more precisely a random search, is executed on the training set, with 250 iterations for each algorithm. Only the best parameters of the HPO are used for each algorithm during the validation of the test set. The resulting scoring values for each algorithm are shown in Table 3. Each entry shows the mean and the variance of the scoring metric, which corresponds to a non-stratified, non-shuffled K-Fold Cross-Validation with $k = 3$. For the evaluation of the algorithms the scoring measurements accuracy, F1-score and Matthews correlation coefficient (MCC) [33] were selected to ensure a high degree of interpretation.

Results. An overview of the detection performance of the algorithms is shown in Table 3. In general, all detectors have a higher performance than random classification. This can be seen from the mean values of the results using the MCC score, which are positive ($MCC > 0$). We can appreciate that the MMC- and F1-score provide the most information about the performance since the accuracy score is susceptible to unbalanced data sets. However, the best performing detector using the accuracy score is OLINDDA, with a mean value of 75.7%. But, considering the F1- and MCC-score, it seems reasonable to assume that the detector tends to predict only the normal behaviour. Other detectors have promising results, like the AlphaDetector with a mean F1-score of around 50%, followed by LSAnomaly and LODA-offline. Thus, anomaly detectors (second part of the table) tend to show higher performance than novelty detectors, i.e., MINAS, NDTDet, OLINDDA, CSND, which detect agglomeration of anomalies. Overall, the results can be interpreted as promising, but the high standard deviation should be taken into account.

5   Conclusion and Future Work

We introduced the NDNET library, a collection of implementations of various anomaly and novelty detection algorithms that share a common interface. The library also provides the *mCANDIES* sub-package - a framework on its own that implements the CANDIES methodology. In two case studies we presented how the NDNET library is useful for researchers. Either to develop novelty detectors tuned to specific applications or to easily investigate existing data sets with different anomaly and novelty detectors.

In the first use-case Sect. 4.1, we have shown that CANDIES can be used to explore the objective domain in design optimization problems to find some promising designs in an efficient way. The best design in the data set was found after 428 evaluations of the computer simulation. This results in a total of 5572 simulations being saved in our example. This result shows that due to the simple applicability of NDNET even untypical problems can be easily adapted to novelty and anomaly detection and at the same time provide an additional benefit, which is worth investigating further.

The second use-case Sect. 4.2 shows the capability of NDNET to handle high dimensional data sets with additional pre-processing using PCA to reduce the computational cost. The results show that the failures in the test data are of a novelty nature rather than an anomaly. Further investigations due to the high variation of the scores are required.

In future work, we will extend the existing framework with deep learning-based anomaly and novelty detectors (i.e. AutoEncoders, GANs, Bayesian Networks) and also provide new tools to evaluate novelty detection algorithms.

Acknowledgment. This research has been partly funded by the German Ministry for Education and Research (BMBF) within the projects "Ein Organic-Computing-basierter Ansatz zur Sicherstellung und Verbesserung der Resilienz in technischen und IKT-Systemen (OCTIKT)" (01IS18064C) and the project "AI based Monitoring and Experimental Evaluation (AIMEE)" (01IS19061) and further funded by the Federal Ministry for Economic Affairs and Climate Action (BMWK) within the project "KI-basierte Topologieoptimierung elektrischer Maschinen (KITE)" (19I21034C).

References

1. Pimentel, M.A., Clifton, D.A., Clifton, L., Tarassenko, L.: A review of novelty detection. Signal Process. **99**, 215–249 (2014)
2. de Faria, E.R., de Leon Ferreira, A.C.P., Gama, J.: MINAS: multiclass learning algorithm for novelty detection in data streams. Data Min. Knowl. Discov. **30**(3), 640–680 (2016)
3. Vatanen, T., Kuusela, M., Malmi, E., Raiko, T., Aaltonen, T., Nagai, Y.: Semi-supervised detection of collective anomalies with an application in high energy particle physics. In: The 2012 International Joint Conference on Neural Networks (IJCNN), pp. 1–8. IEEE (2012)
4. Gruhl, C., Sick, B., Tomforde, S.: Novelty detection in continuously changing environments. Futur. Gener. Comput. Syst. **114**, 138–154 (2021)
5. Gruhl, C., Sick, B.: Novelty detection with CANDIES: a holistic technique based on probabilistic models. Int. J. Mach. Learn. Cybern. **9**(6), 927–945 (2018)
6. Spinosa, E.J., de Carvalho, F., de Leon, A., Gama, J.: Novelty detection with application to data streams. Intell. Data Anal. **13**(3), 405–422 (2009)
7. Chandola, V., Banerjee, A., Kumar, V.: Anomaly detection: a survey. ACM Comput. Surv. (CSUR) **41**(3), 1–58 (2009)
8. Babcock, B., Babu, S., Datar, M., Motwani, R., Widom, J.: Models and issues in data stream systems. In: Proceedings of the Twenty-First ACM SIGMOD-SIGACT-SIGART Symposium on Principles of Database Systems, pp. 1–16 (2002)
9. Vakilinia, S., Zhang, X., Qiu, D.: Analysis and optimization of big-data stream processing. In: IEEE Global Communications Conference (GLOBECOM), pp. 1–6. IEEE (2016)
10. Aberer, K., Hauswirth, M., Salehi, A.: A middleware for fast and flexible sensor network deployment. In: Proceedings of the International Conference on Very Large Data Bases (VLDB 2006), pp. 1–4 (2006)
11. Alzghoul, A., Löfstrand, M., Backe, B.: Data stream forecasting for system fault prediction. Comput. Ind. Eng. **62**(4), 972–978 (2012)
12. Gruhl, C.: Novelty detection in multivariate data stream with probabilistic models. Ph.D. thesis, University of Kassel (2022)
13. Pedregosa, F., et al.: Scikit-learn: machine learning in Python. J. Mach. Learn. Res. **12**, 2825–2830 (2011)
14. Zhao, Y., Nasrullah, Z., Li, Z.: PyOD: a Python toolbox for scalable outlier detection. J. Mach. Learn. Res. **20**(96), 1–7 (2019). https://jmlr.org/papers/v20/19-011.html
15. Lavin, A., Ahmad, S.: Evaluating real-time anomaly detection algorithms–the Numenta anomaly benchmark. In: ICMLA, pp. 38–44 (2016). arXiv:1510.03336
16. Faria, E.R., Gama, J., Carvalho, A.C.: Novelty detection algorithm for data streams multi-class problems. In: Proceedings of the 28th Annual ACM Symposium on Applied Computing, pp. 795–800 (2013)
17. Gruhl, C., Sick, B., Wacker, A., Tomforde, S., Hähner, J.: A building block for awareness in technical systems: online novelty detection and reaction with an application in intrusion detection. In: iCAST, pp. 194–200. IEEE (2015)
18. Fisch, D.: Intelligente technische Systeme mit der Fähigkeit zum kollaborativen Wissenserwerb, Dissertation, Universität Kassel (2011)
19. Hoffmann, H.: Kernel PCA for novelty detection. Pattern Recogn. **40**(3), 863–874 (2007)

20. Schölkopf, B., Williamson, R.C., Smola, A.J., Shawe-Taylor, J., Platt, J.C.: Support vector method for novelty detection. In: Advances in neural Information Processing Systems, vol. 12, pp. 582–588 (2000)
21. Gruhl, C., Tomforde, S.: Ohodin-online anomaly detection for data streams. In: 2021 IEEE International Conference on Autonomic Computing and Self-Organizing Systems Companion (ACSOS-C), pp. 193–197. IEEE (2021)
22. Breunig, M.M., Kriegel, H.-P., Ng, R.T., Sander, J.: LOF: identifying density-based local outliers. In: SIGMOD, vol. 29, pp. 93–104. ACM (2000). https://dl.acm.org/citation.cfm?id=335191.335388
23. Pevný, T.: LODA: lightweight on-line detector of anomalies. Mach. Learn. **102**(2), 275–304 (2016)
24. Liu, F.T., Ting, K.M., Zhou, Z.-H.: Isolation forest. In: Eighth IEEE International Conference on Data Mining, pp. 413–422. IEEE (2008)
25. Tan, S.C., Ting, K.M., Liu, T.F.: Fast anomaly detection for streaming data. In: Twenty-Second International Joint Conference on Artificial Intelligence, pp. 1511–1516 (2011)
26. Rousseeuw, P.J., Driessen, K.V.: A fast algorithm for the minimum covariance determinant estimator. Technometrics **41**(3), 212–223 (1999)
27. Quinn, J.A., Sugiyama, M.: A least-squares approach to anomaly detection in static and sequential data. Pattern Recogn. Lett. **40**, 36–40 (2014)
28. Ahmad, A., Bici, M., Campana, F.: Guidelines for topology optimization as concept design tool and their application for the mechanical design of the inner frame to support an ancient bronze statue. Appl. Sci. **11**(17) (2021)
29. Verstraete, T., Coletti, F., Bulle, J., Vanderwielen, T., Arts, T.: Optimization of a U-bend for minimal pressure loss in internal cooling channels-Part I: Numerical method. J. Turbomach. **135**(5) (2013)
30. Bishop, C.M.: Pattern Recognition and Machine Learning. Information Science and Statistics, Springer, Heidelberg (2006)
31. Van der Maaten, L., Hinton, G.: Visualizing data using t-SNE. J. Mach. Learn. Res. **9**(11) (2008)
32. Botache, D., et al.: Towards highly automated machine-learning-empowered monitoring of motor test stands. In: IEEE International Conference on Autonomic Computing and Self-Organizing Systems (ACSOS), pp. 120–130 (2021)
33. Chicco, D., Jurman, G.: The advantages of the Matthews correlation coefficient (MCC) over F1 score and accuracy in binary classification evaluation. BMC Genomics **21**(1), 1–13 (2020)

Organic Computing to Improve the Dependability of an Automotive Environment

Timo Kisselbach[1]🄳, Simon Meckel[2], Mathias Pacher[1(✉)],
Uwe Brinkschulte[1(✉)], and Roman Obermaisser[2(✉)]

[1] Goethe University Frankfurt, Frankfurt, Germany
{kisselbach,m.pacher,brinksch}@em.uni-frankfurt.de
[2] University of Siegen, Siegen, Germany
{simon.meckel,roman.obermaisser}@uni-siegen.de
https://www.es.cs.uni-frankfurt.de/ , https://networked-embedded.de/es

Abstract. The aim of our research is to implement and evaluate Organic Computing methods in a real vehicle environment and thus increase the reliability of the vehicle's steering system. For this purpose, the steering system is simulated using an Organic Computing approach, which is extended with explicit fault diagnosis capabilities. In order to achieve the goals set by the demands of the automotive industry, several development steps are necessary. This paper outlines the research gaps and potentials as well as the approaches we envision to tackle these challenges. The starting point is a general concept involving three Electronic Control Units (ECUs) that act as active redundancy in the event of a component failure, e.g., an ECU failure. Next, the Organic Computing middleware in terms of an Artificial Hormone System in combination with Artificial DNA will be implemented and examined on real automotive hardware, resulting in a highly-reliable, resource- and cost-efficient fail-operational system. Beyond the classical working principles of Organic Computing to overcome ECU failures, our project implements system-level fault diagnosis to additionally monitor ECU performance in the context of the steering system. Forecasting, detecting and identifying faults in the system enables fault-specific recovery actions, e.g., preventive service migration or degradation. Overall, we combine promising relative work to an Organic Computing approach for a vehicle steering system with an industrial partnership with the goal of a functional ECU. After successful deployment, tests will be documented with suitable vehicle hardware in a corresponding simulation environment. This paper provides insight into the early stages of our research project.

Keywords: Organic computing · Artificial DNA · ADNA-based organic computing · Artificial hormone system · Fault diagnosis · Autonomous driving · Vehicle demonstrator · Vehicle steering system

Supported by Federal Ministry for Economic Affairs and Climate Action.

1   Introduction

Autonomous driving requires the interaction of a large number of sensors, actuators, and data processing in the form of an ensemble of embedded systems. Unexpected behavior and unforeseeable faults in the system, e.g., failures of electronic control units, may repeatedly occur [1]. To ensure safe operation, it is essential that such faults do not lead to an accident. In this regard, so-called safety-critical systems are designed to tolerate faults whereby the application determines the degree of fault-tolerance, e.g., requiring the system to be fail-operational (potentially with degraded performance) in case of a fault.

Having a focus on vehicle electronics, the high-safety requirements (as also formulated in the ISO 26262 standard) for autonomously driving vehicles demand the use of additional active redundancies, e.g., Electronic Control Units (ECUs). A vehicle must tolerate and overcome faults during operation, as the driver cannot be considered a kind of redundancy anymore.

Considering both the ever-increasing complexity of modern vehicles and the competitive market environment, it is of utmost importance to establish efficient use of the available hardware resources. For example, 1 : 1 redundancy [2] means running the same function in parallel on two identical ECUs. If one ECU fails, the other ECU continues to perform the function. For efficiency reasons, current approaches are aiming to reduce the active redundancy [3]. With n : 1 redundancy, only a single ECU is kept as a backup ECU, which can replace a failed ECU. Accordingly, the parallel operation of a function, e.g., vehicle steering system, on at least three identical ECUs is necessary for majority redundancy for autonomous driving. Reducing active redundancy makes sense for several reasons:

- It defuses the lack of semiconductors and chips in times of semiconductor crisis.
- It saves costs for operation and maintenance as fewer parts are installed.
- It protects the environment since less energy and raw materials are required along the entire value chain. In addition, there is less waste.
- It reduces waiting times for the final product, which can favor customers' purchasing decisions.

1.1   Scope

This work aims to demonstrate Organic Computing methods for a vehicle steering system with a vehicle simulator and to deepen approaches for a real vehicle environment like [1]. Using Artificial DNA (ADNA) as a description language for an application (i.e., a system service described in terms of tasks and their dependencies, e.g., the steering of a vehicle) and the Artificial Hormone System (AHS) as middleware to allocate such tasks to processing elements of a distributed system (e.g., on ECUs in a modern vehicles' computing and communication infrastructure) is particularly advantageous, as it leads to significantly improved system reliability with low hardware resource demands, while at the same time considerably reducing system complexity.

Organic Computing has been extensively evaluated in simulations and prototypic implementations, e.g., in [4] and related works. However, the specific requirements of the automotive industry, especially with regard to autonomous driving, must be considered if Organic Computing is to reach market maturity.

The project SelfAutoDOC addresses this gap and demonstrates the feasibility and the advantages of an Organic Computing approach in a real hardware vehicle demonstrator by implementing and verifying steering functionalities for autonomous driving. For this, the expertise of the involved partners, i.e., from two universities, from the automotive sector, and from an automotive supplier company complement each other perfectly.

The remainder of the paper is structured as follows: The next section gives an overview of the related work and the research gap. Thereafter, Organic Computing is explored in more detail by introducing the working principles of ADNA and AHS. Next, the extensions of classical Organic Computing based on fault diagnosis are presented. The paper continues with a discussion of the challenges of our Organic Computing approach in the automotive use case with respect to the market readiness of implementations of self-X properties in the vehicle environment. The next section addresses necessary adaptations to a test platform before the paper ends with a discussion of the results and a conclusion.

2   Related Work

Research in the field of self-organizing systems has been going on for several years [5]. The basic principles deal with emergent behavior and reproduction, among other things. The Autonomic Computing project of IBM and DARPAS [6] examines the self-organization of IT servers in networks. Several so-called *self-X properties* were implemented in the MAPE (Monitor, Analyze, Plan, and Execute) cycle. It realizes these self-X properties such as self-optimization, self-stabilization, self-configuration, self-protection, and self-healing.

In Germany, improving the controllability of complex embedded systems is the goal of the Organic Computing initiative [7], founded in 2003. For this purpose, proven organizational principles from biology are transferred to embedded computing systems. International research programs are e.g., [8]. The DoDOrg project first introduced the decentralized AHS [9]. For embedded systems in the automotive sector, self-organization is described in [10]. In the presented approach, DNA-like structures are integrated into automotive ECUs to improve self-organization and self-healing functions. In contrast to centralized self-healing and self-adaptive approaches for automotive systems with optimized task planning like in [11], the Organic Computing approach of this paper works without explicit monitoring and is self-optimizing.

The continuing shortage of semiconductors is fueling the reduction in the number of built-in ECUs. Companies like Tesla are taking a practical approach and are said to reduce the number of ECUs available for some vehicles to maintain sales figures and delivery dates [12]. This brings the driver back into focus as a redundancy. Tesla uses two ECUs for the power steering in the so-called *dual-control steering system.* The absence of the second ECU reduces the level of vehicle autonomy. This is divided into five levels and ranges from level 1 assisted driving to level 5 autonomous driving [13]. If the second control unit is missing, the possible functionality of the vehicle delivered directly from the factory is reduced. For the affected vehicles, the autonomy level drops from level 3, highly automated driving, to level 2, partially automated driving [12]. This means that functions in the area of driverless driving are no longer accessible without first visiting the workshop, although the necessary software update for the level 3 service would be available [12].

Teslas' reduction of redundancy such as the second ECU for the steering should be viewed critically and requires extensive work. Research projects such as AutoConf start here [3]. Another research project is SelfAutoDOC. It uses the OC approach and focuses on using the self-X properties in a vehicle environment. The OC approach makes it possible to transfer the functions of an ECU to other ECUs and thereby create any redundancy.

With the help of an ADNA and AHS simulator, the self-X properties can be analyzed. An ADNA-Editor allows designing an ADNA on a graphical level [18]. An Autonomous Guided Vehicle (AGV) is available for evaluation as a test vehicle [14]. The designed ADNA can be tested directly on the AGV. In addition, a vehicle simulator is available [15]. Based on an extended physical model, the control succeeds in simulating the braking system, engine, and transmission. More complex scenarios can be easily checked with this, which allows the failure resilience to be tested with little effort. The transformation from fail-safe to fail-operational systems is essential in systems that are becoming more and more complex. The simulator allows transparent and cost-efficient development.

The verification of safety features in automotive applications at design time reduces the effort for later adjustments and optimizations. Two approaches are presented in [16], one of which places value on a minimal response time and the other focuses on system reliability.

Runtime verification is used in [17] to check non-functional aspects like reliability and performance in adaptive systems. This is important because adaptive systems adapt to a changing environment and model assumptions can thus change during runtime.

3   ADNA and AHS Concept

Organic Computing takes biological processes in mammals as a blueprint and transfers them to classic multi-core computers. The Deoxyribonucleic Acid (DNA) and the hormone system are adopted in the form of so-called *Artificial DNA* (ADNA) and *Artificial Hormone System* (AHS), respectively. In this way, the self-X properties of organisms become usable for information technology. For example, organisms are self-organizing, self-configuring, and self-healing. Based on biology, this means for a classic embedded system that functions are assigned and executed independently by computing cores.

ADNA and AHS serve as tools. The ADNA contains building instructions for a function according to its biological model of the DNA. A so-called *ADNA*

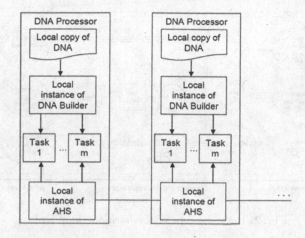

Fig. 1. Basic concept of the ADNA working principles [4].

Processor contains a local copy of the DNA and creates a local instance of the function with a so-called *DNA Builder*. Upon system startup, tasks relevant to the function are provided by the DNA processor and are waiting to be executed by a computer node [4]. Figure 1 abstracts the interaction of ADNA and AHS.

The AHS is a decentralized middleware approach. It manages the distribution and assignment of tasks. According to its biological model, hormones are released and distributed in the system via a control circuit, the so-called *hormone loop*. Figure 2 highlights the function principles of the hormone loop [18]. PE is the processing element (indexed by γ), T the task (indexed by i), E the eager value, Em the modified eager value, S the suppressor, and A the accelerator. In the notation, received values are superscripted and sent values are subscripted. Finally, the $\sum$-sign computes the modified eager values Em as a sum of the local (static) eager values E, received suppressors S, and received accelerators A. If the eager value $a = Em_{i\gamma}$ is larger than the received eager value $b = Em^{i\gamma}$, i.e., $(a > b\ ?)$, PE_γ will take over the task T_i, otherwise it will be executed by other PEs with appropriate eager values. Corresponding to Fig. 2, the following three hormones control the assignment of tasks:

Eager Values – are static suitability values. They are set by the developer separately for each PE according to its suitability for performing a particular task. At each hormone cycle, eager values are converted into modified eager values and sent to all PEs. In turn, received (modified) eager values are compared with the locally modified eager values (for each task) at each PE. The PE with the largest eagerness value takes over the task and executes it. When tasks are started so-called *suppressor* and *accelerator hormones* are additionally sent.

Suppressors – are paid out globally and subtracted from static eager values. This prevents multiple instantiations of tasks in the system. This closes the control loop and leads to a stable execution of the tasks.

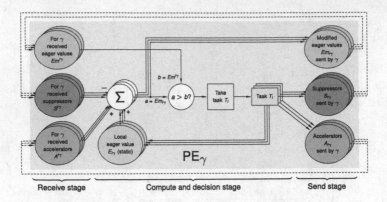

Fig. 2. Basic concept of the hormone loop [18].

Accelerators – are only distributed to neighboring PEs and increase the static eager value of a receiving PE. This leads to the clustering of cooperating tasks and thus to an optimization of the communication distance between related tasks.

4 Fault Diagnosis

Organic Computing in combination with the AHS that organizes task allocations to processing elements in distributed systems inherently overcomes certain fault scenarios, in particular processing element failures. In combination with techniques of active fault diagnosis, Organic Computing enables to identify a broader range of fault cases (e.g., sensor failures) and also looming fault potentials in a fine-granular manner, so that the reliability and availability of system services get significantly increased by means of targeted system interactions, e.g., reconfigurations, degradations.

In a self-organizing runtime environment, a diagnosis model (in the form of a diagnosis ADNA) must also adapt continuously. This is possible by means of a meta-level (automotive diagnosis ontology, e.g., based on AUTOSAR) from which the diagnosis ADNA is derived. The ontology forms the basis for the formal description of diagnostic data (e.g., features derived from sensor measurements) and their relationships to each other. In addition to the existing domain expertise, multivariate analysis methods (e.g., principal component analysis, PCA), among others, help to reveal the characteristic relationships of the information relevant to fault diagnosis.

The encoding of the diagnosis model in ADNA is enabled by the definition of diagnostic ADNA basic building blocks, followed by the development of synthesis algorithms. The latter map the concepts from the ontology to the given physical resources of the real system, yet, such diagnosis models (derived from semantics) may have ambiguities.

For optimization and evaluation of the diagnosis models in the self-organizing OC runtime environment, an existing test bench with the automotive application forms the starting point. By extending it with fault injection according to a fault model, a development environment is created to extract diagnostic features e.g., from sensor data, data from the application, data from the network (e.g., timing), and data from the operating system. For such ADNA optimizations, genetic algorithms are suitable since ADNA can be perfectly represented in the form of a genome. Through targeted artificial mutations of the composition of the basic operators, the synthesized initial solution of the diagnosis ADNA can be modified initially in the design process (as well as concurrently at system runtime) and improved in terms of an objective function (diagnostic coverage and confidence of fault cause identification).

Based on the identified fault causes, the necessary interactions with the system are communicated via the AHS, which causes a self-organizing reconfiguration. For this purpose, strategies are developed for all fault cases defined in the failure model (e.g., degradation possibilities for certain services) and integrated into the self-healing mechanisms.

5 Challenges with the Organic Computing Approach

5.1 Accessing Sensors and Actuators

The Organic Computing approach poses challenges to both fault diagnosis and the implementation on changed hardware structures as general portability to different target hardware is initially not given with the OC approach. Although the ADNA is highly portable, varying resource parameters (recall Fig. 3) of the target hardware might torpedo an easy adaptation of different sensors and actuators. This, however, is of utmost importance for proper system operation and, implicitly, for producing sound fault diagnosis results.

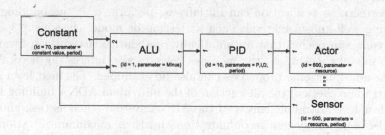

Fig. 3. Closed control loop as ADNA.

5.2   Development Tools and Simulations

The high standards of the automotive industry, such as the ISO 26262, represent a particular challenge for the SelfAutoDOC project. To fulfill the requirements for safety and compatibility of the ECU to be developed, it is essential to combine our Organic Computing approach with the development tools of the automotive industry. This can be done, for example, in the open development environment AUTOSAR [19]. Another candidate here is the MotionWise middleware, a series-proven safety software platform for automated driving [20].

To investigate the behavior of ADNA and AHS, extensive simulations and tests have to be performed. Of interest are the communication processes, the self-healing mechanisms, the interaction of ADNA and AHS, but also the real-time capability of the system and its deployment in a real simulation environment. As outlined in Sect. 5.1, the resource parameters must match different hardware to guarantee correct sensor and actuator control. Vehicle simulators such as [15] can be used to test the behavior.

5.3   System Verification

Recall Sect. 2, a framework for testing algorithms for self-organizing systems is presented in [21]. Due to its flexibility and that of its environment, it is difficult in some situations to distinguish misbehavior from correct behavior (which may even be suboptimal). The framework handles a large number of states and nested loops. In [22], an approach to investigate algorithms for self-organizing systems in isolated environments with probabilistic environment profiles is presented. The evaluations show that various faults, particularly design faults, are found within an acceptable time frame.

The validation and verification will be approached in a targeted manner since a very specific system has been selected with the ADNA. Factors such as the functional correctness of the system and non-functional properties such as compliance with time limits, clock periods, etc. must be examined. The functional correctness verification can initially be performed at the building block level using well-known methods such as testing or model checking [23]. Naturally, recent approaches that automatically modularize the given software and perform model checking on the modules [24] are also interesting here. At this level, the non-functional properties can also be examined. The next level is then the correctness check of the interaction of the individual ADNA building blocks. At the last level, dynamic effects of the ADNA system (such as task allocation times, decisions on system reconfiguration and their maximum duration, etc.) are then investigated. A detailed specification of the ADNA system is used for this purpose.

6   Adaption to a Test Platform

Various challenges have to be overcome in the process. Since the target hardware is not yet available, the first tests are carried out with a simple test setup. It consists of three multi-core processor elements (PE) and a diagnostic computer in the shared network. This allows different development stages to be tested in advance. First, the experimental setup is presented. From this, individual milestones are derived and discussed, as can be seen in the Figs. 6, 7, 8 and 9.

Three Raspberry Pis (RPi) type 3b were chosen as PEs to serve as ECU replacements. Their four computing cores each have enough power for a wide range of applications. The experiment is controlled via a notebook, which runs the fault diagnosis. An identical instance of the vehicle steering system runs on each PE. All communications take place via Ethernet. Figure 4 shows the current experimental setup.

Fig. 4. Experimental setup with three Raspberry Pis.

6.1 General Autonomous Driving Approach

As a general approach for autonomous driving, three ECUs are envisaged as active redundancy. In the event of faults, the ECU data is compared with each other and the vehicle is to be steered on a majority basis. With the help of control and diagnostics, individual ECUs can be manipulated selectively to examine faults and system behavior. Figure 5 shows the schematic structure.

6.2 Autonomous Driving with Organic Computing

While the general approach mentioned in Sect. 6.1 may already be standard, our Organic Computing approach brings independence and reliability due to the ADNA and AHS.

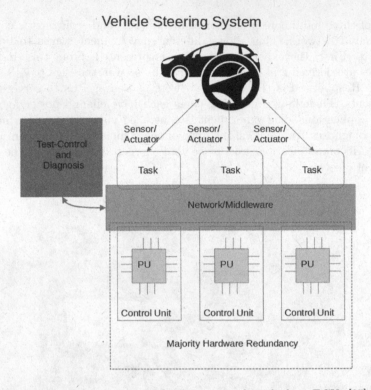

Fig. 5. General autonomous driving approach with three ECUs [25].

OC Implementation – First, the ADNA must be emulated for the vehicle steering system, with the AHS acting as middleware that also accesses the network. The ADNA contains the blueprints for the vehicle's steering function. At system startup, the required tasks are provided and distributed by the AHS to the PEs. The goal is to run identical instances on all three ECUs. The purpose of the diagnosis is to detect, identify, and predict system faults and to initiate recovery actions as a complement to classical majority control. Figure 6 shows the development step. AHS and ADNA are implemented on the target hardware. Three ECUs are shown as active redundancy.

OC Stress Test – It is planned to manipulate individual ECUs in a targeted manner and to investigate the self-healing properties. The failure of individual PEs, but also of individual sensors or actuators will be examined. Utilizing diagnosis, a targeted evaluation of the system behavior will be performed. Figure 7 shows a possible fail-operational case, i.e., a lost sensor. With the implemented diagnosis the fail operation will be examined. From this stage, safe operation in the vehicle is already possible and research priorities are being set, especially concerning self-healing properties.

Implementation of an Organic Computing Software Redundancy – The next step is to develop and implement OC software redundancy to increase

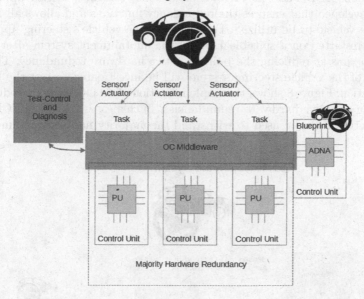

Fig. 6. Concept behind the OC autonomous driving approach with three ECUs [25].

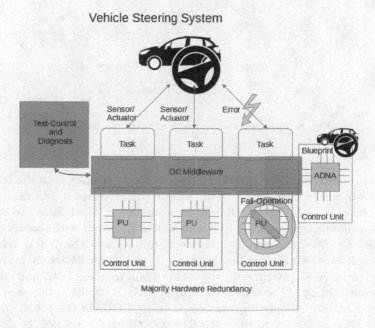

Fig. 7. Failure operational case, i.e., a lost sensor [25].

system reliability or to reduce the number of ECUs installed. This is possible by extending the ADNA and the AHS. A control loop for safety-critical applications will be developed that ensures the redundancy functions and allows all ECUs of the entire vehicle to be utilized. For example, the vehicle's steering application could be restarted on a suitable ECU of the infotainment system after a fault. This step aims at reducing the built-in active hardware redundancy. Then, the behavior of the vehicle steering system will be investigated to test the limits of the reduction. Figure 8 shows the implementation of an OC software redundancy with reduced active hardware redundancies. In this case, any other ECU in the vehicle network can be used to withstand the majority hardware redundancy.

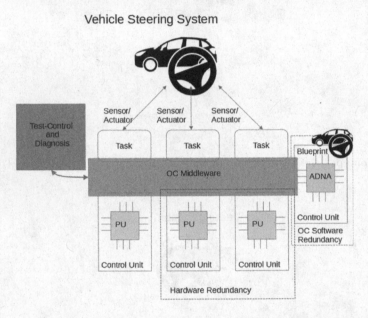

Fig. 8. Implemented OC software redundancy [25].

Final Stage: Stress Test of OC Software Redundancy – In the last step, detailed tests will be carried out to investigate the extended self-healing properties and the reduction of active hardware redundancy. The failure and recovery of the steering function on other ECUs, as well as problems with sensors or actuators, will be verified through diagnostics. Figure 9 shows the final development step. OC software redundancy means that a total of three ECUs are available as active redundancy at any time. In the event of failure, the ADNA and AHS perform the self-healing of the vehicle steering system. If one ECU fails, the ADNA blueprint is able to resume its function on other ECUs in the vehicle network. To do this, it is necessary to solve the ID issues. With the help of the diagnosis, it is possible to document fail-operation cases and analyze the self-healing.

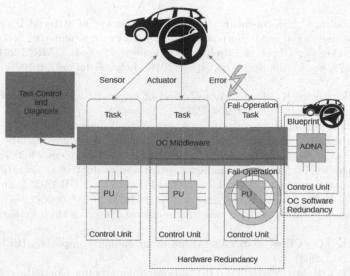

Fig. 9. Final stage of the OC autonomous driving approach for a possible vehicle steering system [25].

7 Conclusion

This paper presents an approach to how to implement an Organic Computing solution in a vehicle environment in the research project SelfAutoDOC. To this end, methods and related challenges have been highlighted to which the respective project participants contribute with their expertise, previous work, and various building blocks to successfully bring Organic Computing to the automotive domain.

The paper presents the main tests on an experimental hardware platform. The results are to be further verified through extensive diagnostics and simulated tests up to market readiness. The necessary steps on the test level have been highlighted.

Particular attention is paid to the objective of keeping the number of electronic control units as low as possible while maintaining the required redundancy level, which saves costs and protects the environment. In summary, an Organic Computing approach is implemented in a concrete test setup for a vehicle environment with a step-by-step expansion of the functional scope. After successful tests with the presented structure consisting of RPi and Ethernet, further tests with typical vehicle hardware (ECUs) and associated networks (CAN, TSN, TTEthernet) follow. Publications follow according to the current state of research. In the end, a functional solution on an ECU is expected.

References

1. Brinkschulte, U., Fastnacht, F.: Applying the concept of artificial DNA and hormone system to a low-performance automotive environment. In: Schoeberl, M., Hochberger, C., Uhrig, S., Brehm, J., Pionteck, T. (eds.) ARCS 2019. LNCS, vol. 11479, pp. 87–99. Springer, Cham (2019). https://doi.org/10.1007/978-3-030-18656-2_7
2. Yi, C.H., Kwon, K., Jeon, J.W.: Method of improved hardware redundancy for automotive system, pp. 204–207 (2015)
3. AutoKonf, Automatisch rekonfigurierbare Aktoriksteuerungen für ausfallsichere automatisierte Fahrfunktionen, Federal ministry of education and research. https://www.elektronikforschung.de/projekte/autokonf. Accessed 26 July 2022
4. Brinkschulte, U.: Prototypic implementation and evaluation of an artificial DNA for self-descripting and self-building embedded systems. EURASIP J. Embed. Syst. **2017**(1), 1–16 (2017). https://doi.org/10.1186/s13639-016-0066-2
5. Jetschke, G.: Mathematik der Selbstorganisation. Harry Deutsch Verlag, Frankfurt (1989)
6. Kephart, J.O., Chess, D.M.: The vision of autonomic computing. IEEE Comput. **36**, 41–50 (2003)
7. VDE/ITG (Hrsg.), VDE/ITG/GI-Positionspapier Organic Computing: Computer- und Systemarchitektur im Jahr 2010, GI, ITG, VDE (2003)
8. CSIRO, centre for complex systems (2009). http://www.dar.csiro.au/css/. Accessed 26 July 2022
9. Brinkschulte, U., Pacher, M., Renteln, A.: An artificial hormone system for self-organizing real-time task allocation in organic middleware. In: Organic Computing. UCS, pp. 261–283. Springer, Heidelberg (2009). https://doi.org/10.1007/978-3-540-77657-4_12
10. Weiss, G., Zeller, M., Eilers, D., Knorr, R.: Towards self-organization in automotive embedded systems. In: González Nieto, J., Reif, W., Wang, G., Indulska, J. (eds.) ATC 2009. LNCS, vol. 5586, pp. 32–46. Springer, Heidelberg (2009). https://doi.org/10.1007/978-3-642-02704-8_4
11. Klöpper, B., Honiden, S., Meyer, J., Tichy, M.: Planning with utility and state trajectory constraints in self-healing automotive systems. In: Fourth IEEE International Conference on Self-Adaptive and Self-Organizing Systems, SASO 2010, Budapest, Hungary, 27 September - 1 October 2010, pp. 74–83. IEEE Computer Society (2010). https://doi.org/10.1109/SASO.2010.16
12. Kolodny, L.: CNBC: tesla cut a steering component from some cars to deal with chip shortage, sources say. Published 7 Feb 2022, Updated 8 Feb 2022. https://www.cnbc.com/2022/02/07/tesla-cut-a-steering-component-to-deal-with-chip-shortage.html. Accessed 26 July 2022
13. Maurer, J.M., Gerdes, C., Lenz, B., Winner, H.: Autonomes Fahren: Technische, rechtliche und gesellschaftliche Aspekte. Springer, Heidelberg (2015)
14. Brinkschulte, U.: Technical report: Artificial DNA - a concept for self-building embedded systems. ArXiv CoRR abs/1707.07617 (2017). http://arxiv.org/abs/1707.07617. Accessed 25 July 2022
15. Brinkschulte, M.: Development of a vehicle simulator for the evaluation of a novel organic control unit concept. In: Reussner, R. H., Koziolek, A., Heinrich, R. (eds.) INFORMATIK 2020, pp. 883–890. Gesellschaft für Informatik, Bonn (2021). https://doi.org/10.18420/inf2020_79

16. Xie, G., Zeng, G., Liu, Y., Zhou, J., Li, R., Li, K.: Fast functional safety verification for distributed automotive applications during early design phase. IEEE Trans. Ind. Electron. **65**(5), 4378–4391 (2018)

17. Filieri, A., Ghezzi, C., Tamburrelli, G.: A formal approach to adaptive software: continuous assurance of non-functional requirements. Form. Asp. Comp. **24**, 163–186 (2011). https://doi.org/10.1007/s00165-011-0207-2

18. Hutter, E., Brinkschulte, U.: Towards a priority-based task distribution strategy for an artificial hormone system. In: Brinkmann, A., Karl, W., Lankes, S., Tomforde, S., Pionteck, T., Trinitis, C. (eds.) Architecture of Computing Systems - ARCS 2020. Lecture Notes in Computer Science, vol. 12155, pp. 69–81. Springer, Cham (2020). https://doi.org/10.1007/978-3-030-52794-5_6

19. Brinkschulte, U., Hutter, E., Fastnacht, F.: Adapting the concept of artificial DNA and hormone system to a classical AUTOSAR environment. In: 2019 IEEE 22nd International Symposium on Real-Time Distributed Computing (ISORC). IEEE (2019)

20. TTTechAuto: MotionWise. https://www.tttech-auto.com/products/safety-software-platform/motionwise/. Accessed 25 July 2022

21. Eberhardinger, B., Anders, G., Seebach, H., Siefert, F., Reif, W.: A framework for testing self-organization algorithms. GI Softwaretechniktrends **35**(1), 1–2 (2015)

22. Eberhardinger, B., Anders, G., Seebach, H., Siefert, F., Knapp, A., Reif, W.: An approach for isolated testing of self-organization algorithms. In: de Lemos, R., Garlan, D., Ghezzi, C., Giese, H. (eds.) Software Engineering for Self-Adaptive Systems III. Assurances. LNCS, vol. 9640, pp. 188–222. Springer, Cham (2017). https://doi.org/10.1007/978-3-319-74183-3_7

23. Baier, C., Katoen, J.P.: Principles of Model Checking. MIT Press, Cambridge (2008)

24. Kleine Büning, M., Sinz, C.: Automatic modularization of large programs for bounded model checking. In: Ait-Ameur, Y., Qin, S. (eds.) ICFEM 2019. LNCS, vol. 11852, pp. 186–202. Springer, Cham (2019). https://doi.org/10.1007/978-3-030-32409-4_12

25. Butterflytronics: Auto, und, Lenkung Symbol. Copyright. License: CC Version 4.0. Disclaimer: original symbol implemented, changes in size may made. https://icon-icons.com/de/symbol/Auto-und-Lenkung-Rad-transport-Fahrzeug/123460

A Context Aware and Self-improving Monitoring System for Field Vegetables

Nils Lüling[1]($\boxtimes$), Jonas Boysen[2], Henning Kuper[1,2], and Anthony Stein[2]

[1] Department of Technology in Crop Production, University of Hohenheim, Garbenstraße 9, 70599 Stuttgart, Germany
nils.lueling@uni-hohenheim.de, henning.kuper@kaluha.de
[2] Department of Artificial Intelligence in Agricultural Engineering, University of Hohenheim, Garbenstraße 9, 70599 Stuttgart, Germany
{jonas.boysen,anthony.stein}@uni-hohenheim.de

Abstract. Camera-based vision systems are becoming increasingly influential in the advancing automation of agriculture. Smart Farming technologies such as selective mechanical or chemical weeding are already firmly implemented processes in practice utilizing intelligent camera technology. The capabilities of such technologies recently advanced with the implementation of Deep Learning-based Computer Vision algorithms which proved their applicability in the agricultural domain by successfully solving classification, object detection and segmentation tasks. Due to the demanding environment of agricultural fields and the increasing dependence of farmers on the correct and reliable functioning of such systems, we propose to utilize agronomic context of a field to obtain a self-improving system for camera-based detection and segmentation of cabbage plants. For this purpose, we trained and tested a neural network for instance segmentation (Mask R-CNN) with different datasets of white cabbage (*brassica oleracea*). In our work, the relevant context parameters are the expected height of the plants as well as the color of the plant pixels. A cost-efficient camera setup utilizing a Structure from Motion (SfM) approach was used to gain complementary depth images. Knowledge gaps in our system appearing in form of missed or poorly detected and segmented plants can be closed by means of an Active Learning approach. This leads to an improvement in our experiments by up to 27.2% in terms of mean average precision.

Keywords: Smart Farming · Active Learning · Cabbage · Instance segmentation · Organic Computing · Context-awareness · Self-improvement

1 Introduction

With the digitization reaching agricultural farms, robotics and autonomous systems show increased use in agricultural fields. These systems are utilized in, e.g., mechanical or chemical weeding and need to observe their working environment to perform and evaluate their work. A steadily growing demand for automated systems in agriculture results from the increasing difficulty in finding qualified and affordable workers. This trend is particularly evident in field vegetable production, as the majority of costs is

M. Schulz et al. (Eds.): ARCS 2022, LNCS 13642, pp. 226–240, 2022.
https://doi.org/10.1007/978-3-031-21867-5_15

human labor [7]. The most time-consuming tasks are harvesting and mechanical weed control, which are becoming increasingly important due to the growing demand for sustainably produced food [27]. For this purpose, intelligent vision systems are subject of research using Computer Vision methods to extract features of the working environment. With the recent advances in Deep Learning-based Computer Vision, these vision systems gain new potential in agricultural contexts [18].

The classification, localization and segmentation of vegetable plants on images serves as a starting point for automated detection of plant growth, yield prediction or weed control. These Computer Vision tasks can be solved with a Convolutional Neural Network (CNN) performing instance segmentation such as Mask R-CNN [11]. For these data-intensive models, a substantial amount of annotated training data is required and the pixel-wise annotation of the images is a highly time-demanding task [2]. Even if sufficient training data is available, the broad variety of different environment conditions in agricultural fields such as different lighting conditions, plant stadium or soil color may hinder a model to generalize well [19]. An ongoing annotation of new data and automated fine-tuning of models could lead to continual model self-improvement.

Organic Computing is a systems engineering paradigm concerned with building intelligent systems that possess so-called self-x properties rendering their behavior 'lifelike', i.e., allowing these systems to act robustly and flexibly in complex real world environments. Among these properties, self-adaptation, self-optimization and self-learning (often summarized as self-improvement) as well as self-healing belong to the most investigated ones. In this work, we render a monitoring system for field vegetables self-improving by enabling it to detect knowledge gaps [28] in its detection capability and propose a means how to automatically close these gaps using an Active Learning approach. Therefore, we endow the system with basic context-awareness and a self-reflection capability.

Active Learning strategies relieve the annotator by, e.g., allowing the system to only queue images for annotation for which its prediction is uncertain [26]. We propose to leverage and extend these learning strategies by making our system aware of agronomic context and thus transform it into a self-adaptive OC system. This context in the form of the height and the color of the crops can be utilized to allow the system to identify that there is a crop plant in the image with high probability and further allow the identification of knowledge gaps in the model. In our scenario, the system is also enabled for unsupervised annotation utilizing a dynamic context-based segmentation method.

Our work aims to increase the robustness and adaptivity of our system by equipping it with autonomous learning behavior. This work contributes to a workflow allowing a model to continuously adapt its parametrization by increasing its experiences with images under consideration of the agronomic context and the uncertainty of the model itself. Through our dynamically adapting threshold segmentation by color and depth information, plants can be annotated automatically. This enables more robust autonomous robot systems on vegetable fields with minimal sensor effort. We evaluate the influence on the mean average precision of our model when our system is aware of its context and utilizes it for autonomous learning behavior. For this purpose, we experimentally investigate the performance of instance segmentation of white cabbage on several own datasets containing real-world.

2 Related Work

For a robust use of RGB images with Deep Learning-based systems in agricultural fields, an enormous amount of annotated data is required for a given crop, as the appearance of the plant changes greatly depending on the growth stage and the environmental conditions. In the research literature, different combinations of sensors are implemented to improve their systems. The general intention of these combinations is to increase detection accuracy and improve robustness against external influences. Many approaches use near-infrared in addition to the RGB channels to complement the algorithms [16, 17]. Gai et al. [9] combine RGB images with depth images from a Kinect v2 sensor to improve the detection of broccoli and leaf lettuce under high weed pressure. The additional information provided by the combination of both sensors led to an improvement in performance compared to using the sensors individually. Farooq et al. [8] use hyperspectral images to detect weeds. By using additional spectral bands, the detection accuracy of the CNN was improved in contrast to the Histogram of Oriented Gradients (HoG) method. The fusion of several sensors increases the depth of information on which the models can capitalize.

The training data of a CNN is crucial for its performance. Preprocessing, acquisition, generation and duplication are of great interest to the systems. Typical data augmentation methods are noise reduction, image scaling, normalization and general image correction [29]. Lottes et al. [15] use a Gaussian Blur algorithm for each channel (red, green, blue and near infra-red) of the individual images to remove noise from the training data. Jiang et al. [12] prepared their data using a contrast-limited adaptive histogram equalization (CLAHE) algorithm to increase image contrast aiming to create reduced variation due to lighting conditions. Semi-supervised learning or AI-supported data annotation can lead to improved datasets with less time effort [3, 6, 32] have developed an image annotation tool specifically for use in the agricultural sector. Among other tools, they use semi- and fully automatic methods to speed up the annotation process.

In the agricultural domain, an OC-system has already been researched in the form of a holistic optimization approach to a tractor [13]. They realized their approach by using an Observer/ Controller architecture, which is typically used in OC. Their goal is to increase output efficiency in the complex system of a Fendt Vario tractor. Active Learning strategies have been applied to the recognition of crop and weed on hyperspectral images [21], the estimation of ear density on RGB images [20], the weed identification [33] and the detection of panicles in cereal crops [4].

3 Approach

Organic Computing systems are commonly designed based on the well-known Multi-layer Observer/Controller architecture (MLOC) [31]. This work mainly focuses on improving the observer components in the reactive (also called adaptation layer) as well as the proactive (often also referred to as reflection layer) layers 1 and 2. In the reactive layer 1, we enhance the system state by means of adding context-information and thus making the system context-aware. In layer 2, the self-reflection capability is addressed in our work by allowing the system to reason upon its confidence scores in reliably detecting vegetables and use this information to detect knowledge gaps that are then closed with an Active Learning approach. In view of the utilization of the proposed enhanced vision system within an intelligent robotic system capable of applying measures to the monitored crops, a more detailed description of the controller components constitutes part of future work.

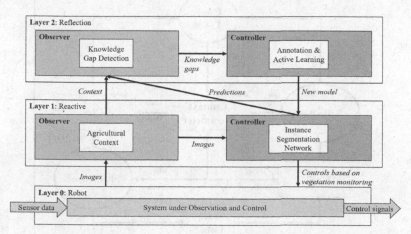

Fig. 1. Overview of our MLOC system of self-improving vegetables monitoring (adapted from [22]).

In our case, the first layer of our system displayed in Fig. 1 observes its environment through the RGB image and further processes the image to calculate context information. The controller of this first layer contains the instance segmentation network and performs the detection and segmentation of the cabbage plants which can be utilized for vegetation monitoring [18] and may lead to controls for a robot in future works. In the second layer, our system will reflect on its decision of the detection and segmentation. The observing part of this reflecting layer is providing self-awareness to our system by detecting knowledge gaps [28] through comparing the predictions of the first layer with the agricultural context. If the confidence level of a prediction is low, the system will reflect its prediction on the agronomic context and reveal knowledge gaps. If a knowledge gap is detected, the controller of this layer will retrain the instance segmentation network contained in the controller of our decision layer and thus makes our system self-adaptive.

3.1 Proposed Algorithm

To utilize the proposed MLOC for our experiments, we developed an algorithm including the calculation and awareness to agricultural context, the self-reflection of the predictions, the unsupervised training data generation and the Active Learning component. This algorithm is displayed in the form of a float chart in Fig. 2. The algorithm aims to use context parameters to check the segmentation of the Mask R-CNN as well as to perform a post-segmentation by the context parameters. In doing so, an attempt was made to deal with all detection situations that could occur in a practical application.

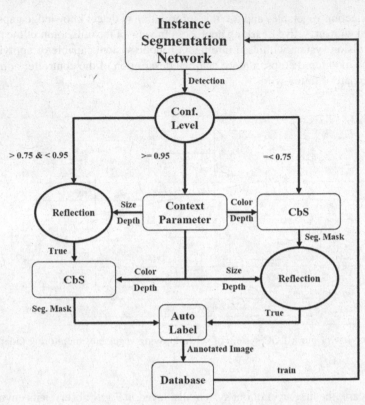

Fig. 2. Active Learning process including Context-based Segmentation (CbS) for automated annotation

In our algorithm, a detection of the instance segmentation network can have three different confidence levels. If the confidence level is less than 0.75, no successful detection was performed by the Mask R-CNN and no segmentation mask is available. The confidence level is greater than 0.75 but less than 0.95. Therefore, there is a high probability that a successful detection has taken place, but the segmentation is probably insufficient. The last possibility is a confidence level greater than 0.95. In this case, the algorithm assumes a successful and sufficiently accurate detection and segmentation. With these accurate detections, the context parameters are determined.

The context parameters always refer to the segmented area of a detection with a confidence level greater 0.95. The color, size and depth information of the segmented area is recorded and averaged over all plants. The hue channel of the HSV color space is used for color information, because all color information is located in this channel and is therefore easier to process. The context parameters behave dynamically, as they are influenced by each new segmentation with high confidence levels. The context parameters of depth and color are used to create an orientation value that can guide the subsequent steps. For this purpose, the color values (H) and the depth information (D) of the segmented areas are averaged and an origin vector is calculated from these two values as depicted in Fig. 3. The vector length $(\overrightarrow{DH})$ and the angle α_{mean} to the X-axis are used as context parameter for the subsequent segmentation.

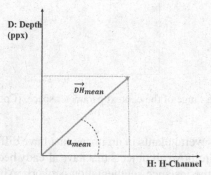

Fig. 3. Agricultural Context in the form of depth and color information.

If a prediction has a confidence level between 75% and 95%, it counts as a knowledge gap and the size and depth of the segmented area are compared with the context parameters (size and depth) of the predictions with a confidence level greater 0.95. If the size and the depth information of the segmented area do not lie within a certain tolerance range, it is a false positive detection and the knowledge gap cannot be closed by including the image in a new training data set. If the size of the segmentation and the depth are similar to the context data, the image is processed further. In this further step, the plant needs to be segmented which is done by the Context based Segmentation (CbS) step in which a binary mask is generated from the color and depth information. The CbS is carried out in three steps:

1. In the first step, the algorithm checks the length and angle of the orientation vector from the context parameters color and depth from the previously successfully segmented plants. These values adjust to the current situation depending on new segmentations with high confidence levels. For the image to be processed, the angle and length of the respective vector is calculated for each pixel. The segmentation of a pixel only takes place if the length as well as the angle are in a tolerance range to the context parameters. Figure 4 visualizes the tolerance range (orange area) and the context parameters (green vector).

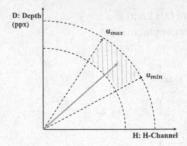

Fig. 4. Tolerance range of the context parameter space. (Color figure online)

2. Since there may be several plants in an image that have different confidence levels, the second step is to remove all objects that have already been examined or successfully segmented by the instance segmentation network. After that, only the largest remaining object is segmented.
3. Finally, the size and depth information of the binary mask is compared to the context parameters of size and depth. If these comparison results in values within a tolerance range, the annotation mask is completed.

If the Mask R-CNN does not detect an object or the Object has a confidence level below 0.75, a binary mask is computed by the previously described CbS. The size as well as the depth information of the largest object in the binary mask is compared with the context parameters, to check whether the prediction of the Mask R-CNN is a false negative or a true negative. If the values resulting from the comparison are within a certain tolerance range, the image and the mask can be used for automatic annotation.

For automated annotation, the contour of the binary object is traced and the pixel positions are saved and transferred to the appropriate annotation format. As a final step, the newly annotated images are added to the original dataset and the original Mask R-CNN is re-trained with the new dataset. An 80 to 20 split takes place, adding the newly annotated images to the original training and evaluation dataset. In the subsequent training of the Mask R-CNN, only the last layers of the network are re-trained.

3.2 Experimental Setup

Dataset Recording. Four datasets of different growth stages were created for the analysis of the Active Learning Process. A standard GoPro camera (Hero 7, GoPro Inc., San Mateo, CA, USA) was used to capture the training and test images from a vertical perspective without shading or artificial exposure. The camera was moved across the rows at a recording frequency of 60 Hz and a resolution of 1920 × 1440, with constant height of 900 mm and speed of 1 m/s to produce high-quality depth images by a structure from motion approach [19].

For subsequent application in the field, the camera system should be attached to the robot platform Phoenix [25]. The caterpillar tracks and the generally good field conditions in vegetable cultivation ensure a relative smooth camera movement. The displayed cabbage is a storage cabbage of the cultivar Storidor, grown with a row width

A Context Aware and Self-improving Monitoring System   233

of 600 mm and a planting distance of 600 mm. Table 1 shows sample images from the used trainings data sets with their according growth stage and average plant coverage. Most of the cabbage plants are recorded in macro stage 1 of the BBCH scale. The pictures of the vegetation exhibit sporadic weeds, but the weed pressure is in general low. The soil partly contains residues from the previous crop [19].

Table 1. Datasets overview

Dataset	(1)	(2)	(3)	(4)
RGB image				
Growth stage	BBCH 15	BBCH 16	BBCH 17	BBCH 19
Plant coverage (avg. %)	16.2	40.0	41.0	67.2

Software and Dataset Setup. The Mask R-CNN [1] is mainly based on the libraries Tensorflow GPU 1.3.0 [14, 23, 30]. The segmentation through the color and depth information, the automated labelling, as well as the depth image calculation were implemented with MATLAB (Matlab R2020a, The MathWorks Inc., Natick, MA, USA). The complete training and the following steps were carried out with a computer with an AMD Ryzen Threadripper 2920X 12-core processor 64 GB RAM and a 24 GB graphics card (GeForce RTX 3090, Nvidia corporate, Santa Clara, CA, USA).

A comparatively small data set is used to better analyze the influences of the procedure. A major advantage of the presented algorithm is its adaptivity to changing conditions by adjusting the context parameter values and the inclusion of new data in the training data set of the neural network. For a better analysis of the adaptivity of the process, the initial network was trained only with images of one growth stage (Dataset 3). The starting dataset consists of 180 training images, 20 evaluation images, with a resolution of 512x512 pixels.

For the evaluation of the algorithm, 5 test data sets are created with 120 images each, consisting of equal parts of the four different growth stages. This serves to analyze the development of the mAP [5], as new training images from different growth stages are added with each run of the algorithm. To avoid overfitting, different image augmentation techniques (shift, rotation, scaling, mirroring) are used before each training epoch The Mask-RCNN is trained with one class over 15 epochs utilizing stochastic gradient descent, an image batch size of four and a learning rate of 0.0001.

Depth Image Calculation. Due to its cost-effectiveness and versatility, depth information acquisition using a SfM approach is widely used for agricultural applications [10, 24] (Fig. 5). The linear movement of the camera at a constant height and speed, the short distance between camera and object as well as the static environment offer good conditions for an SfM method. To validate the calculated depth images, a reference scale was placed in the field to conduct the tests [18].

Fig. 5. Comparison of an RGB image (a) and a calculated structure from motion depth image (b)

4   Results

An important process step in the optimization of segmentation accuracy by the presented algorithm lies in CbS. Faulty segmentation by the CbS leads to faulty annotation, whereby incorrect features are learned in the subsequent training run. Table 2 shows the different stages of the algorithm, from the four different growth stages after one algorithm run.

The first image, shows the angle of the two-dimensional vector of color and depth information of each pixel. With this angle and the length of the vector, a binary image is segmented. In the raw binary image from data set 2, it can be seen that only the left plant was insufficiently segmented. The right plant was segmented with a high confidence level and is removed from the binary image by the segmentation mask. In the third image, only the largest binary object is still visible in the image. The fourth image shows the original RGB image with automated generated annotation points visualized in color. Due to the automatic adjustment of the orientation parameters, the annotation accuracies are very high even with different growth parameters or exposure situations.

For the initial network, only images from dataset 3 were used to investigate the adaptation of the Active Learning process and the CbS to the different growth stages and environmental parameters. Each process run consists of two steps. In the first step, the initial network is evaluated with the first test data set. The mAP results of this evaluation are in Tables 3 and 4 in the second row. In the second step, all confidence levels of the detections are analyzed. The detections with a confidence level higher than 0.95 form the context parameters, all those with a lower confidence level go through the active learning process and are segmented and annotated automatically. In the first run, 104 images (R1) were re-annotated and added to the initial training set. As the accuracy of the Mask R-CNN increases, the number of newly annotated images decreases.

Table 2. Qualitative results of the CbS algorithm

Dataset	Angle (Rad)	Binary Raw	Binary	RGB
Dataset (1)				
Dataset (2)				
Dataset (3)				
Dataset (4)				

Every Algorithm run is evaluated by a new test data set, consisting of 30 images from each growth stage dataset. The initial network was then further trained with the extended training dataset. This process was repeated five times, increasing the training dataset up to 544 images. After each training run, the mean average precision values (mAP) of the four different test data sets were calculated. Table 3 shows the mAP results of the increasing training datasets by the CbS Algorithm.

Table 3. Quantitative results CbS Algorithm

Training Dataset	Experiences	Dataset 1 (mAP)	Dataset 2 (mAP)	Dataset 3 (mAP)	Dataset 4 (mAP)	Average
T1	R1(104)	27.05	39.58	57.61	14.36	34.65
T2(T1 + R1)	R2(62)	55.75	64.41	62.74	69	62.97
T3(T2 + R2)	R3(62)	65.75	67.25	72.16	63.67	67.21
T4(T3 + R3)	R4(46)	57.58	73.16	79.91	64.16	68.70
T5(T4 + R4)	R5(70)	59.08	74.75	67.75	70.25	67.96

The mAP values of the training dataset T1 show good results only for the test images of growth stage dataset 3, as these have the same growth stage as the training dataset. The images of growth stage dataset 1, 2 and 4 have only been segmented very poorly, as they have other growth stages and other environmental situations. The high number of images that have been run through the algorithm and re-annotated also show the poor performance of the initial network. The subsequent algorithm runs increasingly include images from the other datasets in the training dataset, increasing the segmentation accuracy of Mask R-CNN by almost 100% from a mAP value of 34.65 to 67.96 after 4 runs. Table 4 shows the mAP results of the same training datasets as in Table 3 but without the automated annotation. To evaluate the CbS and the automated annotation process, the images have a ground truth (gTruth) annotation.

Table 4. Quantitative results ground truth annotation.

Training Dataset	Experiences	Dataset 1 (mAP)	Dataset 2 (mAP)	Dataset 3 (mAP)	Dataset 4 (mAP)	Average
T1	R1(104)	27.05	39.58	57.61	14.36	34.65
T2(T1 + R1)	R2(62)	65.83	63.41	61.41	68.83	64.87
T3(T2 + R2)	R3(62)	71.83	69.33	69.5	62.5	68.29
T4(T3 + R3)	R4(46)	63.83	74.42	79.83	66.33	71.1
T5(T4 + R4)	R5(70)	68.08	76.63	70.41	73.83	72.16

The results in Table 4 show the high accuracy of context-based segmentation and automated annotation. The basic course of the mAP values over the five test data sets is comparable to the values from Table 3. As expected, there is a slightly higher segmentation accuracy with the ground truth values of up to 6.4% for training dataset T5.

Figure 6 shows the mAP results of the five test data sets for four consecutive algorithm runs. The CbS graph shows the results from Table 3. The gTruth graph shows the results from Table 4. The Initial Network graph shows the mAP results of the Mask R-CNN with an unchanged initial dataset over the same number of training epochs as the Active Learning approach. All three training variants start with the same initial network and the same training and test data set. New experiences can only be generated through a knowledge gap in the test data set. After each algorithm run, the Mask R-CNN try to close these gaps, due to the active learning process, which distinguishes the CbS and gTruth curve from the initial dataset curve. It can be seen that with a constant dataset, the maximum segmentation accuracy is reached much sooner than when new data is constantly added to the training dataset. The comparison between the CbS curve and the gTruth curve shows how close the Active Learning process with automated annotation is to the possible optimum. On average, the segmentation accuracy is only 3.4% lower.

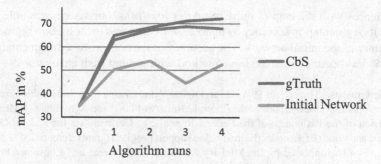

Fig. 6. Mean average precision results of five test data sets.

5 Discussion

The confidence level is an important indicator for the context parameters and indirectly for the CbS. Since the context parameters can only change slowly due to a continuous averaging of the values, false positive detections only have a minor negative influence. However, if the algorithm does not have any context parameters at the beginning, the CbS cannot perform and false-positive detections have an enormous influence on the further behaviour of the algorithm. For a practical application, it is therefore advisable to capture context parameters from the training data set and take them as starting values. In addition, the context parameters should not be averaged over all previous values, but limited to a certain number in order to react more quickly to new circumstances.

As could be seen especially in dataset 4, the CbS can only successfully segment plants that do not overlap with other plants. If a plant has an overlap, the CbS cannot differentiate between the plants and includes both plants as one in the training data set. For applications in the field of mechanical or chemical weed control, the influence of overlapping plants is minimal, as they are only applied in earlier growth stages. At later times, for an application for automated harvesting or vegetation monitoring, the CbS cannot be used. The results so far are based on only one training dataset. For a statistical validation of the results, several different training data sets would have to be created to determine the variance of the results. In addition, the networks should not be trained with a fixed number of epochs, instead they should be trained until convergence.

6 Conclusion

Through the context parameters of size, color and height of field vegetables and the ability to detect knowledge gaps, the Active Learning process embedded into our OC system led to increased mAP. This process is based on a context-based segmentation algorithm that uses the context parameters color and height of detections with a high confidence level, to resegment poorly segmented plants. Through a subsequent automated annotation, these defectively segmented plants are selected for additional training of the instance segmentation network. This continuous self-adaptation to the current environment leads to an increased segmentation accuracy of the neural network. In our experiments, five consecutive runs led to our OC system detecting 544 knowledge gaps which are converted to experiences with the help of our CbS. After four runs, our system was able to self-improve its segmentation accuracy by up to 27.7% compared to the highest segmentation performance of the initial network. The accuracy of the context-based segmentation was only 3.4% less accurate than the same method with ground truth annotations.

Acknowledgments. The project DiWenkLa (Digital Value Chains for a Sustainable Small-Scale Agriculture) is supported by funds of the Federal Ministry of Food and Agriculture (BMEL) based on a decision of the Parliament of the Federal Republic of Germany via the Federal Office for Agriculture and Food (BLE) under the innovation support program (grant reference 28DE106A18). DiWenkLa is also supported by the Ministry for Food, Rural Areas and Consumer Protection Baden-Württemberg.

References

1. Abdulla, W.: Mask R-CNN for object detection and instance segmentation on Keras and TensorFlow (2022). https://github.com/matterport/Mask_RCNN. Accessed 03 Sep 2022
2. Beck, M.A., Liu, C.-Y., Bidinosti, C.P., Henry, C.J., Godee, C.M., Ajmani, M.: An embedded system for the automated generation of labeled plant images to enable machine learning applications in agriculture. PLoS One **15**(12), 1–23 (2020)
3. Boysen, J., Stein, A.: AI-supported data annotation in the context of UAV-based weed detection in sugar beet fields using deep neural networks. In: Gandorfer, M., Hoffmann, C., El Benni, N., Cockburn, M., Anken, T., Floto, H. (eds.) 42. GIL-Jahrestagung, Künstliche Intelligenz in der Agrar- und Ernährungswirtschaft 2022, pp. 63–68. Gesellschaft für Informatik e.V., Bonn (2022)
4. Chandra, A.L., Desai, S.V., Balasubramanian, V.N., Ninomiya, S., Guo, W.: Active learning with point supervision for cost-effective panicle detection in cereal crops. Plant Methods **16**(34), 1–16 (2020)
5. COCO. Detection evaluation (2022). http://cocodataset.org/#detection-eval. Accessed 03 Sep 2022
6. dos Santos Ferreira, A., Freitas, D.M., Da Silva, G.G., Pistori, H., Folhes, M.T.: Unsupervised deep learning and semi-automatic data labeling in weed discrimination. Comput. Electron. Agric. **165**, 104963 (2019)
7. Ducket, T., Pearson, S., Blackmore, S., Grieve, B., Wilson, P., Gill, H. et al.: Agricultural robotics: the future of robotic agriculture. arXiv e-prints. https://arxiv.org/abs/1806.06762 (2018)
8. Farooq, A., Hu, J., Jia, X.: Weed classification in hyperspectral remote sensing images via deep convolutional neural network. In: IGARSS 2018 - 2018 IEEE International Geoscience and Remote Sensing Symposium 2018, pp. 3816–3819. IEEE, Valencia (2018)
9. Gai, J., Tang, L., Steward, B.L.: Automated crop plant detection based on the fusion of color and depth images for robotic weed control. J. Field Rob. **37**(1), 35–52 (2020)
10. Gene-Mola, J., Sainz-Cortiella, R., Rosell-Polo, J.R., Morros, J.R., Ruiz-Hidalgo, J., Vilaplana, V., et al.: Fuji-SfM dataset: A collection of annotated images and point clouds for Fuji apple detection and location using structure-from-motion photogrammetry. Data Brief **30**, 105591 (2020)
11. He, K., Gkioxari, G., Dollár, P., Girshick, R.: Mask R-CNN. arXiv e-prints. https://arxiv.org/abs/1703.06870 (2018)
12. Jiang, Y., Li, C., Paterson, A.H., Robertson, J.S.: DeepSeedling: deep convolutional network and Kalman filter for plant seedling detection and counting in the field. Plant Methods **15**(141), 1–19 (2019)

13. Kautzmann, T., Wuensche, M., Geimer, M., Mostaghim, S., Schmeck, H.: Holistic optimization of tractor management. In: Solutions for Intelligent and Sustainable Farming: Land-Technik AgEng 2011, pp. 275–281. VDI-Verlag, Hannover (2011)
14. Keras (2022). https://keras.io/getting_started/intro_to_keras_for_engineers/. Accessed 03 Sep 2022
15. Lottes, P., Behley, J., Chebrolu, N., Milioto, A., Stachniss, C.: Robust joint stem detection and crop-weed classification using image sequences for plant-specific treatment in precision farming. J. Field Rob. **37**(1), 20–34 (2020)
16. Lottes, P., Hoeferlin, M., Sander, S., Muter, M., Schulze, P., Stachniss, L.C.: An effective classification system for separating sugar beets and weeds for precision farming applications. In: 2016 IEEE International Conference on Robotics and Automation (ICRA) 2016, pp. 5157–5163. IEEE, Stockholm, Sweden (2016)
17. Louargant, M., Jones, G., Faroux, R., Paoli, J.-N., Maillot, T., Gée, C., et al.: Unsupervised classification algorithm for early weed detection in row-crops by combining spatial and spectral information. Remote Sens. **10**(5), 761–779 (2018)
18. Lüling, N., Reiser, D., Griepentrog, H.W.: Volume and leaf area calculation of cabbage with a neural network-based instance segmentation. In: Stafford, J.V. (eds.) Precision Agriculture 2021: Proceedings of the 14th European Conference on Precision Agriculture, pp. 719–726. Wageningen Academic Publishers, Wageningen (2021)
19. Lüling, N., Reiser, D., Stana, A., Griepentrog, H.W.: Using depth information and color space variations for improving outdoor robustness for instance segmentation of cabbage, In: 2021 IEEE International Conference on Robotics and Automation (ICRA) 2021, pp. 2331–2336. IEEE, Xi'an, China (2021)
20. Madec, S., Jin, X., Lu, H., De Solan, B., Liu, S., Duyme, F., et al.: Ear density estimation from high resolution RGB imagery using deep learning technique. Agric. For. Meteorol. **264**, 225–234 (2019)
21. Moshou, D., Kateris, D., Pantazi, X.E., Gravalos, I.: Crop and weed species recognition based on hyperspectral sensing and active learning. In: Stafford, J.V. (ed.) Precision agriculture '13, pp. 555–561. Wageningen Academic Publishers, Wageningen (2013)
22. Müller-Schloer, C., Tomforde, S.: Organic Computing – Technical Systems for Survival in the Real World, 5th edn. Springer, Cham (2017). https://doi.org/10.1007/978-3-319-68477-2
23. Python 3.6.0 (2022). https://www.python.org/downloads/release/python-360/. Accessed 03 Sep 2022
24. Reiser, D., Kamman, A., Vázquez Arellano, M., Griepentrog, H.W.: Using terrestrial photogrammetry for leaf area estimation in maize under different plant growth stages. In: Stafford, J.V (eds.), Precision Agriculture 2019: Proceedings of the 12th European Conference on Precision Agriculture 2019, pp. 331–337. Wageningen Academic Publishers, Wageningen (2019)
25. Reiser, D., Sehsah, E.-S., Bumann, O., Morhard, J., Griepentrog, H.W.: Development of an autonomous electric robot implement for intra-row weeding in vineyards. Agriculture **9**(1), 18–30 (2019)
26. Settles, B.: Active learning literature survey. Technical report 1648, University of Wisconsin Madison (2009)
27. Smith, P., Gregory, P.: Climate change and sustainable food production. Proc. Nutr. Soc. **72**(1), 21–28 (2013)
28. Stein, A., Tomforde, S., Diaconescu, A., Hähner, J., Müller-Schloer, C.: A concept for proactive knowledge construction in self-learning autonomous systems. In: 2018 IEEE 3rd International Workshops on Foundations and Applications of Self* Systems (FAS*W) 2018, pp. 204–213. IEEE, Trento, Italy (2018)
29. Szeliski, R.: Computer Vision: Algorithms and Applications, Chapter 5: 2nd edn. Springer, Cham (2022). https://doi.org/10.1007/978-1-84882-935-0

30. Tensorflow (2021). https://www.tensorflow.org/install/pip. Accessed 22 Nov 2021
31. Tomforde, S., Prothmann, H., Branke, J., Hähner, J., Mnif, M., Mueller-Schloer, C.: Observation and control of organic systems. In: Müller-Schloer, C., Schmeck, H., Ungerer, T. (eds.) Organic Computing—A Paradigm Shift for Complex Systems. Autonomic Systems, vol. 1, pp. 325–338. Springer, Basel (2011). https://doi.org/10.1007/978-3-0348-0130-0_21
32. Wspanialy, P., Brooks, J., Moussa, M.: An image labeling tool and agricultural dataset for deep learning. arXiv e-prints. https://arxiv.org/abs/2004.03351 (2020)
33. Yang, Y., Li, Y., Yang, J., Wen, J.: Dissimilarity-based active learning for embedded weed identification. Turk. J. Agric. For. **46**(3), 390–401 (2022)

Semi-model-Based Reinforcement Learning in Organic Computing Systems

Wenzel Pilar von Pilchau[1]([✉]) [iD], Anthony Stein[2] [iD], and Jörg Hähner[1]

[1] University of Augsburg, Augsburg 86159, Germany
wenzel.pilar-von-pilchau@uni-a.de
[2] University of Hohenheim, Stuttgart 70599, Germany

Abstract. Reinforcement Learning (RL) can generally be distinguished into two main classes: model-based and model-free. While model-based approaches use some kind of model of the environment and exploit it for learning, model-free methods learn with the complete absence of a model. Interpolation-based RL, and more specifically Interpolated Experience Replay (IER), comes with some properties that fit very well into the domain of Organic Computing (OC). We demonstrate how an OC system can benefit from this concept and attempt to place IER into one of the two RL classes. To do so, we give a broad overview of how both of the terms (model-based and model-free) are defined and detail different model-based categorizations. It turns out that replay-based techniques are quite on the edge between both. Furthermore, even if interpolation based on stored samples could be classified as a kind of model, the general way of using the interpolated experiences remains replay-based. Here, the borders get blurry and the classes overlap. In conclusion, we define a third class: semi-model-based. Additionally, we show that some architectural approaches of the OC domain fit this new class very well and even encourage such methods.

Keywords: Interpolated experience replay · Reinforcement learning · Model-based · Model-free · Organic computing

1 Motivation

With the rapid evolution of technical solutions, inevitably, the complexity of modern systems increases. Such systems, implemented into real world scenarios, face difficult problems that they need to solve. Disturbances have to be handled in a way that the system remains functional and even non-critical, but formerly unseen, situations can be a challenge. Organic Computing (OC) [16,17,34] is a rather young discipline that tries to address these issues. To do so, OC systems aim for robustness and autonomy in a way that they can function properly in an unsecure and possibly changing environment with as little input from the outside as possible. To understand the dynamics of the environment, adapt to new situations and disturbances and recognize changes that may occur over time, an OC system should be able to learn in some way.

M. Schulz et al. (Eds.): ARCS 2022, LNCS 13642, pp. 241–255, 2022.
https://doi.org/10.1007/978-3-031-21867-5_16

In Machine Learning (ML), different approaches of how to learn exist, but Reinforcement Learning (RL) [32] is the discipline that can adapt to situations in a very flexible and self-adaptive way as it repeatedly goes through a cycle of trial-and-error to understand the environment it interacts with. While ML generally fits the scope of OC, RL can be seen as the learning technique that brings the most beneficial properties. For example, it is capable of online learning which describes the process of constantly continuing to learn and this can be used to adapt for changes in the world dynamics. Furthermore, the general concept of how RL happens resembles the architecture of a typical OC system [17].

Generally, RL can be distinguished into the two classes model-based and model-free. While model-free approaches try to learn and approximate a form of the value function by interacting with the environment (a prominent example is Q-Learning [38]), model-based approaches take another route and aim for an approximation of the world dynamics itself (e.g. Dyna-Q [30]). Pilar von Pilchau et al. presented an approach called Interpolated Experience Replay (IER) [21] that uses the model-free Deep Q-Network (DQN) [28], but also creates synthetic experiences like model-based approaches often do. In contrast to classic model-based methods, IER does not generate synthetic experiences based on an approximated model but uses past experiences in combination with interpolation. A synthetic experiences is an experience that is not generated by interacting with the environment but in some other way. IER can be used to reduce the amount of exploration (actual interactions with the environment) which can be costly in real world scenarios. As OC systems are often situated in this kind of settings they can benefit from the IER in a way that keeps insecure/exploratory actions to a minimum.

The main contribution tries to classify the IER into the two classes model-based and model-free. To attempt this classification, a good understanding of the terms is required. Thus, we provide rigorous definitions after a deep dive into the respective literature. It turns out that the IER satisfies conditions from both classes and can be located right in-between them. We therefore introduce the new class semi-model-based. In addition, we show how OC systems can benefit from interpolation-based RL methods such as IER and that the Multi-layer Observer/Controller (MLOC) architecture even encourages such approaches.

The remainder of the paper is structured as follows. We start with an in-depth definition of the terms model-free and model-based in Sect. 2 and follow this with a short description of the IER. In Sect. 4 we define and differentiate interpolation and approximation. The main contribution follows in Sect. 5 and discusses the position of IER between model-based and model-free resulting in the definition of the new class semi-model-based. How OC systems relate to this new class is shown in Sect. 6. An overview of some related work is given in Sect. 7 and the paper is concluded in Sect. 8.

2   Model-Based and Model-Free Reinforcement Learning

The following section is mainly based on: Sutton and Bartos *Reinforcement Learning: An Introduction* [32].

2.1   The Model

First of all, we give a very short introduction to the RL cycle. An agent interacts with an environment and receives in every time step t a description of the actual state of the environment S_t (in this theoretical definition there are no measurements and corresponding uncertainties involved). Based on this information it chooses an action A_t that is executed and results in a new state S_{t+1} coupled with a corresponding reward R_t which are both received by the agent.

To understand the concepts of model-free and model-based RL, it is necessary to define the term model. The *model* in RL is defined as a model of the environment and therefore should be able to fulfil the tasks of the environment. These are the calculation of a follow-up state and a reward based on a given state-action pair.

To describe this in a more specific way, it is necessary to understand, that a RL problem can (usually) be described as a finite Markov Decision Process (MDP) and be formalized in the following way:

1. The finite set of all possible states s is described as the state space: $s \in S$.
2. The finite set of all possible actions a is described as the action space: $a \in A$.
3. The probability that the agent ends up in a particular state s' after starting in a specific state s and executing a specific action a is described as the state-transition function:

$$p(s'|s,a) = Pr\{S_{t+1} = s'|S_t = s, A_t = a\},$$

   for all $s', s \in S$ and $a \in A(s)$.
4. The expected reward that is received after starting in a specific state s, executing a specific action a and ending up in a specific state s' is described as the reward function:

$$r(s,a,s') = \mathbb{E}\{R_{t+1}|S_t = s, A_t = a, S_{t+1} = s'\},$$

   for all $s', s \in S$ and $a \in A(s)$.

Based on this formalization, the model can be described as the combination of the state-transition function and the reward function.

2.2   Model-Free Reinforcement Learning

The term model-free RL is generally describing all RL techniques that learn in the absence of a model of the environment. Here, *learning* often means the estimation of a *value function*. Such functions estimate how good it is for the agent to be in a given state (or how good it is to execute a given action in a given state). To express this in a scalar value, typically the expected future rewards (also called expected *return*) hold as a good metric. Rewards the agent can expect in the future are directly dependant on the taken actions. The particular way the agent chooses an action in a given state is called *policy*.

In a formalized way, a policy is a mapping from states to probabilities of performing each possible action. $\pi(a|s)$ therefore is the probability that the agent chooses action a in the state s while following the policy π. In RL, changes to the agent's policy as a result of experience is paramount.

Returning to the value functions, $v_\pi(s)$ denotes the state-value function of state s when the agent follows the policy π and yields the expected return when starting in s and following π thereafter. The state-value function $v_\pi(s)$ and the action-value function $q_\pi(s,a)$ can formally be described as follows:

$$v_\pi(s) \doteq \mathbb{E}_\pi\left[G_t|S_t = s\right] = \mathbb{E}_\pi\left[\sum_{k=0}^{\infty} \gamma^k R_{t+k+1}\middle| S_t = s\right],$$

$$q_\pi(s,a) \doteq \mathbb{E}_\pi\left[G_t|S_t = s, A_t = a\right] = \mathbb{E}_\pi\left[\sum_{k=0}^{\infty} \gamma^k R_{t+k+1}\middle| S_t = s, A_t = a\right],$$

with G_t denoting the return starting at time t and γ being a constant to discount future rewards.

The value functions v_π and q_π can be estimated from experience, but what we want to do is to maintain them as parametrized functions and adjust the parameters to better match the observed states.

A fundamental property of these type of functions used in RL is that they satisfy recursive relationships. The Bellmann equation for v_π is denoted as follows:

$$v_\pi(s) \doteq \sum_a \pi(a|s) \sum_{s',r} p(s',r|s,a)\left[r + \gamma v_\pi(s')\right], \text{ for all } s \in S,$$

with $p(s',r|s,a)$ being the probability that reward r is received in state s', after starting in state s and executing action a. This is basicly the model of the environment but in model-free RL we receive the corresponding distribution by traversing the state space.

To determine how the agent should behave in a given state, it can simply choose that action that maximizes the value. A basic RL approach that does so is Q-Learning [38]. But there are of course more sophisticated approaches like DQN [12,13] and its extensions [3,4,37]. The class of these methods, that learn a value function and derive a policy from it is called value-based. Another class that takes a different route is called policy-based and methods from this field directly parametrize the policy and try to optimize it according to the expected return. An example is the REINFORCE algorithm [33]. A third class of RL methods aims to bring the former mentioned approaches together and such algorithms are known as actor-critic methods. These approaches parametrize both, a value function and a policy and try to optimize them together. Examples of actor-critic algorithms are A3C [11], DDPG [9] and PPO [25].

2.3   Model-Based Reinforcement Learning

Model-based RL was defined by Moerland et al. [14] as:

Definition 1. *Model-based reinforcement learning is a class of MDP algorithms that (1) use a model, and (2) store a global solution.*

Thereby, a global solution is either a value function or a policy. Furthermore, they found two subclasses:

1. *Model-based RL with a learned model.* Here, both, a model and a global solution is learned. An example is Dyna [31].
2. *Model-based RL with a known model.* A model of the environment is known upfront and used to learn the global solution. An example is AlphaZero [27].

The idea behind having a model is to use it for planning. If a model is at hand, it can be used to simulate experience, this describes the process of feeding an input (state-action-pair) to the model and receiving an output (reward and follow-up state).

Given a starting state and a policy, we are able to receive a whole sequence of state-action-reward-state 4-tuples. We *simulate* the environment with the model and create *simulated experiences.* The term planning is used for every computational process that produces or improves a policy for interacting with the modelled environment, given a model as input:

$$\text{model} \xrightarrow{\text{planning}} \text{policy}$$

Actions are used to traverse the state space and value functions are computed over states. Planning methods share a common structure that is based on two basic ideas: (1) they involve computing value functions as a key intermediate step towards improving the policy or learn the policy directly, and (2) they compute value functions/policies by update operations applied to simulated experiences:

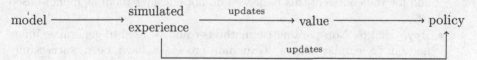

Referring to the learning process described in Sect. 2.2, it can be seen that both learning and planning focus on the estimation of value functions or policies by backing-up update operations. They do in fact differ in the utilized experiences. Planning uses simulated experiences that are generated by a model whereas learning methods make use of real experiences generated by the environment. This means nevertheless, that they share a common structure and algorithms can be transferred between them.

According to Moerland et al. [14] model-based methods (for a learned model) can be distinguished into the following categories addressing the three main considerations: what type of model do we learn, what type of estimation method do we use and in what region should our model be valid?

Type of Model. Moerland et al. set their focus here on dynamics models (learning the state-transition function). As mentioned above, the reward function is also part of the model, but as it is usually easier to learn it can be ignored for the distinction into the following three classes:

- *Forward model*: $(S_t, A_t) \rightarrow S_{t+1}$. Predicting the follow-up state given a current state and chosen action. Most of the model-based RL techniques follows this path, and an example is Deep Dyna-Q [18].
- *Backward/reverse model*: $S_{t+1} \rightarrow (S_t, A_t)$. Predicting the start state and chosen action to end up in a given state. Prioritized sweeping [15] uses this approach.
- *Inverse model*: $(S_t, S_{t+1}) \rightarrow A_t$. Predicting the action that needs to be performed to traverse from a given state into another. This technique is for example used in RRT planning [7].

Estimation Method. The method of approximating a model is often a form of supervised learning and can be distinguished into the following classes:

- *Parametric*: this is the most common approach for model approximation. There are two main subgroups:
  - *Exact*: This concludes tabular methods, containing a separate entry for every possible transition.
  - *Approximate*: Function approximation can reduce the required number of parameters and enable generalization. Nowadays, most of the time neural networks are used for this purpose [2].
- *Non-parametric*: Methods from this class directly store and use data to represent the model.
  - *Exact*: Replay buffers [10] could be considered non-parametric versions of tabular transition models, but even if the line between model-based RL and replay buffer methods is very thin, this is a discussable statement [36] and for the course of this paper we do not consider them as model-based RL.
  - *Approximate*: Non-parametric methods could be used to generalize information to similar states. Gaussian processes have been successfully applied to do so [1].

Region in Which the Model is Valid. The following classes specify the area of the state space where the model is valid:

- *Global*: This is the main approach for most of the methods and means the approximation of the dynamics of the entire state space.
- *Local*: In contrast to the global approach, local methods only approximate local dynamics and discard the local model afterwards. This approach is often used in the control community [8].

3   Interpolated Experience Replay

Pilar von Pilchau et al. presented an approach called Interpolated Experience Replay [19–21] which is an enhancement of the classic replay buffer used in DQN. While the basic replay buffer can be described as a memory that remembers experiences generated by interacting with the environment, the IER uses these true experiences to generate synthetic ones by means of interpolation.

The assumption of the authors is that true experiences resemble gathered information of the environment that can be exploited. Therefore, next to learning an action-value function (DQN) and traversing the problem space, interpolated experiences are generated to populate the replay buffer together with true experiences. An important finding was that interpolations spread completely random over the state space did rather harm instead of helping the learning progress. It turned out to be beneficial to stick to the distribution created by the policy and interpolate in its neighbourhood. [22]

The technique, from a general point of view, can be described in the following way: In every step, draw a query point s_q in the neighbourhood of a true sample drawn from the policy distribution and find all neighbouring experiences. Neighbouring experiences are the ones that start in a state neighbouring the query point. According to an action-selection method, one or more actions a_q are chosen for the synthetic experience(s). The true experiences matching the selected action(s) form the set of sampling points and based on them the reward $\hat{r}$ and the follow-up state $\hat{s}$ are interpolated. The final synthetic experience $\hat{e}$ is assembled of the query point, one of the selected actions and the interpolated reward and follow-up state: $\hat{e} = (s_q, a_q, \hat{r}, \hat{s})$.

The actual replay buffer consists out of two separate memories, one for the true samples and one for the synthetic ones. As the most benefit is expected in the exploration phase, the synthetic buffer shrinks over time and in direct dependence to the amount of gathered true experiences.

Both, synthetic, as well as true experiences are drawn at random from the replay buffer and are used to update the action-value function.

4   Interpolation vs. Approximation

The task of finding a function $\tilde{f}(x)$ that fits either a real valued function $f(x)$ of the real valued variable x or a given table of data (x_i, y_i) can be solved by *interpolation* or *approximation*. [26]

Approximation is thereby defined as finding a function $\tilde{f}(x)$ that minimizes a norm of the difference of the values for the searched function $\tilde{f}(x_i)$ and the given table $||\tilde{f} - y||$ with vectors $\tilde{f} = \{\tilde{f}(x_i)\}$ and $y = y_i$. Or rather, in case of $f(x)$, minimizes a norm of the difference of the values for the searched and the given function $||\tilde{f}(x) - f(x)||$. Interpolation on the other hand tries to find a function $\tilde{f}(x)$ that fits the given function or data in specific points, such that holds: $\tilde{f}(x_i) = f(x_i)$ or $\tilde{f}(x_i) = y_i$. [26]

Both approaches are in fact quite similar and only differ in the estimated values for the given points. We call the given data points also sampling points

s_i, and for them applies: $s_i = (x_i, y_i) = (x_i, f(x_i))$. Nevertheless, there are some benefits that determine the cases when to use which method. Given a table of data $(x_i, y_i), i = 0, 1, \ldots, n$ there are two main differences:

1. If the amount of given data is (very) high—n is (very) high—interpolation turns out to be not practical. This effect even grows with the amount of noise in the data. The given data should be approximated with a smooth line through the "datacloud".
2. If there is only a small amount of data available and it is reasonable or even necessary that $\tilde{f}(x)$ fits the values y_i at x_i or $f(x_i)$ perfectly, then interpolation turns out to be better than approximation. [26]

5   Semi-model-Based Reinforcement Learning

To bring everything together, we start with a categorization of IER into the three main categories of model-based RL from Sect. 2.3:

1. **Type of model**: As IER uses true experiences stored in the real-valued replay buffer as sampling points to interpolate rewards and follow-up states, it can be classified as *forward model*.
2. **Region in which the model is valid**: Interpolated experiences are created from surrounding sampling points and the interpolation model is discarded afterwards. This falls clearly into the *local* region category.
3. **Estimation method**: As we do not learn a model that we parametrize, the parametric class can be excluded. As stated in Sect. 2.3 replay buffer methods could be considered as model-based approaches, but we do not. We go with this assumption as the range of predictions that these "models" can make is very limited to, not only the exact experienced transitions of the learners past, but additionally only to those that are currently stored in the buffer. This means that no form of generalization is possible as well. The second argument also holds for parametric and exact methods like Dyna, but in contrast, these methods are capable of covering a bigger area of the state space (they do not forget) and in addition can model stochastic state-transitions way better than a simple fraction of past transitions does. In fact, experiences in a replay buffer can be seen as true experiences, even though off-policy ones. We come to this assumption because they are not directly generated from an interaction with the environment but drawn from a memory. If they are considered true experiences, they can not be simulated ones and considering the definition that model-based methods use synthetic samples to learn, replay buffer methods do not satisfy this requirement. This consideration could be interpreted to be true for tabular models as well, but the main difference here is that replayed experiences are drawn from the distribution created from a developing/converging policy and can therefore be seen as off-policy experiences while reused experiences from a tabular model do not follow such a distribution. Indeed, there are researchers who describe the usage of replay methods as a way to avoid a conventional model [36]. So,

the underlying replay buffer functionality does not fit in here, even if the line is thin. Interpolation, which we use on top, can not be considered as an exact approach apart from the values equal to the sampling points and therefore does not fit the non-parametric and exact class as well. The only remaining candidate among the traditional classes is non-parametric and approximate. Here, the line is very thin again. The general concept of interpolation based on stored true experiences could be classified as a non-parametric model. Then again, interpolation is a different thing than approximation (cf. Sect. 4) and it remains at least discussable if such methods fit in here. Nevertheless, the simulated experiences are used in a replay-based manner which is regarded as model-free learning in general (see above). As we add interpolated samples into the mix this is of course not true anymore for all updates and IER combines planning and learning in a stochastic manner which at least differs from classic model-based RL approaches in the way that they usually have a clear separation of these phases. In conclusion, we do not consider IER as a whole to meet the requirements of a non-parametric model to the fullest.

The question may arise why IER uses interpolation instead of approximation in the first place. Looking at the two different situations from Sect. 4, IER clearly fits the second one. The replay buffer is of limited size and throws away experiences when its maximum size is reached. First of all, the amount of sampling points for an interpolation is restricted to the replays maximum size. And furthermore, predictions are needed for very specific local areas and as the true experiences are expected to be distributed over the sate space this number can be expected to be rather small. Of course all of this depends on the chosen maximum size of the replay buffer and the problems state space, but we can expect to rather have few than many sampling points and this scenario favours interpolation. In classic RL, sampling points usually come without noise (non-deterministic environments are an exceptional case) which requires that the points are matched exactly, also favouring interpolation. Of course in real world scenarios (that are OC systems often applied to) this is not true, but the first point still holds.

Focusing on value-based and model-free RL techniques like DQN, IER also expresses some beneficial features of model-based approaches. The generation and usage of synthetic experiences is of course one of them. In early exploration phases, the learner is assisted with interpolated transitions that try to cover unexplored areas. This effect could be classified as model-based RL, but over time the generation of synthetic experiences is reduced and the method focuses on model-free Q-updates. Under the assumption that interpolation would fit the model-based RL definition, IER still would be a method that shifts from model-based to model-free and might even shift back if concept drifts occur.

According to [5] classification and categorization can be defined and distinguished as follows: Classification involves the assignment of each entity to one and only one class, whereas categorization is described as the process of dividing the world into groups of entities that share some similarities. The main difference is that classes can not overlap whereas categories can.

In conclusion, IER could be categorized as a model-free, as well as a model-based RL method depending on the point of view and the definition of single aspects, as in fact the line is very thin. But on the other hand, if we wanted to classify it we would need to commit for one class, and, following the former argumentation, this is neither easy nor explicit. Therefore, we introduce a class right in-between model-based and model-free and call it *semi-model-based*. Following this new option, IER is to be classified as a semi-model-based RL approach.

6   Interpolation-Based RL in Organic Computing

An architectural approach for OC systems is the generic *Observer/Controller*-architecture, more specifically the *Multi-Layer Observer/Controller*-architecture (MLOC) [17]. Even if there do exist other approaches beside it, we focus on this one because it is the architecture that is tied to OC the closest and has even been set into close relation to RL [29]. The MLOC architecture is composed of 4 layers. At the bottom sits *layer 0* which is the productive system and, in the OC domain, is often called *System under Observation and Control* (SuOC). Here manageable resources are encapsulated via well-defined interfaces that enable monitoring (observation) as well as configuration (control). We consider the SuOC to be deployed in a *Non-Stationary Environment* (NSE) that continuously challenge the MLOC with unforeseen situations and external disturbances. *Layer 1* is called the runtime adaptation layer and deploys a feedback control loop by periodically observing the internal system state and adapting the SuOC accordingly. A form of online RL approach is often situated in this layer. *Layer 2* is known as the offline learning layer and its main functionality is the monitoring of layer 1. If a critical situation (unknown state or disturbance) is detected, then an internal model of the SuOC is used to find a solution. The model can be an upfront known simulation or even a parametrized model that is trained during runtime. Critical exploration is outsourced to this layer so that situations in which the SuOC might be harmed can be reduced to a minimum. The last layer is called collaboration layer and is responsible for communicating with entities from the outside such as the user or neighbouring MLOC instances.

An IER implemented into an OC system based on a MLOC architecture would look the following way: First of all, the online learning DQN instance is located in layer 1 and continuously interacts with the SuOC to generate new insights in the form of true experiences. We call the replay buffer used on this layer D_{l1} and this buffer is composed of true and simulated experiences and has a maximum length of l_1. When the maximum length is reached, new samples replace old ones in a FIFO manner. Minibatches drawn at random from D_{l1} are used continuously to perform Q-updates and train the online DQN. The true experiences generated by interacting with the SuOC follow the trajectory $\tau = ((S_1, A_1), \ldots, (S_n, A_n))$ with $t = 1 \ldots n$. Even if neural networks are capable of generalisation, it requires a lot of samples (in form of experiences) to understand the dynamics of the environment. This results in a lot of exploration which can be costly in real world scenarios. Reasons for that are among others energy, abrasion and possible damage to either the OC system or entities in the environment. To reduce exploration, synthetic experiences can be generated in layer 2. Therefore, the real experiences stored in D_{l1} are copied to a sampling-point-buffer called D_{l2}. This storage is of length l_2 and can be bigger than l_1 resulting in $l_2 \geq l_1$. The benefit of remembering true experiences longer than layer 1 does is an increased accuracy for interpolations, whereas sticking too long to old samples in layer 1 can result in unstable learning. Asynchronously, in an offline manner, layer 2 triggers interpolations in areas surrounding τ. To realize that, a state s_t is drawn uniformly from τ and the querypoint s_q is drawn uniformly from the corresponding ball of radius r: $B_r(s_i) = \{y \in \mathbb{R}^n : |x - y| \leq r]\}$. Using the interpolation technique described in Sect. 3 simulated experiences can be generated and added to D_{l1} which helps with the exploration around τ and therefore can result in reduced exploration needed in the real world. This effect was shown in detailed evaluations in [21, 22].

As mentioned above, we consider the system to operate in a NSE and we can therefore expect concept drifts (changes in the world dynamics) to occur which require the agent to relearn the environments dynamics at least for local areas. Consequentially, exploration is required to adapt. A mechanic that is able to detect concept drifts would trigger the reset of D_{l2}, and probably also D_{l1}, and the new dynamics could be learned with a reduced amount of exploration. An approach that would reduce exploration even more would require a technique that is able to not only detect when a concept drift occurs, but also where. In this case only stored experiences from that area would be deleted and all the still valid sampling points could be kept.

The MLOC architecture described above is typically realized with rule-based learning approaches and one representant of such is the Organic Traffic Control (OTC) [23]. The authors use Learning Classifier Systems (LCSs) to generate rules that configure traffic lights for a crossroad. Here, on layer 1, an online version of an LCS reacts in real time to changing traffic volumes. The rules feature evaluation metrics such as fitness, expected payoff, expected error and experience. The expected payoff resembles a state-action-value and is mainly used, among the other metrics, to optimize the rule set. According to our definition of model-free RL methods from Sect. 2.2 the learning approach on layer 1 can be classified as such.

If unforeseen or unknown situations occur, the offline layer is triggered. Here a Genetic Algorithm (GA) generates new rules of minimum quality in interaction with a simulation of the underlying environment. A simulation that is given upfront holds as model, but a GA performs optimization and does not learn. So, layer 2 on its own can not be classified as model-based RL. In combination with layer 1 on the other hand it fulfils the requirements of storing a global solution and the usage of a model. Another requirement says that simulated experiences have to be used, and this is not the case, instead we use the model to produce new rules. Furthermore, in contrast to the typical model-based RL approach, the triggering of the model is restricted to special cases instead of a general assistance for the global solution.

The classification of this system in one of the classes model-free or model-based is not easy and obvious and the OTC tends to be in-between both. Therefore, it could be classified as a semi-model-based RL approach. Furthermore, the OC system that implements IER follows the argumentation of Sect. 5 and turns out to be a semi-model-based RL approach as well. In conclusion, it can be seen that the MLOC architecture pairs well with approaches of this type, as the separation between the online component and the offline and model-based component encourages them.

7   Related Work

Van Seijen and Sutton show in [36] for the first time an exact equivalence between the sequence of value functions found by a model-based method and by a model-free method with replay. The used replay method differs from the traditional replay functionality [10] such that, instead of the presentation of old samples to the learning agent, update targets of old samples are recomputed based on current information and updates are redone. They introduce an algorithm called forgetful LSTD(λ) that can be interpreted as a model-free or model-based method depending on its parametrization. The presented approach and the resulting statements are limited to linear approaches. Even if they show a close relation between replaying experience and exploiting a model, the case that they find equal learning functions is restricted to specific situations. In contrast to the Interpolated Experience Replay, LSTD(λ) is not able to create completely new experiences.

Van Hasselt et al. [35] compare parametric models with experience replay methods. They state that replay-based agents are often classified as model-free, but do share many characteristics of model-based methods. They point out the ability to plan which they define as the usage of additional computation to improve the agent's value function and policy without additional data. Furthermore, they discuss how model errors may cause issues when a parametric model in a replay-like setting is used. In contrast to [36], the authors focus on nonlinear approaches and compare the model-based SimPLe [6] with Rainbow DQN [4] that utilizes a replay buffer. It is shown that a data efficient version of Rainbow DQN can outperform SimPLe in experiments on Atari 2600 video games. In the end they state that they consider a non-parametric model approach, like interpolation applied to a replay, as model-based. We disagree with this statement and haven provided an alternative classification.

Sander develops in [24] a method called Bayesian Interpolated Experience Replay that is very similar to the Interpolated Experience Replay presented by Pilar von Pilchau et al. [22]. In contrast to the described method above, it uses sampled mixup coefficients and is designed for, and evaluated on, robotic control tasks. The approach is classified as a combination of model-based and model-free methods and therefore in a similar way as we do.

8   Conclusions

We started with an in-depth definition of the terms model-free and model-based RL. This built the basis for the attempted classification of the IER into one of these classes. While IER can be categorized as a forward type model that focuses on local areas, the categorization of the estimation method turned out the be not that obvious. Replay-based approaches were interpreted as a way of avoiding conventional models and were assigned to the model-free class. IER uses interpolation on top of a replay buffer and this combination can not easily be located into either the model-based nor the model-free class. To overcome this state of uncertainty, we introduced a new class located right in-between model-based and model-free called semi-model-based. As IER focuses on model-free DQN updates, but gets assistance from a model-like local interpolation approach based on stored experiences, we classify it as semi-model-based.

Furthermore, we showed how IER and interpolation-based RL approaches can be beneficial for OC systems. Based on an exemplary combination of the MLOC architecture with IER, along the original OTC approach, a classification into model-based or model-free was attempted, finding that both must be classified semi-model-based Additionally, we could show that the general architectural approach of MLOC encourages the semi-model-based class.

The categorization/classification of replay-based RL methods is defined differently by different researchers taking different perspectives. We tried to contribute our part to this discussion and offer a new perspective with the introduction of a new class in-between. Of course this debate is not over yet and future contributions might strengthen one or the other side.

References

1. Deisenroth, M., Rasmussen, C.E.: PILCO: a model-based and data-efficient approach to policy search. In: Proceedings of the 28th International Conference on machine learning (ICML-11), pp. 465–472. Citeseer (2011)
2. Goodfellow, I., Bengio, Y., Courville, A.: Deep Learning. MIT press (2016)
3. van Hasselt, H., Guez, A., Silver, D.: Deep reinforcement learning with double q-learning. In: Proceedings of the AAAI Conference on Artificial Intelligence, vol. 30, no. 1 (2016). https://doi.org/10.1609/aaai.v30i1.10295, https://ojs.aaai.org/index.php/AAAI/article/view/10295
4. Hessel, M., et al.: Rainbow: combining improvements in deep reinforcement learning (2017). https://doi.org/10.48550/ARXIV.1710.02298
5. Jacob, E.K.: Classification and categorization: a difference that makes a difference (2004). publisher: Graduate School of Library and Information Science. University of Illinois
6. Kaiser, L., et al.: Model-based reinforcement learning for atari. arXiv preprint arXiv:1903.00374 (2019)
7. LaValle, S.M., et al.: Rapidly-exploring random trees: a new tool for path planning. publisher: Ames. IA, USA (1998)
8. Levine, S., Abbeel, P.: Learning neural network policies with guided policy search under unknown dynamics. Adv. Neural Inf. Process. Syst. **27** (2014)

9. Lillicrap, T.P., et al.: Continuous control with deep reinforcement learning (2015). https://doi.org/10.48550/ARXIV.1509.02971
10. Lin, L.J.: Reinforcement learning for robots using neural networks. Carnegie-Mellon Univ Pittsburgh Pa School of Computer Science, Technical report (1993)
11. Mnih, V., et al.: Asynchronous methods for deep reinforcement learning. In: International Conference on Machine Learning, pp. 1928–1937. PMLR (2016)
12. Mnih, V., et al.: Playing Atari with deep reinforcement learning. CoRR abs/1312.5602 (2013). http://arxiv.org/abs/1312.5602
13. Mnih, V., et al.: Human-level control through deep reinforcement learning. Nature **518**(7540), 529–533 (2015)
14. Moerland, T.M., Broekens, J., Plaat, A., Jonker, C.M.: Model-based reinforcement learning: a survey (2020). https://doi.org/10.48550/ARXIV.2006.16712
15. Moore, A.W., Atkeson, C.G.: Prioritized sweeping: reinforcement learning with less data and less time. Mach. Learn. **13**(1), 103–130 (1993). https://doi.org/10.1007/BF00993104
16. Müller-Schloer, C., Schmeck, H., Ungerer, T.: Organic Computing-a Paradigm Shift for Complex Systems. Springer, Cham (2011). https://doi.org/10.1007/978-3-0348-0130-0
17. M üller-Schloer, C., Tomforde, S.: Organic computing - technical systems for survival in the real world. Birkh äuser (2017). https://doi.org/10.1007/978-3-319-68477-2
18. Peng, B., Li, X., Gao, J., Liu, J., Wong, K.F., Su, S.Y.: Deep dyna-Q: integrating planning for task-completion dialogue policy learning. arXiv preprint arXiv:1801.06176 (2018)
19. Pilar von Pilchau, W.: Averaging rewards as a first approach towards interpolated experience replay. In: Draude, C., Lange, M., Sick, B. (eds.) INFORMATIK 2019: 50 Jahre Gesellschaft für Informatik - Informatik für Gesellschaft (Workshop-Beiträge), pp. 493–506. Gesellschaft für Informatik e.V., Bonn (2019). https://doi.org/10.18420/inf2019_ws53
20. Pilar von Pilchau, W., Stein, A., Hähner, J.: Bootstrapping a DQN replay memory with synthetic experiences. In: Merelo, J.J., Garibaldi, J., Wagner, C., Bäck, T., Madani, K., Warwick, K. (eds.) Proceedings of the 12th International Joint Conference on Computational Intelligence (IJCCI 2020), 2–4 November 2020 (2020). https://doi.org/10.5220/0010107904040411
21. Pilar von Pilchau, W., Stein, A., Hähner, J.: Synthetic experiences for accelerating DQN performance in discrete non-deterministic environments. Algorithms **14**(8), 226 (2021). https://doi.org/10.3390/a14080226
22. Pilar von Pilchau, W., Stein, A., Hähner, J.: Interpolated experience replay for continuous environments. In: Proceedings of the 14th International Joint Conference on Computational Intelligence (IJCCI 2020), 24–46 October 2022, p. to appear (2022)
23. Prothmann, H., et al.: Organic traffic control. In: Müller-Schloer, C., Schmeck, H., Ungerer, T. (eds.) Organic Computing — A Paradigm Shift for Complex Systems. Autonomic Systems, vol. 1, pp. 431–446. Springer, Cham (2011). https://doi.org/10.1007/978-3-0348-0130-0_28
24. Sander, R.M.: Interpolated experience replay for improved sample efficiency of model-free deep reinforcement learning algorithms. Ph.D. thesis, Massachusetts Institute of Technology (2021)
25. Schulman, J., Wolski, F., Dhariwal, P., Radford, A., Klimov, O.: Proximal policy optimization algorithms (2017). https://doi.org/10.48550/ARXIV.1707.06347

26. Schwarz, H., Köckler, N.: Interpolation und approximation. In: Numerische Mathematik, pp. 91–182. Vieweg+Teubner Verlag (2011). https://doi.org/10.1007/978-3-8348-8166-3_4

27. Silver, D., et al.: A general reinforcement learning algorithm that masters chess, shogi, and Go through self-play. Science **362**(6419), 1140–1144 (2018)

28. Silver, D., et al.: Mastering the game of Go without human knowledge. Nature **550**(7676), 354–359 (2017). https://doi.org/10.1038/nature24270

29. Stein, A., Tomforde, S., Diaconescu, A., Hähner, J., Müller-Schloer, C.: A concept for proactive knowledge construction in self-learning autonomous systems. In: 2018 IEEE 3rd International Workshops on Foundations and Applications of Self* Systems (FAS*W), pp. 204–213 (2018). https://doi.org/10.1109/FAS-W.2018.00048

30. Sutton, R.S.: Integrated architectures for learning, planning, and reacting based on approximating dynamic programming. In: Porter, B., Mooney, R. (eds.) Machine Learning Proceedings 1990, pp. 216–224. Morgan Kaufmann, San Francisco (CA) (1990). https://doi.org/10.1016/B978-1-55860-141-3.50030-4

31. Sutton, R.S.: Dyna, an integrated architecture for learning, planning, and reacting. ACM Sigart Bull. **2**(4), 160–163 (1991)

32. Sutton, R.S., Barto, A.G.: Reinforcement Learning: An Introduction. MIT press (2018)

33. Sutton, R.S., McAllester, D., Singh, S., Mansour, Y.: Policy gradient methods for reinforcement learning with function approximation. Adv. Neural Inf. Process. Syst. **12** (1999)

34. Tomforde, S., Sick, B., Müller-Schloer, C.: organic computing in the spotlight. CoRR abs/1701.08125 (2017)

35. Van Hasselt, H.P., Hessel, M., Aslanides, J.: When to use parametric models in reinforcement learning? Adv. Neural Inf. Process. Syst. **32** (2019)

36. Vanseijen, H., Sutton, R.: A deeper look at planning as learning from replay. In: International Conference on Machine Learning, pp. 2314–2322. PMLR (2015)

37. Wang, Z., Schaul, T., Hessel, M., Hasselt, H., Lanctot, M., Freitas, N.: Dueling network architectures for deep reinforcement learning. In: International Conference on Machine Learning, pp. 1995–2003. PMLR (2016)

38. Watkins, C.J.C.H., Dayan, P.: Q-learning. Mach. Learn. **8**(3), 279–292 (1992). https://doi.org/10.1007/BF00992698

Deep Reinforcement Learning
with a Classifier System – First Steps

Connor Schönberner[(✉)] and Sven Tomforde

Intelligent Systems, Department of Computer Science, Kiel University,
Kiel, Germany
{cos,st}@informatik.uni-kiel.de

Abstract. Organic Computing enables self-* properties in technical systems for mastering them in the face of complexity and for improving robustness and efficiency. Key technology for self-improving adaptation decisions is reinforcement learning (RL). In this paper, we argue that traditional deep RL concepts are not applicable due to their limited interpretability. In contrast, approaches from the field of rule-based evolutionary RL are less powerful. We propose to fuse both technical concepts while maintaining their advantages – allowing for an applicability especially suited for Organic Computing applications. We present initial steps and the first evaluation of standard RL scenarios.

Keywords: Evolutionary reinforcement learning · Deep reinforcement learning · Learning classifier systems · XCS · Organic computing

1 Introduction

In recent decades, technical systems have become increasingly complex and interwoven [33]. This leads to challenges in controllability - Organic Computing (OC) is a field that aims to maintain this controllability by increasing the autonomy of systems and establishing self* properties [35]. Typically, productive parts are wrapped by additional observer/controller structures [34] establishing autonomous, self-learning behaviour, which results in systems acting more robustly, efficiently and flexibly.

A central aspect of such a runtime decision on appropriate behaviour is the establishment of control structures based on reinforcement learning (RL) concepts [16]. Especially in the field of OC, the Extended Classifier System (XCS) based on Wilson's work has established itself as a key technology for this. Examples include traffic control [25], network control [32], testing [26] or surveillance systems [31], but also in robotics [36]. Current developments show that fundamentally deep RL approaches lead to significantly better results in complex problems such as computer games [28,40]. However, they suffer from a lack of interpretability and explainability - whereas the XCS-based solutions enable a strongly improved comprehensibility of decision-making due to the explicit knowledge representation and the clear algorithmic structure.

M. Schulz et al. (Eds.): ARCS 2022, LNCS 13642, pp. 256–270, 2022.
https://doi.org/10.1007/978-3-031-21867-5_17

In this paper, we present an initial approach that aims to merge two approaches based on current practices in the field. To this end, we present initial approaches and analyse learning behaviour on standard RL problems.

The remainder of this paper is organised follows: First, Sect. 2 introduces the XCS. It explains how the canonical system and several important extensions work. Next, Sect. 3 provides an overview of Neural Learning Classifier System (LCS) and Deep LCS. Following, Sect. 4 presents which neural concepts are selected and how they are modified for the Deep XCS experiments. The latter is then explained, showcased, and evaluated in Sect. 5. Eventually, Sect. 6 summarises the results and provides a short outlook.

2   Background: The Extended Classifier System

XCS is a Michigan-style LCS introduced by Wilson [37]. It is seen as the most prominent and researched LCS, which was originally introduced and implemented by Holland and Reitman [11]. In general, LCS can be seen as evolutionary reinforcement learning (ERL) systems since they combine a version of Holland's genetic algorithm (GA) [10], which is a form of evolutionary algorithm, with an RL scheme.

The core elements of an LCS are its classifiers. Whereby, one classifier $cl := (C, a, p, \varepsilon, F, \dots)$ consists of a *condition* C, the *action* a it advocates, the *prediction* p of the payoff, the current prediction *error* ε as an error estimation for the previous predictions, its accuracy-based fitness value F, which is defined an inverse to the prediction error [37], and additional bookkeeping parameters. All currently "alive" classifiers are collected in the population $[P]$.

Originally, XCS was designed to only process binary input, XCSR [38] alleviated this by introducing hyperrectangle conditions making XCS better suited for OC applications whose real-world data is usually of real-valued nature. A hyperrectangle condition is an ordered sequence of real bounds that span a hyperrectangle in an n-dimensional problem space with $n \in \mathbb{N}$. Such a condition can be encoded as matrix $C = [L, U]$ with two column vectors $L = (l_1, \dots, l_n)$ and $U = (u_1, \dots, u_n)$. Whereby, the i-th row vector of C corresponds to an interval $[l_i, u_i]$ with $l_i, u_i \in \mathbb{R}$ and $1 \leq i \leq n$. It *matches* the observation $\sigma(t) = (x_1, \dots, x_n)$ for $x_i \in \mathbb{R}$ if $l_i \leq x_i \leq u_i$ for discrete timesteps $t \in \mathbb{N}$. In addition, the constant prediction of XCS was replaced with a computed prediction with the introduction of XCSF [39] and later lifted to quadratic and polynomial prediction [14]. The latter additions allow XCS to deal with more complex problems.

Figure 1 shows a schema of XCS' structure and sketches its main loop with arrows. For each new timestep t, XCS forms a *match set* $[M]$ out of all classifiers whose condition matches the current observation $\sigma(t)$. If $|[M]| = 0$ or the amount of unique actions in $[M]$ is less than the given threshold θ_{mna} the *covering* mechanism adds new classifiers to $[P]$ and $[M]$ matching $\sigma(t)$. Following, the match-set is used to calculate the *prediction array* PA. It has one entry per action. The entry of an action a, called *system prediction* for a, is computed as

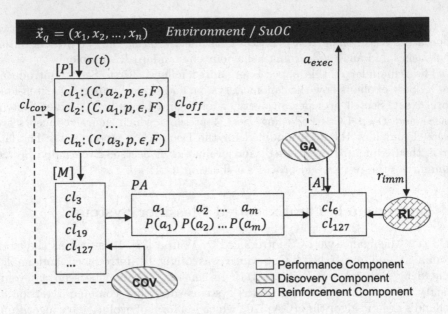

Fig. 1. Schematic of the general XCS architecture, cf. [30]. For simplicity here given for single-step problems.

a fitness-weighted average of all prediction values of those classifiers advocating a. Formalised this means

$$P(a) = \frac{\sum_{cl \in [M]|cl.a=a} cl.p \cdot cl.F}{\sum_{cl \in [M]|cl.a=a} cl.F}.$$

PA is utilised to select the system response, i.e. the action for the current time step, following an exploration/exploitation strategy which is also called an *action selection regime*. All actions that advocate this action are then collected in the *action-set* $[A]$. The same action is passed to the environment, which executes it and passes the resulting reward back to the XCS. Next, the RL component updates the classifiers of the current action-set $[A]$ or the preceding action-set depending on whether XCS is faced with a single- or multistep problem.

The steady-state niche GA of XCS also operates on action sets and usually gets active after the RL update. It is called if the time difference to its last call exceeds the given threshold θ_{GA}. It follows the same case distinction as the RL update. The GA exerts an evolutionary pressure on the population of XCS, which enables the system to evolve maximally general and accurate classifiers. This is encompassed by Wilson's generalisation hypothesis [37]. In their formal investigations, Butz identified several pressures active within the population and theoretically confirmed the hypothesis [7].

For more details about the implementation of a canonical XCS, including update formulas, the GA, and hyperparameters, the reader is referred to the algorithmic description of Butz [6].

3   Approaches to Neural and Deep LCS

Driven by the success story of ANN, an integration of shallow ANNs (i.e. ANNs with less than two hidden layers) into LCS variants has been proposed. The Pittsburgh-style LCS PANIC from 1995 is one if not the first LCS with a neural component. It utilises an ANN as a global prediction mechanism [9].

In 2002, Bull and O'Hara [5] created the first Neural XCS by introducing the concept of *neural rules*. These replace the condition and action of a classifier with one shallow ANN. Consequently, such a neural rule fulfils the role of conditions, i.e. matching observations, as well as choosing the not-constant action of a classifier. Multiple publications advanced this concept of neural rules, e.g. neural rules were combined with backpropagation within an XCS to perform a local search [18] and to train action sets with backpropagation and gradient descent [20]. In the area of anticipatory LCS, neural rules were combined with an additional feedforward ANN predicting the next observation [19].

Another neural component for LCS is *neural prediction*, which replaces the prediction mechanism within classifiers with an originally shallow ANN. Consequently, an LCS can fully rely on shallow ANNs by using neural rules as well as neural prediction which was the case in the work of O'Hara and Bull [17] as explained by Lanzi and Loicono [12]. However, they also showed that neural prediction does not require the usage of neural rules. In addition, neural prediction networks can be trained using backpropagation with the predicted payoff as target. Regarding the GA, they mutated the number of neurons in the hidden layer of their shallow ANNs for neural prediction [12]. Further experiments by the same authors focused on function approximation with a GA, investigating how to evolve the architecture of neural prediction networks [15]. Another angle for neural components is to compute the action of XCS with an ANN as done in XCSCA [13].

Yet another direction has been explored by Dam et al., who build on the supervised learning classifier system (UCS) [8] in order to apply their neural UCS (NLCS) on classification. They replace only the action of classifiers of NLCS with a shallow ANN. This decision was made because they did not want to lose the interpretability of UCS, which they feared might suffer when condition and action are replaced by one single ANN.

CN-LCS [4], which is inspired by the NLCS of Dam, is probably the first Deep LCS and utilises CNNs for deep (neural) prediction. This new system was designed to be applied for Database Intrusion Detection. Aside from swapping shallow ANNs against CNNs, CN-LCS changes more aspects of NLCS: Instead of dividing the solution space into niches via conditions, each classifier is trained on the entire set of current queries that are filtered using so-called chromosomes [4]. As a result, each classifier acts as a global solution to the problem. This makes CN-LCS more similar to a Pittsburgh-style LCS than a Michigan-style LCS [22].

The first Michigan-Style and Deep XCS was created in 2019 and focused on autoencoding [24]. In a second version, it was applied to classification in 2021 [22]. This Deep XCS is action-agnostic, assigning each classifier the same dummy action. As a result, its prediction array generation calculates one single global prediction, to which each classifier in the match set contributes its prediction vector. The latter includes one classification probability for each class of the problem. A classifier advocates the class that is the most probable according to its prediction. Above that, the system includes several genetic operators specialised for ANN.

As a summary of the previous discussion, there have been several Neural LCS in the past of which some have been applied to RL, but they relied on shallow ANNs and often outdated design choices such as using sigmoid units. CN-LCS is UCS-inspired which renders its findings not directly applicable to RL. The Deep XCS of Preen et al. [23] investigated unsupervised [24] and supervised learning [22]. Their findings cannot be directly applied to RL due to both being action-agnostic and their computation of the global prediction. All in all, there exists no approach to Deep LCS for RL applicable for OC purposes.

4   Approach: Concepts for a Deep XCS

As a first step toward an OC-ready Deep XCS, we keep the algorithmic structure of XCS as introduced in Fig. 1 and investigate two deep learning-based modifications: a) neural conditions and b) deep (neural) prediction. We, therefore, rely on RL variants of XCS and utilise the standard learning routine. In the following, we briefly summarise the two variants:

a) Neural conditions have already been proposed by Preen et al. [22,24] The authors used shallow ANNs for this purpose. These ANNs have n inputs for an n dimensional input space, one non-linearly activated hidden layer with an arbitrary number of units and a linearly activated output layer with exactly one unit. As activation functions for the hidden layer rectified linear units (ReLU) or exponential linear units (SELU) have been examined previously. Such a neural condition matches an observation $\sigma(t)$ if the activation of its output unit is higher than 0.5. Covering of neural conditions is done by randomly drawing weights from a Gaussian Normal Distribution until the neural condition matches the observation that needs to be tackled. Moreover, neural conditions are explicitly not trained with backpropagation and an optimiser. Only the GA is allowed to modify them. At least to our knowledge, this form of neural conditions has not been applied to RL problems before. Consequently, we experimented with the unaltered neural conditions to assess their applicability.

b) Deep prediction is based on the concept of shallow neural prediction proposed by Lanzi and Loicono [12]. This prediction mechanism employs a feedforward ANN with one sigmoid-activated hidden layer that was only allowed to feature a low amount of units, i.e. 1, 5, 10, and mutated up to 15 by their GA component, in their experiments. In addition, these ANNs have one linearly activated output unit that is directly interpreted as the action value of the classifier's action and their input layer corresponds to an n-dimensional observation $sigma(t) = (x_1 \dots x_n)$. Those ANNs are trained using backpropagation.

More precise information about the training logic is not provided by the authors, it is assumed that they used ordinary stochastic gradient descent (SGD). The authors applied their extension to function approximation and to the GridWorld problem.

Overall, we retain the semantics in our intent to elevate the concept to deep prediction. However, the shallow ANN is replaced with a DNN featuring an arbitrary number of non-linearly activated hidden layers and an arbitrary number of units per layer. Instead of sigmoid units, we choose ReLUs and SELUs to improve the learning performance. For training the DNNs, we rely on backpropagation and SGD with momentum.

The mutation operator of the GA considers the number of neurons to potentially find better fitting architectures for the neural components, based on the insights presented in [12, 22]. The idea [12] to train mutated offspring with their parents' experience is not investigated. Preen et al. additionally used weight mutation, mutation for the layer-specific learning rates, and so-called connection mutation. The latter deactivates a weight with a certain probability, setting it to zero and excluding it from SGD updates. The same operator can also reactivate previously deactivated weights by setting them to a random value. This genetic operator is conceptually similar to dropout layers. For neural conditions, weight mutation and connection mutation are applicable and are the only source for improvement for these conditions.

Neural conditions, neural predictions, as well as the described GA operators, have been implemented for the Python-based xcsfrl implementation [1], which is an improvement of the XCSF implementation Piecewise [2]. In addition, experience replay (ER) for XCS [29] was implemented for xcsfrl. Furthermore, experiments without ER were conducted with newly created experimental setups using Preen and Pätzel's XCSF [23]. One key difference to the experiments of Preen and Bull is that their experiments are action agnostic, which means they are not directly transferable to RL. CNNs for deep prediction are considered future work.

5   Evaluation

Several experiments were designed and conducted to evaluate the proposed concepts of a Deep XCSF for RL.

5.1   Experimental Design

For the Deep XCS experiments, the 6-Real Multiplexer Problem (RMP) [38] was selected as an exemplary single-step problem together with an implementation of Maze4 [23], and Frozen Lake [21] as multi-step problems. Two devices were used for the experiments a server cluster provided by the Intelligent Systems Group at Kiel University and a desktop PC. The server's hardware includes an AMD EPYC™ 7002 CPU, four NVIDIA® GeForce 2nd Gen RTX 3090 TURBO 24GB GDDR6X GPUs and has 8 times 16 GB DDR4 3200MHz ECC registered memory and an 4 TB Intel NVME-SSD. The desktop PC employs an Intel i9 9900 CPU, a NVIDIA® 1070 GTX GPU, and 32 Gigabyte DDR4 RAM.

As mentioned, both the extended xcsfrl and the XCSF of Preen and Pätzel were used for experiments. Each experiment was usually repeated 20 times and their statistics averaged over all those runs. After collecting the data, the results were statistically tested using the one-sided and two-sided Wilcoxon Signed Rank test and a significance level of 0.05.

5.2   6-RMP Experiments

Several experiments were conducted with the 6-RMP, employing xcsfrl extended for Neural and Deep XCSF. For these, the alternating exploration/exploitation (E/E) strategy was chosen.

For the experiments in this environment, each run was terminated after 50, 000 steps and used its own random seed. In first series of experiments compared an XCSF, a Neural Prediction XCSF as well as a Deep Neural Prediction XCSF and were all run on the cluster. The XCSF used hyperrectangles in UBR and linear prediction with the NLMS update rule. The hyperparameters for the XCSF [1,2] were $N = 800$, $\beta = 0.2$, $\gamma = 0.95$, $\alpha = 0.1$, $\eta = 1$, $error_0 = 0.01$, $\nu = 5$, $\theta_{del} = 20$, $\delta = 0.1$, $error_{init} = 0$, $f_{init} = 0.01$, $weight_{init_{min}} = weight_{init_{max}} = 0$, $\mu_{init} = 0.001$, $\mu = 0.04$, $\chi = 0.5$, $\theta_{ga} = 12$, $\theta_{sub} = 20$, $\tau = 0.5$, $x_0 = 10$, $m_0 = 0.1$, $r_0 = 1$, $ga_{sub} = True$, $as_{sub} = False$, and $v = 0.5$. Both other XCSF share most of these hyperparameters since they also use hyperrectangles. The shallow ANN of the Neural Prediction XCSF has one hidden layer with five ReLUs. Similarly, the DNN of the Deep Neural Prediction XCSF has three fully connected ReLU activated hidden layers with five units and a fully connected output layer with one unit. Both use $\eta = 0.1$ and $\omega = 0.9$ for their SGD updates and weight clamping.

Table 1. Average rewards of 20 runs in the 6-RMP - showing rewards over the first 500, all, and the last 500 steps. Arrows indicate an increase or decrease compared to the respective mean of XCSF. Bold numbers indicate a significant difference

6-RMP	First 500	Overall	Last 500
Deep prediction	**0.603** ↑ ±0.06	**0.907** ↓ ±0.042	**0.984** ↓ ±0.022
Neural prediction	**0.601** ↑ ±0.062	**0.885** ↓ ±0.047	**0.979** ↓ ±0.023
XCSF	0.594 ± 0.06	0.961 ± 0.016	0.997 ± 0.004

As can be seen in Table 1 the average reward of the XCSF outperforms the other algorithms overall. This is also reflected in their significantly higher system error, which is a quantity coined by Wilson [37].

Interestingly, those XCSF that use neural prediction networks perform significantly better in the first 500 steps than XCSF. In contrast, they perform worse in the last 500 steps. Both circumstances are covered by Table 1. This means that

XCSF might learn the 6-RMP slower in the first steps than the configurations with neural prediction but outperforms them after the beginning. Nonetheless, Neural and Deep Prediction XCSF approach the performance of XCSF so that the difference in the last 500 steps becomes comparably small. It is assumed that the known bad sample efficiency of ANN might cause the difference in learning speed between XCSF and the two neural prediction variants. A longer training time or different hyperparameters might lead to an even less distinct result.

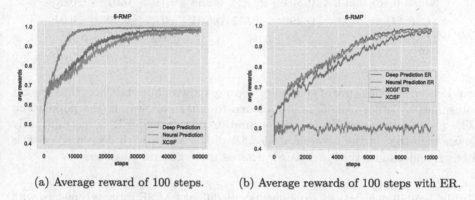

(a) Average reward of 100 steps.   (b) Average rewards of 100 steps with ER.

Fig. 2. XCSF vs. Neural vs. Deep prediction XCSF in the 6-RMP.

Furthermore, neural prediction, deep prediction, and default XCSF have been combined with experience replay (ER) in another series of experiments. They use the same XCSF-related hyperparameters as the aforementioned experiments. ER utilised a initial warm-up capacity of 1000 experiences, has a total replay memory capacity of 10, 000, and draws four experiences out of its replay memory in the replay procedure. Each experiment with activated ER was run for 20, 000 steps due to the considerably longer wall clock time that was needed and quicker convergence tendency of neural and deep prediction when ER was activated. Surprisingly, ER led to divergence in each run of the XCSF. This is either caused by an unidentified bug that only has a significant impact with activated ER or a side effect of the NLMS Update Rule. The latter could be true because ER led to improved learning performance in the Cart Pole problem employing the same implementation when using the RLS Update Rule instead of NLMS [27].

As can be seen in Table 2, ER led both other systems to a significant improvement in terms of reward metric compared to the baseline XCSF, outperforming it clearly. This is especially true for the last 500 episodes. In the first 500 episodes, the baseline XCSF still outperforms both other variants in the first 500 episodes. In addition, the XCSF with deep prediction significantly outperforms the one with neural prediction. Neural and Deep Prediction with ER enabled the XCSF to beat the baseline in terms of system error while maintaining a smaller population and leading to more general classifiers. The classifier ratio in Table 3 means the average ratio between all micro and macro classifiers in the population. It

Table 2. Average rewards for the first 500 steps, all steps, and the last 500 steps in the 6-RMP in the experiments with different XCSF variants combined with ER. Arrows indicate relative change compared to the baseline XCSF. Bold numbers indicate statistical significance determined by Wilcoxon Signed Ranked tests between the baseline XCSF and the specific variant.

6-RMP	First 500	Overall	Last 500
Deep prediction ER	**0.488 ↓** ±0.072	**0.861 ↑** ±0.039	**0.986 ↑** ±0.012
Neural prediction ER	**0.501 ↓** ±0.07	**0.858 ↑** ±0.038	**0.978 ↑** ±0.015
XCSF ER	**0.499 ↓** ±0.052	**0.501 ↓** ±0.05	**0.505 ↓** ±0.049
XCSF	0.594 ± 0.06	0.831 ± 0.052	0.969 ± 0.025

can be seen as a measure of generality because only unique classifiers that are not subsumed by other classifiers are allowed to enter and stay in the population. The classifier ratio of XCSF with neural prediction and ER is insignificantly lower than that of the baseline while that of the XCSF with deep prediction is higher, underlining that this XCSF evolved more general classifiers.

Table 3. Additional data for experiments with different XCSF variants combined with ER in the 6-RMP. Arrows indicate relative change compared to the baseline XCSF. Bold numbers indicate statistical significance determined by Wilcoxon Signed Ranked tests between the baseline XCSF and the specific variant. The micro-macro-ratio of the "Neural Prediction with ER" is marked * because the shown mean might be lower, but the test indicates that the XCSF actually has a lower micro-macro-ratio.

6-RMP	System Error	$[|P|]$	$clfr^*_{mfrac}$	Clfr-Ratio
Deep Pred. ER	**0.148 ↓** ±0.039	**436.782 ↓** ±38.14	**0.199 ↑** ±0.061	**1.8 ↑** ±0.182
Neural Pred. ER	**0.155 ↓** ±0.041	**478.75 ↓** ±37.091	**0.191 ↑** ±0.061	**1.597*↓** ±0.148
XCSF ER	**0.5 ↑** ±0.051	**553.035 ↑** ±16.359	**0.118 ↓** ±0.144	**1.353 ↓** ±0.037
XCSF	0.19 ± 0.056	497.136 ± 30.705	0.149 ± 0.05	1.611 ± 0.107

5.3 Frozen Lake Experiments

The experiments for the Frozen Lake were conducted in FrozenLake-v1 using the XCSF library of Preen and Pätzel [23]. It seems to be the case that there have been no Neural XCSF experiments with Frozen Lake prior to this work.

The experiments used a set of 20 randomly generated seeds that were shared between all algorithms such that the i-th experiment uses the same seed for each algorithm. As an E/E strategy exponentially decaying epsilon-greedy was chosen. It used a decay factor of 0.995 decaying the epsilon from 1 until 0.1.

Five different algorithms were compared: An XCSF, an XCSF with neural conditions, and three variants of XCSF with neural prediction. The experiments for the XCSF and the "Neural Prediction XCSF" were run on the desktop computer and the other experiments on the cluster. The same hyperparameters and seeds were used on both devices. The XCSF utilises hyperrectangles in Centre-Spread-Representation and quadratic prediction using the recursive least square (RLS) update rule. It used the hyperparameters: $N = 1000$, $error_0 = 0.001$, $\beta = 0.2$, θ_{EA}, $\alpha = 0.1$, $\nu = 5$, EA subsumption and action-set subsumption, $\theta_{sub} = 100$, $teletransportation = 100$. For hyperrectangles $min = 0$, $max = 1$ and $spread_{min} = 0.1$ were chosen. The remaining ones are set by default, which includes $\lambda_{RLS} = 1$, $\tau_{RLS} = 0.1$ and a scale-factor $\delta_{RLS} = 1000$. The hyperparameters are explained in the documentation of Preen and Pätzel [23].

Table 4. Average rewards of 20 runs in the Frozen Lake - showing rewards over the first 500, all, and the last 500 episodes. Arrows indicate increase or decrease compared to the respective mean of XCSF. Bold numbers indicate a significant difference. Italic numbers indicate that there is no statistical difference.

FrozenLake-v1-8 × 8	First 500	Overall	Last 500
XCSF	0.180 ± 0.140	*0.658 ± 0.292*	0.744 ± 0.310
Neural prediction XCSF	**0.055** ↓ ± 0.09	*0.645* ↓ ± 0.301	**0.799** ↑ ± 0.281
N. Pred 5 units + unit mut	**0.055** ↓ ± 0.115	**0.661** ↑ ± 0.206	**0.864** ↑ ± 0.080
N. Pred w. all mut	**0.014** ↓ ± 0.055	**0.148** ↓ ± 0.298	**0.247** ↓ ± 0.396
XCSF with neural conditions	**0.037** ↓ ± 0.076	**0.173** ↓ ± 0.313	**0.187** ↓ ± 0.362

The shallow ANN for the first variant of neural prediction has 256 units in its single scaled SELU activated layer. It uses $\eta = 0.001$ and $\omega = 0.9$ for the SGD updates. Lastly, the XCSF with neural conditions corresponds to the other XCSF in all but its conditions. For them, it uses a shallow ANN with one neuron and SELU activation.

The average rewards of this experimental series are collected in Table 4. Overall, the difference between the average rewards of XCSF and Neural XCSF in the experimental series over 20 runs, consisting of 4000 episodes, is not statistically significant. This means that both algorithms perform equally well over the complete duration of the experiments. In contrast, the XCSF performs better in the first 500 episodes, while in the last 500 the Neural XCSF outperforms the XCSF. This means that the Neural XCSF may learn Frozen Lake slower but exceeds XCSF in the long run.

On top of that, the second variant, a neural prediction with five units in its hidden layer and unit mutation, which adds and removes units from the hidden layer, outperforms both XCSF and the other neural prediction variant, compare Table 4. It is also significantly better than those two variants in the last 500 episodes. This shows that incorporating neuro-evolution is beneficial for RL problems. Future work should assess which architectures are explored by unit mutation and should test how well it works for deep prediction.

The third variant of XCSF with neural prediction has the same amount of units as the first one but uses all genetic operators of Preen and Pätzel [23], i.e., weight mutation, unit mutation, SGD learning rate mutation, and connection mutation. The results of this variant suggest that one, the combination or the hyperparameters of those operators negatively impact the learning success since it is far behind the other two variants employing neural prediction. It could be that connection mutation is not beneficial for ANNs used for value-based RL. Moreover, the Gaussian distribution-based weight mutation might harm the learned behaviour leading to catastrophic forgetting [3].

Not well performing in Frozen Lake was the XCSF with neural conditions. Its performance is far below both Neural XCSF and XCSF, which can be seen in the plots in Fig. 3a. These results might be partially explainable by the low amount of units in its layer and unused unit mutation. Another experimental comparison in Subsect. 5.4 compares three variants of neural conditions with each other, where this neural mechanism proved to be more successful.

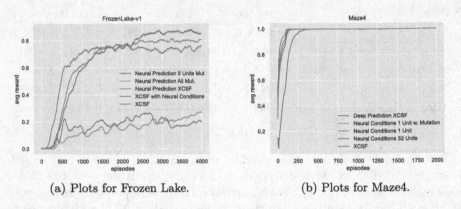

(a) Plots for Frozen Lake.   (b) Plots for Maze4.

Fig. 3. Average reward over 100 episodes in Frozen Lake and Maze4.

5.4 Maze4 Experiments

Summarised, five XCSF variants were compared in experiments in the Maze4 environment provided by Preen and Pätzel [23]. This includes one with deep prediction, three XCSF with neural conditions, and an ordinary XCSF. All experiments were run on the aforementioned cluster. There is no shallow neural prediction included in this overview because no shallow architecture has been found yet that solves the chosen variant of Maze4. This series uses exponentially decaying epsilon-greedy as an E/E strategy. The XCSF employs linear prediction with an RLS update and otherwise uses the same hyperparameters as reported in Subsect. 5.3. The DNN for the deep prediction networks has two fully connected hidden layers and one fully connected output layer. Its hidden layers with 128 and 512 units use SELU, $\eta = 0.001$, and $\omega = 0.9$.

As an optimal value for average steps needed to complete Maze4, Preen and Pätzel [23] hard-coded 3.5 steps, which was probably determined with a value iteration technique. XCSF and the XCSF with deep prediction come close to this value in the course of the experiments and can learn the environment without major occurrences of diverging runs. All in all, this was expected because Maze4 is one environment, in which XCS and XCSF have been tested several times. Figure 2 shows the plots of different quantities of both results. Overall, the XCSF achieves a significantly higher average reward. This is also true for the first 500 episodes. However, there is no difference in average rewards in the last 500 episodes.

All in all, this can be interpreted as that the Deep XCSF learns Maze4 slower than XCSF. However, over time its performance reaches or comes near to the performance of the XCSF depending on whether the step metric or average reward is seen as more important. This means the difference might mainly be caused by the sample inefficiency of DNNs.

Another set of experiments compares different setups of XCSF using neural conditions with each other. The resulting plots are depicted in Fig. 3b. They show that neural conditions actually work in RL, which is the most important result of experimenting with neural conditions for this thesis. This was not the case in the conducted experiment with Frozen Lake but might have been caused by a wrongly chosen configuration of the neural condition networks. The conducted experiments compare neural conditions with one unit, one unit with unit mutation, and 32 units against the baseline XCSF, whose data was already compared with the aforementioned XCSF with deep prediction. The hyperparameters are equal to those of the other Maze4 and Frozen Lake experiments. As can be seen in Table 5, the performance in the metric average rewards is similar for all four algorithms and none actually manages to outperform the baseline.

While the difference compared to XCSF is statistically significant, the variants with neural conditions instead of hyperrectangles are able to compete with it and nearly reach its performance: This is true for the overall performance as well as for the performance in the last 500 episodes. Among the three setups of neural conditions, the 32 unit variant performs better than the one unit variant with unit mutation, which performs better than the one unit variant without unit mutation compared over all 2000 episodes. Surprisingly, this is not the case in the last 500 episodes: Here, the variant with one unit outperforms both other variants and reaches a very similar mean compared to XCSF, despite being still worse in a statistically significant sense. This difference in the last 500 episodes is hard to explain. Maybe the mutation and more units lead to a slight overgeneralisation. Future work should assess neural conditions further and test them for more complex problems.

All in all, the findings indicate that neural conditions are not able to outperform hyperrectangles in Maze4. This either means that the current form of neural conditions is not appropriate for RL with XCSF or that they are not able to outperform hyperrectangles for smaller input spaces. In this case, the input has a size of 8. This might change with larger input spaces. Further research is required to investigate this.

Table 5. Shows the average reward over 100 episodes of the different systems in the first 500, overall, and the last 500 episodes of the experiments in Maze4. Arrows next to the numbers indicate the relative performance compared to XCSF. Bold numbers indicate a statistical significance affirmed by Wilcoxon Signed Rank Test. Italic numbers indicate that there is no statistically significant difference.

Maze4	First 500	Overall	Last 500
Deep prediction XCSF	**0.816** ↓ ±0.054	**0.954** ↓ ±0.014	*1.0* ± 0.0
Neural Cond. 1 Unit w. Mut	**0.948** ↓ ±0.032	**0.987** ↓ ±0.008	**1.0** ↓ ±0.001
Neural Cond. 1 Unit	**0.94** ↓ ±0.03	**0.985** ↓ ±0.008	*1.0* ± 0.0
Neural Cond. 32 Units	**0.959** ↓ ±0.024	**0.989** ↓ ±0.007	**1.0** ↓ ±0.002
XCSF	0.97 ± 0.022	0.992 ± 0.006	*1.0* ± 0.0

6   Conclusion

In this paper, we presented an approach for an initial Deep XCSF building upon neural conditions and (deep) neural prediction. We showed that neural and deep neural prediction outperform the chosen baseline XCSF in the 6-RMP if used together with ER and even without ER in the Frozen Lake environment. In addition, we demonstrated that neural conditions and deep prediction lead to successful learning in the Maze4 problem, even if it was not able to outperform the baseline in the used variant of Maze4.

In the current work, performance improvements and additional experiments with ER, architectures including different optimisers, and environments including OC applications such as the Organic Traffic Control system are investigated. For future experiments with CNNs, investigation on how to improve neural conditions is required. Finally, the explainability of Deep XCSF variants will be further investigated.

References

1. Bishop, J.: xcsfrl. https://github.com/jtbish/xcsfrl. Accessed 09 May 2022
2. Bishop, J.T., Gallagher, M.: Optimality-based analysis of XCSF compaction in discrete reinforcement learning. In: Bäck, T., et al. (eds.) PPSN 2020. LNCS, vol. 12270, pp. 471–484. Springer, Cham (2020). https://doi.org/10.1007/978-3-030-58115-2_33
3. Bodnar, C., Day, B., Lió, P.: Proximal distilled evolutionary reinforcement learning. In: Proceedings of AAAI Conference on AI, vol. 34(4), pp. 3283–3290 (2020)

4. Bu, S.-J., Cho, S.-B.: A hybrid system of deep learning and learning classifier system for database intrusion detection. In: Martínez de Pisón, F.J., Urraca, R., Quintián, H., Corchado, E. (eds.) HAIS 2017. LNCS (LNAI), vol. 10334, pp. 615–625. Springer, Cham (2017). https://doi.org/10.1007/978-3-319-59650-1_52

5. Bull, L., O'Hara, T.: Accuracy-based neuro and neuro-fuzzy classifier systems. In: Proceedings of GECCO 2002, p. 7 (2002)

6. Butz, M., Wilson, S.W.: An algorithmic description of XCS. In: Revised Papers from the 3rd IWLCS, pp. 253–272. IWLCS 2000, Springer (2000). https://doi.org/10.1007/s005000100111

7. Butz, M., Kovacs, T., Lanzi, P., Wilson, S.: Toward a theory of generalization and learning in XCS. IEEE Trans. on Evol. Comp. 8(1), 28–46 (2004)

8. Dam, H., Abbass, H., Lokan, C.: Xin Yao: neural-based learning classifier systems. IEEE Trans. Knowl. Data Eng. 20(1), 26–39 (2008)

9. Giani, A., Baiardi, F., Starita, A.: PANIC: a parallel evolutionary rule based system. In: Proceedings of (EP)95, pp. 753 771 MIT Press (1995)

10. Holland, J.H.: Adaptation in Natural and Artificial Systems: An Introductory Analysis with Applications to Biology, Control, and Artificial Intelligence. University of Michigan Press, Ann Arbor (1975)

11. Holland, J.H., Reitman, J.S.: Cognitive systems based on adaptive algorithms. In: Waterman, D., Haey-Roth, F. (eds.) Pattern-directed inference systems, pp. 313–329. Academic Press (1978)

12. Lanzi, P.L., Loiacono, D.: XCSF with neural prediction. In: 2006 IEEE International Conference on Evolutionary Computation, pp. 2270–2276. IEEE (2006)

13. Lanzi, P.L., Loiacono, D.: Classifier systems that compute action mappings. In: GECCO 2007: Proceedings of the 9th Annual Conference on Genetic and Evolutionary Computation, pp. 1822–1829 (2007)

14. Lanzi, P.L., Loiacono, D., Wilson, S.W., Goldberg, D.E.: Extending XCSF beyond linear approximation. In: GECCO 2005: Proceedings of the 7th annual conference on Genetic and evolutionary computation, pp. 1827–1834 (2005)

15. Loiacono, D., Lanzi, P.L.: Evolving neural networks for classifier prediction with XCSF. Technical report, AIRLab, Milano, Italy and IlliGAL, University of Illinois at Urbana Champaign (2014)

16. Müller-Schloer, C., Tomforde, S.: Organic Computing - Technical Systems for Survival in the Real World. Birkhäuser (2017)

17. O'Hara, T., Bull, L.: Prediction calculation in accuracy-based neural learning classifier systems. UWELCSG 04–004, UWE Bristol, England (2004)

18. O'Hara, T., Bull, L.: A memetic accuracy-based neural learning classifier system. In: Proceedings of CEC05, vol. 3, pp. 2040–2045. IEEE (2005)

19. O'Hara, T., Bull, L.: Building anticipations in an accuracy-based learning classifier system by use of an artificial neural network. In: 2005 IEEE Congress on Evolutionary Computation, vol. 3, pp. 2046–2052 (2005). ISSN: 1941–0026

20. O'Hara, T., Bull, L.: Backpropagation in accuracy-based neural learning classifier systems. In: Kovacs, T., Llorà, X., Takadama, K., Lanzi, P.L., Stolzmann, W., Wilson, S.W. (eds.) Learning Classifier Systems, pp. 25–39. Springer, Cham (2007)

21. OpenAI: frozen lake - gym documentation. https://www.gymlibrary.ml/environments/toy_text/frozen_lake/. Accessed 15 May 2022

22. Preen, R.J., Bull, L.: Deep learning with a classifier system: initial results. arXiv:2103.01118 [cs] (2021)

23. Preen, R.J., Pätzel, D.: XCSF. https://github.com/rpreen/xcsf (2021). Accessed 03 May 2022

24. Preen, R.J., Wilson, S.W., Bull, L.: Autoencoding with a classifier system. IEEE Trans. Evol. Comput. **25**, 1079–1090 (2021)

25. Prothmann, H., Tomforde, S., Branke, J., Hähner, J., Müller-Schloer, C., Schmeck, H.: Organic Traffic Control. In: Müller-Schloer, C., Schmeck, H., Ungerer, T. (eds.) Organic Computing — A Paradigm Shift for Complex Systems, vol. 1, pp. 431–446. Springer, Cham (2011). https://doi.org/10.1007/978-3-0348-0130-0_28

26. Rosenbauer, L., Stein, A., Maier, R., Pätzel, D., Hähner, J.: XCS as a reinforcement learning approach to automatic test case prioritization. In: Proceedings of GECCO 2020, pp. 1798–1806 (2020)

27. Schönberner, C.: Deep Reinforcement Learning with a Classifier System. Master's thesis, Kiel University, Kiel, Germany (2022)

28. Silver, D., Schrittwieser, J., Simonyan, K., Antonoglou, I., et al.: Mastering the game of go without human knowledge. Nature **550**(7676), 354–359. Nature Publishing Group (2017)

29. Stein, A., Maier, R., Rosenbauer, L., Hähner, J.: XCS classifier system with experience replay. In: Proceedings of GECCO20, pp. 404–413. ACM (2020)

30. Stein, A., Rauh, D., Tomforde, S., Hähner, J.: Interpolation in the extended classifier system: An architectural perspective. J. Sys. Arch. **75**, 79–94 (2017)

31. Stein, A., Rudolph, S., Tomforde, S., Hähner, J.: Self-learning smart cameras - harnessing the generalization capability of XCS. In: IJCCI17, pp. 129–140 (2017)

32. Tomforde, S., Hähner, J.: Organic network control: turning standard protocols into evolving systems. In: Lio, P., Verma, D. (eds.) Biologically Inspired Networking and Sensing - Algorithms and Architectures, pp. 11–35. IGI Global (2012)

33. Tomforde, S., Hähner, J., Sick, B.: Interwoven systems. Inform. Spektrum **37**(5), 483–487 (2014)

34. Tomforde, S., Prothmann, H., Branke, J., et al.: Observation and Control of Organic Systems. In: Müller-Schloer, C., Schmeck, H., Ungerer, T. (eds.) Organic Computing — A Paradigm Shift for Complex Systems, pp. 325–338. Springer, Cham (2011). https://doi.org/10.1007/978-3-0348-0130-0_21

35. Tomforde, S., Sick, B., Müller-Schloer, C.: Organic computing in the spotlight. arXiv:1701.08125v1 [cs.MA] (2017)

36. von Mammen, S., Tomforde, S., Höhner, J., et al.: OCbotics: an organic computing approach to collaborative robotic swarms. In: 2014 IEEE Symposium on Swarm Intelligence, pp. 1–8 (2014)

37. Wilson, S.W.: Classifier fitness based on accuracy. Evol. Comput. **3**(2), 149–175 (1995)

38. Wilson, S.W.: Get real! XCS with continuous-valued inputs. In: Lanzi, P.L., Stolzmann, W., Wilson, S.W. (eds.) IWLCS 1999. LNCS (LNAI), vol. 1813, pp. 209–219. Springer, Heidelberg (2000). https://doi.org/10.1007/3-540-45027-0_11

39. Wilson, S.W.: Classifiers that approximate functions. Nat. Comput. **1**(2), 211–234 (2002)

40. Wurman, P.R., Barrett, S., Kawamoto, K., MacGlashan, J., Subramanian, K., Walsh, T.J., et al.: Outracing champion Gran Turismo drivers with deep reinforcement learning. Nature **602**(7896), 223–228 (2022)

GAE-LCT: A Run-Time <u>GA</u>-Based Classifier <u>E</u>volution Method for Hardware <u>LCT</u> Controlled SoC Performance-Power Optimization

Anmol Surhonne[1]([✉]), Nguyen Anh Vu Doan[1,2], Florian Maurer[1], Thomas Wild[1], and Andreas Herkersdorf[1]

[1] Technical University of Munich, Arcisstrasse 21, 80333 Munich, Germany
anmol.surhonne@tum.de
[2] Fraunhofer IKS, Hansastrasse 32, 80686 Munich, Germany

Abstract. Learning classifier tables (LCTs) are classifier based and lightweight hardware reinforcement learning building blocks which inherit the concepts of learning classifier systems. LCTs are used as a per-core low level controllers to learn and optimize potentially conflicting objectives e.g. achieving a performance target under a power budget. A supervisor is used at the system level which translate system and application requirements into objectives for the LCTs. The classifier population in the LCTs has to be evolved in run-time to adapt to the changes in the mode, performance targets, constraints or workload being executed. Towards this goal, we present GAE-LCT, a genetic algorithm (GA) based classifier evolution for hardware learning classifier tables. The GA uses accuracy to evolve classifiers in run-time. We introduce extensions to the LCT to enable accuracy based genetic algorithm. The GA runs as a software process on one of the cores and interacts with the hardware LCT via interrupts. We evaluate our work using DVFS on an FPGA using Leon3 cores. We demonstrate GAE-LCT's ability to generate accurate classifiers in run-time from scratch. GAE-LCT achieves 5% lower difference to IPS reference and 51.5% lower power budget overshoot compared to Q-table while requiring 75% less memory. The hybrid GAE-LCT also requires 12 times less software overhead compared to a full software implementation.

Keywords: Model-free control · Learning classifier systems · Run-time management · DVFS · Reinforcement learning · Genetic algorithms

1 Introduction

Resource management strategies for multi/many core systems require sharing resources (power, memory bandwidth etc.) among applications in order to

We thank our project partners in the IPF project and acknowledge the financial support from the DFG under Grant HE4584/7-1.

achieve application requirements (e.g. quality of service (QoS), response time) and adhere to system constraints (e.g. power budgets, temperature). Traditional management strategies rely on heuristics or control theory to achieve their goals, which require a certain *a-priori* knowledge of the system configuration, accurate model of the system and the transient behaviour of application being executed. This makes them rigid to adapt to changing system goals or constraints, emerging workloads or changing system dynamics e.g. hardware variations or environmental effects. Machine learning (ML) based management strategies have proven to adapt to the varying system, environment and application changes by learning from their experiences, resulting in improved management decisions. These strategies require very little to no *a-priori* knowledge of the system.

Reinforcement learning (RL) is a type of machine learning where the learning agent learns to perform a task through trial and error. Tabular Q-learning is the most common type of reinforcement learning used in resource management in SoCs for e.g. in dynamic voltage and frequency scaling (DVFS) [2,6,19], task scheduling [20,23] and dynamic power management (DPM) [7,15]. They are easy to implement and are human interpretable. Tabular Q-learning based ML controllers have a major drawback, that the number of entries in the table grows exponentially with the number of states and actions. Implementing a tabular Q-learning based agent in hardware requires a large amount of memory [18].

The Autonomic System on Chip (ASoC) [4] project introduced Learning Classifier Tables (LCTs) [21], a light weight classifier-based machine learning hardware building block inheriting the concepts of reinforcement learning (Q-learning) found in learning classifier systems (LCS). LCTs have been applied as controllers for workload management and DVFS in [8]. LCS based systems address the state-space problem of tabular Q-learning by generalizing over it's experience [5]. Classifier application and assessment with LCTs are shown to be done in the order of few milliseconds, hence the evolutionary exploration of the state space which typically takes thousands of iterations can be accomplished in seconds.

This work replaces the design-time classifier generation of the ASoC project [1] by a GA-based classifier evolution at run-time. In ASoC, the classifiers were generated and explored by means of offline simulation. This approach ensured that only classifiers that passed certain stability criteria were adopted into the LCT for run-time exploration and exploitation. However, this resulted (a) in a static population of condition-action pairs, and even more (b), was limited by the simulation coverage as well as simulation model accuracy. Furthermore, such a design time approach can hardly keep pace with varying workloads and dynamically changing goals and constraints of the SoC environment.

Hence, we propose a GA-based classifier evolution (GAE) at run-time in combination with the proven LCT-based classifier exploration and exploitation (GAE-LCT). The GAE dynamically adjusts the population based on the effectiveness of the classifiers and runs as a software process on the MPSoC application cores. However, introducing a new, unexplored classifier at run-time bears uncertainties in respect to the stability of the system in consequence of the applied action. Therefore, the GAE limits the allowed action range of new classifiers to stay compliant to the recovery mechanism reported in [16]. This mechanism ensures the return to a proven valid operation point for the CPU in case a defined margin zone (power budget) for a critical system constraint (i.e. tdp) has been reached. Thus, we can guarantee that our new online GAE-LCT will never violate a critical system constraint.

Towards this goal, the main contributions of this paper are:

- A run-time GA-based classifier evolution method for learning classifier tables (GAE-LCT) for run-time SoC performance-power optimization. The GA uses accuracy as a metric for evolution.
- Enhancing the GA with a classifier validity check (CVC) to generate valid classifiers. Extensions to the LCT to enable accuracy-based GA.
- Range based LCTs which provide more flexibility and effective representation of classifiers. An action selection strategy based on match set error for improved exploration-exploitation in learning.
- Empirical analysis of performance, power budget overshoots and resource utilization.

The paper is organized as follows. Section 2 offers an overview about learning based SoC management. Section 3 introduces the range based LCT and extensions, its states and actions, and objective and reward function. The proposed GA-based classifier evolution is described in Sect. 4. Section 5 illustrates the experimental setup and results of this work.

2   Background and Related Work

Tabular Q-learning based resource management is the simplest form of RL. Various works exist which apply tablular Q-learing to dynamic voltage and frequency scaling (DVFS) [2,6,19], task scheduling [20,23] and dynamic power management (DPM) [7,15]. However tabular Q-learning suffers from scalability problems since the size of the table grows exponentially w.r.t. the number of states and actions.

Deep Q-learning using neural networks (DQN) has recently become very popular in resource management. Gupta *et al.* [10] use DQN to determine the number of cores and the frequencies in a heterogeneous MPSoC to obtain the best performance-per-watt (PPW) and Zhang *et al.* use double-DQN for energy efficient scheduling. These techniques face some primary challenges such as: large input data, highly hardware dependent, high processing overheads, response time and hardware footprint etc. [17]. Using DQNs for optimization problems with conflicting and ever changing objectives is cumbersome. Further, DQN based techniques are not easily human-interpretable making their decisions hard to analyze, especially when used in mixed-critical systems.

Learning classifier systems are another class of reinforcement learning techniques which have recently gained attention. LCS based controllers are easily human-interpretable just like the tabular Q-learning and scalable although not on the same scale as neural networks. Hansmeier *et al.* in [12] use XCS to schedule tasks on heterogeneous MPSoC. Learning classifier tables are a class of LCS which are light weight hardware based learners used in resource management. Zeppenfeld *et al.* in [21] use LCTs for DVFS and workload management in MPSoCs. SOSA [8] by Donyanavard *et al.* is a cross-layer hardware/software hierarchical resource manager which utilize LCTs as low-level controllers and supervisory control theory to manage the targets and constraints for the LCTs. Maurer *et al.* propose an archive based backup mechanism [16] to restrict and control the emergent behaviour seen in LCTs.

3   Range-Based LCT and Extensions

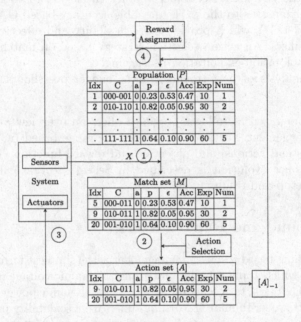

Fig. 1. Working of LCT.

LCTs are hardware based machine learning building blocks which inherit the concepts of reinforcement learning found in LCS. The LCT implementation in this work is based on [8,22]. LCTs consists of a population $[P]$ of size N classifiers. Initial LCTs were designed on strength based LCS and hence each classifier consisted of condition (C), action (a) and the prediction payoff (p). In this work, the condition (C) is a collection of sub-conditions C_i, where $1 \leq i \leq \zeta$ and ζ is the number of different sensory inputs to the LCT. Each sub condition C_i of a classifier is a pair $(C_{i,min}, C_{i,max})$. A classifier matches an input state $X = \{x_1, x_2, ..., x_\zeta\}$ if and only if $C_{i,min} \leq x_i \leq C_{i,max}$ for all $i \in [1, \zeta]$. The action represents the action to be applied to the system. Prediction (p) is updated using a learning rate β, prediction in the previous iteration (p_{-1}) and reward R as:

$$p = p_{-1} + \beta(R - p_{-1}) \tag{1}$$

Figure 1 depicts the operation of a learning classifier table. The LCT works periodically and performs the following steps in each iteration:

1. The LCT reads the current state of the system $(X = \{x_1, x_2, ..., x_\zeta\})$ and compares it to the classifiers in the population $[P]$. All the classifiers that match the input constitute the match set $[M]$.
2. Depending on the selection algorithm (exploration vs. exploitation), an action is selected from the classifiers in the match set $[M]$. All classifiers which propose the taken action constitute the action set $[A]$.
3. The proposed action is applied to the system. The effects of the action on the system is evaluated in the next LCT iteration. Simultaneously, a reward is received from the reward assignment unit.
4. The reward depicts the effectiveness of the action (a_{-1}) taken in the previous iteration and is used to update the prediction (p) of the classifiers in $[A_{-1}]$.

3.1 LCT Extensions to Enable Accuracy-Based GA

Accuracy-based LCS has been shown to provide better performance and smaller population sizes compared to strength based systems [14]. Therefore, we added the following parameters to the LCT to enable accuracy-based GA (Fig. 1) as also suggested by [3].

– The classifier error ($\epsilon \in [0, 1]$) which is updated as:

$$\epsilon = \epsilon_{-1} + \beta(\mid R - p \mid - \epsilon_{-1}) \tag{2}$$

– The classifier accuracy ($Acc \in [0, 1]$) which is calculated as:

$$Acc = Acc_{-1} + \beta(\kappa - Acc_{-1}) \tag{3}$$

$$\kappa = \begin{cases} 1, & \text{if } \epsilon \leq \epsilon_0 \\ 0, & \text{otherwise} \end{cases} \tag{4}$$

where, ϵ_{-1} and Acc_{-1} are the classifier error and accuracy in the previous LCT iteration, ϵ_0 is the threshold error and κ is the raw accuracy. The genetic algorithm uses accuracy as fitness for classifier evolution.
– Experience (Exp) represents the number of times the classifier has been applied to the system.
– Numerosity (Num) represents the number of copies of a classifier with the same condition and action present in the population.

3.2 Exploration-Exploitation Strategy

RL agents are constantly faced with the decision of exploration and exploitation, risking short term costs but potentially improving performance in the long run. In this work, we use an exploration-exploitation strategy depending on the average error in the match set [13]. In this strategy, the average error (E_{avg})

in the match set with size N_{match_set} is calculated for each LCT iteration. The exploration probability is determined as:

$$p_{explore} = \frac{E_{avg}}{N_{match\_set}} \tag{5}$$

During exploration a random action is selected and during exploitation the action with the maximum prediction is selected.

3.3 States and Actions

Dynamic voltage and frequency has been used in modern processors for performance-power optimization, energy reduction and temperature control. We use DVFS to evaluate our work. The goal of the LCT is to find an optimal policy in order to achieve the performance/QoS metric (IPS) within a constraint (Power budget). A supervisor is used at a system level to set the IPS and power budgets depending on application and system requirements [6,8,17].

- The current frequency (f), CPU utilization (u) and Instructions-per-second (IPS) constitute the input state of the LCT i.e. $X = \{f, u, IPS\}$. The CPU utilization is calculated as:

$$u = 1 - \frac{\#cycles\_cpu\_stalled}{\#cycles\_total} \tag{6}$$

  where $\#cycles\_cpu\_stalled$ is the number of cycles the CPU was stalled due to cache or branch misses. $\#cycles\_total$ is the number of cycles per LCT interval at maximum CPU frequency (f_{max}).
- The frequency, utilitization and IPS are binned into 8, 16 and 16 bins and hence they require 3, 4 and 4 bits to represent their values respectively.
- The actions which can be applied by the LCT are increase ($+1$) or decrease (-1) in frequency of the processor by a unit step. The voltage level is scaled proportionally w.r.t. the frequency.

3.4 Objective and Reward Function

The objective and reward function are used to evaluate the effectiveness of the action taken and to provide immediate feedback to the controller. The objective function (Δ) is used to set the optimization objective of the LCT. The objective function (Δ) requires the controller to provide a certain IPS reference (IPS_{ref}) but is limited by a power budget ($power_{budget}$). A supervisor considers the application and system requirements and provides the IPS reference and the power budget to the LCT. Any action that reduces the difference to the (IPS_{ref}), reduces the objective function, and thus receives a higher reward and vice versa. The objective function Δ is defined as:

$$\Delta = \frac{|IPS - IPS_{ref}|}{IPS_{max}} \tag{7}$$

The reward function (R) is used to enforce constraints and provide rewards to the LCT actions. A reward of 0 is provided if the controller violates the power budget. The reward function (R) is defined as:

$$R = \begin{cases} 1 - \Delta, & \text{if } power \leq power_{budget} \\ 0, & \text{otherwise} \end{cases} \tag{8}$$

4   GA-Based Classifier Evolution

The LCT is implemented in hardware and the GA-based classifier evolution (GAE) is implemented in software, running on the processing core the LCT is controlling. The GAE consists of covering operator, crossover and mutation, subsumption, addition and deletion strategy. Figure 2 depicts the block diagram of the GAE and its interaction with the hardware LCT. Figure 2 shows the timeline of the covering and GA operations for an experimental run. In order to generate meaningful and effective classifiers, we first analyze the state space the LCT works on (Sect. 4.1). We define a classifier validity check (CVC) to ensure the classifiers cover valid state spaces. The hardware and software parts interact with each other via interrupts.

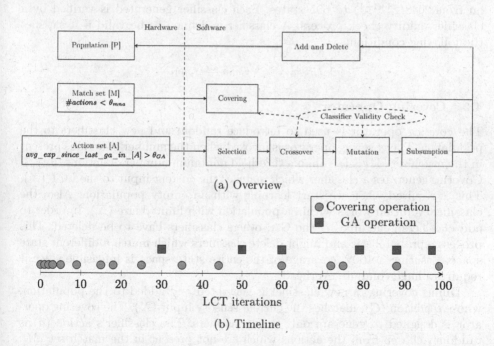

(a) Overview

(b) Timeline

Fig. 2. Overview and timeline of hardware LCT and software GA operation.

4.1   State Space Analysis and Classifier Validity Check

Real world systems are subject to physical limitations. There exists correlations between the different sensory inputs of the system and certain combination of the inputs are physically impossible to occur. For example, number of L2 cache misses cannot be greater than the L1 cache misses. This is important for classifier evolution to prevent generating classifiers which apply to these never occurring inputs. To achieve this, we analyze the state space of the system and implement a classifier validity check (CVC) to generate classifiers within the valid state space. This requires knowledge about the physical limitations of the system. The CVC restricts the state space a classifier matches by limiting the minimum $(C_{i,min})$ and/or maximum $(C_{i,max})$ of the sub-conditions C_i depending on the inequalities between the sensors they match.

In the considered case study, $\{f, u, IPS\}$ are used as our sensory inputs to the LCT. Hence the condition of a classifier is

$$C = \{(C_{f,min}, C_{f,max}), (C_{u,min}, C_{u,max}), (C_{IPS,min}, C_{IPS,max})\} \tag{9}$$

We know that:

$$IPS = IPC * f \quad and \quad IPC \propto u \tag{10}$$

Using the above relationship we reduce the state space the GA has to operate on from $2048(2^{3+4+4})$ to 695 states. Each classifier generated is verified by a classifier validity check process. A classifier is defined to be valid if it satisfies the following condition:

$$C_{IPS,max} \leq C_{u,min} * C_{f,min} \tag{11}$$

4.2   Covering Operator

The covering operator is used to introduce random and new classifiers to the population. The covering operator is invoked when the number of actions present in the match set $[M]$ is less than a threshold minimum number of actions (θ_{mna}). Covering generates a classifier which matches the current input to the LCT (X). This is required when we start learning with an empty population. Also, the classifier evolution works within a population with limited size (N). In order to add classifiers generated by the GA, others classifiers have to be deleted. This process is probabilistic and might delete classifiers which match a different state space. Ensuring a 100% coverage of the entire state space is infeasible since it requires a huge compute overhead.

During covering, a new classifier is generated and added to the population, whose condition (C), matches the current sensory input (X). The covering operator is designed to generate only valid classifiers. The classifier's action (a) is randomly chosen from the actions which are not present in the match set $[M]$. This process is repeated until the threshold minimum number of actions (θ_{mna}) in the match set is met. Typically θ_{mna} is the number of actions supported by the system. The covering operator always generates valid classifiers by the following steps:

- Read the current state of the system $X = \{x_1, x_2, ..., x_\varsigma\}$.
- Generate a list of all classifiers whose sub-conditions (C_i) are in the span of δ_i from x_i, i.e. $(C_{i,min}, C_{i,max}) = (x_i - [0, \delta_i], x_i + [0, \delta_i])$, where $1 \leq i \leq \varsigma$ and $\delta_i \in \mathbb{N}_0$.
- Check this list for validity using CVC. Delete invalid classifiers.
- This results in $\prod_{i=1}^{\varsigma} (2\delta_i + 1)$ calculations per invocation.
- Select one classifier from this list and set the action a by randomly selecting the actions not present in match set $[M]$ but allowed by the system (θ_{nma}).

4.3   Crossover, Mutation and Subsumption

The genetic algorithm operates only on the classifiers in the action set $[A]$. It is invoked when the average experience of the classifiers in the action set since their last participation in the GA execution is greater than a threshold experience (θ_{GA}). In such a scenario, two parent classifiers are selected from the action set based on classifier accuracy.

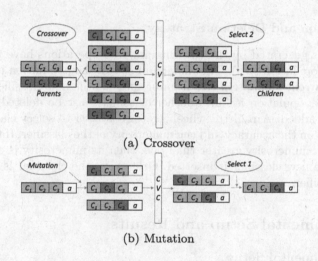

(a) Crossover

(b) Mutation

Fig. 3. Crossover and Mutation in the GA. CVC is the classifier validity test.

Crossover is performed on the selected parents with a probability $P_{crossover}$ (Fig. 3a). We use a two point crossover, where one of the sub-conditions C_i are swapped between the two parent classifiers. Swapping ensures that meaningful information from both parents are inherited by their children classifiers.

After crossover, the children classifiers are mutated with a probability $P_{mutation}$ (Fig. 3b). Mutation can be performed on either the condition or the action or both. When operated on the classifier condition, we employ the mutation operator to perform local search where the values $C_{i,min}$ and/or $C_{i,max}$ of any sub condition C_i is either increased or decreased by 1. This enables both specification and generalization of classifier sub condition with equal probability. When operated on the classifier action, the action of the classifier is modified to any of the other actions permissible in the system.

The crossover and mutation operator always generate valid classifiers by the following steps:

- Make a list of all children classifiers that can be obtained by the performing the crossover (or mutation) operation on the parents.
- Check the children classifiers for validity. Delete invalid children classifiers.
- For a system with ζ different input sensors, this results in $\frac{\zeta!}{(\zeta-2)!}$ (or 2ζ) calculations per invocation.
- Select two (or one) children classifiers as products of crossover (or mutation).

The children classifiers are then checked for subsumption by the parent classifiers. A parent classifier subsumes a child if it is sufficiently accurate and experienced, and it logically covers all the states of the child classifier. For subsumption, the error of the parent classifier (ϵ) be lower than the threshold error (ϵ_0) and the experience (exp) be greater than the experience threshold (θ_{sub}).

4.4   Addition and Deletion Strategy

The classifiers generated by the covering and GA operations have to be added back to the population ($[P]$). The maximum size of the population is a constant (N). If the current population size is lower than N, the new classifier is directly added. If the population is full, another classifier must be deleted first before a new one is added. A roulette wheel strategy is used to select classifier to be deleted based on the accuracy and the numerosity of the classifier. If the classifier selected has a numerosity greater than one, then its numerosity is decremented by 1, and the new classifier is inserted. Otherwise, the classifier is replaced by the new classifier.

5   Experimental Setup and Results

5.1   Experimental Setup

We implement our experiment in hardware on a Xilinx Virtex-7 FPGA using Gaisler's SPARCv8 library (GRLIB) to evaluate our methodology. We use a three-core Leon3 system with L1 cache, connected to a main memory (DRAM module) via AHB bus using the general purpose configuration provided by Gaisler [9]. We use benchmarks from MiBench [11] to form the workload to evaluate the system. Our goal is to generate workloads with varying CPU intensiveness. We use a randomized subset of these benchmarks and serialize them in random order to create 4 workload mixes. Their CPU utilization in our setup varies from 40% to 100%. We determine the control parameters of the GAE-LCT by empirical analysis. The LCT operates every 5ms. However it must be noted that since the LCT is implemented in hardware, it can operate at much lower time interval in the order of a few hundred microseconds. We use 5 ms time interval in order to efficiently extract debug data without any loss. The results depicted in this work are obtained with the following parameters: $N = 128$, $\beta = 12.5\%$, $\theta_{nma} = 2$, $\delta = 1$, $P_{crossover} = 70\%$, $P_{mutation} = 5\%$, $\theta_{GA} = 16$, $\epsilon_0 = 0.0625$, $\theta_{sub} = 24$.

5.2 Resource Utilization

Table 1. Comparison of hardware and software utilization.

	LUTs	Registers	RAM	% SW overhead
Bare-leon3	8586	5438	32 kB	–
Q-Table - hardware	120	40	4 kB	0%
Q-Table - software	0	0	0	0.1–0.2%
GAE-LCT	392	143	1kB	0.5–1%
Full Software LCS	0	0	0	12–15%

Table 1 compares the resource utilization of our GAE-LCT work to a hardware Q-table and a completely software LCS. We also compute the overhead of the GAE-LCT against a bare leon3 core. The performance of a software LCS with the same encoding, reinforcement and evolution components and parameters is similar to the GAE-LCT and hence is omitted in the performance analysis in Sect. 5.3. We evaluate the hardware resources used in LUTs, registers and RAM on our FPGA and also the overhead in software time utilized. The GAE-LCT requires 200% more LUTs and 250% more registers compared to a hardware Q-table agent. The LCT requires 1 kB of RAM compared to the 4 kB of RAM needed by the Q-table in our experimental setup. The resources required by the GAE-LCT scale linearly with the population size of the LCT and the Q-table scales exponentially with the number of states and actions. We also observe that the GAE-LCT increases the number of LUTs, registers and BRAMs by 3%, 2.5% and 4.7% respectively relative to a bare Leon3 core. We assume the sensors and actuators are already part of the MPSoC system.

In software, we compare the overhead in software execution time utilized by the GAE-LCT, a software Q-table and a software LCS agent. We repeat our experiments with the different workload mixes, IPS and power targets, objective functions and report the average value obtained. The GAE-LCT has an overhead of 0.5–1% of software time while the software Q-table has 0.1%–0.2% overhead and the software XCS has 12–15% overhead. The GAE-LCT has a lower overhead since it is not invoked every 5ms, but only when the covering or GA criteria are met.

5.3   Performance

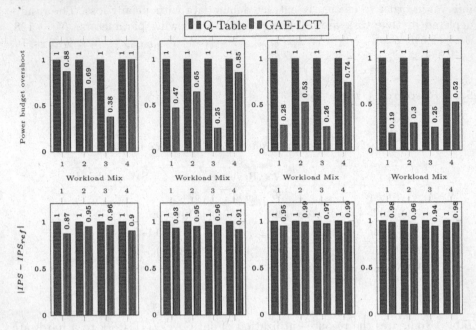

Fig. 4. Power budget overshoot and $|IPS - IPS_{ref}|$ for 4 workload mixes and 4 power budgets. IPS_{ref} is set to IPS_{max} to maximize performance under 4 different power budgets ($0.9P_{max}$, $0.75P_{max}$, $0.6P_{max}$ and $0.45P_{max}$). All values normalized to Q-table. (Lower is better)

Run-Time Learning. In order to evaluate the effectiveness of our work, we compare the performance of GAE-LCT to the performance of a tabular Q-learning agent. Tabular Q-table is the most popular RL agent which is widely used in run-time resource management. We explicitly do not compare against neural-network based approaches since they require significant design time effort and they are not human interpretable. We use the IPS difference ($|IPS - IPS_{ref}|$) and power budget overshoots as metrics for our evaluation. In order to have a fair evaluation, we start our experiments with an empty classifier population in the LCT. Hence, all classifiers generated over time are a result of the covering and the genetic algorithm. We set the goal of both the agents ($IPS_{ref} = IPS_{max}$) to maximize performance under different power budgets. We run each of the 4 workload mixes with the different power budgets and average the obtained values over 10 runs. Each run executes for 3000 LCT iterations. Figure 4 summarizes the results of our experiments. We normalize all values to that of the Q-table. On average, we observe that GAE-LCT has 51.5% lower power budget overshoot and 5% lower IPS difference compared to the Q-table approach. We achieve maximum improvement of 75% in power budget overshoots and 13% in IPS difference and minimum improvement of 1% and 2%

respectively. The GAE-LCT is able to provide better performance due to it's ability to use the genetic operators to evolve accurate classifiers, generalize over its experiences and approximate the state space whereas the Q-table approach has to learn for each individual state separately.

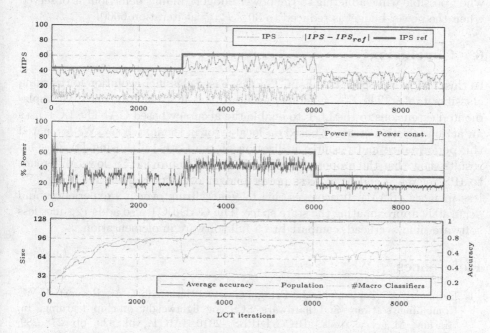

Fig. 5. GAE-LCT showing its ability to self-adapt to changing IPS references and power budgets.

Self-adapting to Run-Time Changes. In order to show the ability of GAE-LCT to adapt to changing workloads, performance targets and power budgets, we present one representative run for a workload mix from our experiments. Figure 5 shows the MIPS, % Power, average accuracy in population, population size and #Macro classifiers. At the start of the experiment, the population is empty and hence the population parameters are zero. Initially the supervisor requires an IPS reference of 43.75MIPS within a power budget of 60% P_{max}. At the start, the error in the population is high and hence the accuracy is low. This leads to more exploration (iterations 0–500) by the action selection strategy as the GAE-LCT tries to generate accurate classifiers. This can also be seen with the high number of power budget overshoots. Over time the accuracy in the population increases leading to more exploitation and GAE-LCT maintains the MIPS withing 5% of the reference and lower budget overshoots.

At iteration 3000, the supervisor increases the IPS reference to 62.5MIPS while maintaining the power budget. This leads to a change in rewards received by the classifiers which increases their error and reduces accuracy, increasing the exploration rate. This is observed in the reduction in average accuracy after iteration 3000. GAE-LCT adapts to the change in IPS reference by exploring and evolving the classifiers. GAE-LCT is able to provide the required IPS throughput when possible while adhering to the power budget. Similar behaviour is observed when the power budget is reduced to 30% P_{max} at iteration 6000.

6   Conclusion

In this work, we proposed GAE-LCT, a GA-based classifier evolution for learning classifier tables. The GA generates accurate classifiers in run-time. We implemented extensions to the LCT to enable the accuracy based GA. The LCT uses an action selection strategy based on local error in the match set. We evaluated the performance and resource utilization of the GAE-LCT using DVFS. Our results show that the proposed GAE-LCT is able to provide 5% lower difference to IPS reference and 51.5% less power budget overshoots while requiring 75% less memory (RAM). It achieves this by generalizing over it's experiences and accurately approximating the state space. The GAE-LCT also adds 12 times less software time overhead, compared to a full software implementation.

References

1. Bernauer, A., Zeppenfeld, J., Bringmann, O., Herkersdorf, A., Rosenstiel, W.: Combining software and hardware LCS for lightweight on-chip learning. In: Hinchey, M., et al. (eds.) BICC/DIPES -2010. IAICT, vol. 329, pp. 278–289. Springer, Heidelberg (2010). https://doi.org/10.1007/978-3-642-15234-4_27
2. Bitirgen, R., Ipek, E., Martinez, J.F.: Coordinated management of multiple interacting resources in chip multiprocessors: a machine learning approach. In: 2008 41st IEEE/ACM International Symposium on Microarchitecture (2008)
3. Bolchini, C., Ferrandi, P., Lanzi, P.L., Salice, F.: Evolving classifiers on field programmable gate arrays: migrating XCS to FPGAs. J. Syst. Archit. **52**, 516–533 (2006)
4. Bouajila, A., et al.: Autonomic system on chip platform. In: Müller-Schloer, C., Schmeck, H., Ungerer, T. (eds.) Organic Computing–A Paradigm Shift for Complex System, vol. 1, pp. 413–425. Springer, Basel (2011). https://doi.org/10.1007/978-3-0348-0130-0_27
5. Butz, M.V., Kovacs, T., Lanzi, P.L., Wilson, S.W.: How XCS evolves accurate classifiers. In: Proceedings of the Third Genetic and Evolutionary Computation Conference (GECCO-2001) (2001)
6. Chen, Z., Marculescu, D.: Distributed reinforcement learning for power limited many-core system performance optimization. In: 2015 Design, Automation & Test in Europe Conference & Exhibition (DATE) (2015)
7. Dhiman, G., Rosing, T.S.: Dynamic power management using machine learning. In: Proceedings of the 2006 IEEE/ACM International Conference on Computer-Aided Design (2006)
8. Donyanavard, B., et al.: SOSA: self-optimizing learning with self-adaptive control for hierarchical system-on-chip management. In: Proceedings of the 52nd Annual IEEE/ACM International Symposium on Microarchitecture (2019)

9. Gaisler, J., Catovic, E., Isomaki, M., Glembo, K., Habinc, S.: Grlib IP core user's manual. Gaisler research (2007)

10. Gupta, U., Mandal, S.K., Mao, M., Chakrabarti, C., Ogras, U.Y.: A deep Q-learning approach for dynamic management of heterogeneous processors. IEEE Comput. Archit. Lett. **18**, 14–17 (2019)

11. Guthaus, M.R., Ringenberg, J.S., Ernst, D., Austin, T.M., Mudge, T., Brown, R.B.: MiBench: a free, commercially representative embedded benchmark suite. In: Proceedings of the Fourth Annual IEEE International Workshop on Workload Characterization (2001)

12. Hansmeier, T.: Self-aware operation of heterogeneous compute nodes using the learning classifier system XCS. In: Proceedings of the 11th International Symposium on Highly Efficient Accelerators and Reconfigurable Technologies (2021)

13. Hansmeier, T., Platzner, M.: An experimental comparison of explore/exploit strategies for the learning classifier system XCS. In: Proceedings of the Genetic and Evolutionary Computation Conference Companion (2021)

14. Kovacs, T.: Strength or accuracy? Fitness calculation in learning classifier systems. In: Lanzi, P.L., Stolzmann, W., Wilson, S.W. (eds.) IWLCS 1999. LNCS (LNAI), vol. 1813, pp. 143–160. Springer, Heidelberg (2000). https://doi.org/10.1007/3-540-45027-0_7

15. Liu, W., Tan, Y., Qiu, Q.: Enhanced Q-learning algorithm for dynamic power management with performance constraint. In: 2010 Design, Automation & Test in Europe Conference & Exhibition (DATE) (2010)

16. Maurer, F., Donyanavard, B., Rahmani, A.M., Dutt, N., Herkersdorf, A.: Emergent control of MPSOC operation by a hierarchical supervisor/reinforcement learning approach. In: 2020 Design, Automation & Test in Europe Conference & Exhibition (DATE) (2020)

17. Pagani, S., Manoj, P.S., Jantsch, A., Henkel, J.: Machine learning for power, energy, and thermal management on multicore processors: a survey. IEEE Trans. Comput.-Aided Design Integr. Circ. Syst. **39**, 101–116 (2018)

18. Rajat, R., Meng, Y., Kuppannagari, S., Srivastava, A., Prasanna, V., Kannan, R.: QTAccel: a generic FPGA based design for q-table based reinforcement learning accelerators. In: Proceedings of the 2020 ACM/SIGDA International Symposium on Field-Programmable Gate Arrays (2020)

19. Shen, H., Lu, J., Qiu, Q.: Learning based DVFS for simultaneous temperature, performance and energy management. In: Thirteenth International Symposium on Quality Electronic Design (ISQED) (2012)

20. Wang, Y.C., Usher, J.M.: Application of reinforcement learning for agent-based production scheduling. Eng. Appl. Artif. Intell. **18**, 73–82 (2005)

21. Zeppenfeld, J., et al.: Applying ASOC to multi-core applications for workload management. In: Müller-Schloer, C., Schmeck, H., Ungerer, T. (eds.) Organic Computing–A Paradigm Shift for Complex Systems. Autonomic Systems, vol. 1, pp. 461–472. Springer, Basel (2011). https://doi.org/10.1007/978-3-0348-0130-0_30

22. Zeppenfeld, J., Bouajila, A., Stechele, W., Herkersdorf, A.: Learning classifier tables for autonomic systems on chip. INFORMATIK 2008. Beherrschbare Systeme-dank Informatik. Band 2 (2008)

23. Zhang, Q., Lin, M., Yang, L.T., Chen, Z., Li, P.: Energy-efficient scheduling for real-time systems based on deep Q-learning model. IEEE Trans. Sustain. Comput. **4**, 132–141 (2017)

Author Index

Printed in the United States
by Baker & Taylor Publisher Services

Printed in the United States
by Baker & Taylor Publisher Services